MW01515525

THE GREAT WAR

BOOK SOLD
NO LONGER R.H.P.L.
PROPERTY

RICHMOND HILL
PUBLIC LIBRARY

DEC 07 2015

CENTRAL LIBRARY
905-884-9288

Kellen Kurschinski, Steve Marti, Alicia Robinet, Matt Symes, Jonathan F. Vance, editors

FROM MEMORY TO HISTORY
THE GREAT WAR

WLU PRESS

WILFRID LAURIER
UNIVERSITY PRESS

Wilfrid Laurier University Press acknowledges the support of the Canada Council for the Arts for our publishing program. We acknowledge the financial support of the Government of Canada through the Canada Book Fund for our publishing activities. This work was supported by the Research Support Fund.

LAURIER 🍁
Inspiring Lives.

Canada Council
for the Arts

Conseil des Art
du Canada

ONTARIO ARTS COUNCIL
CONSEIL DES ARTS DE L'ONTARIO

Library and Archives Canada Cataloguing in Publication

The great war : from memory to history / Kellen Kurschinski, Steve Marti, Alicia Robinet, Matt Symes, Jonathan F. Vance, editors.

Scholarly essays that arose from The Great War: From Memory to History Conference held at the University of Western Ontario, November 10–12, 2011.
Includes bibliographical references.
Issued in print and electronic formats.
ISBN 978-1-77112-050-0 (pbk.).—ISBN 978-1-77112-052-4 (epub).—
ISBN 978-1-77112-051-7 (pdf)

1. World War, 1914–1918—Social aspects—Canada. 2. Collective memory—Canada. 3. Memory—Social aspects—Canada. 4. War and society—Canada. 5. World War, 1914–1918—Art and the war. 6. World War, 1914–1918—Monuments—Canada. 7. World War, 1914–1918—Influence. 8. World War, 1914–1918—Canada.
I. Kurschinski, Kellen, editor

D524.7.C3G74 2015   940.3'71   C2015-901587-1
                                              C2015-901588-X

Front-cover image: detail from *Gassed*, an oil painting of 1919 by John Singer Sargent (1856–1925). The image is in the public domain and was retrieved as an item in the Google Art Project from wikipedia.org. Cover design by Blakeley Words+Pictures. Text design by Janette Thompson (Jansom).

RICHMOND HILL
PUBLIC LIBRARY

DEC 07 2015

CENTRAL LIBRARY
905-884-9288

© 2015 Wilfrid Laurier University Press
Waterloo, Ontario, Canada
www.wlupress.wlu.ca

This book is printed on FSC˚ certified paper and is certified Ecologo. It contains post-consumer fibre, is processed chlorine free, and is manufactured using biogas energy.

Printed in Canada

Every reasonable effort has been made to acquire permission for copyright material used in this text, and to acknowledge all such indebtedness accurately. Any errors and omissions called to the publisher's attention will be corrected in future printings.

No part of this publication may be reproduced, stored in a retrieval system, or transmitted, in any form or by any means, without the prior written consent of the publisher or a licence from the Canadian Copyright Licensing Agency (Access Copyright). For an Access Copyright licence, visit http://www.accesscopyright.ca or call toll free to 1-800-893-5777.

FSC
www.fsc.org

MIX
Paper from
responsible sources
FSC® C004071

CONTENTS

Section Three · SEEING AND FEELING MEMORY

INTRODUCTION

John Babcock, 18 February 2010
August Bischof, 4 March 2006
Frank Buckles, 27 February 2011
Claude Choules, 4 May 2011
Erich Kästner, 1 January 2008
Mikhail Krichevsky, 26 December 2008
Pierre Picault, 20 November 2008
John Campbell Ross, 3 June 2009

There are millions of names on thousands of memorials to the First World War, but over the span of just a few years these few were singled out as the last of their kind: the last surviving veterans of the Great War. Politicians debated the scale of commemoration that would mark their interment. Journalists and photographers tried to record what they could of their recollections and reflections. Artists, writers, and musicians composed works that could tell their stories. All tried to convey the meaning of these men's passing as the last living connections to that far-off war that ushered in the twentieth century. By 2011, the Great War had passed from memory to history.

This passing was the theme of a conference hosted by Western University. The conference invited participants to promote an international, interdisciplinary discussion of the memory of the First World War, which has often been constructed and interpreted through the lens of the nation-state. The conference chose to emphasize an international approach to memory in order to reveal parallel patterns in the production and consumption of cultural memories by comparing these processes as they took place in different national traditions. In particular, the conference sought to situate the scholarship on Canadian memory of the First World War within a broader body of work.

Understanding the transition from memory to history necessitates an interdisciplinary approach. While history can be defined as a separate academic discipline, memory is a complex, composite construction that can be analyzed and examined through any field of the arts, humanities, and social sciences. In November 2011, the conference assembled historians, literary scholars, art historians, educators, genealogists, and students from across Canada, the United States, Europe, and Australia to share their views on the memory, commemoration, and teaching of the Great War. By inviting participants from a variety of disciplines, the conference was able to demonstrate how authors and artists have engaged with historical events to produce works of art, literature, and visual media that have combined with the work of historians to shape and reshape the war memory.

Though academic in nature, the conference recognized the most important element in shaping memory: the public. Artists, writers, or historians may each try to define a historical event in their own terms, but it is the public's acceptance or rejection of those terms that ultimately shapes memory. To reinforce the importance of public participation in shaping memory, traditional academic presentations were placed alongside other manifestations of public commemoration. Family historians spoke about their efforts to understand the experiences of fathers and uncles who rarely spoke about the war; uncovering wartime trauma through research provided a means to explain and illuminate the shadows of familial tensions. Educators spoke about the challenges of teaching a narrative of the Great War that is inclusive, nuanced, and conforms to the curriculum. Immersing students in the subject through computer games, family history, or first-person compositions are some of the methods used to address that most difficult task: maintaining a teenager's interest. Primary and secondary school students reflected on the meaning of the Great War through art projects that were showcased in a static display, with poems and poppy collages conveying a sense of mourning and loss. The Canadigm Group set up the three-dimensional imaging equipment it used to scan dozens of regimental badges that soldiers had carved on the chalk walls of tunnels in the Vimy Ridge sector nearly a century earlier, while Veterans Affairs Canada mounted a public outreach exhibit; both displays sought to make battlefield artifacts accessible and tangible to the wider public. The conference also coincided with the local Remembrance Day service in downtown London, and participants were encouraged to observe the ceremony. With the Canadian Forces still engaged in combat operations in Afghanistan, the addresses during the service drew on events from the current conflict to make connections with the legacies of the First World War. The themes of the ceremony revealed how Canadian memory continues to shift in response to contemporary experience. These examples of public commemoration echoed a recurring theme of the conference papers: capitalizing on broader interest in the First World War to build stronger connections beyond the academic world, and thereby reconstituting the bond that was severed by the passing of the last surviving veterans.

The Great War: From Memory to History presents a selection of scholarly essays that reflect the conference goal of promoting academic engagement across national and disciplinary boundaries. Scholars have long been interested in the collective memory of the Great War as it evolved in the decades after the Armistice of 11 November 1918. These analyses centred on participants, especially veterans and those who had lost loved ones to the war; and they all sought to understand the construction of memory by and within societies dominated by people who had a deep personal stake in the war and its cost. Credit for inaugurating the field may go to Paul Fussell, whose classic *The Great War and Modern Memory* (1975) argued that the war destroyed the High Diction of the Victorian world and ushered in an age of ironic, modernist expression. Fussell's book inspired a legion of followers among literary scholars, and had a major impact in other disciplines, as well. Among the foundational works by historians are Modris Eksteins's magisterial *Rites of Spring: The First World War and the Coming of the Modern Age* (1989), a tour de force that sees the advent of modernism in Stravinsky and the Ballets Russes, in the *Frontsoldaten* of the Great War, in Charles Lindbergh and the Spirit of St. Louis; George L. Mosse's enormously influential *Fallen Soldiers: Reshaping the Memory of the World Wars* (1990), which argued that the Myth of the War Experience was used in Germany (and elsewhere) to draw consolation, explanation, and justification from a ruinous war; and Jay Winter's *Sites of Memory, Sites of Mourning: The Great War in European Cultural History* (1995), describing how the visceral need for consolation among grief-stricken Europeans led them to embrace traditional modes of expression, not reject them.

These seminal works ushered in a wave of scholarship that explores the memory of the First World War through different themes and in different national contexts.[1] Even the most cursory survey of that literature reveals its breadth and catholicity.[2] Scholars of veterans' organizations have considered the culture of the ex-soldier, finding nostalgia for the simpler days at the front, disillusionment at a youth lost for no clear purpose, and all opinions in between. The organizations themselves might have been radical or conservative—or they might simply have been opportunistic.[3] At the same time, much has been learned from studying the ex-soldier—not in a collective, corporate sense, but as novelist, memoirist, or poet, as dramatist, sculptor, or artist, as composer or historian—to understand how the war experience was manifest in culture.[4] But the memory of the Great War was also created by those who did not fight, some of whom, after the war, had to explain themselves—from the politician who faced awkward questions on the hustings to the father who faced them at home ("What did you do in the war, Daddy?"). Their responses say as much about each individual experience as they do about social expectations of proper conduct in the wake of the war.

The study of war memorials has revealed much about the language of remembrance, the roles of different levels of government in commemorative projects, gendered aspects of mourning, and the spatial dimensions of memorialization in the urban landscape.[5] The same might be said of analyses of annual observances—Armistice Day, Remembrance Day, Memorial Day, Langemarck Tag, Anzac Day—their waxing and waning, the parades and speeches that marked them, the scattered attempts to undermine or reinvent them.[6] Scholars have looked at battlefield tourism, individual journeys or mass pilgrimages, ex-soldiers returning to the sites they knew so well or grieving relatives visiting for the first time a place where their world changed.[7] Because of the centrality of death to the memory of the war, mourning practices have fascinated scholars from various disciplines.[8] Much of this work has been done from the perspective of gender, with studies that focus on mothers and widows of fallen soldiers.[9] We have yet to see significant work on the father as mourner, but the impact of the war memory on children is beginning to draw attention. Researchers on childhood have examined how the war was taught in schools in the interwar era, how it continued to dominate toys and games, and the fortunes of the cadet movement as it sought to carry on under the legacy of the war.

Taken together, these studies have given us a more complex and textured understanding of the legacy of the Great War. Some members of the Generation of 1914, to use Robert Wohl's apt phrase, remembered it just as an empiricist historian might: as a slaughter of mind-boggling proportions in which millions of young men lost their lives in unspeakable conditions because their generals and politicians were blinkered, unimaginative, and stupid. But it is now clear that other people remembered the war as a once-in-a-lifetime opportunity to achieve great things, to fight in defence of sacred values, or to give one's life for a cause one believed in. And we know

now that this memory was not necessarily a reactionary plot to bolster the conservatism of the old order; it was also a powerful source of consolation, a way to explain events and losses that were otherwise inexplicable. The emergence of a social memory is the creation of a usable past; many people around the world were able to transform the experience of the Great War into a usable past.

Building on foundations laid by earlier writers, the 2011 conference invited scholars from different disciplines to consider the memory of the war in traditional ways, but also to reflect on how that memory has been, and will continue to be, reshaped by generations with no personal connection to the events—as the war moves from the realm of personal memory to that of history. The academic presentations, only a portion of which are included in this collection, represented a broad range of themes, geographical contexts, and disciplines. Collectively, these works drew connections across geographic and disciplinary boundaries to illuminate the memory of the Great War at a significant crossroads.

In a 2011 article, Swedish historian Peter Englund argued that "[w]hen the past turns into history a part of its complexity gets lost, not least because of the overwhelming need to turn a confusing and chaotic reality into a neat and tidy narrative."[10] The chapters in Section One examine the processes by which official and unofficial histories and literature are combined to construct and codify narratives of the First World War. Thomas Hodd and William Stewart consider the creation of history, examining how the *Canada in Flanders* series was written while the conflict was in progress, and how one general, Sir Richard Turner, has been remembered and re-evaluated by later generations of historians. Zachary Abram's chapter, "Canon Fodder: The Canadian Canon and the Erasure of Great War Narratives," examines the cultural shift brought about in Canada by the founding of the literary canon that altered the perception of the nation's military culture. Abram demonstrates that despite the initial success of Canadian First World War novels—particularly those written by veterans—these books were critically neglected in the years after the formation of the national canon. Clearly, one must understand not only which memories of the Great War a nation chooses to remember, but how those memories were selected and shaped.

By the same token, public commemoration of the last veteran of the First World War was an international phenomenon that reflected national idiosyncrasies of popular memory and embodied the broader narratives that defined the meaning of the war in the public memory of each national context. The passing of an otherwise anonymous individual captured the public imagination almost everywhere; it fostered publicity, curiosity, and a determination for public commemoration. These efforts suggest that it was not the individuals who were remembered, but their war. This metonymic relationship is mirrored in the Great War detective fiction that Marzena Sokolowska-Paryz examines. She demonstrates a two-fold effect of the detective fiction format: it enables a reader's suspenseful engagement, drawing one in to examine critically the meaning of the Great War; while, at the same time, the detective's investigation reveals a means of examining the "truth" of the war. The article suggests that the genre inscribes the potential to heal a traumatic past. Sokolowska-Paryz, like Abram and the other authors in this section, demonstrate that an analysis of Great War narratives reveals their ability to diminish the space between memory and history.

In every national context, the last surviving veteran who received the widest public commemoration was a male soldier. The importance of the last soldier in public commemorations of the First World War—in preference to the last nurse, the last munitions worker, or even the last airman or sailor—reflected the strength of the dominant narratives that emerged from the war. However, parallel to these stories are the memories and histories of others whose experiences have been forgotten or otherwise marginalized. Section Two interrogates why certain narratives persisted over others; these chapters seek to rediscover experiences of the war that were not always considered popular or significant. For instance, while Aboriginal Peoples and French Canadians have long been a part of Canada's national memory of the war, their collective experience has been obfuscated by nationalist imperatives, as Brian MacDowall and Geoff Keelan illustrate; Veysel Şimşek describes a similar process in Turkey. The desire to reintroduce actors or events into the broader narratives of the First World War also led to corrections of public memory, such as in the Shot at Dawn movement to pardon those executed for cowardice, which Bette London examines in "The Names of the Dead: 'Shot at Dawn' and the Politics of Remembrance." London sees the absence of names in memorials and books of remembrance at a time of intensified commemoration and remembrance as an act of "unremembrance." By inscribing the names of the executed soldiers in the public record, London argues, the Shot at Dawn movement made the absent present and narrowed the gap between the private and public memory of these once-forgotten soldiers. Like the other authors in this section, London, MacDowall, and Keelan consider why and how certain perspectives and experiences of the First World War have long been unprivileged or unremembered.

The passing of the last human connection to the First World War also motivates attempts to maintain or re-create a personal or emotional connection by means of public commemorations. Such efforts reflect a desire to understand the war not just as a narrative, but as an experience. The memory of the First World War has been shared not only in prose; narratives were also communicated as subtext through other media. Personal memoirs could evoke visceral reactions to death or trauma, while visual media recreated and projected scenes and images that only soldiers could have witnessed. A common concern voiced at the conference was how educators might engage students in the war as it recedes further into the past. Drawing upon visceral or tangible war memories—those that can be seen or felt—may enable students to understand the war better. The process of propagating the memory of the war as an experience, rather than as a narrative, raises questions about the possibility of sharing private, intimate events as public spectacles.

Section Three examines how writers, artists, photographers, sculptors, and filmmakers used their own particular media to convey wartime experiences to a mass audience. Alice Kelly's chapter examines deathbed narratives in published nurses' memoirs and contrasts these with popular perceptions of femininity, motherhood, and sacrifice. Chapters by Robert Morley and Mark Connelly examine how idealized cinematic depictions of the war in the air and at sea were mediated by the need to present seemingly authentic recreations of battle that would accord with public perceptions of the war. Also drawing on memory in its tangible manifestations, Mark A.R. Facknitz considers kitsch as that which fetishizes grief, noting its appeal to mass culture, such as the crowds that view commemorative sites. Facknitz clarifies the concept of kitsch and interrogates the ethics and aesthetics of Great War memorials, such as the *Tranchée des Baionnettes* (Bayonet Trench) at Verdun and the Canadian memorial at Vimy Ridge, which turn former battlefields into focal points for public mourning and commemoration. Michèle Wijegoonaratna takes the enquiry in the direction of high culture, exploring how German artist Otto Dix structured his war experience in his work. In these studies, we see the degree to which personal experiences of the First World War conformed to public expectations when disseminated through various media.

The release of this collection comes at a particularly important juncture in our developing understanding of what the war of 1914–18 meant to those who participated in it, and, perhaps more importantly, to those who felt (and continue to feel) its lasting impact. During the centenary, debates about the Great War's meaning, legacy, and lessons will be thrust into the public spotlight as former belligerents craft their own unique programs of national commemoration and remembrance. Undoubtedly, narratives that emphasize themes of national unity, sacrifice, and, in certain cases, victory will colour official interpretations of the war. In the absence of veterans and with few witnesses left from those fateful years, the onus will fall on scholars to contextualize, challenge, or enhance these interpretations through their work and public influence. *The Great War: From Memory to History*, and the conference that spawned it, were directed at this fundamental objective of scholarly engagement with the public.

As they have in the past, political imperatives will undoubtedly shape what aspects of the Great War and its legacy are privileged over others in official centenary celebrations. In the wake of one of the worst international financial crises since the Great Depression and with the political and economic stability of Europe under increasing strain, there is evidence to suggest that some countries will use the centenary as a means of bolstering national pride through the celebration of past achievements. The Government of Canada's current plans suggest that the official commemoration of the Great War will take on a celebratory tone, emphasizing the war as a defining "nation-building" experience. According to the Department of Canadian Heritage, the main objective of the centenary, in connection with contemporaneous anniversaries for the Second World War, will be to "build an awareness on how the war efforts shaped the Canada we know today, promote a sense of national pride, and create a legacy for generations to come."[11] Highlights include expanded exhibits at the Canadian War Museum, a new, privately funded national memorial (to be launched officially on 1 July 2017, Canada's 150th birthday), the digitization of previously unavailable First World War documents, and a new Education Centre to be constructed at the Canadian National Vimy Memorial. The planned commemorations indicate a continued emphasis on the connection between Canadian nationhood and Canada's participation in the Great War.

The Australian and New Zealand celebrations will have an equal if not greater national significance. In what is being dubbed the "Anzac Centenary," on 25 April 2015 thousands of Australian and New Zealand nationals travelled to Gallipoli to celebrate the hundredth anniversary of their most important national holiday. In a similar approach to Canada's centenary celebrations, popular appeals to the "Anzac Myth" will underscore national unity and a common heritage as a counterbalance to increasing globalization and multiculturalism. But as Jane McGaughey reminds us in her chapter, Gallipoli was not just an Australasian campaign; for Ireland and Newfoundland, the Dardanelles also became a critical element in identity formation. At the other end of the spectrum is the United States, where the centenary (which in any case would not begin until 2017) has elicited little interest. The importance of the US Civil War sesquicentennial perhaps offers a partial explanation for this lack of attention, but Kimberly J. Lamay Licursi's article about the unsuccessful attempts to write official state histories of the American war effort suggests that the "ocean of apathy" has had a long shelf life.

Military triumphs and narratives of sacrifice will have to be weighed carefully against the brutal realities of the war's human cost. How, for example, will the 500,000 casualties sustained during the Battle of Verdun influence France's efforts to honour its war dead and underscore national unity in the face of present-day economic turmoil and state austerity? Will the 1917 army mutinies fit into a narrative that emphasizes collective sacrifice for the survival of the Republic? Official British plans include special ceremonies and commemorative events on key dates, including the Battle of the Somme, which has long served as a horrifying symbol of senseless slaughter for the British public. This particular commemorative approach suggests that the centenary will privilege a celebration of the Great War over its remembrance, although heated debates in British newspapers and on television suggest that alternative voices will not easily be silenced.

For the victors and the defeated alike, regional and international politics have raised difficult questions about how the First World War can be remembered. Indeed, some observers have implored politicians and organizers of national celebrations to acknowledge Germany's and Austria-Hungary's roles in escalating the July Crisis into a European War, thus far with only limited effect. In contrast to the French or British, the Germans have shown little interest in devoting significant resources toward the centenary, a move that has drawn criticism from some scholars wary of a reactive approach to commemoration. With the exception of a joint French-German museum in Alsace and a patchwork of exhibits planned in Berlin and other major cities, it appears that Germany, at least officially, will spend 2014–18 acting primarily as a collaborator on projects that promote "reconciliation," rather than critically engaging in debates about its own memory.

The theme of reconciliation has featured prominently in preliminary centenary commemorations. British, French, and German heads of state came together at Notre-Dame-de-Lorette in November 2014 to unveil the "Ring of Remembrance," a circular memorial displaying the names of

579,606 soldiers from all sides on gold tablets, without distinction of rank or nationality. Celebrations of the Christmas truce in December 2014 presented narratives of the shared hardship of the trenches and the common humanity of opposing soldiers, momentarily united through sport. Reconciliation, however, has its limits. The announcement that a Japanese flag would be flown during Brisbane's Anzac Day ceremonies in 2015 has angered Australian veterans of the Second World War.[12] Even though Japan was an ally to the British Empire during the First World War and escorted the first Australian Imperial Force as it sailed to Egypt, this fact is overshadowed by the memory of Japanese atrocities against Australian prisoners of war during the Second World War. The absence of Russian representation at European commemoration ceremonies reveals how current events continue to complicate old enmities.

What is important is to engage critically with the political and cultural institutions and personalities that will play a formative role in laying out the framework for commemoration at the international, national, and local levels. Scholars, as custodians of history and memory alike, must help to equip those who will participate or bear witness to these exercises in remembrance, with a clear understanding of how memory is related to yet distinct from "the past." Indeed, a key theme in many of the essays in this collection is the malleability of memory. Narratives that privilege the experiences of a few over those of many present not only a problem of scholarly interpretation, but can also undermine or devalue competing narratives that are just as worthy of recognition and exploration. So much is clear in the articles by Dan Bullard, on African veterans of the Great War and the use and abuse of their experiences, and Mary Chaktsiris, on Canada's internment of enemy alien civilians and its historical legacy. Many centenary celebrations will no doubt focus on the combat experience of the Western Front and the ultimate sacrifice paid by everyday soldiers, but does this sufficiently encapsulate how the war was fought and by whom? What of the disabled and able-bodied veterans who returned home, or the countless civilians who toiled and grieved on the home front, or were subjected to injury, disease, displacement, famine, or even genocide? How might countries that emerged from the ashes of empire interrogate their own collective interpretations? What of those who remain marginalized to this day? Although collective memory often grants primacy to the "national experience," the essays in this collection show that the diversity of the war's participants shaped postwar commemoration and memory-making, deliberately crafting interpretations of the Great War in response to particular circumstances. These divergent memories of the First World War reveal that scholars still have much to learn about how these memories are written into history.

NOTES

1. To avoid an uncomfortably long introduction, we have made no effort to provide an exhaustive bibliography in these notes, but have confined the references to major monographs and edited collections. Interested readers will find no shortage of journal articles, conference papers, and research reports (many of them referred to in the chapters that follow) on any of these subjects.

2. Jay Winter, *Remembering War: The Great War between Memory and History in the 20th Century* (New Haven: Yale University Press, 2006); Dan Todman, *The Great War: Myth and Memory* (Bloomsbury Academic, 2007); Kate Kennedy and Trudi Tate, eds., *The Silent Morning: Culture and Memory After the Armistice* (Manchester: Manchester University Press, 2013); T.G. Ashplant, Graham Dawson, and Michael Roper, eds., *The Politics of War Memory and Commemoration* (London: Routledge, 2000); Elena Lamberti and Vita Fortunati, eds., *Memories and Representations of War: The Case of World War I and World War II* (Amsterdam: Rodopi, 2009); Angela Gaffney, *Aftermath: Remembering the Great War in Wales* (Cardiff: University of Wales Press, 1998); Janet S.K. Watson, *Fighting Different Wars: Experience, Memory, and the First World War in Britain* (Cambridge: Cambridge University Press, 2004); Nuala C. Johnson, *Ireland, the Great War and the Geography of Remembrance* (Cambridge: Cambridge University Press, 2003); Mark David Sheftall, *Altered Memories of the Great War: Divergent Narratives of Britain, Australia, New Zealand and Canada* (I.B. Tauris, 2010); Jonathan F. Vance, *Death So Noble: Memory, Meaning and the First World War* (Vancouver: UBC Press, 1997); Alistair Thomson, *Anzac Memories: Living with the Legend* (Melbourne: Oxford University Press, 1994); Ross J. Wilson, *Cultural Heritage of the Great War in Britain* (Ashgate, 2013); Stefan Goebel, *The Great War and Medieval Memory: War, Remembrance and Medievalism in Britain and Germany, 1914–1940* (Cambridge: Cambridge University Press, 2007); Jason Crouthamel, *The Great War and German Memory: Society, Politics and Psychological Trauma, 1914–1945* (Liverpool: Liverpool University Press, 2010); Tim Grady, *The German-Jewish Soldiers of the First World War in History and Memory* (Liverpool: Liverpool University Press, 2012); Mark A. Snell, ed., *Unknown Soldiers: The American Expeditionary Forces in Memory and Remembrance* (Kent State University Press, 2008); Steven Trout, *On the Battlefield of Memory: The First World War and American Remembrance, 1919–1941* (Tuscaloosa: University of Alabama Press, 2012); Karen Petrone, *The Great War in Russian Memory*

(Bloomington: Indiana University Press, 2011); Daniel J. Sherman, *The Construction of Memory in Interwar France* (Chicago: University of Chicago Press, 1999).

3. Deborah Cohen, *The War Come Home: Disabled Veterans in Britain and Germany, 1914–1939* (Berkeley: University of California Press, 2001); Benjamin Ziemann, *Contested Commemorations: Republican War Veterans and Weimar Political Culture* (Cambridge: Cambridge University Press, 2013); Thomas A. Rumer, *The American Legion: An Official History, 1919–1989* (New York: M. Evans, 1990); Stephen R. Ortiz, *Beyond the Bonus March and GI Bill: How Veteran Politics Shaped the New Deal Era* (New York: New York University Press, 2010); Antoine Prost, *In the Wake of War: Les anciens combattants and French Society* (Oxford: Berg, 1992); Chris Millington, *From Victory to Vichy: Veterans in Inter-war France* (Manchester: Manchester University Press, 2012); Marina Larsson, *Shattered Anzacs: Living with the Scars of War* (Sydney: University of New South Wales Press, 2009).

4. David Taylor, *Memory, Narrative and the Great War: Rifleman Patrick MacGill and the Construction of Wartime Experience* (Liverpool: Liverpool University Press, 2013).

5. Alex King, *Memorials of the Great War in Britain: The Symbolism and Politics of Remembrance* (Oxford: Berg, 1998); Mark Connelly, *The Great War: Memory and Ritual. Commemoration in the City and East London, 1916–1939* (Woodbridge: Boydell Press, 2002); K.S. Inglis, *Sacred Places: War Memorials in the Australian Landscape* (Carlton South: Melbourne University Press, 1998); Bruce Scates, *A Place to Remember: A History of the Shrine of Remembrance* (Cambridge: Cambridge University Press, 2009); Marilène Patten Henry, *Monumental Accusations: The Monuments aux Morts as Expressions of Popular Resentment* (New York: Peter Lang, 1996).

6. Adrian Gregory, *The Silence of Memory: Armistice Day, 1919–1946* (Oxford: Berg, 1994); Ted Harrison, *Remembrance Today: Poppies, Grief and Heroism* (London: Reaktion, 2012).

7. David Lloyd, *Battlefield Tourism: Pilgrimage and the Commemoration of the Great War in Britain, Australia and Canada, 1919–1939* (Oxford: Berg, 1998); Ian McGibbon, *New Zealand Battlefields and Memorials of the Western Front* (Auckland: Oxford University Press, 2001); Julie Summers, *Remembering Fromelles: A New Cemetery for a New Century* (London: Commonwealth War Graves Commission, 2010); David Crane, *Empires Of The Dead: How One Man's Vision Led to the Creation of WWI's War Graves* (General Books, 2013).

8. Tanja Luckins, *The Gates of Memory: Australian People's Experiences and Memories of Loss and the Great War* (North Fremantle: Fremantle Arts Centre Press, 2004).

9. Suzanne Evans, *Mothers of Heroes, Mothers of Martyrs: World War I and the Politics of Grief* (Montreal: McGill-Queen's University Press, 2007); John W.

Graham, *The Gold Star Mother Pilgrimages of the 1930s: Overseas Grave Visitations by Mothers and Widows of Fallen U.S. World War I Soldiers* (Jefferson, NC: McFarland, 2005).

10. Peter Englund "Remembering the First World War: Touched from a Distance," *History Today* 61, no. 11 (November 2011).

11. "The World War Commemorations, 1914–1920," Heritage Canada, http://www.pch.gc.ca/eng/1389645310511 (accessed 8 January 2014).

12. "Japanese flag likely to cause a flap as it flies above Anzac Day parade," *Brisbane Courier Mail*, 22 Februrary 2015.

SECTION ONE

MEMORY AND MAKING NARRATIVES

CANON FODDER
The Canadian Canon and the Erasure of Great War Narratives

ZACHARY ABRAM

In the decade after the disputed peace that ended the First World War, the Canadian literary market was inundated with novels about the war. From 1919 to 1929, more than twenty war novels were published in Canada.[1] These novels are remarkably homogeneous in both theme and form. The typical First World War novel follows a set formula established by Ralph Connor, the era's most popular writer. These novels can be characterized as Romantic and nationalistic. Written to adhere to the Protestant British values of a community that was staunchly pro-war at the outset of the conflict, these war narratives continue the national project Daniel Coleman identifies as "British Canadian White Civility," the assumption, "so prevalent it often goes unnoticed, that Canada's status as a liberal, progressive, and humane nation derives from British … racial and cultural values."[2] These novels were Romances, which sought to entwine the First World War, and Canada's performance in it, with an unstoppable march towards progress.

When the markets crashed in 1929, and the world settled in for what would turn out to be a protracted economic depression, these Romantic panegyrics to the glory of war became untenable. It was only in the ideological vacuum created by the Great Depression that the Canadian anti-war novel was able to emerge as antidote to the nationalist myth-making typified by Connor's *Sky Pilot* novels. There was a concerted effort by authors to represent the war as it was and to do so from the perspective of the average enlisted man. The most important and enduring Canadian anti-war novel is Charles Yale Harrison's *Generals Die in Bed* (1930), a blistering indictment of war as violent folly. Few novels match its intensity and its humanity.

Harrison posits himself as the anti-Connor in the novel's opening pages. When a meek chaplain figure scolds the enlisted men for engaging in ribaldry, he is promptly dispatched by one of the men: "Shut up, Sky Pilot."[3] The implication is clear.

Whether Romantic or radical, novels written by Canadian veterans were remarkably well received. Charles Yale Harrison was an international bestseller, and *Generals Die in Bed* was named the "best of the war books" by the *New York Evening Standard*. G.H. Sallans's *Little Man* (1942), David Walker's *The Pillar* (1952), and Lionel Shapiro's *The Sixth of June* (1955) all won the Governor General's Award for fiction. Between 1915 and 1977, there were over eighty novels published about the world wars (Appendix A) to serve a readymade readership market. Between 1940 and 1960, thirty-three novels benefited from the seemingly insatiable market of the war-book boom. After 1960, however, the publication of Canadian war novels dropped off dramatically. What accounts for this shift in readership? This chapter argues that forces, official or not, within Canadian culture have systematically diminished the violent effects of the First World War in favour of a more peaceful postwar portrait in order to adhere to Canada's new "national reputation as a populace committed to community values, multiculturalism, political compromise, peaceful government, and international peacekeeping."[4]

Using *Generals Die in Bed* and Hugh MacLennan's *Barometer Rising* (1941) as case studies, so chosen because they are both worthy novels and archetypal (the best anti-war novel and the best nationalistic war novel), this chapter attributes the relegation of worthy Canadian war novels to two distinct, but related factors: an accelerated, deliberate, and politicized process of canonicity and a subsequent critical prejudice, brought on by the work of Evelyn Cobley and Linda Hutcheon, toward war novels that cannot be viewed through the lens of postmodernism, post-structuralism, or historiographic metafiction. Both of these factors buttressed the self-conscious reinvention of Canadian identity as part of the larger nationalist project of the 1950s and '60s. When compared to a canonical text, like Timothy Findley's *The Wars*, the reasons for the erasure of earlier First World War narratives become even more evident.

The process of Canadian canonicity is difficult to elucidate. It is, by equal measure, self-conscious and mysterious. It has, at various times, been called "weak" and a "non-canon."[5] Unlike in the United States or Great Britain, the Canadian canon did not emerge gradually as the product of centuries of scholarship. It was engineered at the behest of a government insecure about the lack of Canadian literature being taught as a separate subject in Canadian schools. This insecurity was a direct result of the World Wars and the emergence of the United States as the world's premier superpower. These developments provoked unprecedented state intervention into Canadian cultural affairs to guard against American ascendancy and cultural hegemony, prompting the Royal Commission on National Development in the Arts, Letters and Sciences in 1951. The Massey Report was "concerned with nothing less than the spiritual foundations of our national life," and the commissioners set about to search for "what can make our country great, and what can make it one." The report gave a frank and sometimes unflattering portrayal of Canadian cultural life: "If modern nations were marshaled in the order of the importance which they assign to those things with which this inquiry is concerned, Canada would be found far from the vanguard; she would even be near the end of the procession." Some of the reasons are suggested in the report: vast distances, a scattered population, its relative short history as a nation, and, most troublingly, "easy dependence on a huge and generous neighbour."[6] These factors all pointed toward the need for state patronage of the arts to be administered by a separate agency.

Eventually, the Massey Report led to the establishment of that agency, the Canada Council for the Arts, in 1957, which provided funds for writers and publishers. Thanks to official government intervention and the deliberate shift in school curricula, there was a demand for affordable Canadian titles. Critic Malcolm Ross responded by helping Jack McClelland engineer a paperback revolution in 1958 with the establishment of the New Canadian Library. The NCL "proved invaluable to an emergent group of scholars who were eager to make Canadian literature a substantial part of their teaching and research careers."[7] Essentially, the establishment of the Canadian canon was necessary in order to continue the postwar project of cultural protectionism and a desire to elevate Canadian cultural contributions.

Prior to the First Word War, the predominant perception of Canadian literature was that there was no real canon to speak of. Frank Davey writes, "Canadian literature was not taught as an independent subject in Canadian schools. There was no canon."[8] Northrop Frye described the possibility of a Canadian canon as but "a gleam in a paternal critic's eye."[9] Therefore, the canon had to be formed in a remarkably short period of time. As one critic puts it: "It is startling to realize that Canadian literature was canonized in fewer than twenty years ... [It was] canonization run rampant."[10] This rampant canonization, then, can be attributed to a single period and a group of largely homogenous actors—Canadian academics of the 1960s and 1970s. Canadian canonicity did not truly begin until the establishment of the New Canadian Library and the publication of the *Literary History of Canada* in 1965. These measures were supported by numerous academic conferences in Fredericton in 1970 and Calgary in 1973 before reaching near consensus in February 1978 at the University of Calgary conference on the Canadian novel. The Calgary conference, organized by Malcolm Ross, was the first to be so transparent about its agenda to establish a canon by creating a list of the one hundred "most important" Canadian novels. It was a controversial four days; one presenter, Robert Kroetsch, felt the need to plead with the assembly, "please, no blood, no loud noises, no pissing in each other's boots."[11]

Many critics of the conference dismissed the process out of hand. In his opening address, Kroetsch issued a stern warning: "We are engaged in a kind of pantheon-making among the living. We occupy the most treacherous ground."[12] The main criticism of the conference was that it was nothing more than a crass marketing stunt in order to promote Ross's New Canadian Library, which, at that point, had just over one hundred "classics" in its paperback catalogue. Ross spent the duration of the conference deflecting accusations that the entire endeavour was engineered in order to afford legitimacy to the works selected for the NCL during a period of economic stagnation for the publishing industry. Ross would describe the conference as "the most painful experience of [his] life."[13]

The results of the February 1978 Calgary conference were problematic. The list of the supposed ten most important Canadian novels is narrow and deficient (Appendix B). Eight of the ten were written in the twenty-five years immediately preceding the conference, and there is only one French Canadian selection, Gabrielle Roy's *The Tin Flute*. Ultimately, the selections of the Calgary conference privilege a certain kind of Canadian cultural nationalism, literary realism, and commitment to mimesis. Robert Lecker writes that the early founders of the Canadian canon got "what they have always wanted: an image of themselves and their values." For him, those values included: "A pre-occupation with history and historical placement; an interest in topicality, mimesis, verisimilitude, a documentary presentation; a bias in favour of the native over the cosmopolitan; a concern with traditional over innovative forms; a pursuit of the created over the uncreated, the named before the unnamed; an expression of national self consciousness; a valorization of the cautious, democratic, moral imagination before the liberal, inventive one; a hegemonic identification with texts that are ordered, orderable, and safe."[14]

It is the privileging of this kind of Canadian-ness that has relegated worthy war novels to the critical margins. The historical and political climate of the 1960s and '70s did not allow the point of view espoused by most veteran-penned Canadian war novels to prosper in mainstream discourse. The vast majority of Canadian war novels follow the "grand adventure" paradigm of war writing. In these novels, war is represented as an exercise undertaken to prove one's worth and test one's mettle. These novels did little to disabuse Canadians of the persistent myth that "war is an exercise in manly prowess, deadly for some, glorious for most."[15] Most of these novels are long forgotten due to their interchangeable plots and stock characters, but many simply do not fit with the widely held conception of war as an unforgivable transgression against civilization. These writers refused to be good modernists, and therefore history has dismissed them as propagandists. For Paul Fussell, "Every war is ironic because every war is worse than expected. Every war constitutes an irony of situation because its means are so melodramatically disproportionate to its presumed ends."[16] It is extremely difficult to read Canadian novels of the First World War, particularly those written between 1915 and 1929, and detect even the slightest hint of irony or incredulity. While these writers may not have the depth or style of the kinds of authors favoured by Fussell, the readiness of critics to dismiss these patriotic Romances has led to the erasure of First World War narratives in general that do not fit that paradigm.

The election of Lester B. Pearson in 1963 further signalled a shift in Canadian culture. Pearson's election and government marked a distinct departure from the Canadian values of the war and postwar eras. This shift was cemented semiotically by the changing of the Canadian flag in 1965. Pearson even called the new flag, which dispensed with the Union Jack in favour of the Maple Leaf, a symbol of "our new nationalism." Peter C. Newman called it "transfer of power from one generation to the next" and "a triumph of the Canadian present over the Canadian past,"[17] ushering in the ascendancy of forward thinking Canadianism at the expense of an outmoded British version of Canada.

In his most famous essay, "The Implications of a Free Society," Pearson lays out his political ideology represented by the metaphor of "walking in the middle of the road." This adherence to ideological neutrality would come to represent Canadian foreign policy for decades: "The Middle Way, unlike extremism in political doctrine, has positive faith in the good will and common sense of most people in most circumstances."[18] Pearson guided Canada to the middle of the road throughout his time as prime minister;

this is significant because it was under Pearson, a man known as the architect of international peacekeeping and a recipient of the Nobel Peace Prize, that Canada began to identify itself as the "Peaceable Kingdom" and point to its 5,000-mile undefended border as a point of pride. J.L. Granatstein and Norman Hillmer argued, "if nations must have images, it is certainly better for Canadians to think of themselves as umpires, as morality incarnate, than as mass murderers or warmongers."[19]

The Canadian cultural shift from noble warrior to stoic peacekeeper has had a profound effect on attempts to theorize Canadian war literature. The image of Canadians as "storm troops" has not been welcome since the adoption of peacekeeping as an official policy under Pearson. Although Canadians remained proud of their performance in the First World War and owed a great deal of their autonomy to how they acquitted themselves in Europe's trenches, the idea of peace began to hold a tighter grasp on the Canadian psyche.

In 2002, three in ten Canadians reported "peacekeeping" as the most positive contribution that Canada as a country makes to the world.[20] The fact that, as of 2009, Canada ranked 49th in peacekeeping among participating countries has not deterred its persistence as a national myth. As Heike Harting and Smaro Kamboureli write, "This vision of Canada as an engineer and custodian of global civility reflects a politically comforting national imaginary domestically." For them, peacekeeping is "a persistent cultural fable."[21] The myth of the "blue helmet" would only get a chortle from the soldiers of *Generals Die in Bed* or *Barometer Rising*.

This ideological shift has a tremendous impact on the production and reception of First World War narratives. It is under these auspices that novels that engage more directly with humanitarian narratives gain prominence. Hugh MacLennan seems to anticipate the vaunted middle path as a political ideology in his First World War novel, *Barometer Rising*. Neil Macrae, a soldier returning to Halifax has a nationalistic epiphany: "For almost the first time in his life, he fully realized what being a Canadian meant ... this nation undiscovered by the rest of the world and unknown to itself, these people neither American nor English, nor even sure what they wanted to be, this unborn mightiness, this question mark, this future for himself, and for God knew how many millions of mankind!"[22] Although MacLennan's vision seems to be congruous with Pearson's idea of the middle path, MacLennan does not espouse the right kind of Canadian nationalism. His desire for Canada to serve as alchemist between England and the United States does not fit with Pearson's "new nationalism."

MacLennan's treatment of the First World War is remote and does not convey the proximity to experience that defines most veteran-penned novels. MacLennan set his novels in Canada rather than at the point of conflict itself. MacLennan's wife convinced him that the reason his first two novels had not been successful was due to the fact that he had set them in the United States and Europe rather than his native Canada. She told him, "Nobody's going to understand Canada until she evolves a literature of her own, and you're the fellow to start bringing Canadian novels up to date."[23] The main flaw in MacLennan's war writing is that he rarely affords his soldiers any nuance as characters. They merely serve as ideological types. They are the terrain upon which MacLennan can level a wider nationalist critique. In *Barometer Rising*, the Halifax Explosion signals a startling shift from late Victorian certainty to modern irony. MacLennan's view of history, however, is, according to Robert D. Chambers, "overlaid with a sense of inevitability."[24]

As the foremost writer of the first generation to grow up in the shadow of the First World War, MacLennan was profoundly influenced by it and sought to create a literature of the home front. *Barometer Rising, Two Solitudes* (1945), and *The Watch That Ends the Night* (1959) form a loosely connected trilogy that documents the impact of global conflict on Canada. Yet he depicts no grisly battles or scenes in the trenches. His novels depict Canada at war as a country fraught with domestic strife and in perpetual identity crisis. As Peter Webb points out, "MacLennan's home front ... is not a safe haven from war but a domestic battleground."[25]

MacLennan's main literary mission was to advance Canadian national progress. Surprisingly, he often wrote negatively of nationalism in general; he called it an "aberration of the religious impulse."[26] Yet many of his characters come to exemplify just this aberration. Neil Macrae represents Canada's potential as a nation—if it is able to distinguish itself from Great Britain within the Empire. The Canadian relationship to the British Empire is personified in the town of Halifax, "for it was her birthright to serve England in time of war and to sleep neglected where there was peace. It was a bondage Halifax had no thought of escaping ... for the town figured more largely in the calamities of the British Empire than in its prosperities."[27] The new nationalism that would be codified by Pearson depends on Canada's independence *from* Britain. Neil is Canada's potential if that bondage can be broken: "The life he led in Europe and England these past two years had been worse than an emptiness. It was as though he had been able to feel the old continent tearing out its own entrails as the ancient civilizations had done before it. There was no help there."[28] The war, however, serves only to heighten the *nóstos*—the return home. The soldier's trauma is soothed by a renewed commitment to Canada. For Neil, Canada was immune to the trauma experienced by other participant nations: "[The war] was not going to do to Canada what it had done to Europe … no matter what the Canadians did over there, they were not living out the sociological results of their own lives when they crawled through the trenches of France."[29] Though Neil strives to break away from the Old World, he still defines himself in relation to Great Britain, which renders MacLennan's brand of nationalism anathema to Pearson's. MacLennan's commitment to national optimism in the face of such violence and his unwillingness to afford his soldiers nuance beyond allegory renders him an outlier in Canadian war literature. Unfortunately, his didacticism came at the expense of a more humane and realistic portrayal of the Canadian soldier. In better war novels, like *Generals Die in Bed*, the possibility for redemption is there, but it is personal and individual rather than national and collective.

Like *Barometer Rising*, *Generals Die in Bed* also seems to embody many of the supposed values of the founders of the new Canadian canon. It is staunchly realist and committed to historical verisimilitude. Harrison saw the First World War as the nullification of the individual: "Out on rest we behaved like human beings; here we are merely soldiers." The war is defined by malevolent monotony: "We do not know what day it is. We have lost count. It makes no difference whether it is Sunday or Monday. It is merely another day—a day on which one may die."[30] *Generals Die in Bed* remains largely unknown, however, on the outside of mainstream Canadian critical discourse. Hannah Arendt's work on the nature of bureaucracy provides a useful entry point into understanding the discrepancy between value and canonical recognition. The new Canadian canon, given its connections to official government efforts like the Massey Report or postwar education reforms, is, for all intents and purposes, a bureaucracy. The canon is an institution unto itself and institutions have a mandate to which they must adhere if they wish to continue serving as an administrative arm of the government.

The core meaning of the Greek word *kanon*, the etymological root for the English term, is "rule" or "measure," and then, but only by extrapolation, "correct" or "authoritative." It is, by definition and origin, an ideologically loaded term. For Arendt, bureaucracy can only function if it cloaks its mechanisms in a sort of "pseudomysticism," which is "the stamp of bureaucracy when it becomes a form of government. Since the people it dominates never really know why something is happening, and a rational interpretation of laws does not exist, there remains only one thing that counts, the brutal naked event itself. What happens to one then becomes subject to an interpretation whose possibilities are unlimited by reason and unhampered by knowledge."[31] Critics, who seek to understand Canadian canonicity and the criteria according to which works are admitted and others are not, assume there to be logic and order to the process when there is not. Why one book is included at the expense of another is nearly impossible to determine absolutely. Indeed, that is the very point of a bureaucracy and how it is able to maintain power. Trying to match novels with a set of canonical criteria, as Lecker does, in an attempt to understand Canadian canon-formation, is futile because no such criteria exist, and to search for them fails to recognize the importance of pseudomysticism to a bureaucracy. In *Strange Bedfellows*, George Woodcock recognizes the difficulty of consciously engineering culture: "We slip into the assumption that culture can be planned. Culture can never be wholly conscious—there is always more to it than we are conscious of; and it cannot be planned because it is also the unconscious background of all our planning."[32] Thanks to its mystical underpinnings the canon is open to an infinite number of interpretations, none of which brings anyone closer to the naked event itself. While some texts may gain admittance to the canon by adhering to these supposedly rigid criteria, others are admitted for less obvious reasons.

As the Korean War came to an uneasy close in 1953, Canada entered into a period of peace unknown in the twentieth century. Under Pearson and Trudeau, Canadian troops were deployed in various peacekeeping capacities abroad and were engaged domestically in Quebec during the October Crisis of 1970; for the most part, however, Canada managed to avoid large-scale international conflicts. As the decades wore on, fewer and fewer Canadian veterans wrote of their experiences abroad, and the reading public grew tired of these narratives.

There may be no accounting for the taste of the reading public. It is likely, though, that the publishing industry saturated the market with war novels written by veterans. To appropriate the terminology of military psychology, the reading and critical public began to suffer from a kind of war-lit fatigue, and the Canadian imagination began to drift from wartime exploits to peacekeeping's more palatable forbearance. The favourable climate for war novels in the 1940s and '50s meant that second-rate works like *Little Man* and *Remember Me* could not only be published but be successful. *Generals Die in Bed* or *Barometer Rising*, two sophisticated novels, have been unfairly lumped in with the innumerable novels published during the war novel's bull market. During the 1960s and especially the '70s, the drought in the publication of war novels truly set in. There were passing references to the wars in *The Studhorse Man* (1969) by Robert Kroetsch and *Fifth Business* (1970) by Robertson Davies, but war was reduced to a minor theme in Canadian novels. The rapidity with which the Canadian literary canon was established, and its inherent biases, certainly played a role in the erasure of First World War narratives from the Canadian literary limelight, but it was subsequent trends in literary theory that ensured these novels would remain on the periphery of critical discourse.

This marginalization is most evident in the case of *Generals Die in Bed*. Postmodern critics have had qualms over the impulse of First World War writers to memorialize and commemorate their fellow soldiers. Erich Maria Remarque famously dedicates *All Quiet on the Western Front* to "a generation which was destroyed by the war—even when it escaped its grenades."[33] Such a dedication is problematic for a critic like Cobley: "the commemorative gesture thus finds itself compelled to name the unnameable again and again."[34] Despite her qualms, there is a unique quality to the war novels written by veterans, defined by their proximity to the experience, which would prove impossible to replicate in subsequent decades. The Canadian veterans, like Harrison, who chose to write about their experience, were of a generation for whom death became commonplace. Like Remarque, Harrison's dedication is universal in scope: "*To* the bewildered youths—British, Australian, Canadian, and German—who were killed in that wood a few miles beyond Amiens on August 8th, 1918, I DEDICATE THIS BOOK."[35]

In her book *Representing War: Form and Ideology in First World War Narratives*, Cobley issues a critique of the type of "commemorative gesture" found in Harrison and Remarque. She investigates the way in which "modes of representation generate critiques of the war which nevertheless remain complicitous with the Enlightenment values which the experience of war can do nothing but undermine," and she analyzes novels about the First World War to show how their formal properties derive from conservative ideological assumptions that contradict the authors' overtly radical critiques of the war and the cultural values that sustained it. Cobley is skeptical of the desire of writers who fictionalize their own war experience to "set the record straight, to tell it as it had been." She believes the schism between experience and subsequent text to be insurmountable: "The impulse to 'set down what can be remembered' is complicated not only by the recognition that the horrors of mass slaughter were ultimately beyond words … the opposition between experience and text looms as an absolute division, allowing for no translation that is not also a distortion."[36] For Paul Fussell, novels like Harrison's are complicit in the way in which the "drift of modern history domesticates the fantastic and normalizes the unspeakable. And the catastrophe that begins it is the Great War."[37] For Cobley, the First World War represented a "crisis in consciousness which accelerated the shift from modernity to postmodernity."[38] Therefore, Harrison's attempts, through historical verisimilitude, to represent their war experience accurately were bound to fall short due to the nature of memory and uncritical loyalty to brothers-in-arms.

Although Cobley believes this attitude to be "generally acknowledged," *Generals Die in Bed* resists this interpretation. Harrison's dedication of *Generals Die in Bed* is a deliberate attempt to circumvent the tendencies of the previous generation of war writers. For him, the German soldier, like the Canadian and British soldier, is caught up in a hellish and meaningless conflict far outside his purview where decisions are made well above his pay grade. The narrator notes that the Canadian soldiers never "refer to the Germans as our enemy…. Instead, we call him Heine and Fritz. The nearest we get to unfriendly is when we call him 'square-head.'"[39] The Canadian soldiers develop camaraderie with their German counterparts. There is historical precedent for this type of kinship. The most famous example is the Christmas truce of 1914, when opposing forces met in No Man's Land to exchange gifts and even play soccer. For those in authority, however, dualism is a strategic necessity. "One of the legacies of the war," according to Fussell, is "this habit of simple distinction, simplification, and opposition. If truth is the main casualty in war, ambiguity is another." Harrison reconfigures what Fussell terms the "versus habit"—a "self-other/us-them" mentality that was pervasive in Romantic war literature before the late 1920s. As Fussell points out, "The mode of gross dichotomy came to dominate perception and expression elsewhere, encouraging finally what we can call the modern versus habit: one thing opposed to another, not with some Hegelian hope of synthesis involving a dissolution of both extremes (that would suggest "a negotiated peace," which is anathema), but with a sense that one of the poles embodies so wicked a deficiency or flaw or perversion that its total submission is called for."[40] The Canadian soldiers of *Generals Die in Bed* reject the clean dichotomy of the modern "versus habit." The novel, despite Cobley's misgivings, is in line with Fussell's framework. As the Canadian soldiers pass an encampment of German prisoners, they are overcome not with hate but with empathy: "We pass an encampment for war prisoners. The emaciated looking Germans stand looking, as silent and motionless as owls. One of them waves his hand at us as we ride past. We wave back at them. We throw them cigarettes and cans of bully beef."[41] They share a moment of recognition of the victimhood of the enlisted man on both sides.

The prevalence of this theoretical matrix, embodied by Fussell and Cobley, laid the critical groundwork in the late twentieth century for war literature's marginalization as realist novels that shy away from engaging with the difficulties of the mimetic connection between experience and art. Far from being complicit in what gave birth to what William Golding called "the most violent century in human history,"[42] Harrison and others like him issue a philosophical attack against the rationalism and empty detachment of the Enlightenment project. Ultimately, however, they are relegated to critical obscurity because their popularity and literary achievement contradict the main critical narrative of the twentieth century; that the two World Wars ushered Western society from modernism into postmodernism.

One of the factors that the engineers of the Canadian canon supposedly valued was the mimetic connection between art and life. This connection would become very important to subsequent critics of war literature in the late twentieth century. Foremost among them is Linda Hutcheon, who coined the term "historiographic metafiction" to describe emerging postmodern texts "that, by definition, are self referential or autorepresentative" and "suggest that the mimetic connection between art and life (by which we still seem to want to define the novel genre) has changed."[43] According to Hutcheon, these metafictions, through constant negotiation with the process of writing history, offer a unique avenue through which the reader can engage with and speak constructively about the past, and which acknowledges the writing of history, fiction, or otherwise as an inherently flawed endeavour. Hutcheon hopes that historiographic metafiction will rescue literature from the natural impulse to write *history* and not *histories*. Hutcheon's paradigm, though revolutionary and valid, became so popular and ubiquitous that novels that did not adhere to the tenets set out in her work became secondary as their defenders in the old guard of criticism began to lose power. Again, the war novels that emerged in the years following the First World War found themselves on the outs of mainstream criticism—first not modern enough to satisfy the founders of the Canadian canon, and then not postmodern enough, either. This is not to blame Hutcheon personally for sweeping war novels into history's dustbin, but the sheer ubiquity of her theories about historical fiction was not conducive to the earnest realism employed by many of the novels written during and immediately after the First World War.

In historiographic metafiction, the process of reading is as important as the process of writing. The demarcation between author and reader is unstable. As George Bowering puts it in *Burning Water*, "If you are to identify with anyone it is likely to be the author who may lay his cards on the table & ask your opinion or help in finishing the book."[44] Hutcheon argues that all histories are discursive and constructed by their author: "to write history (or historical fiction) is (equally) to narrate, to re-present by means of selection and interpretation. History (like realist fiction) is *made* by its writer."[45] Timothy Findley fictionalizes this very impulse in *The Wars* and Dennis Duffy notes that the novel represents how stories "do not tell themselves. They do not come to us with beginnings, middles, and ends waiting to be bevelled neatly against each other. They come from scraps and tags, and we order them according to our notions of meaning rather than out of a certainty that it had to have been this way."[46] Historiographic metafiction, like a high school student on a math test, must show its work.

Findley's ardent skepticism toward historical truth is central to his canonical success. It is what sets Findley apart from the Canadian war novelists that preceded him. As Webb notes, "For Connor and Montgomery, moral truth lay in the division of good and evil—with little doubt that Canada was on the side of good.... Anti-war novelists, Harrison in particular, were obsessed with documenting war 'as it really happened.'"[47] An early scene signals the instability of artifacts, even one as seemingly stable as the photograph: "Then you see him: Robert Ross. Standing on the sidelines with pocketed hands—feet apart and narrowed eyes. His hair falls sideways across his forehead. He wears a checkered cap and dark blue suit. He watches with a dubious expression; half admiring–half reluctant to admire."[48] The reader, trained by years of reading history, could be forgiven for taking this account at face value. He or she might not ask how the researcher is able to distinguish between a dark blue suit and a black suit in a black-and-white photograph.

Throughout the novel, Findley pursues a policy one might describe as "near-accuracy." Many of the events and details in the novel are verifiable. The descriptions of gas attacks, flamethrowers, and trench life in general are well researched. For Webb, this commitment to accuracy allows *The Wars*, "for all its ambiguities and wordplay, to appear credible as an authentic piece of historical fiction—which in ways it is."[49] Perhaps Findley is not as far removed from Harrison's or MacLennan's style as one might think. Given the critical climate into which it was published, it is not surprising that only *The Wars* was able to navigate this critical minefield and gain entry into the national consciousness, avoiding erasure by adopting the tropes of a typical historiographic metafiction. Most war novels have not been as lucky. The typical First World War novel does not include self-reflexive characters or any other elements that indicate its potential biases or prejudices. They are sincere accounts of war and the men who fought it, not ironic experiments with a sense of play about reader and writer.

In *Into the Silence: The Great War, Mallory, and the Conquest of Everest* (2011), Wade Davis explores the ways in which the First World War affected climbers George Mallory and Andrew Irvine in their attempt to scale Mount Everest. Of the twenty-six men who went on these expeditions, the vast majority of them had served on the Western Front, and this experience informed their postwar quest for glory at Everest. The most vivid image of the impact the war had on these expeditions is Jack Hazard, who climbed to the top of the North Col with open, bleeding wounds from the Somme, which soaked the tunic of his climbing gear. The wars of the first half of the twentieth century have had an analogous effect on Canadian literature. They are a wound that stubbornly refuses to scab over, no matter the shifts in demographics, policy, or culture. Stephen Greenblatt writes that those who form literary canons have the power to "impose fictions upon the world and ... enforce the acceptance of fictions that are known to be fictions."[50] The rush to codify Canadian culture after the Massey Report resulted in the erasure of war narratives that no longer held the same cultural currency they did upon publication. These novels became instant anachronisms. They are retrograde reminders of Canada's supposedly primitive past. What is irrevocably lost when these novels vanish? In *The Wars*, Timothy Findley writes that veterans of the First World War are "the occupants of memory" and "have to be protected."[51] Novels written by veterans about their experiences deserve the same courtesy.

Appendix A · Canadian Novels about the Two World Wars by Date of Publication: 1910–79[52]

1910–19:

Stirling, Helen. *A Soldier of the King.* 1915
Rae, Herbert. *Maple Leaves in Flanders Fields.* 1916
Dancey, S.N. *The Faith of the Belgian: A Romance of the Great War.* 1916
Connor, Ralph. *The Major.* 1917
McClung, Nellie. *The Next of Kin.* 1917
King, Basil. *The High Heart.* 1917
———. *The Lifted Veil.* 1917
Bell, Frederick. *A Romance of the Halifax Explosion.* 1918
Stead, Robert. *The Cow Puncher.* 1918
Gibbon, J. Murray. *Drums Afar: An International Romance.* 1918
Connor, Ralph. *The Sky Pilot in No Man's Land.* 1919
Blewett, Jean. *Heart Stories.* 1919
Beynon, Francis. *Aleta Day.* 1919
Sinclair, Bertrand. *Burned Bridges.* 1919
McKowan, Evah. *Janet of Kootenay.* 1919
King, Basil. *Going West.* 1919
Arnold, Gertrude. *Sister Anne! Sister Anne!* 1919

1920–29:

Baxter, Beverley Arthur. *The Blower of Bubbles.* 1920
———. *The Parts Men Play.* 1920
King, Basil. *The Thread of Flame.* 1920
Sinclair, Bertrand. *Poor Man's Rock.* 1920
Stead, Robert. *Denison Grant.* 1920
Montgomery, L.M. *Rilla of Ingleside.* 1920
Gibbon, J. Murray. *The Conquering Hero.* 1920
Sinclair, Bertrand. *The Hidden Places.* 1922
King, Basil. *The Happy Isles.* 1923
Sinclair, Bertrand. *The Inverted Pyramid.* 1924
Wilson, Henry Beckles. *Redemption.* 1924
Connor, Ralph. *Treading the Winepress.* 1925
Cox, Carolyn. *Stand By.* 1925
Stead, Robert. *Grain.* 1926
Acland, Peregrine. *All Else Is Folly.* 1929

1930-39:

Beames, John. *An Army Without Banners*. 1930
Harrison, Charles Yale. *Generals Die in Bed*. 1930
Neil, Stephen. *All the King's Men*. 1934
Cobb, Humphrey. *Paths of Glory*. 1935
Filion, Laeticia. *Yolande, la Fiancée*. 1935
Niven, Frederick. *Old Soldier*. 1936
Child, Philip. *God's Sparrows*. 1937
Vinton, V.V. *To the Greater Glory*. 1939

1940-49:

Baird, Irene. *He Rides the Sky*. 1941
Sallans, G.H. *Little Man*. 1942
Heighington, Wilfrid. *The Cannon's Mouth*. 1943
Graham, Gwethylan. *Earth and High Heaven*. 1944
Hutchison, Bruce. *The Hollow Men*. 1944
Child, Philip. *Day of Wrath*. 1945
Roy, Gabrielle. *Bonheur d'occasion*. 1945
Allen, Ralph. *Home Made Banners*. 1946
Meade, Edward. *Remenber Me*. 1946
Nablo, J.B. *The Long November*. 1946
McCourt, Edward. *Music at the Close*. 1947
Shapiro, Lionel. *The Sealed Verdict*. 1947
Elliot, A.J. *The Aging Nymph*. 1948
Haig-Brown, Roderick. *On the Highest Hill*. 1949
Richard, Jean Jules. *Neuf Jours de Haine*. 1949
Garner, Hugh. *Storm Below*. 1949
Birney, Earle. *Turvey*. 1949

1950-59:

Shapiro, Lionel. *Torch for a Dark Journey*. 1950
Elie, Robert. *La fin des Songes*. 1950
Gelinas, Gratien. *Tit-Coq*. 1950
Langevin, André. *Evadé de la nuit*. 1950
Levine, Norman. *The Angled Road*. 1952
Vac, Bertrand. *Deux portes ... une addresse*. 1952
Walker, David. *The Pillar*. 1952

Hemp, Pierre. *Hormidas le Canadien*. 1954

Vaillancourt, Jean. *Les Canadiens Errants*. 1954

Shapiro, Lionel. *The Sixth of June*. 1955

Walker, David. *Harry Black*. 1956

McCourt, Edward. *The Wooden Sword*. 1956

McDougall, Colin. *Executioni*. 1958

Findlay, D.K. *Search for Amelia*. 1958

Gagnon, Maurice. *Les chasseurs d'ombres*. 1959

1960-69:

Allister, William. *A Handful of Rice*. 1961

Childerhouse, R.J. *Splash One Tiger*. 1961

Martel, Stephen. *In the Forest of the Night*. 1961

Jackson, James. *To the Edge of Morning*. 1964

Le Pan, Douglas. *The Deserter*. 1964

Bodsworth, Fred. *The Atonement of Ashleu Morden*. 1964

Allen, Ralph. *The High White Forest*. 1964

Shelley, Sidney. *Bowmanville Break*. 1968

Cornish, John. *A World Turned Turtle*. 1969

1970-79:

Findley, Timothy. *The Wars*. 1977

Appendix B · The Top Ten Canadian Novels according to the 1978 University of Calgary Conference on the Novel[53]

Laurence, Margaret. *The Stone Angel*. 1964.

Davies, Robertson. *Fifth Business*. 1970.

Ross, Sinclair. *As for Me and My House*. 1941.

Buckler, Ernest. *The Mountain and the Valley*. 1952.

Roy, Gabrielle. *The Tin Flute*. 1947.

Richler, Mordecai. *The Apprenticeship of Duddy Kravitz*. 1959.

Watson, Sheila. *The Double Hook*. 1959.

MacLennan, Hugh. *The Watch That Ends the Night*. 1959.

Mitchell, W.O. *Who Has Seen the Wind*. 1947.

Laurence, Margaret. *The Diviners*. 1974.

NOTES

1. Dagmar Novak, *Dubious Glory: The Two World Wars and the Canadian Novel* (New York: Peter Lang, 2000), 7.
2. Peter Webb, "'The Silent Flag in the New Fallen Snow': Sara Jeannette Duncan and the Legacy of the South African War," *Journal of Canadian Studies* 44, no. 1 (2010): 77.
3. Charles Yale Harrison, *Generals Die in Bed* (Toronto: Annick, 2007), 3.
4. Cynthia Sugars, "Review of *White Civility: The Literary Project of English Canada*," *Canadian Literature* 196 (Spring 2008): 137.
5. Robert Lecker, *Making It Real: The Canonization of English-Canadian Literature* (Concord: Anansi, 1995), 104.
6. Royal Commission on National Development in the Arts, Letters and Sciences, *Report* (Ottawa, 1951), 271–72.
7. Janet Friskney, "Case Study: McClelland and Stewart and the Quality Paperback," in *History of the Book in Canada*, ed. Carole Gerson and Jacques Michon (Toronto: University of Toronto Press, 2007), 234.
8. Frank Davey, "Canadian Canons," *Critical Inquiry* 16, no. 3 (Spring 1990): 673
9. Robert Steele, *Taking Stock: The Calgary Conference on the Canadian Novel* (Downsview: ECW, 1982), 21.
10. Robert Lecker, "The Canonization of Canadian Literature: An Inquiry into Value," *Critical Inquiry* 16, no. 3 (Spring 1990): 656.
11. Steele, *Taking Stock*, 12.
12. Ibid.
13. James Adams, "Taking a Shot at a New Canon," *Globe and Mail*, 7 January 2008.
14. Lecker, "The Canonization of Canadian Literature": 657–58.
15. Peter Webb, "Occupants of Memory: War in Twentieth Century Canadian Fiction" (Ph.D. diss., University of Ottawa, 2007), 30.
16. Paul Fussell, *The Great War and Modern Memory* (New York: Oxford University Press, 1978), 7.
17. C.P. Champion, "A Very British Coup: Canadianism, Quebec, and Ethnicity in the Flag Debate, 1964–1965." *Journal of Canadian Studies* 40, no. 3 (Fall 2006): 69.
18. Lester Pearson, "The Implications of a Free Society," in *Words and Occasions: An Anthology of Speeches and Articles from his Papers* (Cambridge: Harvard University Press, 1970), 90–91.
19. J.L. Granatstein and Norman Hillmer, *Empire to Umpire: Canada and the World to the 1990s* (Toronto: Copp Clark Longman, 1994), 350.
20. Lane Anker, "Peacekeeping and Public Opinion," *National Defense and the Canadian Forces* (Department of National Defense, 2008).

21. Heike and Smaro Kambourelli. "Introduction: Discourses of Security, Peacekeeping Narratives, and the Cultural Imagination in Canada," *University of Toronto Quarterly* 78, no. 2 (2009): 660.

22. Hugh MacLennan, *Barometer Rising* (Toronto: McClelland and Stewart, 1989), 102.

23. Elspeth Cameron, *Hugh MacLennan: A Writer's Life* (Halifax: Goodread Biographies, 1983), 133.

24. Robert D. Chambers, "The Novels of Hugh MacLennan," in *Hugh MacLennan: Critical Views on Canadian Writers*, ed. Paul Goetsch (Toronto: McGraw-Hill Ryerson, 1973), 61.

25. Webb, *Occupants of Memory*, 120.

26. Hugh MacLennan, *Cross Country* (Toronto: Collins, 1949), 141.

27. MacLennan, *Barometer Rising*, 51.

28. Ibid., 119

29. Ibid., 300.

30. Harrison, *Generals Die in Bed*, 49, 14.

31. Hannah Arendt, *The Origins of Totalitarianism* (New York: Harvest, 1968), 245.

32. George Woodcock, *Strange Bedfellows: The State and the Arts in Canada* (Vancouver: Douglas and McIntyre, 1985), 17.

33. Erich Maria Remarque, *All Quiet on the Western Front* (New York: Concord, 2004), i.

34. Evelyn Cobley, *Representing War: Form and Ideology in First World War Narratives* (Toronto: University of Toronto Press, 1993), 3.

35. Harrison, *Generals Die in Bed*, i.

36. Cobley, *Representing War*, 3, 6.

37. Fussell, *The Great War and Modern Memory*, 74.

38. Cobley, *Representing War*, 3.

39. Harrison, *Generals Die in Bed*, 23.

40. Fussell, *The Great War and Modern Memory*, 77.

41. Harrison, *Generals Die in Bed*, 85.

42. Eric Hobsbawm, *The Age of Extremes, 1914–1991* (London: Abacus, 1994), 1.

43. Linda Hutcheon, *The Canadian Postmodern* (Toronto: Oxford University Press, 1988), 62.

44. George Bowering, *Burning Water* (Don Mills: General Publication, 1980), 30.

45. Hutcheon, *The Canadian Postmodern*, 66.

46. Dennis Duffy, "Let Us Compare Histories: Meaning and Mythology in Findley's *Famous Last Words*," *Essays on Canadian Writing* 30 (1984–85): 190.

47. Webb, *Occupants of Memory*, 200.

48. Timothy Findley, *The Wars* (Toronto: Penguin, 1986), 6.

49. Webb, *Occupants of Memory*, 203.

50. Robert Lecker, "Response to Frank Davey," *Critical Inquiry* 16, no. 3 (Spring 1990): 682.

51. Findley, *The Wars*, 6.

52. Novak, *Dubious Glory*, 167–69.

53. Steele, *Taking Stock*, 153.

TOO CLOSE TO HISTORY

Major Charles G.D. Roberts,
the *Canada in Flanders* Series, and the
Writing of Wartime Documentary

THOMAS HODD

A considerable body of scholarship has been produced on the life and work of New Brunswick–born author Charles G.D. Roberts. Hailed in his lifetime as the "The Father of Canadian Literature," Roberts was born on 10 January 1860, in Douglas, New Brunswick, near Fredericton. He studied at the University of New Brunswick in the late 1870s and early 1880s, graduating with a B.A. and an M.A. before beginning his career as a school principal and freelance writer. From 1885 to 1895 he was a professor of English and French literature at King's College in Windsor, Nova Scotia. But he resigned from his position at King's College to become a full-time writer, moving first to New York, then overseas in 1907 before returning to Canada in 1925. A prolific writer, over his lifetime Roberts produced more than ten books of poetry, several novels and works of short fiction, and nearly two dozen collections of animal stories. Over the last century, research on Roberts has yielded two biographies, two symposia, and a wealth of essays on his oeuvre. But the majority of criticism has centred on his life and writings while he lived in Canada, between the years 1860 and 1897, and the period from his return to Canada until his death in 1943. Little scholarly attention has been paid to his decade in New York at the turn of the century or the nearly twenty years he spent in Europe from 1907 to 1925.

Of particular note is the lack of scholarship surrounding Roberts's activities and writings during the wartime period of 1914–18. Notwithstanding short sections in literary biographies by Elise Pomeroy and John Coldwell

Adams, the significance of Roberts's involvement in the First World War has gone largely unacknowledged by critics, even though he served as a Legion Frontiersman, trained infantry officers for the King's Liverpool Regiment, worked as a war correspondent with the Canadian War Records Office (CWRO), and wrote Volume III of Sir Max Aitken's *Canada in Flanders* series.[1] Military historians have likewise treated Roberts as little more than a footnote. Despite the popularity and historical contribution of the *Canada in Flanders* series, which was conceived by Beaverbook to chronicle the actions of Canadian soldiers at the front using a combination of war records and eyewitness accounts, Roberts's contribution has received limited treatment.[2] In his study on propaganda in the Great War, for instance, Jeffrey Keshen devotes almost a whole chapter to the CWRO and includes several comments about Aitken's two volumes for *Canada in Flanders*. But in his book Keshen makes no mention of Roberts's third volume; the only time Roberts appears is in a single line meant to qualify for readers who Thede Roberts was.[3] Equally telling is Roberts's absence from most of Tim Cook's ongoing examinations about the writing of the First World War; not until Cook's third attempt does he afford some space to Roberts's contribution to the series, although the bulk of his few, short paragraphs focuses on Sir Arthur Currie's criticism of Roberts's volume.[4] Similarly, Jonathan Vance offers only limited comments about Roberts's contribution to the *Canada in Flanders* series.[5]

As a first step toward rectifying Roberts's marginalization from discussions about *Canada in Flanders*, this essay will offer bio-critical comments about Roberts's military service during the First World War, as well as suggest that his early training in Classics, his reading of history as narrative, and his own experience in historical writing made him uniquely qualified to write Volume III of the series. Moreover, as a corollary to this bio-critical examination, I will offer a comparison of the style and rhetoric between Aitken's first two volumes and that of Roberts's volume in order to suggest that neither man intended *Canada in Flanders* to be read or criticized as a product of flawed, romanticized history—which many historians have argued. On the contrary, both writers recognized that the recording of events too close to history made it impossible for their narratives to be presented as works of historical scholarship. Consequently, they approached their subjects in a manner that reflects more closely the storytelling techniques of the emerging medium of film. The resulting three volumes thus represent an early form of modern documentary narrative that captured in words Canada's transformation from colony to nation during the Great War.

I.

Roberts's military service began at an early age: while studying at the University of New Brunswick in the late 1870s, he joined the 71st York Regiment of Infantry, which at the time formed part of a local militia group. Although I have not found evidence that Roberts's family on his father's side was involved in the military, there was a history of military service on his mother's side: John Murray Bliss, Roberts's great-grandfather, for instance, had been an officer in a local militia, and had also served as provincial aide-de-camp to Major-General Stracey Smyth during the War of 1812. Perhaps inspired by his great-grandfather's military achievements, Roberts passed the exams that qualified him for captaincy, although there is no published proof to suggest that Roberts continued his affiliation with the regiment after his college years.[6]

It was also during this time that Roberts began to articulate some of his ideas about the teaching of history and its link to literature. In 1880, the Chatham, New Brunswick newspaper *The Star* published a talk Roberts had given as the opening paper in a session on history at the fourth annual meeting of the Northumberland Teachers' Institute. He offered an analytical review of the merits of a history textbook, *Archer's History of Canada*, and its limited success as an educational tool. Interestingly enough, Roberts begins his assessment of *Archer's* as a work of literature, not of history: "First look at the book as a literary effort.... It is full to brimming over with most imaginative eloquence with felicities of expression, and graceful and skilful inversions." Equally important is Roberts's concluding statement in which he sounds a patriotic chord for the linking of Canadian history texts to the welfare of the nation-state: "I hope that soon we may be enabled to place in the children's hands such a text book, from the able hands of the author of the present one, as will make Canadian History no longer a bug bear, but the intensely interesting subject which it should be to us, the fruitful mother of loyal love towards this our country, and practice zeal for her future welfare."[7] In essence, he considered that the historical text was a part of the nation's literature, not a separate discipline or discourse, and that Canadian history was of central importance to nation-building.

Eight years later, Roberts would reiterate these ideas in a review of Rev. George Bryce's *Short History of the Canadian People*, which appeared in *Dial*, a leading American literary magazine. He begins by praising the volume for its merits as a story rather than a string of facts: "It carries us easily and rapidly through periods which most of our historians, by a multiplicity of unessential detail, have made for us a weariness to the flesh. In general, it may be regarded as trustworthy and thorough. In a word, it does effectively what it sets out to do, —it tells a story in a way to hold attention." Roberts goes on to quibble with Bryce on the accuracy of a few details, but ends on a personal note. More specifically, he criticizes Bryce's section on "Canadian Literature" for being less than adequate, pointing out that, "We are occupied in the beginnings of a literature ... [so] Let me urge upon Dr. Bryce the desirability, in his next edition, of a less perfunctory survey of this struggling literature, in which his own work occupies so important a place."[8] Once again, Roberts views and places historical texts within the larger framework of a "struggling" national literature. Moreover, in his own *History of Canada*, which he published in 1897 and expanded into a new edition in 1915, Roberts has a section on literature that includes reference to several works of history, as well as poetry and prose. His rationale for doing so? Both genres, he suggests, pertain to "the strong imaginative and intellectual bent of her people."[9]

In short, Roberts read history and viewed the writing and publishing of it as part of a larger nationalist narrative—a mythmaking vision that thirty years later would prove attractive to the nation-building sensibilities of fellow New Brunswicker Sir Max Aitken, who was building his own vision of Canada through the efforts of the Canadian War Records Office.

II.

Despite being in his early fifties at the outbreak of the First World War, Roberts enlisted with the Legion of Frontiersmen in September 1914. Begun in 1904, the Frontiersmen were an independent and self-governing paramilitary organization that by August 1914 had grown to ten thousand members, drawn mostly from "adventurers, pioneers, big-game hunters, ex-soldiers and travellers."[10] While enlisted, Roberts performed various non-combat duties such as drilling and training horses, but he was eager to do more.[11] In a letter to his daughter Edith in mid-September, he wrote: "There's only the war, always the war, with the roar of it almost near enough to hear, & the bulletins coming in every hour, & the lists of the killed & wounded, till I almost cry in the street, & can't speak a word, because I'm not with them in the trenches with a rifle in my hand."[12] Three weeks later, he expressed a similar sentiment to his son, Douglas: "I am coming to the feeling that it would be actual relief and blessed comfort to lie in the trench with my cheek to the rifle & just give oneself, give oneself utterly, for all that we stand for in this war."[13]

Consequently, Roberts applied for a commission in November 1914. He admitted in a letter to George Parkin, his old teacher and mentor from Fredericton: "I am determined to give active personal service in the war."[14] Roberts's choice of terms is deliberate here: he had no desire to be a cog in the war wheel, but instead give "active personal service." Equally telling is his application to the War Secretary, in which he stated plainly that he is "fitted for more responsible work than that of a private soldier" and lists as his references the Canadian writer Sir Gilbert Parker; George W. Perley, the High Commissioner for Canada; and Parkin, who at the time was serving as the director of the Rhodes Trust.[15] The true depth of his commitment to the war effort, though, is expressed in a letter to his family just before Christmas: "In this great & terrible crisis of the world's history one can only give himself utterly & without reserve to the work in hand. I know well what sacrifice I am forcing upon you all, but I do not let myself think of it, lest it should weaken me. I am sure of my duty; for I believe that in such a war as this a man must give nothing less than all."[16]

That same month Roberts received his commission and was promoted to first lieutenant in the King's Liverpool Regiment and began to train infantry officers. Despite being pleased with the appointment and increase in pay, he soon felt the pull of responsibility to serve his own country; by the following spring, he openly mused to Douglas about a transfer: "And our Canadians on the Yser! Oh, how the blood leaps at what they have accomplished & the old heroic manner of it! And they but raw troops! Truly the breed is good! I wonder from time to time if I ought not get myself transferred to a Canadian command."[17] Roberts's expression of nationalism is telling of his character, since by this time he had been living away from Canada for nearly twenty years.

A year later Roberts is promoted to the rank of Captain, and in the spring of 1916 he is part of the force sent to Curragh, the military outpost in County Kildare, Ireland. He notes in a letter to Douglas: "arrived just in time to be in the Sinn Fein rebellion. It has been pretty lively, —but we've got the unspeakable scoundrels in hand now. I can't write particulars, lest the Censor should object to what I say!" Coincidentally, in this same letter he hints at his prospects of becoming part of the Canadian war effort: "I have very strong hopes of being transferred to the Canadian Force, presently, —to the Staff, in London, on a special job, with greatly increased pay. They have promised me the job, but they are slow in putting it through though."[18]

It would take an additional few months, but in the fall of 1916 Roberts was finally transferred to the Canadian Expeditionary Force and promoted to the rank of major. By December of that year he became attached to the Canadian Corps as a special press correspondent, largely through the help of Lord Beaverbrook.[19] He was also asked by Beaverbrook to write Volume III of the *Canada in Flanders* series to chronicle the activities of the 4th Canadian Division's activities in the battles of the Somme—no doubt, in part, because of Roberts's previous experience with historical writing.[20] Consequently, after publishing Volume III Roberts was recalled to the War Records Office in London, where he was tasked with giving the address when a Canadian war photographs exhibition opened at a new centre.[21] Before the war's end he had also begun work on Volume IV, regarding the Battle of Vimy Ridge, but the book was never printed.[22]

Roberts's dedication to give "active personal service" to the war effort is commendable. Not only did he serve for both Canada and imperial Britain, he also served as both a regular soldier and as an officer. Such activities required considerable physical and mental effort, though, and left little time for creativity: Roberts published only three poems about the Great War, and it would take more than twenty years and the Second World War to motivate him to produce any more work of a military nature.[23] But as a writer embedded with the CWRO, Roberts was able to help tell part of the story of the Canadian Corps's exploits through his volume of the *Canada in Flanders* series, an innovative publishing project, which, because of the status and abilities of its two main contributors, demands further examination of its literary methods and rhetorical style than previously offered by historians.

III.

Despite the publishing success of the *Canada in Flanders* series in its own time, the project has garnered little attention in Canadian military historical scholarship.[24] Of the few historians who have afforded space to discussing the series, the majority of them acknowledge it as a part of Aitken's larger war recording efforts but offer little by way of examining the contents of the volumes or Roberts's place in those discussions.

Part of the reason for the easy dismissal of the series lies in the fact that critics have struggled to categorize the volumes. Although most military historians are in agreement that the series offered a largely uncritical per-spective on the war, there is a lack of consistency among critics on how to describe it. Cook, for instance, refers to the volumes as "popular war histo-ries" and "semi-official histories," while Keshen describes Volume I as a "nar-rative."[25] For his part, Vance initially describes the series as "official history," although he later points out that the "CWRO accounts did tend to be closer to romance."[26]

For their part, early reviewers tended to describe the volumes less as history and more as narrative works: Volume I, for instance, was typi-cally categorized as a story rather than a history book; the *Daily Chronicle* even goes so far as to declare that the "Official Historian of the Canadian Expeditionary Force, whoever he may be ... cannot hope to match the vivid narrative" of Aitken.[27] For their parts, Beaverbrook and Roberts were explicit in noting that what they had written was by no means an end prod-uct for historians. In his preface to Volume I, Beaverbrook points out that the ensuing pages are merely his "impressions of the fortunes of the 1st Canadian Division," and that he hoped it would serve as a source text for future, more comprehensive histories: "Nor is there reason to doubt that the official historian of Canada ... will find abundant material for a grave and adequate work."[28] A similar sentiment is offered in Volume II, although this time it is stated more forcibly: "the fog of war lies heavy on the scene of confusion and heroic effort, and if (which is very unlikely) it is to be lifted at all, it must be by the hand of the future historian."[29]

Roberts is also quick to differentiate between what he is writing and what a career historian might produce. In a letter to Macmillan Company president George Platt Brett, Roberts writes that his volume " is dry & bald & official, —though, I trust, reliable.... By & by, when one can see these colossal events in perspective, justly and clearly, I may do some historical work of importance in connection with some limited section of them."[30] Like Beaverbrook, Roberts understood that the most his narrative could offer is "reliability," since proper historical writing can only be undertaken once "one can see these colossal events in perspective." Not surprisingly, these sentiments appear more explicitly near the beginning of Volume III:

> To present an adequate picture of the battle as a whole, or even of the specific part played in it by this or that particular corps, is a task that will tax the powers of the inspired historian, viewing the great subject at such a distance that he can see it as a whole and in its true perspective. The utmost that can be attempted in this unpretending narrative is to

set down the salient facts as to the achievements of our own Divisions, with such detail as can be sifted out, more or less at hazard, while the dust of the stupendous conflict is still in the air.[31]

What Roberts and Beaverbrook both recognized was the need for time and distance from events before proper historical writing could be undertaken; in other words, neither man viewed their books as comprehensive works of history.

But if the volumes were never envisioned as history, to what genre of writing do they belong? Part of the answer can be construed from the series subtitle: "the official story of the Canadian Expeditionary Force." For most readers, the phrase "official story" is likely interpreted along military lines; that is, its content approved and controlled by censors from the Canadian military bureaucracy. But what if the phrase was considered along literary lines as describing an inherent tension between fact ("official") and fiction ("story")? Read in this way, the subtitle could be interpreted as a descriptive term meant to align the series more closely with notions of documentary rather than history.

The idea of documentary is usually associated with film, although the term itself was not coined until 1926 by Scottish-born film producer John Grierson, who would go on to establish Canada's National Film Board twelve years later. But before the term was invented, cinematography was already being employed as a way to document and capture human events; Beaverbrook in particular recognized the powerful storytelling and myth-making techniques of this relatively new medium and included cinematography early in the establishment of the CWRO as part of its arsenal of approaches to recording the Canadian war effort.[32] As a mode of storytelling, documentary provided creators with a theoretical framework within which they could approach human events in a reliable, visual way without requiring the distance of time to legitimize the authenticity of their works. As Bill Nichols describes it, "the documentary form balances creative vision with a respect for the historical world."[33] Of course, a by-product of this approach is the illusion that what is being presented is an objective treatment of the subject. But as Robert Rosenstone points out, even documentary films based on historical events are inherently biased: "All too often, historians who scorn dramatizations are willing to accept the documentary film as a more accurate way of representing the past, as if somehow the images appear on the screen unmediated. Yet the documentary is never a direct reflection of an outside reality but a work consciously shaped into a narrative that—whether dealing with past or present—creates the meaning of the material being conveyed."[34] In short, documentaries may be viewed as reliable without being overly critical, accurate without being governed by the tautology of facts—an ideal approach for Beaverbrook (and later Roberts) by which to tell the story of the Canadian Corps in a timely fashion.

Both of Beaverbrook's volumes can certainly be interpreted for their documentary mode of storytelling. For instance, in Volume I he eschews the authoritative third-person voice in favour of the personal pronoun "I" as a way to create a more intimate and humanizing relationship with the reader: "[T]he evening that I reached the billeting area, I saw several battalions of the Expeditionary Force marching from their billets towards the trenches—they had been at the front for months, yet they stepped as freshly as though they were just home or route-marching in English lanes." At other times Beaverbrook narrates himself into the story in order to create a sense of immediacy, as though the narrative is occurring as he describes it: "I went on foot part of the way here, for so many battalions of men were massed that motor traffic was impossible.... I had just passed the signpost when the comparative peace of morning was awfully shattered by the united roar and crash of hundreds of guns."[35] Obviously Beaverbrook was drawing on his work as a war reporter to help create his narrative, but this first-person form of reportage is also successful in helping to establish the twinned documentary illusion of credibility and authenticity.

Equally effective in both volumes is Beaverbrook's frequent digressions from high-level operational descriptions to low-level narrative episodes of bravery. Although rightly criticized for focusing on the acts of officers in the majority of instances, Beaverbrook nevertheless employed a kind of creative storytelling technique meant to draw the reader's attention to the human dimension of war. The following example is just one of a number of similar illustrative passages: "[Sergeant] Morris led the attack down the German communication trench, and all the members of his party, with the exception of himself, were either killed or wounded. He got to a point at the end of the trench and there maintained himself—to use the cold official phrase—by throwing bombs and by the work of his single rifle and bayonet."[36] It is interesting to note that in the middle of this fictionalized recounting of Sergeant Morris's bravery, Beaverbrook felt compelled to point out the rhetorical difference between stylized writing and the "cold official phrase" of the military historian. From a documentary standpoint, these episodes not only help to humanize the narrative: they also function as further proof that the story being told is based in the real world.

This is not to say that Beaverbrook completely fictionalized his story. On the contrary, his story is a fact-based narrative, and Beaverbrook explicitly stated at different points that his material has come from various reports and despatches, often quoting directly from officers' reports to emphasize the volume's authenticity. Early in Volume I, for instance, he quotes a long excerpt from a speech by General Alderson to the troops, declaring that "General Alderson's methods—his practical and soldierly style—could not be better illustrated than by some extracts from the speech."[37] Volume I also includes several appendices meant to educate and arouse approval from Beaverbrook's home-front readers. Inspirational documents, such as the King's Message to Canadian troops in the First Division before their embarkation for France and several speeches by then Prime Minister Robert Borden, serve to strengthen the book's patriotic perspective. Beaverbrook also included at the end of the first volume a list of casualties, as well as honours and awards granted to officers and soldiers of the First Division, to lend further factual legitimacy to his volume.

The resulting narrative is a continual tension between fact and fiction. On the one hand, Beaverbrook's explanation of strategies and battlefield operations, inclusion of maps, and quotations from speeches and despatches help root the narrative in fact. On the other, his descriptive episodes of bravery serve as creative and stylistic counterpoints that help humanize the narrative and push the volume beyond the kind of cold, objective, and balanced prose required for traditional historical writing. In short, Volume I was meant to serve as one man's perspective on a nation's war effort and as a source document for future scholarly work—not to stand as a representative work of history.[38]

Beaverbrook's documentary approach to recording the efforts of the Canadian Corps continued in Volume II, although he did make adjustments to the book's overall style and structure. Not surprisingly, he maintained his technique of offering an overarching chronological narrative, as well as several detailed operational maps, anecdotes of bravery, and quotations from despatches and reports to lend credibility to the story. Having said that, Volume II offers some significant changes that reflect a refinement of his documentary style. Most pronounced is Beaverbrook's discarding of the centralizing pronoun "I" in favour of the more inclusive, collective pronoun "we" in all but the final chapter. Equally significant is his reduction in appendices from six to one; but this by no means lessens the documentary effect of the volume, since the extracts from a Despatch from Sir Douglas Haig in the appendix are not directly quoted, but supplied via a reputable British newspaper, the *London Gazette*, lending further legitimacy to Haig's words, as well as Beaverbrook's story.

In Volume II, Beaverbrook was also less effusive in his use of patriotic rhetoric to describe the Canadian war effort; it still appears in the second volume, but the sentiments are more restrained in both tone and length. For instance, here is Beaverbrook extolling praise on soldiers in Volume I: "With what devotion, with a valour how desperate, with resourcefulness how cool and how fruitful, the amateur soldiers of Canada confronted overwhelming odds may, perhaps, be made clear even by a narrative so incomplete as this."[39] In Volume II, however, Beaverbrook was less epic in his presentation of acts of heroism, and more willing at times to describe the real cost of such bravery: for example, he mentioned at one point how Private Green, "who actually touched off the wire, was blown to atoms";[40] later he recounted how Lieutenant Owens warded off a German attack so that his men could escape, but "he never returned, and when his party went back to seek him they found him lying on the wet ground with a bullet through his head."[41] Another poignant example of Beaverbrook's increasingly honest assessment of the Canadian Corps is his inclusion of a counter-attack launched against the Germans at Ypres; he declared at the outset that "this chapter is the record of a counter-attack which failed." A few pages later he noted that the counterattack "was to prove, unfortunately, as fallible in execution as sweeping measures hurriedly conceived under the stress of war are apt to be"—although it must be said that by the end of the chapter Beaverbrook felt it necessary to return to patriotic ways and praise the Canadians for having achieved "battle honours."[42] Rather than ignore the truth of the battle, Beaverbrook is forthright in his assessment of the outcome, presenting readers with images of sacrifice and loss, as well acts of bravery.

Vance refers to an undated memo in which "Aitken himself … admitted that the main purpose of the second volume of *Canada in Flanders* was not to document a period of the nation's history but 'to further the Imperial cause by stimulating recruiting in Canada.'"[43] Given the above evidence, however, it is difficult to understand from a content standpoint why Beaverbrook saw Volume II as an effective tool for recruiting. On the contrary, an examination of its rhetoric and style suggests that Beaverbrook was starting to move away from the blatant propagandistic phrases and portrayals of Volume I toward a more nuanced documentary style—an evolution in the series that would change again under the practised pen of Roberts.

III.

At the beginning of Volume III, Roberts signalled to the reader that Canada was no longer a naive colony; through sacrifice it was becoming a mature nation: "In the summer of 1914 Canada was a land of peace, of self-interest, of political warfare, and commercial and agricultural prosperity; and now her thousands lie dead on foreign battlefields; thousands of her sons have returned to her, maimed, broken, and blind; her forward army fights on, continually bleeding yet continually growing in strength."[44] The fulsome, epic praise heaped on Canadian soldiers by Beaverbrook—particularly in the first volume—had become more tempered under the experienced authorship of Roberts. This is not to say that Roberts completely rejected his predecessor's tone or approach. On the contrary, several of the documentary elements Beaverbrook employed in his volumes appear in Roberts's story, significantly the use of maps, inclusion of descriptive anecdotes and episodes of bravery, as well as a didactic approach with respect to explaining operational activities such as tunnelling or barrage tactics. Also in keeping with Beaverbrook's use of appendices, Roberts includes a Chronological Index of the Operations on the Somme at the end of his volume to augment the factual legitimacy of his narrative. But Volume III is not simply an imitation of its predecessors.

One of the significant differences is Roberts's more democratic accounting of the Canadian Corps exploits. Indeed, as W.S. Wallace noted in his review for the *Canadian Bookman*, "Major Roberts' volume is a distinct improvement on its predecessors. There is in it none of that fulsome flattery of prominent officers and politicians which marred the first volume of 'Canada in Flanders.'"[45] Although Roberts mentioned and described acts of bravery by officers, he included many anecdotes of heroism by non-commissioned officers and ordinary soldiers. He also focused more attention on the Corps's non-infantry activities: for instance, in Chapter II he afforded considerable space to recounting the efforts of the Tunnelling Companies, and later described the actions of the Canadian Engineer and Pioneer companies, as well as the Field Ambulances.[46] Equally successful are those places where Roberts used his abilities as an imaginative writer to depict the machine of war, as when he offered what is perhaps one of the earliest documented descriptions of a tank in battle:

> This monster, apparently eyeless, its carapace a daub of uncouth colours, squat and portentous as one of those colossal saurians which we picture emerging from the Eocene slime, had wallowed its slow, irresistible way up over the trenches and shellholes, belching fire from its sides and its dreadful, blind, blunt snout. Bullets and shrapnel fell harmlessly as snowflakes from its impervious shell. Bombs exploded thickly upon it, and, though wrapping it in flame, did no more than deface the fantastic pattern of its paint. Its path, wherever it moved, was spread with panic. In the teeth of the most concentrated fire it waddled deliberately up to the barriers of the Sugar Factory, trod them down without haste or effort, and exterminated a defending machine-gun with its crew. Then, crashing ponderously through or over every kind of obstacle, it made a slow circuit of the Factory, halting stolidly here and there to blot out a troublesome nest of machine-gunners or to preside over the submission of a bunch of horror-stricken Huns. Its work done at this point, it lumbered off to seek adventure elsewhere.[47]

It is worth noting that this tank is mythical rather than heroic in nature. Instead of being a vehicle for propaganda, Roberts portrays it as "a monster" capable of "belching fire" and toppling buildings "without haste or effort." Put another way, this description is not the work of a historian; only a creative writer could have conceived such a wartime vision.

Equally significant is that Roberts offers readers a more balanced narrative than that of his predecessor. Although Beaverbrook included some references to battlefield failure in his second volume, Roberts's narrative moves more obviously from the early successes of Courcelette to the operational failures at Moquet Farm and Regina Trench. His account of Zollern Redoubt, for instance, is not couched in false patriotic rhetoric; instead he notes that the operation was "disorganized in its foundations" and that "the whole attack fell through and was abandoned, and our battalions, angry and bleeding, drew back into their own lines…. As far as the object with which it was undertaken is concerned, the operation was a confessed failure." It is worth mentioning here that the word "failure," a term seldom employed by Beaverbrook, begins to appear frequently in the latter half of the volume. In one two-page span of Roberts's volume the word appears four times, the last instance a difficult phrase for any soldier to read: "The undeniable failure of the operations of October 1st and 8th." Having said that, Roberts was still an unrepentant nationalist, and, like his predecessor, wished to end the story on a positive note. Coincidentally, his nationalist rhetoric in the last chapter closely echoes Beaverbrook's: "Welded now by sacrifice, endurance, prudent and brilliant leaderships, and glorious achievements against the mightiest military Power in the world's history, into a fighting force of incomparable effectiveness, it was no less than their due that the most tremendous tasks should be set to these fiery and indomitable fighters of the North."[48]

Patriotic in tone, Roberts's ending is certainly a biased one. But like Beaverbrook, Roberts's perspective was that of the documentarian, not the official historian, and so his romantic evocation of battled-tested heroes from the North is a fitting image by which to end such a nationalist tale—a tale rooted in fact but inspired by imagination.

IV.

After the publication of Volume III, Sir Arthur Currie declared in a letter to Lieutenant Colonel Harold Daly that Roberts's volume "bears no resemblance to the true story of the period it depicts than a mutton stew does to the sheep itself."[49] Currie also wrote a strongly worded letter to Roberts, criticizing him on the "accuracy" of the events described in his book. Not to be intimidated, Roberts responds with an equally strongly worded defence of his book—a heated exchange recounted by Cook.[50] What is interesting to note about these two pieces of correspondence is not so much their contents but the way Cook's retelling reveals his favouring of the historical figure over the literary one. To his credit, Cook corroborates Currie's criticism by specifying the inaccurate elements in the volume that Currie was alluding to; he also mentions the letter of response Roberts wrote to Currie, in which the former apologized for errors. Cook, however, neglects to point out two important details. First, he fails to report that Roberts attempted to consult with Currie several times on the details of the book before its publication: "When I arrived at Camblain l'Abbe in April last I called upon you within an hour of my arrival. Finding that you were engaged, I reported myself formally, and left with your ADC an earnest request that you would see me at your earliest convenience. I twice repeated the request, and was much disappointed at receiving no response from you." Second, Roberts's letter reveals that what irked Currie most was not so much factual inaccuracies within the volume, but the less-than-primary position afforded to his First Division:

> Referring to paragraphs 4 and 5, may I point out that a great part of Volume II deals with matters in which the First Division was not involved? The first chapter deals entirely with the organization, etc., etc., of the Fourth Division, as the opening chapters of Volume I deal with the organization, etc., etc., of the First Division. Chapter 4 and 5 are entirely taken up with the actual capture of Courcelette; and Chapter 10 with the operations against Desire Trench. Thus four out of the ten chapters of the book deal with subjects not directly involving the First Division. This, you will agree, very substantially reduces the disproportion which you have called attention to.[51]

Cook, however, rejects Roberts's defence. He argues that Currie's demand "for more recognition for his men" was simply the result of a man wishing for a "balanced history."[52] But it is difficult to accept Cook's interpretation of the exchange, not only for his lack of attention to the content of Roberts's letter, but also because Currie had a reputation for knee-jerk reactions against writers who did not portray the military in a positive light; as Vance relates, when Charles Yale Harrison's *Generals Die in Bed* was published, Currie condemned the book before having even read it.[53] In short, Currie's infamous quip about "mutton stew" is less an informed opinion by a careful reader as it is a biased complaint by an ego-driven military commander who mistook Roberts's documentary for history. Yet Cook is content with declaring, at the end of his short assessment of the volume, that Roberts had "indeed written an uneven history of the Canadians on the Somme."[54]

Roberts's volume has also been criticized by Peter Buitenhuis, who declares, among other things, that Roberts had "a more romantic view of battle than Aitken," although he offers little evidence to support this claim. Subsequently Buitenhuis goes on to dismiss the volume in one rhetorical swoop by stating that Roberts "combines some medieval mythology with his interests as a naturalist" to gloss over tough-fought battles.[55] I have found no obvious allusion to medievalism in Roberts's volume; in fact, it is Beaverbrook who refers to the Princess Pats in Volume I as "knights of mediaeval days."[56] Had Buitenhuis bothered to investigate Roberts's life or reading habits, he would have discovered that Roberts received his first degree in Classics—a perspective that is quickly supported by an early description of the attack on Courcelette as a "Homeric bout." More telling is the fact that near the beginning of his volume Roberts declares that, "to present an adequate picture of the battle [on the Somme] as a whole, or even of the specific part played in it by this or that particular corps, is a task that will tax the powers of the inspired historian…. He will need to be a new Thucydides, equipped, not only with grasp and vision, but also with mastery of the magic of words."[57] Thucydides was an Ancient Greek historian, and so even this innocent reference reveals to us that Roberts's sensibility is to a tradition of historical writing and literature in which heroes functioned as a part of the nation's narrative, not as possible romance exploits for propaganda purposes. As to Buitenhuis's second criticism—that Roberts glossed over tough battles—this is also factually inaccurate. Did Roberts soften the realistic details of the carnage of the Somme? Yes. Did he deny that soldiers were killed? No. In fact, in three places in the narrative Roberts quotes significant numbers of casualties, including the 1,267 casualties sustained in the battle of Courcelette; the 5,509 casualties incurred from 27 September to 4 October in the Battle of Regina Trench; and the 2,685 casualties suffered the following week.[58]

What historians like Cook and Buitenhuis have come to interpret as Roberts's "propaganda speak" when he describes the valiant efforts of the soldiers, or portrays them as heroic figures, reveals not so much Roberts's faults as a historian, but a penchant on the part of these historians for reading history with a historical bias—of confusing twentieth-century British colonial ideas about romance with Roberts's classical understanding of heroic narratives for the purposes of nation-building. For Roberts's volume is neither romantic nor a dry piece of mostly accurate history. What Roberts attempted to write was, in his own words, a "reliable" story, one that wove fact with imagination into a kind of documentary narrative that would help provide the necessary literary foundation for a nation struggling to define itself.

V.

Charles G.D. Roberts is a problematic figure for Canadian military historians because he is a writer first and a historian second (or third, or fourth), and thus many critics, it seems, have decided that the best way of dealing with him is barely to mention him at all. His Volume III of the *Canada in Flanders* series—indeed, all three volumes—suffers from a lack of proper scholarly attention because these narratives live outside the generally accepted historical method of writing. By examining the rhetoric and approach in all three volumes, however, one can discern a stylistic evolution in the series from an early romantic form of nationalist documentary to a more balanced and disciplined narrative. And so, perhaps, in an ironic way the subtitle for the *Canada in Flanders* series as the "official story" of the CEF is a fitting one, because it was much more than a form of flawed history or wartime propaganda. Instead, it represents an early form of modern nationalist documentary, and Roberts's third volume stands as the apotheosis, rather than the denouement, of Aitken's original vision.

NOTES

1. E.M. Pomeroy, *Sir Charles G.D. Roberts: A Biography* (Toronto: Ryerson Press, 1943); John Coldwell Adams, *Sir Charles God Damn: the Life of Sir Charles G.D. Roberts* (Toronto: University of Toronto Press, 1986). Pomeroy devotes only ten pages to Roberts's wartime service and the majority of her information is a series of anecdotes showing how clever and charming Roberts was; Coldwell Adams devotes only four pages to describing Roberts's actitivies.

2. Tim Cook, *Clio's Warriors: Canadian Historians and the Writing of the World Wars* (Vancouver: UBC Press, 2006). Cook notes that the first volume went through "four printings in the first month, and twelve printings by March" (16). He also points out that "the series remained authoritative for many Canadians, and if the second and third volumes did not have the same influence as the first groundbreaking effort, they were still important in laying the foundation for subsequent historical interpretations" (26). See also note 27.

3. Jeffrey Keshen, *Propaganda and Censorship during Canada's Great War* (Edmonton: University of Alberta Press, 1996). More embarrassing is the typo in Keshen's article, "The Great War Soldier as Nation Builder in Canada and Australia," in *Shaping Nations: Constitutionalism and Society in Australia and Canada* (Ottawa: University of Ottawa Press, 2002), in which Volume III is wrongly attributed to Theodore (215)—an error committed by Robert McIntosh five years earlier in "The Great War, Archives, and Modern Memory," *Archivaria* 46 (Fall 1998): 26.

4. Tim Cook, "Documenting War and Forging Reputations: Sir Max Aitken and the Canadian War Records Office in the First World War," *War in History* 10, no. 3 (July 2003): 265–95; "Quill and Canon: Writing the Great War in Canada," *American Review of Canadian Studies* 35, no. 3 (October 2005): 503–30; Cook, *Clio's Warriors*. In "Documenting War," Cook echoes Keshen by mentioning Roberts only as the brother of Theodore; in "Quill and the Canon," Cook again ignores Roberts, choosing to use Aitken as the only necessary representative to explain the *Canada in Flanders* series.

5. Jonathan F. Vance, *Death So Noble: Memory, Meaning, and the First World War* (Vancouver: UBC Press, 1997), 165. Vance includes only one page of discussion on the *Canada in Flanders* series, and one short paragraph on Roberts's volume.

6. Pomeroy says little of Roberts's affiliation with the regiment; Coldwell Adams makes no mention of Roberts's early military service. For a description of the life of John Murrary Bliss, see Phillip Buckner's entry in the *Dictionary of Canadian Biography*.

7. Charles G.D. Roberts, "Canadian History—how best to teach the authorized text book," *The Star*, 13 October 1880. http://www.canadianpoetry.ca/confederation/roberts/non-fictional_prose/index.htm.

8. Charles G.D. Roberts, "Bryce's *Short History of the Canadian People*," *Dial* 8, no. 96 (April 1888): 290–92. http://www.canadianpoetry.ca/confederation/roberts/non-fictional_prose/index.htm.

9. Charles G.D. Roberts, *A History of Canada* (Toronto: Macmillan, 1915 [1897]), 428.

10. Michael Humphries, "'The eyes of an empire': the Legion of Frontiersmen, 1904–14," *Historical Research* 85, no. 227 (February 2012): 134.

11. At the outbreak of war, Roberts was fifty-four years old and had been living in England for two years; Coldwell Adams notes that Roberts lied about his age in order to enlist (123).

12. Letter to Edith, 14 September 1914, in *The Collected Letters of Sir Charles G.D. Roberts*, ed. Laurel Boone (Fredericton: Goose Lane, 1989), 300.

13. Letter to Douglas, 4 October 1914, *Collected Letters*, 301.

14. Letter to Parkin, 5 November 1914, *Collected Letters*, 303.

15. Letter to War Secretary, 5 November 1914, *Collected Letters*, 303–4. In spite of his well-placed references, Pomeroy suggests that it was Lieutenant-Colonel Hamer Greenwood (later Viscount Greenwood) who ultimately helped Roberts get his commission (235).

16. Letter to Roberts's family, *Collected Letters*, 305–6.

17. Letter to Douglas, 24 May 1915, *Collected Letters*, 306–7. Coincidentally, Coldwell Adams notes that Roberts had actually applied for a transfer to the Canadian forces during the spring of 1915 (124).

18. Letter to Douglas, 1 May 1916, *Collected Letters*, 310–11.

19. See Pomeroy, 235.

20. By 1916, Roberts had published book reviews on several Canadian history texts, several non-fiction pieces on historical Acadie, and two books on historical subjects, *A History of Canada* (1897) and the lengthy *Discoveries and Explorations in the Century* (1903). Roberts also based his historical novel, *Barbara Ladd* (1902), on the American Civil War, and drew on the mid-eighteenth-century conflict between England and France as inspiration for his three novels about Acadie: *The Forge in the Forest* (1896), *A Sister to Evangeline* (1898), and *The Prisoner of Mademoiselle* (1904).

21. Roberts gave the address for at least two exhibitions—at Stoke-on-Trent on 10 November 1918 (Coldwell Adams, 126) and at Southend on 14 August 1918 (Canadian War Records Office).

22. In a letter to then Lieutenant-General Sir Arthur Currie, Roberts noted that, "I am now engaged upon Volume IV, which deals with Vimy Ridge and your subsequent operations in that region. I shall certainly beg you to examine the manuscript when it is complete, and to favour me with your criticisms and emendations" (11 July 1918, *Collected Letters*, 315).

23. Shortly before he died, Roberts published a small chapbook, *Canada Speaks of Britain and Other Poems of the War* (Toronto: Ryerson Press, 1941); he also edited an anthology of patriotic poetry: *Flying Colors* (Toronto: Ryerson Press, 1942).

24. As others have pointed out, Beaverbrook's volume was an enormous success. In the first three months after publication, it went through twelve editions and sold more than 250,000 copies. See Cook's "Quill and Canon."

25. Cook, "Documenting War," 268; Cook, "Quill and Canon"; Keshen, *Propaganda and Censorship*, 33.

26. Vance, *Death So Noble*, 105, 165.

27. Cited in Lord Beaverbrook, *Canada in Flanders: The Official Story of the Canadian Expeditionary Force*, vol. I (Toronto: Hodder and Stoughton, 1916), 279.

28. Beaverbrook, *Canada in Flanders*, vol. I, xiii.

29. Beaverbrook, *Canada in Flanders: The Official Story of the Canadian Expeditionary Force*, vol. II (Toronto: Hodder and Stoughton, 1917), 132.

30. Letter to Blatt, 23 November 1918, *Collected Letters*, 316.

31. Charles G.D. Roberts, *Canada in Flanders: The Official Story of the Canadian Expeditionary Force*, vol. III (Toronto: Hodder and Stoughton, 1918), 23–24.

32. For a discussion on the role of cinematography in the CWRO, see Vance, *Death So Noble*, 175.

33. Bill Nichols, *Introduction to Documentary*, 2nd edition (Bloomington: Indiana University Press, 2010 [2001]), 6.

34. Robert Rosenstone, "History in Images/History in Words: Reflections on the Possibility of Really Putting History onto Film," *American Historical Review* 93, no. 5 (December 1988): 1179.

35. Beaverbrook, *Canada in Flanders*, vol. I, 19, 35.

36. Beaverbrook, *Canada in Flanders*, vol. I, 127.

37. Beaverbrook, *Canada in Flanders*, vol. I, 29.

38. Beaverbrook, *Canada in Flanders*, vol. I, xiii.

39. Beaverbrook, *Canada in Flanders*, vol. I, 48.

40. Beaverbrook, *Canada in Flanders*, vol. II, 43.

41. Beaverbrook, *Canada in Flanders*, vol. II, 74.

42. Beaverbrook, *Canada in Flanders*, vol. II, 74, 199, 210.

43. Vance, *Death So Noble*, 165.

44. Roberts, *Canada in Flanders*, vol. III, 9.

45. W.S. Wallace, "Clio in Canada, 1918: A Review of Historical Publications of the Year," *Canadian Bookman* (January 1919): 45.

46. Roberts, *Canada in Flanders*, vol. III, 65.

47. Roberts, *Canada in Flanders*, vol. III, 44–45.

48. Roberts, *Canada in Flanders*, vol. III, 77, 100–101, 121.

49. Letter from Currie to Daly, 26 October 1918, cited in Audrey and Paul Grescoe, *The Book of War Letters* (Toronto: McClelland and Stewart, 2005), 197.

50. Tim Cook, *Clio's Warriors*, 27–28.

51. Letter to Sir Arthur Currie, 11 July 1918, *Collected Letters*, 313–15.

52. Cook, *Clio's Warriors*, 28.

53. Vance, "The Soldier as Novelist: Literature, History, and the Great War," *Canadian Literature* 179 (winter 2003): 32; see also Cook, *Clio's Warriors*, 76–77.

54. Cook, *Clio's Warriors*, 28.

55. Peter Buitenhuis, *The Great War of Words: British, American, and Canadian Propaganda and Fiction, 1914–1933* (Vancouver: UBC Press, 1987), 100.

56. Beaverbrook, *Canada in Flanders*, vol. I, 145.

57. Roberts, *Canada in Flanders*, vol. III, 44, 23–24.

58. Roberts, *Canada in Flanders*, vol. III, 66, 89, 102.

STATE WAR HISTORIES
"An Atom of Interest in an Ocean of Apathy"

KIMBERLY J. LAMAY LICURSI

The passing of Frank Buckles, the last American veteran of the First World War, in February 2011 was a fleeting story that prompted very little reflection about the war's meaning in the United States. His family and other supporters unsuccessfully requested that Buckles be allowed to lie in the Rotunda of the Capitol so that his passing might serve as an occasion for remembering and honouring all American veterans of the Great War. Buckles's family was allowed instead to use the amphitheatre at Arlington Cemetery for a service attended by two hundred people. This is in contrast to the French and Canadian governments, which offered state funerals to their last veterans, and the thousands who attended a ceremony for the last British veteran in 2009. Americans greeted Buckles's death in a manner that was not surprising given their general lack of interest in the First World War in favour of the Civil War and the Second World War, which are thought of as, respectively, bigger and better. This neglect is reflected in the fact that the First World War is the only conflict not remembered with a national monument. The American collective disregard for the war is ironic given the tremendous postwar efforts exerted by some to create war histories ensuring that it never be forgotten.

The fervour that swept America during the war focused not only on winning the war, but on memorializing the efforts taken to secure victory. Patriotic Americans formed war history organizations shortly after the declaration of war, as states worked to preserve the stories of their unique contributions to the cause. Many states planned ambitious multi-volume tributes, but the vast majority failed to publish anything. Efforts lacked funding, local historians failed to engage civic support for the projects, citizens sought to forget the war as quickly as possible, and, most importantly, soldiers rebuffed data-collecting efforts. Historians were left wondering how to create a lasting tribute to personal sacrifice when soldiers refused to contribute their names to a list of those who served. The war was a taboo conversation topic in the years after the armistice—much less a subject for triumphant, commemorative writing. State historians' attempts to engage the public to write war histories were met with overwhelming opposition on many fronts.

The lack of American interest in the First World War, especially across the two decades over which memory had time to take root before the Second World War, defies logic in two ways. First, it ignores the unwritten rule that societies recognize and lionize soldiers for their sacrifices.[1] Second, forgetting war means forgetting its social and cultural implications, disregarding its hard-earned lessons, thereby risking a repetition of historical mistakes. The conventional wisdom that war teaches some of the most important historical lessons would seem to suggest that the First World War should have served some didactic purpose for Americans. Americans had every reason to remember this war. It propelled the country onto the world stage in a compelling and enduring way. Yet the effort to create war histories met with insurmountable obstacles in the field. Historians were unable to facilitate collective acts of remembrance that might sustain collective memory of the war.[2] This refutes the notion that Americans blithely accepted the war and its ramifications.

By 1919, thirty-five states had made systematic efforts to collect and preserve historical data about the war. Many delegated the task to the state historian, a war history committee, a war records commission, or a historical agency. These organizations solicited information from soldiers, war agencies, churches, schools, government agencies, and a host of other sources. The National Board for Historic Service (NBHS) was formed in 1917 as an outlet for historians who wanted to offer public service during the war, much like the public service that was offered by scientists, engineers, or munitions workers.[3]

Government officials and historians had several motivations for collecting war information. First, there was a genuine desire to preserve the names of those who served. The branches of the armed services kept records on soldiers, but did not arrange them according to political boundaries and had never published the information. Second, reminding people of the nation's collective effort in support of the cause might help to preserve a united front after the war. Third, historians expressed concern that studies of the Civil War were hampered by a lack of first-person information from soldiers. The personal recollections of soldiers would fill this void. The NBHS dissolved at the close of the war and was succeeded by the National Association of State War History Organizations (NASWHO), which aimed to collect and preserve war-related records. A core group of fifteen or sixteen states, including New York and Virginia, collaborated through NASWHO to discuss issues related to their respective projects for many years after the war.

New York, Virginia, and Kansas have extant archives of records that document the collection process undertaken to produce their respective war histories. Their experiences establish a pattern of behaviour over a diverse geographic area that demonstrates a pervasive apathy, if not disdain, for remembrance in postwar America. All three states focused most of their time, as did other states, on attempting to collect individual war service records. The desire was borne as much of necessity as of historical curiosity, since no central record of the soldiers from each state was available until years after the war. The testimony of soldiers was the only way to compile lists of those who served and where they fought.[4]

NEW YORK

"[There was] a silly spirit prevalent with some men who think they acquire a sort of big boy credit by replying, 'I want to forget the war.'"

Five hundred thousand New Yorkers went to war and made up more than ten percent of the nation's soldiers.[5] For seven years, State Historian James Sullivan challenged, shamed, and cajoled citizens and historians to fulfill their patriotic duty and document the men who served. When the state legislature supported the plan to record New York's war, it also authorized the appointment of 1,500 local historians to serve as Sullivan's field staff.[6] Securing the appointment of this army of historians would be one of the biggest obstacles Sullivan faced. Many municipalities never appointed a historian or delayed doing so until well into the 1920s. Those historians who were appointed were thwarted by ambivalence, and even antipathy, about war remembrance, and a large number of the historians reported disappointment in their inability to extract information from soldiers and war service organizations. A recalcitrant public would be Sullivan's second major obstacle.

Reports from local historians suggested a strong sense of disillusion-ment. In Sinclairville, the historian reported finding "a very strange con-dition among the soldier boys, their relatives and friends. None of them, or perhaps not more than one in ten seem to care to give me ... the details [of their service]."[7] Numerous historians wrote to Sullivan apologizing for paltry returns and long delays. In Fairfield, just five out of fifty soldiers sup-plied the requested information.[8] In Hudson Falls, local officials reported that the "men were too careless to participate," and collected the stories of only twenty out of three hundred soldiers.[9] Dr. Sullivan told one distraught historian that there was no generalization to be made about the situation: "In some cases the men and women have entered into the spirit of the mat-ter with vim and energy.... In others they have been what we might popu-larly term 'the limit.' What creates this state of mind is difficult to say."[10]

Letter after letter to Sullivan indicated individual and communal apathy toward the project. One historian wrote that Civil War veterans were proud of their service and would share their stories freely. When he sought out the stories of Great War veterans, he claimed: "never have I worked with greater zeal or spent more time and effort than on the subject in question [soldier questionnaires] and never have I met with as little response and manifest interest on the part of those who ought to have been interested." Even after begging soldiers, he could get no response.[11]

By November 1922, Plattsburgh City historian George Bixby decried the meagre responses from soldiers and municipal war agencies and pub-lished a statement in the local paper urging "all persons and families inter-ested in having proper credit given to the city, its martyrs, its ex-service men ... to do their part in furnishing information."[12] Bixby had elevated those who died in the war to the status of martyrs to encourage partici-pation, but his request met with little response.[13] Historians mailed ques-tionnaires once, twice, even three times, with little effect. Personal visits soliciting information were often met with a stern refusal. One historian noted that soldiers did not even seem to know, or care to share, the unit in which they enlisted. Veterans told the Saratoga Springs historian that, "they got little recognition for their sacrifice and suffering and felt that it was use-less for me to try [and] give them any now."[14]

Despite eight years of considerable effort, New York State officials never published a history of the State's role in the war. However, some com-munities were more successful in publishing localized histories of New Yorkers in the First World War, including at least ten counties (Albany, Chautauqua, Erie, Franklin, Jefferson, Monroe, Oneida, Otsego, and Yates).

Many municipalities also published works that ranged in scope from brief pamphlets to multi-volume publications.

Many of the histories that came to fruition were a direct extension of the state's propaganda infrastructure. County Defense Committees were established during the war in all sixty-two New York State counties. After the armistice, these committees were authorized to continue work until May 1920 to prepare county honour rolls of those who served and died.[15] In Oneida County, the Defense Committee published a notice requesting the names of all servicemen and women from the war for the purposes of preparing the roster for the honour roll, urging residents to "Do it as a Duty." Through rosters from the National Guard, recruiting stations, and draft boards, the Defense Committee estimated 8,100 people had served in various civilian and military roles. When the roll was published several months later, the Committee had received response cards from only 364 individuals. The Committee's chairman suggested the poor response rate "must bring unpleasant reflections and regrets to the minds of those who failed to render that co-operation so solicitously sought."[16] Although Oneida County published a war history, it consisted of little more than an imprecise list cobbled together from different war agencies, without significant community support and input.

Emmett Harrison, the compiler and publisher of *Yates County in the World War 1917–1918*, appeared to have succeeded where others had failed. A reviewer lauded Harrison for the amount of information, including photographs, he was able to extract from some soldiers. However, while Harrison was successful at compiling full reports on select soldiers, he was forthright in his admission that his task did not have universal support. The reviewer absolved Harrison of responsibility, stating "that there were some [soldiers] that he could not get is evidently no fault of his own, but of a silly spirit prevalent with some men who think they acquire a sort of big boy credit by replying, 'I want to forget the war.'"[17]

Erie and Monroe Counties both made outstanding efforts to compile the two largest war histories produced in New York. In 1920, Erie County and the City of Buffalo, through the Committee of One Hundred, produced a 733-page tome, reportedly at a cost of $40,000, outlining the illustrious work of the county during the war. The first 450 pages are dedicated to the years leading up to war, civilian efforts on the home front, and histories of the units containing many Buffalo and Erie County soldiers. The publication, however, required little or no interaction with veterans and their families. The roster lists only the soldier's name, occasionally with rank and unit affiliation. There are no photographs, except for those of local elected officials and dignitaries, and little distinction is made to recognize those who died in service. The book is a compilation of documents produced by wartime propaganda agents with the addition of an incomplete roster of soldiers at the end.[18]

A group of Monroe County historians undertook a much more substantive effort. In three volumes totaling an overwhelming 3,300 pages, the City of Rochester and Monroe County crafted an extremely detailed account of citizens' and soldiers' contributions to the war effort. The county hired ex-servicemen to assist with the collection of data. Even veterans, however, met with resistance in gathering information from fellow soldiers. The ex-servicemen told organizers that veterans engaged in both open and covert opposition to the solicitations for information because "they think the country has been ungrateful to them for not supplying them with jobs or with a bonus."[19] Ultimately, county officials formed teams of volunteers to blanket the streets and counteract apathetic soldiers. The Red Triangle Club, an outgrowth of the YMCA during the war, fanned out across the county in seven teams, each composed of a captain and four other members. The Club was made up primarily of young women who would use all the resources at their disposal to secure information on the county's war heroes.[20]

The tactic was successful, and a small army of hard-working individuals created the *World War Service Record of Rochester and Monroe County, New York*. The first volume memorialized those who had died and included photographs of the majority of the deceased.[21] The second volume is a thorough accounting of more than 23,000 men and women who served during the war. Each individual is identified by name, address, place of birth, date of entry to service, places of service (including training camps), and discharge date. Of those included, just over 3,000 were civilians on the home front.

It seems that an organized, well-financed cadre of individuals willing to track down soldiers helped overcome the apathy evident in other communities. There are, however, a few other factors that may have contributed to the County's success. First, the county claims that 11,064 of 20,211 soldiers volunteered for service (the remainder having been drafted), a fifty-five percent enlistment rate, almost double the national average of twenty-eight percent.[22] The City of Rochester was also particularly solicitous of returning soldiers, bestowing on each soldier an honour medal, hung from a ribbon of blue, white, and gold, with the inscription "For Democracy, Liberty & Justice." It appears that they also gave similar medals for "Mothers of

Defenders of Liberty."[23] These efforts attest to stronger community support for the war, and created an environment of gratitude that may have made soldiers more amenable to participation. Monroe County's effort and the resulting volumes were unique among New York's communities. Their success was not primarily based on enthusiastic and voluntary participation of soldiers, but a determined community effort to recognize war service that garnered striking results.

Monroe County historians were also very inclusive in their data collection efforts and made significant efforts to capture the activities of Italians, Poles, Canadians, French, Lithuanians, Ukrainians, Armenians, and Greeks, many of whom were not naturalized citizens. Rochester officials queried the Italian Consular Office to secure the names of reservists who were recalled to the Italian Army. There is much less evidence of outreach to African American communities. Of all the New York publications reviewed, African American soldiers are only readily evident in two local histories, and in one of these, they are represented by a separate list for "colored soldiers."

Ultimately, the purposeful exclusion of black soldiers is mostly moot, as so few soldiers are represented in the limited war histories that were published. African Americans joined white New York veterans who were missing from the public record, many of the latter, at least, of their own accord. As the record in Virginia will demonstrate, however, it is just as likely that African American soldiers refused to participate as it is that they were excluded. The indifference and outright opposition expressed by soldiers in New York was evident in Virginia as well, and the sizable population of black soldiers there was not an exception to this rule.

VIRGINIA

"I am already beginning to feel like an atom of interest in an ocean of apathy as regards war history."

Governor Westmoreland Davis created the Virginia War History Commission (VWHC) in 1919. The commission was made up of sixteen community leaders and chaired by Arthur Kyle Davis, president of Southern Female College in Petersburg. The Commission oversaw local branches set up in Virginia's one hundred counties and twenty-one cities.[24] Davis's 121 local commissioners would serve the same role as Sullivan's locally appointed historians. Davis also had between one and six field workers who canvassed the state in an attempt to keep commission members on target.[25]

Davis asked commissioners to collect individual service records along with several other categories of information, including:

1. Virginians of Distinguished Service
2. Prewar Conditions and Activities
3. Virginia Churches in War Time
4. Virginia Schools and Colleges in the War
5. Draft Law and Virginia Organizations
6. Economic and Social Conditions
7. The Red Cross in Virginia
8. War Work and Relief Organizations
9. War Letters, Diaries and Incidents
10. Post War Conditions and Activities

However, as in New York, the Commission stressed the importance of collecting individual service records, telling county commissions that the collection of service records was the "gravamen of the history. The history will fail of its purpose unless we have a fairly accurate roster of all Virginia troops with something more than a mere list of names."[26] They had no idea how prescient that claim would be. The success of each county commission was rated, largely, on the number of records collected. So, while the county commissions exhibited limited success collecting reports on other topics, their efficacy would be rated according to the number of soldiers' records collected, which was, more often than not, meagre.[27] The four-page questionnaire sent to veterans was more comprehensive than New York's, and included queries about their attitudes toward military service, the effect of their experiences at training camps and overseas, the effect on religious beliefs, and any changes in the soldiers' overall state of mind after the war.

Davis asked county and local commissions to appoint a chairman to coordinate data collection efforts, including questionnaires. Many of those appointed seem to have been obligated rather than volunteered, and the roster of commissioners was continually updated with resignations and replacements. By the end of 1923, forty-six of one hundred counties stopped responding to letters from the VWHC, had no chairman in place, or had submitted no reports.[28] Without the constant prodding of War History Commission field agents, it is unlikely that most county organizations would have been appointed at all, a situation analogous to the appointment of local historians in New York State. In Richmond, the field agent found that none of the named members of the county committee had agreed to serve, and "most had positively refused the use of their names."[29]

Field workers who submitted regular progress updates to Davis often bemoaned the lack of interest in the topic. One reported, "I am already beginning to feel like an atom of interest in an ocean of apathy as regards war history."[30] The effort suffered from two fundamental problems: an inability to keep commission members active in the counties; and, in those counties where commissioners made some attempt to complete their task, an inability to get soldiers to share their war histories. Virginia's war history foundered on a double-barrelled problem of community and veteran indifference.

An American Legion officer wrote Arthur Kyle Davis that he believed Virginians were apathetic about a war history because they did not care about soldiers and that their efforts on the battlefield were not appreciated. The Legion official noted that he would not lobby the legislature for funding for a war history because, "if what the young men of the state did consti- tutes meritorious and patriotic service, you may depend that a history will be made of the same, for outstanding appreciative work will always become known." He believed that, "the record of service and sacrifice of those who bore the brunt of this war is not history if we have to beg for money to com- pile it in book form; no more than the compliments in a eulogy delivered by a paid agent." In effect, he argued, if society does not provide the momen- tum for such a memorial to be completed, then "what some of us think is history is only unimportant events to the majority." [31]

In Richmond, county organizers had the police bring veterans sur- veys with the admonition that they would be back to collect the completed forms. This strong-arm tactic may or may not have produced significant results. Of the six or seven thousand soldiers recruited from Richmond, at least 2,500 were recipients of hand-delivered questionnaires, and 2,814 are extant in the archive.[32] In Shenandoah County, high school students solicited responses as part of a competition for prizes. This strategy may have garnered some success, as the county submitted records for sixty-six percent of its soldiers.[33]

Most field reports contained some reference to the attitudes of ex- soldiers and citizens, which generally ranged from general apathy to bitter opposition. Approximately one in seven of the extant veteran question- naires in the Library of Virginia archive indicate a negative opinion of the war. Soldiers mentioned the senselessness of war, disgust over the way government handled disabled soldiers, and criticism of the way enlisted men were treated. One veteran disclosed that war "is a horrible useless waste of our young men," while another offered that a new law was in order to ensure that, "a few of the flat-top-desk-officers of the last war, and as many of the war profiteers as the army can accommodate, be induced into the service to help fight the next war."[34] Veterans recognized the inequities of the system that sent them to fight, and resentment for those who stayed home festered just under the surface for many.

African American veterans exhibited the same cynicism. Some expressed a fear that signing government papers of any type would only result in their obligation to serve in a future war.[35] Others took the opportunity to snub the government because of any complaint they had with government organizations during the war. A field officer reported, "everybody who had a grievance against the Red Cross, Liberty Bond or any war organization has told it to me and then positively refused to cooperate with the History Commission."[36] Many scholars, including Jennifer Keene, have explored the state of mind of the returning soldier and written of the grudge many held against a government that sent them to fight for unclear purposes and welcomed them home to a dry country suffering from both high prices and high unemployment. One soldier put it very succinctly: "We fought for democracy and you gave us Spanish Influenza and prohibition."[37] Black soldiers, particularly in the South, cited the added injury of Jim Crow. One black veteran had been turned away at Red Cross headquarters because of his colour, and "still nursed his wrath all through the war and promised to not assist anything."[38] After the war, black soldiers faced ridicule and hostility in many Southern towns, black officers were prohibited from staying in the army, and most veterans were barred entry to the newly formed American Legion. A black newspaper reported, "For valor displayed in the recent war, it seems that the Negro's particular decoration is to be the 'double-cross.'"[39]

While African-American veterans may have faced greater tension as they returned as victorious soldiers back to a segregated South, officials courted them for their war stories as vigorously as those of white soldiers. There was no lack of black Virginians in the war—thirty percent of the state population—and fully twenty-five percent of the forces sent from the State were African American.[40] Early in the war, county history committees were charged with gathering the records of both white and black soldiers, but it soon became evident that almost no information was coming in from African American soldiers or war-related organizations. As it turned out, only one white chairman "attempted to do anything for the Negroes."[41] By February 1920, a plan was in place to appoint a "Board of Negro Collaborators" to assist in compiling African American information, as "it will have a good effect on some of our critics to the North when they find that we have treated the negroes not only with justice in allowing them to have a separate and distinct representation, but with generosity in making it interesting and sympathetic."[42] However, even after the appointment of black collaborators, African Americans were less than forthcoming with information. Interestingly, but perhaps predictably, members of the war history commission found that either the Board of Collaborators was negligent in pursuing the information or African Americans were not fulfilling their patriotic duty.[43]

Virginia fielded thirteen black officers during the war, four of whom completed war history questionnaires. One of those officers, First Lieutenant Edward Dabney, exuded pride in his service when answering the question, "What was your attitude toward military service in general and toward your call in particular?" He responded, "Being an officer answers that in full." Officers were more likely to complete questionnaires both because they were professionals and because they had a larger stake in the war and more to brag about. A sample of five hundred of the Virginia surveys found that the distribution "skewed heavily in favor of those higher in rank, better educated, more literate, and more eager for one reason or another to record their experiences."[44]

Ultimately, however, most soldiers, African American or white, joined in an unwitting solidarity of silence about their war service. The State of Virginia was unable to produce the four-volume war history it had envisioned. As late as 1923, Davis told John Pollard, the president of William and Mary College, that only six cities and twelve counties had provided war information that could be considered adequate. Davis asked Pollard to consider a plan under which the colleges in Virginia would send students throughout the state during the summer to collect the information.[45] No such plan was implemented.

With the prospect of a comprehensive history fading, Davis focused his energies on publishing volumes of source materials that could be used by future historians. The War History Commission ultimately produced seven volumes of the material that it had compiled, all edited by Davis. The first, published in 1923, is a roster of Virginians who were recognized for wartime heroism by either the American government or one of its allies. Volumes two, three, and four provide documentation on Virginia's war agencies, clippings from state newspapers, and copies of war letters, diary entries, and soldiers' letters. Volumes five, six, and seven include information on Virginia military organizations and Virginia communities in wartime.

Less than half of Virginia's communities submitted material for a war history, and far fewer would publish anything independently. There are only eight extant, independently published community histories in the Library of Virginia. Of these, only one was not merely a reprint of the brief history (typically less than thirty pages) that was submitted to the War History Commission. Seven of these eight histories provided a few narrative paragraphs on a varying number of the original fifteen topics suggested by Davis. None included a roster of soldiers or of those awarded medals or honors, and only one contained a roster of those who killed or wounded in action. None contained photographs.[46] One of the seven, from the City of Norfolk, was not even completed by community members, but compiled by Davis to serve as a model for other communities.

Davis, assisted by county and city commissioners, came up short in the quest to document Virginia's soldiers. His best effort to memorialize Virginia's contributions to the war only amounted to a small fraction of what he had hoped to collect. Virginia citizens and veterans were uninterested in packaging the war story for future generations. Many soldiers bore grudges against state agencies and found the recognition effort "too little, too late." Citizens were sick of war and craved a return to normalcy. In their apathy, Virginians failed to acknowledge the sacrifices of those who had waged war on their behalf, and their attitude would have long-term implications for collective memory of the First World War.[47] After a protracted battle, the VWHC had collected information on approximately fifteen percent of its veterans.

KANSAS

"Is it possible that any do not now wish the fact recorded that they fought against Germany in 1917 and 1918?"

The war history campaign in Kansas was not guided by the same vision as either Sullivan in New York or Davis in Virginia, and its scope was not nearly as comprehensive. The effort to collect war information in Kansas was also much less formal than those in Virginia and New York, and a simpler approach did not garner better results. The Kansas Historical

Society, based in Topeka, initiated the effort to collect the records of select Kansas servicemen and pursued the cause without a formal staff, local historians, or committees. Society staff placed ads in local newspapers and worked directly with community and war organizations, including the Grange, American Legion auxiliary organizations, the Military Sisterhood, and Gold Star Mothers. Their efforts focused on two divisions in which many Kansans served, the 89th and 35th. The 89th contained the 353rd "All Kansas" Regiment and was based at Camp Funston in Fort Riley. The 35th Division had the most Kansans, close to ten thousand, and was made up of a combination of Kansas and Missouri National Guard units.[48] The adjutant general in Kansas published a list of Kansas soldiers who died during the war and their next of kin, but it was derided by William Connelly, secretary of the Kansas Historical Society, as "inaccurate and really of very little value."[49]

Connelly appealed directly to family members in newspaper ads, suggesting "friends and relatives of these soldiers are certainly proud of their record overseas. They would always regret it if there should be any failure on the part of any one to do all possible to make this record complete. As you love your soldier husband, son or sweetheart, send his letters, his photograph."[50] Once the War Society of the 89th Division published its own history in 1920, Connelly focused only on the 35th, arbitrarily disregarding the service of Kansans in other divisions.[51]

Early efforts were guided by the desire to have an archive of information for future reference with only vague notions of publishing the material at some point.[52] What is clear is that the Historical Society never invested much time in compiling information other than individual war service records. Unlike the efforts in New York and Virginia, the effort in Kansas did not include the activities of wartime organizations, schools, or government agencies; they were totally focused on publishing a complete list of Kansas soldiers with relevant biographical information.[53]

The Society appears to have been working without any official direction from either governor or legislature, the latter having failed to appropriate any funds for the collection of materials.[54] Instead, it was an effort directed by the Historical Society involving different partners at different times. One of the first partners was the National Military Sisterhood of America, conceived in 1917 by the wife of a general in the Kansas National Guard to help the families of soldiers. Chapters sprung up around the state, as well as in Missouri, Oklahoma, Iowa, and Colorado during and after the war.[55] The Military Sisterhood sought basic information on Kansas soldiers, including the nationality of the soldier and his parents, when and where he had served, and copies of wartime letters and photographs.[56] It is difficult to estimate how successful the Sisterhood was in this endeavor, but only a few surveys survive at the Kansas Historical Society. American Legion Auxiliary groups, the Gold Star Mothers, and Grange posts also assisted the Society at various times. This resulted in a hodge-podge of forms in the archive with varying types and amounts of information.

The Gold Star Mothers limited membership to the surviving mother, daughter, wife, or sister of a soldier who died while in service, and, as such, the organization focused largely on the desire to memorialize the dead. At the first meeting of the Gold Star Mothers in Kansas in 1921, they pledged to "collect and preserve the history and keep fresh the memory of the men and women who gave their lives at home or abroad."[57] In 1922, they sent a bulletin to American Legion Auxiliary chapters about the urgency of collecting this information by the end of the year. This deadline was never met, and a refined plan emerged in 1923 when the Order of the Gold Star announced it would sponsor a book memorializing "the 3,000 Kansas boys who gave their lives for America." Plans called for a five-hundred-page document with five biographies to a page and approximately eighty-five words allotted to each soldier.[58] However, the project remained incomplete as of 1927, when a renewed call was made to complete the book by 1928. Ultimately, nothing was ever published.[59]

As in New York, Kansas veterans were memorialized in numerous county histories compiled by local organizations. At least eight such books were produced between 1919 and 1921. Six of these books were significant publications including relatively substantive lists of those who served.

Marion County holds the distinction of presenting the highest proportion of soldiers in the pages of their memorial book—close to one hundred percent. Only twenty-seven records were listed as "unobtainable," and the collection of 801 soldier vignettes, including almost seven hundred photographs, backed up that claim.[60] The Red Cross Home Service carefully compiled soldiers' war histories and printed a complete roster on the front page of the local paper, indicating which soldiers had not yet submitted information and asking anyone in the community to submit a questionnaire (included in the paper) with the required information. This means that it was not necessary for veterans, or even close family members, to participate in a complete accounting.[61] The organizers indicated that the collection of information was a "long and arduous task," which took, at the very least, nine months of dedicated effort. As in Monroe County, New York, public

librarians, local historians, and public officials that there was something about the war worth remembering.

Fortunately, New York, Virginia, and Kansas all retain the archives of information collected after the war. In some states, the material was forgotten as quickly as the war, and archives were lost. Ultimately, the sparse war service records collected in New York, Virginia, Kansas, and other states are all that remain to document the service of millions of American soldiers after a fire at the National Archives in St. Louis in 1973 consumed the vast majority of First World War Army personnel records, furthering the public's disconnection from this war.[68] War data is most accessible in Virginia, where all fifteen thousand soldier questionnaires are available through an online database. In Kansas, researchers can access an alphabetical index of soldier questionnaires. In New York, researchers must comb through the reports submitted by each historian.

Officials in New York, Virginia, and Kansas each took a different approach to the creation of war histories, whether it was the appointment of 1,200 local historians, the creation of 120 local commissions, or the use of a solitary agency, but all failed to meet either of their goals: the collection of individual war service records or the publication of narrative war histories. They were unable to produce war histories because many soldiers and citizens wanted to forget the war, not write paeans to it. Soldiers shared culpability, but their reticence to relive what was, to many, a disagreeable experience is both understandable and typical of soldiers from many wars. The task of memorializing soldiers would have seen greater success if communities had evidenced the gratitude and respect that war histories were supposed to embody. This is the crux of what the legionnaire in Virginia had told Davis: "If what the young men of the state did constitutes meritorious and patriotic service, you may depend that a history will be made of the same, for outstanding appreciative work will always become known." However, friends, family, and the larger community were complicit in the rejection of the war, and manifested an attitude that discouraged soldiers from talking about their experiences, and, by extension, discouraged the creation of war histories. They ignored their unwritten obligation to engage in acts of remembrance to keep alive the memory of those who fought.

The state tried to uphold this obligation, particularly in New York and Virginia, although the motive for action was likely a mix of appreciation and self-preservation. The state benefitted by holding up soldiers as paragons of sacrifice and duty, effectively sanctioning the decision to go to war and setting an example for future generations to follow if the nation was threatened again. Where the state failed, some communities succeeded in creating memorial volumes that extolled the sacrifices of their native sons and daughters. The hundredth anniversary of the First World War has once again brought the war into the public consciousness. These vital yet incomplete archives will serve as a starting point for understanding those who served, and why Americans have forgotten them and the war they fought.

NOTES

1. Jay Winter, *Remembering War: The Great War Between Memory and History in the 20th Century* (New Haven, CT: Yale University Press, 2006), 4–5, 279–82.
2. Ibid. Winter argues that acts of remembrance can be facilitated by historians, and these collective acts of remembrance foster and sustain collective memory.
3. Newton D. Mereness, ed., *American Historical Activities during the War* (Washington: Government Printing Office, 1923), 161, 165.
4. The adjutant general of the Army was provided an appropriation to share data with the states, but it was slow in coming and often inaccurate. A test case discussed by NASWHO in December 1920 found that Delaware collected data on 235 dead soldiers, while the adjutant general only recorded 123. NASWHO Meeting Minutes, 28 December 1920. Working Files for a Publication on New York in The First World War, 1917–1925 (A3166), New York State Archives, Albany, New York (hereafter NYSA).
5. Statistics Branch, General Staff, War Department, 8 March 1920, Historical Research Working Files 1795–1945 (A3167), NYSA. New York also lost more men than any other state; over 14,000 soldiers died.
6. James Sullivan to Karl Singewald, 1 December 1920, Historical Research Working Files (A3167), NYSA. The five boroughs of New York City were not included in the bill authorizing the appointment of local historians; they were added through an amendment in 1921. Of the five, only Brooklyn submitted any information to the state.
7. Charles M. Reed to James Sullivan, 10 March 1921, Historical Research Working Files (A3167), NYSA.
8. James Sullivan to Delight Keller, 19 August 1922, Historical Research Working Files (A3167), NYSA.
9. L.R. Lewis to James Sullivan, 13 February 1922, Historical Research Working Files (A3167), NYSA.
10. James Sullivan to Edgar J. Klock, 21 December 1921, The First World War Veterans' Service Data (A0412), NYSA.
11. Edgar J. Klock to James Sullivan, 20 December 1921, The First World War Veterans' Service Data (A0412) NYSA.

12. George S. Bixby, "City Historian Asks for Military Records," *Plattsburg Sentinel*, 10 November 1922.

13. "Material for the War History," *Plattsburgh Sentinel*, 26 December 1922.

14. Evelyn M. Barrett to James Sullivan, 20 October 1922, The First World War Veterans' Service Data (A0412), NYSA.

15. William A. Orr, State Defense Council, to County Defense Committees, 3 December 1918, Historical Research Working Files (A3167), NYSA.

16. Oneida County Honor Roll, Oneida County Defense Committee, Utica, New York, The First World War Veterans' Service Data (A0412), NYSA.

17. Review of "Yates County in the World War 1917–1918," *Quarterly Journal of the New York State Historical Association* 11, no. 2 (April 1921): 105.

18. Daniel J. Sweeney, ed., *History of Buffalo and Erie County 1917–1918* (Committee of One Hundred, 4 July 1919).

19. "Much Data Already Gathered for War History of Former Service Men of Rochester," *The Record*, March 1922.

20. "Historical Society in One of Its Most Important Works," *Rochester Post Express*, 15 March 1920.

21. Monroe County reported 609 war dead and the New York State adjutant general reported 447, another example of the poor quality of the adjutant general's records. Part of this discrepancy may be because Monroe County also reported deaths of home-front workers.

22. Jennifer Keene, *Doughboys: The Great War and the Remaking of America* (Baltimore: Johns Hopkins University Press, 2003), 2.

23. Edward F. Foreman, ed., *World War Service Record of Rochester & Monroe County, New York* (Rochester: Rochester Public Library, 1928, 1930, and 1934).

24. "About the World War I History Commission Questionnaires Collection," Library of Virginia, Richmond, Virginia (hereafter LOV), http://www.lva .virginia.gov/public/guides/opac/wwiqabout.htm (accessed 13 October 2010).

25. Arthur Kyle Davis, ed., *Publications of the Virginia War History Commission, Source Volume VII, Virginia Communities in War Time* (Richmond: State Capitol, 1927), 3.

26. C.R. Keiley, Secretary of the War History Commission, to County Committee Chairmen, 20 September 1919, Virginia War History Commission, Series XI, Office Files, 1917–27, Boxes 151–55, LOV.

27. War History Commission Annual Report, Virginia War History Commission, Series XI, Office Files, 1917–27, Box 152, Folder 5, LOV.

28. Progress Report, Virginia War History Commission, Series XI, Office Files, 1917–27, Box 160, Folder 4, LOV.

29. Letter to C.R. Keiley, 24 August 1920, Virginia War History Commission, Series XI, Office Files, 1917–27, Box 156, Folder 1, LOV.

30. Walter F. Beverly to Col. C.R. Keiley, Virginia War History Commission, Series XI, Office Files, 1917–27, Box 152, Folder 7, LOV.

31. Letter from G.M. Harrison to Arthur Kyle Davis, 14 February 1922, Virginia War History Commission, Series XI, Office Files, 1917–27, Box 165, Folder 1, LOV.

32. "Police Supply 2,500 Men with War Record Blanks," *Richmond Times Dispatch*, 8 March 1921. The police were sent to the homes of white veterans, while students of Virginia Union University canvassed black veterans.

33. "About the World War I History Commission Questionnaires Collection," Library of Virginia, http://www.lva.virginia.gov/public/guides/opac/wwiq about.htm (accessed 9 November 2010). Field Report from 1922 or 1923, Virginia War History Commission, Series XI, Office Files, 1917–27, Box 160, Folder #4, LOV.

34. J. Jefferson Looney, "I Really Never Thought War Was So Cruel," *Virginia Cavalcade* 50, no. 3 (Summer 2001): 128–30.

35. Lillian Webb Naylor to Julia Sully, 16 March 1920, Virginia War History Commission, Series XI, Office Files, 1917–27, Box 160, Folder #4, LOV.

36. Report of Ora Stokes, 31 August 1920, Virginia War History Commission, Series XI, Office Files, 1917–27, Box 158, Folder 2, LOV.

37. "Returning Troops Decry Dry Nation," *Knickerbocker Press* (Albany), 20 April 1919.

38. Report of Ora Stokes, LOV.

39. Arthur E. Barbeau and Florette Henri, *The Unknown Soldiers: Black American Troops in The First World War* (Philadelphia: Temple University Press, 1974) 172–74. Barbeau and Henri also explore the "Red Summer" of 1919 and the effect of returning black servicemen on the race riots the year after the war ended.

40. W. Allison Sweeney, *History of the American Negro in the Great World War* (Negro Universities Press, 1969 [1919]). Some 141,714 white soldiers and 34,796 black soldiers were inducted from Virginia. Campbell Gibson and Kay Jung, "Historical Census Statistics on Population Totals By Race, 1790 to 1990, and By Hispanic Origin, 1970 to 1990, For The United States, Regions, Divisions, and States," Population Division, United States Census, 2002, http://www.census.gov/population/www/documentation/twps0056/twps0056.html (accessed 14 December 2010).

41. Julia Sully to W.S. Morton, chairman of the Charlotte County War History Commission, Virginia War History Commission, Series XI, Office Files, 1917–27, Box 158, Folder #4, LOV.

42. Julia Sully to Arthur Kyle Davis, 23 February 1920, Virginia War History Commission, Series XI, Office Files, 1917–27, Box 158, Folder #5, LOV.

43. Letter to T.C. Erwin from Chairman Arthur Kyle Davis, 4 October 1920, Virginia War History Commission, Series XI, Office Files, 1917–27, Box 158, Folder #4, LOV.

44. Looney, "I Really Never Thought War Was So Cruel," 127.

45. Arthur Kyle Davis to John Garland Pollard, 17 January 1923, Virginia War History Commission, Series XI, Office Files, 1917–27, Box 153, Folder #8, LOV.

46. The seven histories are from the counties of Hanover, Fluvana, Dickenson, Cumberland, and Scott, and the cities of Clifton Forge and Norfolk.

47. See Jay Winter, *Remembering War: The Great War Between Memory and History in the 20th Century* (New Haven: Yale University Press, 2006), 4–5, 279–82. Winter calls remembrance "an act of symbolic exchange between those who remain and those who suffered or died. They went through much; they lost or gave much; we give the little we can—starting with recognition and acknowledgement and then moving on, at times, to material expressions of both."

48. "World War I," Kansas State Historical Society, http://www.kshs.org/kansapedia/world-war-i/12247 (accessed 17 November 2010). Harry Truman served with the 35th Division as part of the Missouri National Guard.

49. William Connelly to Mrs. Hugh Bay, 1 June 1921, Kansas State Historical Society, Topeka (hereafter KSHS), Manuscript Collection (MC) 49, Box #1.

50. "To Prepare Histories of Two Famous Divisions," KSHS MC 49, Box #1.

51. George English, Jr., *History of the 89th Division* (War Society of the 89th Division, 1920). The history includes a roster of officers and a listing of soldiers who were wounded, but no general roster of the men who served.

52. William Connelly to John Beaton, 23 May 1919, KSHS, MC 49, Box #1.

53. William Connelly to Mrs. Hugh Bay, 1 June 1921 KSHS, MC 49, Box #1.

54. William Connelly to W.A. Bevis, 9 July 1919, KSHS, MC 49, Box #1. There is very limited extant information about the Historical Society's effort to collect data, as there are almost no administrative records detailing the process.

55. Nellie Charles Terrill, "The Military Sisterhood of the World War, 1917–1919," KSHS, Manuscripts, Military Sisterhood 1917–24, Box #1.

56. Nellie C. Terrill to Kansas Women of the Military Sisterhood, 25 October 1918, KSHS MC 49, Box #1.

57. "Gold Star Mothers Meet," *Topeka Capital*, 9 April 1922.

58. Draft layout plan for book, no known author, KSHS, Manuscript Collection 49: 27.01. The document assumes 2,500 war dead from Kansas.

59. 1924 and 1927 Annual Convention Meeting Minutes, American Legion Auxiliary, Kansas Department, KSHS.

60. Records issued by the Kansas State Adjutant General's Office indicate that 817 men enlisted from Marion County.

61. "Marion County Service Men," *Marion Record*, 7 August 1919.

62. *Kansans Who Served in the World War*, 4 vols. (Kansas Adjutant General, n.d.).

63. *Honor Roll, Crawford County, Kansas, 1919* (Kansas City: Union Bank Note Company, 1919).

64. "Batteries Greeted by Cheering Thousands of the Home Folks," *Pittsburg Daily Headlight*, 8 May 1919.

65. Advertisement, *Pittsburg Daily Headlight*, 19 April 1919.

66. W.H. Lightfoot, *Our Heroes in Our Defense, Labette County, Kansas* (Kansas: Commercial Publishing, 1921).

67. John Wilson, *Russell County in the War* (Russell, KS, 1921).

68. Mitchell Yockelson, "They Answered the Call: Military Service in the United States Army during World War I, 1917–1919" *Prologue* 30, no. 3 (Fall 1998), http://www.archives.gov/publications/prologue/1998/fall/military-service-in -world-war-one.html (accessed 14 December 2010).

THE GREAT WAR IN DETECTIVE FICTION

MARZENA SOKOLOWSKA-PARYZ

Our contemporary understanding of the Great War is determined by the narrative mode we select as our analytical tool for re-entering the past. The war may be studied through the prism of national histories, the history of one eminent individual whose decisions shaped the course of the conflict, or memoirs and autobiographies that prioritize personal memory over grand history. These are all variants of the documentary narrative, constructing a story of the Great War on the foundations of historical facts and actual human experience. One cannot ignore, however, the importance of fictive narratives in shaping our historical consciousness. According to Pat Barker, fiction is superior to historical and sociological studies insofar as it is "the only form that makes you think deeply and feel strongly, not as alternative modes of reaction, but as part of a single, unified reaction."[1] The focus of my discussion is historical detective fiction about the Great War. Charles Todd, Anne Perry, Jacqueline Winspear, Ben Elton, and Rennie Airth have all produced immensely popular and critically acclaimed novels. By adopting the conventions of this particular literary genre for the purpose of re-remembering the Great War, they effectively prove its capacity to diminish "historical distance" by "mak[ing] the historical scene as vivid and palpable as possible."[2]

Historical detective fiction about the Great War may be set either during the conflict or in its aftermath. In Ben Elton's *The First Casualty* (2005), Inspector Douglas Kingsley must solve a murder case amidst the ongoing battle of Passchendaele. Anne Perry's chaplain-detective Joseph Reavley is forced to unravel murder cases in each year of the Great War in a cycle of five novels: *No Graves as Yet* (2003), *Shoulder the Sky* (2004), *Angels in the Gloom*

(2005), *At Some Disputed Barricade* (2006), and *We Shall Not Sleep* (2007). The temporal embedding of the action in the novels by Elton and Perry is evocative of their interest in the Great War as a historical event, and their use of the detective fiction format serves the purpose of diminishing the "affective and ideological distances"[3] typical of historical narratives. When the reader is caught up in the suspense of who was killed and why, then she/he is inevitably drawn into the meaning of the Great War, contained in the motivations for the crime. Charles Todd's Inspector Ian Rutledge, Rennie Airth's Inspector John Madden, and Jacqueline Winspear's Maisie Dobbs are all veterans of the Great War working on crime cases in the conflict's aftermath, the 1920s and 1930s. Inspector Rutledge makes his first appearance in *A Test of Wills* (1996), to be followed by (so far) sixteen novels; Maisie Dobbs is first introduced in *Maisie Dobbs* (2003), and has since then re-appeared in (so far) ten more novels. Joseph Madden solves his first case in *River of Darkness* (1999), and is challenged by further murder mysteries in *The Blood-Dimmed Tide* (2003), *The Dead of Winter* (2009), and *The Reckoning* (2014). The embedding of the action in the postwar period is indicative of the authors' interest in the legacy of the Great War; hence the foregrounding of traumatic memory which testifies to the perpetual presence of the past: "in the traumatic memory the past defines and determines the present actions and thinking of the rememberer."[4] In the novels by Todd, Winspear, and Airth, it is not only the detectives who are burdened with haunting pasts. In the course of their investigations, they will inevitably uncover traumatic memories at the heart of the community, symptomatic of a social crisis that needs healing.

Historical detective fiction about the Great War provides valuable insight into the meanings of this paradigmatic conflict of the twentieth century for our contemporary, post-memory culture. It is indisputable that the memory of the Great War has become—by now—history, but it should also be acknowledged that this memory is concomitantly "translated" into fictive *stories*, which not only demand that we "remember" this conflict, but also persuasively tell us *how* we should "remember" it. What the literary genre of historical detective fiction offers us is "the rediscovery of [history's] elided potentialities, as well as an often highly conflicted struggle over what should be remembered and what should be forgotten."[5] My analysis will focus on the following issues: the commemorative function of historical detective fiction, the epistemological implications of the uses of war poetry in the selected novels, the social and political "re-reading" of the conflict through contemporary detective fiction conventions, the diverse narratives of the Great War present in post-memory culture (propagation of the futility myth versus returns to the "just war" theory), and, finally, the use of the psychopathic killer as a means of investigating the spheres of convergence between murder and killing in wartime.

The novels by Elton, Perry, Winspear, Airth, and Todd are representative of the prevalent commemorative trend in contemporary fiction about the Great War, which in turn is indicative of the social phenomenon of individualization of memory through an empathic reconnection to a family past: "To this day, through the study of genealogy, through retelling family stories, the war is kept alive as a vivid moment in popular history.... What today's readers find in this literature is that their family stories are part of a wider code, perhaps even a 'master code' of stories about how we in the twentieth century got to be where we are."[6] Dedications preceding novels about the Great War are very common, and authenticate the fictional (re)constructions of the past by testifying to the author's personal commitment to the subject matter. The fact that a family member had experienced the Great War (regardless of whether he was killed, wounded, or emerged unscathed) validates the narrative through the family history and allows the text to be classified as commemorative fiction.

Perry's detective-chaplain, Joseph Reavley, is actually named after her grandfather, whom she never had a chance to meet but about whom she heard from her grandmother. Winspear has written a meticulous account of her battlefield tour of the Somme area and the former Ypres Salient entitled "Skylarks above No Man's Land."[7] Airth's *River of Darkness* is more accurately defined as a police procedural in which "the actual methods and procedures of police work are central to the structure, themes, and action."[8] Yet when asked why he chose to locate the action in the interwar period, he admitted that he had been inspired by a family story he discovered by sheer coincidence: "I was going through some old family albums and came across a scrapbook which my grandparents had kept in memory of their elder son who was killed in the First World War.... From then on I began to read more about that terrible conflict and the deep scars it left on society."[9]

Commemoration serves to consolidate the historical consciousness of the nation by designating the past events that deserve to be remembered and thus constructing a sense of a distinctive collective identity: "The core meaning of any individual or group identity, namely, a sense of sameness over time and space, is sustained by remembering; and what is remembered is defined by the assumed identity."[10] It has been noted, however, that commemorative practices have undergone a significant evolution toward globalization and democratization: "To those familiar with memorial injunctions and inscriptions such as 'Lest we forget,' 'We shall remember them,' 'Passant, souviens-toi!,' that duty is scarcely new. In recent years, it has, however, acquired fresh connotations, has come to mean not simply the need to update memorials to incorporate the conflicts ... but inclusiveness, that is, memorials need to cater also for the sectional memory of groups previously excluded from collective acts of remembrance, occluded or marginalized by official ambivalence or indifference."[11] The most notable aspect of the novels by Todd, Winspear, Airth, Perry, and Elton is their refusal to go beyond a nationally restricted perspective on the Great War. The "Englishness" of their novels is propounded by characters and setting. This may seem predictable in the case of English authors, but Rennie Airth was born in South Africa, whereas Charles and Caroline Todd (mother and son writing under the pen name of "Charles Todd") are Americans. They explained in an interview that their interest in the Great War prompted the choice of an English protagonist because "it was their war, and [the United States] just went over to help them win it. Our role was shorter, our losses lighter and our ability to absorb the impact greater."[12]

The primary indicator of "Englishness" in the selected novels is the fact that they foreground solider poets as the beholders of the "truth" of the Great War. This category of "Englishness" is not determined by the nationality of the authors (Todd, Airth) or by the nationality of the soldier poets quoted in the novels (e.g., John McCrae, Canadian, or Alan Seeger, American). Every nation involved in the Great War had its representative (i.e., most popular) poets, and there also exists an international canon of Great War poetry perpetuated by means of anthologies and studies, yet it would be hard to find any national post-memory literature that devotes as much attention to soldier poets as English literature. Robert Goddard's *In Pale Battalions* uses Charles Sorley's poem as an interpretative frame for the war story in the same way Susan Hill used Wilfred Owen's poetry for the construction of her plot in *Strange Meeting*. The ending of Sebastian Faulks's *Birdsong* is an evident echo of Owen's "strange meeting" between an English and a German officer. Geoff Akers has written a novel about Isaac Rosenberg entitled *Beating for the Light*, and Jill Dawson has recently published a novel about Rupert Brooke entitled *The Great Lover*. War poets appear as characters in James Lansdale Hodson's *Return to the Wood* and John Harris's *Covenant with Death*, and one cannot omit, of course, Pat Barker's *Regeneration* trilogy, with her fictive representations of Siegfried Sassoon, Wilfred Owen, and Robert Graves. The meeting of Sassoon and Owen at Craiglockhart is also the subject of Stephen MacDonald's play *Not About Heroes*.

This tendency to put forth war poets as the hierophants of the Great War is visible also in historical detective fiction. Airth's *River of Darkness* uses as its introductory epigraph a quotation from Sassoon's "To the War-Mongers." The novel is divided into four parts, each preceded by quotations from Great War poetry: Owen's "Anthem for the Doomed Youth," Rose Macauley's "Picnic July 1917," Graves's "Sick Leave," and Seeger's "Rendezvous." Winspear's *Maisie Dobbs* opens with a fragment from Owen's "Disabled." The titles of each of Anne Perry's five novels demonstrate a literary borrowing: *No Graves as Yet* is taken from G.K. Chesterton, *Shoulder in the Sky* from A.E. Housman, *Angels in the Gloom* from Sassoon, *At Some Disputed Barricade* from Seeger, and *We Shall Not Sleep* from McCrae. The Todd mother-and-son tandem do not use epigraphs; still, in the second novel of the series, *Wings of Fire*, the victim of murder proves to be a war poet, whose works Ian Rutledge read in the trenches, "marveling that anyone could have captured so clearly what men felt out there in the bloody shambles of France."[13]

The title of Elton's novel is taken from the famous remark made by Senator Hiram Johnson in 1917 that "the first casualty when war comes, is truth."[14] This quotation contains the clue to the reasons for the murder of Captain Alan Abercrombie, a renowned war poet. He had gained fame by writing poems in the manner of Rupert Brooke, a fact stated in his obituary: "Viscount Abercrombie published two volumes of patriotic verse that have brought much comfort to soldiers and civilians alike.... He will perhaps be best remembered for his poem "Forever England" which was inspired by ... 'The Soldier.'"[15] In the course of his service, Abercrombie changed his views on the war and the type of poetry that was needed. He decided to write about the war as realistically as possible, in the style of Siegfried Sassoon. According to Abercrombie's murderer, "[Brooke's] poetry inspired people, it did not rub their noses in the horror they had to live with anyway. It lifted them up," whereas Sassoon was a "whining little shit," "windy turd," and "we can do without war heroes turning conchie on us."[16] The victim's "truth" of the Great War was a threat to the soldiers' morale and therefore he had to be silenced. The twist is that the man who wanted to safeguard the soldiers against disenchantment was the perpetrator of the crime, his personal integrity destroyed by the brutal realities of trench warfare.

Historical detective fiction is defined as "crime fiction that is entirely set in some particular historical period, but which was not written during that period."[17] This literary convention imposes significant constraints on the author's imagination: "This is a type of novel which cannot claim the artistic autonomy of most literary genres, because readers expect a considerable degree of verisimilitude and historical accuracy.... It is, therefore, always required to subordinate imagination, the play of the signifier, unity or textuality, to the final authority of historical realism."[18] Historical detective fiction thus has its pitfalls. It must resurrect a past world that has little in common with the reality of the contemporary reader. It involves a necessary reconstitution of methods of detection that are obsolete from today's point of view. Douglas Kingsley, Maisie Dobbs, Ian Rutledge, and John Madden solve crimes in a manner reminiscent of the works of Agatha Christie, Dorothy Sayers, or Michael Innes, and yet they are professionals, in contrast to "the Miss Marples, Hercules Poirots, Peter Wimseys, and Gideon Fells of classic detective fiction [who are] an eccentric or wealthy amateur."[19] Joseph Reavley is an amateur detective, but the fact that he is a chaplain provides him with an authority to solve crimes insofar as he embodies the "solidity [and] morality" necessary to defend the "traditional [social] order."[20]

In the interwar period, detective fiction retained its distinctive autonomy as a genre, refusing to embrace the subject matter of the war or its repercussions in the present. Conventionally, crimes could not be situated in wartime: "The motives for all crimes in detective stories should be personal. International plots and war politics belong in a different category of fiction—in secret-service tales, for instance. But a murder story must be kept *gemütlich*, so to speak. It must reflect the reader's everyday experiences, and give him a certain outlet for his own repressed desires and emotions."[21] Elton's and Perry's novels enact an ostentatious breakaway from this precept by their hybrid genericism: a combination of detective story, combat narrative, and political thriller. In classic detective fiction, the aftermath of the Great War is untainted by the past: "The Golden Age fixation with the upper class, or the upper middle class, is further compounded in British fiction of the period by the fact that the physical and social settings are so isolated from postwar depression that it is as if the Great War never happened."[22] The reason for this reticence resided in the genre's aim to construct an idealized image of the society absolved from crime through the efforts of the detective. Portraying the society realistically, in foregrounding "the devastation of the Great War and the social and economic upheaval of 1920s and 1930s depression," would be, in terms of the genre's social conservatism, counterproductive.[23]

Against such a backdrop, the stories by Todd, Winspear, and Airth appear not only far more democratic in scope, incorporating a much larger variety of social classes, but also reflect today's "culture of memory" obsessed with "the past [as] memory, personal and social, traumatic and repressed, involuntary and planned."[24] The crimes that the detectives must solve invariably bring about the return of the repressed, forcing Maisie Dobbs, Ian Rutledge, and John Madden to confront their haunting memories. Detection of crime is thus also a process of healing the psychological scars of a past war. Moreover, an understanding of the crime is often impossible without the knowledge of a particular war experience that contains the reasons for the murder, or, alternatively, a murder in the aftermath of the war has connections with an event that took place during the conflict. The Great War is thus conspicuously omnipresent in times of peace, permeating both personal and social life.

Contemporary detective fiction and its generic derivatives have responded to the demands of modern societies by foregrounding "regional and local detectives" as well as figures of detectives representing a "remarkable ethnic and gender diversity."[25] One is no longer surprised to find progressive feminist women fighting for justice, lesbians and homosexuals, Jews and Native Americans. In consequence, detective fiction has shown a significant evolution from its conservative beginnings: "the detective story has expanded to accommodate a much greater diversity of social values and ideologies until, in the aftermath of the Cold War, it seems on the verge of becoming a truly global mythos."[26] The detectives in the works of Elton, Perry, Winspear, Airth, and Todd reflect the social democratization characteristic of contemporary detective fiction by putting forth war experience as the primary indicator of respectability and reliability. Though class distinctions exist in the world they occupy, the English society is so ravaged by the war that social distinctions lose much of their significance. People are judged by what they did and what happened to them in wartime. Rutledge's and Madden's service on the Somme accounts for their special status; war service is important for Maisie Dobbs, a young working-class woman, who manages to achieve a successful career as private detective very much because she had been a nurse at the front.

The Great War, however brutal and tragic, is depicted as a catalyst of social change. When Elton's Inspector Kingsley is freed from prison (where he finds himself after refusing to serve in the army) so that he can undertake a mission on the Western Front under a new identity, he recognizes in the voices of his "saviours" an alien social world:

> He had heard voices like theirs many times before. Languid, relaxed voices, effortlessly confident and commanding. Kingsley had been listening to these voices all his life, voices that simply assumed the

authority which men who spoke in a different accent had to earn. Kingsley remembered those voices from his youth, when his grammar school rugby team had faced one of the nearby public schools. When some progressive-minded headmaster from Harrow or Winchester had thought it proper that his boys should mix briefly with the sons of the next class down.[27]

It turns out, as the intricate plot unfolds, that one of these men is the murderer. He is the epitome of a disease destroying the upper class at the core. This is most explicitly shown in the fact that this man, brought up to dominate others, proves to be a brutal rapist and a killer. His death at the end of the novel is evocative of the demise of a degenerate social class.

In Perry's first novel, society is divided according to class. In the subsequent novels, set in the time of the war, the former students of Cambridge are now officers, and the local men—farmers and workers—are private soldiers. Perry depicts an idealized version of the Pals Battalions phenomenon, with strong emphasis on the comradeship of men forged by the war. The unity of officers and privates is best shown in *At Some Disputed Barricade*, where two officers and ten private soldiers kidnap their commanding officer and enact a mock court-martial for one reason only: because Major Northrup was an irresponsible CO whose reckless decision had resulted in unnecessary deaths at Passchendaele. When caught, this group of men is defended during the court-martial by Joseph Reavley, who says:

> Many of us will never leave here. We know that, and we accept it. Almost all of us came here because we wished to, we came to fight for the land and the people we love, our own people… But in order to walk into hell, we need the loyalty of our brothers, whether of blood and kin, or of common cause…. If you will follow a man into the darkness and the mouth of the guns, then you have to know beyond question that he will do the same for you, that he will give all he has to be the leader you believe him to be.[28]

This speech represents Reavley's strongly felt beliefs that war is a test of the moral worth of men, and he deliberately uses the plural pronoun that obliterates class distinction. What matters in war is the brotherhood of men, based on a firm sense of responsibility and empathy. Paradoxically, the Great War created a more just and humane society, as stated in *We Shall Not Sleep*: "The old rules of how to behave have been swept away.

Distinctions in social class are blurred more and more all the time. We've been forced to see the courage, intelligence and moral value of men we used barely even to notice."[29]

One of the purposes of historical narratives is to elicit "moral responses" as part and parcel of our comprehension of the past, and "one of the most basic forms of moral response is remembrance."[30] The basic question remains, of course, how the past should be remembered. Elton's *The First Casualty* draws on a tradition of war literature that includes not just war poetry but also the memoirs and novels representing the disenchantment school that dominated the interwar years. The obvious predecessors are Robert Graves, Frederic Manning, Henry Williamson, Richard Aldington, Edmund Blunden, and A.D. Gristwood, who, with many other ex-servicemen authors, constructed what Samuel Hynes labelled "the myth of war," where "story and way of telling the story converge, tone determining the selection of events and events determining tone, until a complete coherent story emerges."[31] The myth of the Great War offers a historical and ethical evaluation of the conflict as an unnecessary one, in which all gains were horrendously disproportionate to the loss of human life. It is telling that Elton's novel begins with an iconic view of a soldier, weighed down by the equipment he has to carry, drowning in the mud of Passchendaele, his death epitomizing the senselessness of the war: "No gains of any significance anyway. There had not been in the battle before this one, nor had there been in the one preceding that."[32] Kingsley is a textual construct whose purpose in the novel is to enter the hell of war only to corroborate a literary "truth" of its futility.

Irony is as important as disenchantment for understanding Elton's novel. Paul Fussell famously states that, "every war constitutes an irony of situation because its means are so melodramatically disproportionate to its presumed ends. In the Great War eight million were destroyed because two persons ... had been shot."[33] Fussell's statement is echoed in Inspector Kingsley's repudiation of the conflict as one that "offends [his] sense of logic" and "[his] sense of scale." The argument that Great Britain entered the war for moral reasons in order to defend "a small, brave [nation] like gallant Belgium when that country [was] brutally attacked and occupied" is ironical, for, as Kingsley states, "I think it strange that we feel no similar obligation to the peoples of the African Congo whom 'gallant' Belgium has happily attacked, subdued and fiendishly brutalized in a manner which I dare say exceeds any current German excesses on the Continent." Kingsley aptly observes that to seek one murderer on a battlefront amidst the carnage that is taking the lives of millions is illogical: "Civilization is now entirely villainous, murdering its own, murdering all it sees…. It does seem like something of a farce that the British army should hold a murder investigation."[34] The irony is that the victim of murder would have most probably been killed sooner or later in combat; and the exoneration of the man accused of the murder is equally ridiculous, for sparing his life means allowing him to return to the front where he will most certainly be killed. According to Kingsley, fighting for the freedom of other nations veils the truth of "the abuse of the poor, abuse of the Irish, abuse of women."[35]

There exists, however, a different story of the Great War, providing the ideological basis for Perry's detective series. Her predecessors include Ian Hay's *The First Hundred Thousand*, Graham H. Greenwell's *An Infant in Arms*, Sidney Rogerson's *Twelve Days on the Somme*, Charles Edmonds's *A Subaltern's War*, John Harris's *Covenant with Death*, and James Lansdale Hodson's *Return to the Wood*. These works are evocations of the greatness of the "Tommy Atkins" spirit of endurance in the trenches, and apotheoses of a British Empire founded on a willing brotherhood of nations fighting for a common cause. The ethos of duty permeates these texts, a duty to the nation and fellow soldiers on the front. The poet figure central to Perry's novels is, predictably, Rupert Brooke.

The most intriguing character in Perry's novels is the elusive Peacemaker, whose identity is not revealed until the last novel in the series. He is a self-appointed Messiah whose aim is to prevent the shedding of English blood in a futile conflict. His disciples include a student at Cambridge, an ardent pacifist, and a journalist whose antiwar convictions can be traced back to the Boer War. The Peacemaker is a man who wants peace at any cost, even at the cost of murder. In *No Graves as Yet*, Joseph and Matthew Reavley come across a document that reveals the Peacemaker's true intentions, a treaty between Great Britain and Germany: "Britain would stand aside and allow Germany to invade and conquer Belgium, France, and of course Luxembourg, saving the hundreds of thousands of lives that would be lost in trying to defend them. In return, a new Anglo-German empire would be formed with unassailable power on land and sea."[36] Perry deconstructs British imperialism by a simple ploy; the murderer's faith is a political doctrine that aims to subjugate nations under the rule of the chosen few, as opposed to the ethical, humanist attitude of the Reavleys. Why did Englishmen fight in the most terrible of wars and why did they endure the most horrific conditions? Perry's answer is clear. The purpose was to defend the moral integrity of England: "The things Christ taught of honour, of courage, and of love are always true, in any imaginable world."[37]

In Elton's *First Casualty*, an officer is killed because he wants to reveal the truth of the horror of war. This murder is an essentially immoral act, aimed at suppressing this truth, and therefore justice was delivered when the perpetrator was killed. In Perry's *Shoulder in the Sky*, Joseph Reavley is ready to risk his own life and personal integrity to prevent a reporter from publishing an account of the brutal realities of war, even kill him, and this is a moral act, intended at safeguarding the morale of the English soldiers, who must persist in their effort to save England: "To think of the land he loved so fiercely it was like part of his own being, desecrated [like Belgium], was unbearable."[38] In her sequence of novels, Perry conjures an image of an enemy that reminds one of the notorious Bryce Report of 1915, as well as novels such as Gabrielle and Marguerite Yerta's *Six Women and the Invasion* or Annie Vivanti Chartres's *Outrage*, published in the interwar period, where "the German soldier [is a] cruel savage, living and acting outside the limits of decent human behavior."[39] Reavley envisages the occupation of England: "German soldiers would be sleeping under the thatched roofs, tearing up the gardens, perhaps killing the beasts to provide food, shooting those people who resisted. Women he had known all his life would be confused and humiliated, ashamed to smile or to be seen to offer a kindness."[40] This may appear to be an anachronistic 'adaptation' of the anti-German propaganda of the time of the Great War: "More than any other factor, the myth of the rape of Belgium came to be accepted as fact following the publication of the infamous Bryce report in May 1915."[41] Yet, when one reads the following passage: "The laws would be changed…. Travel would be restricted…. All newspapers would be censored…. Food would be rationed…. The collaborators would be rewarded, the betrayers and profiteers, the vulnerable, the weak, the bribable, deceivable, the terrified would drift with sheeplike obedience,"[42] it becomes clear that the fears of Perry's protagonist are simply a-chronological, reflecting the fate of Europe under the occupation of the Third Reich.

For Perry, Imperial and Nazi Germany are interchangeable. In 1918, there appeared a very interesting memorial-book, written by A. St. John Adcock, dedicated to soldier-poets killed in the Great War. This tribute also contained an evocation of England as the absolute opposite of Germany. England is described as holding a moral superiority over Germany on the strength of its "racial instincts, long traditions and peace-time training."[43] In Perry's novels, the responsibility for the war resides with Germany. From the beginning the war, however, Germany did more than just pose a threat to the freedom of other nations. War unleashed a moral Armageddon that affected all people involved. The crimes committed by Englishmen were the evidence that the nation had been infected by a disease, which, unless stopped, would destroy its very foundations. That is why Joseph Reavley accepts the role of the detective amidst the carnage on the front, for solving the crimes and bringing the criminals to justice is, symbolically, a means of curing the evil permeating the hearts and minds of the Englishmen: "the fact that justice was impartial was one absolute in a world descending into chaos. Truth was one certainty worth pursuing, finding and clinging on to."[44]

Following W.H. Auden's delineation of the basic formula of detective fiction, William W. Stowe defines the genre as "a ritual exercise on the localization and expulsion of guilt." When the crime is solved and the culprit removed, the society is absolved: "Politically, morally, and epistemologically, detective fiction tends to affirm, rather than to question, to take social structures, moral codes, and the ways of knowing as givens, rather than subjecting them to thorough, principled criticism."[45] Moral expatiation of the English society lies at the core of Winspear's Maisie Dobbs series, though she takes this formula a step further, embedding it very specifically in the context of a necessary acceptance of society's collective guilt, which must lead to a recognition of its moral responsibility for the past: "guilt stems from perceiving the self as responsible for an event that violates internalized moral standards as expectations ... because guilt reflects an acceptance of responsibility for a moral violation that results in harm to another, it should create a willingness to take corrective action to make up for the self's wrongdoing ... guilt may be experienced when the moral violations of a social group that one is associated with are made salient."[46] The author crafts each crime in such a way as to make plain that the reason it was committed resides in the past conflict. Thus, unravelling the mysteries involves an inevitable return to the Great War. The resurfacing memory of the war signifies both acceptance of social culpability and atonement for the harm that was inflicted: "Maisie did not speak but instead began to remove the pins that held her long black hair in a neat chignon. She turned her head to one side and lifted her head ... she revealed a purple scar weaving a path from just above her hairline at the nape of her neck, through her hair and into her scalp. 'Long hair, Billy, hides a multitude of sins.'"[47]

Maisie's first case, which starts out with a seemingly uncomplicated task to find evidence of adultery, leads her to a strange place called "The Retreat," the inhabitants of which are ex-servicemen hiding from society because of their ghastly physical wounds. One by one, these men disappear. They are shot at dawn and buried under their Christian names in one big cemetery. These crimes are a reenactment of the executions of English soldiers, shot at dawn during the war for alleged cowardice: "in very many cases they were often unfortunate helpless victims, least able to help themselves … these ill-educated, inarticulate individuals were frequently exhausted through the strains of constant horrific trench warfare that drained their resolve—and ultimately their life blood."[48] The criminal reenactment is a moral evaluation of wartime executions as unjust and immoral, but it also transfers the guilt from wartime military authorities to postwar society, forcing it to look on the standards it had expected of its soldiers and the ostracism of men who failed to fulfill these expectations. The shot-at-dawn cases are thus depicted as victims of a social ethos of masculinity that found its horrifying consequences in an excessively punitive military justice system. Winspear's explicit implication that the executions of soldiers were morally wrong is typical of the manner in which the shot-at-dawn cases tend to be represented in British literature and film. As Bette London points out, British military executions are a staple theme of literary, documentary, and cinematic narratives intent on perpetuating the interpretation of the Great War as a futile conflict.[49]

In contrast to Maisie Dobbs, whose role as a detective is to expose the collective guilt of English society, Todd's Inspector Rutledge solves crimes to atone for his individual guilt. Rutledge is a very contrived character, the effect of the authors' wish to render him both historically plausible and universally meaningful. Their research included interviews with "veterans of all the wars in the 20th century." The purpose of Inspector Rutledge, the veteran with a mind ravished by the Great War, was to convey "a defining of the human spirit, of one man striving to triumph over his nightmares. Rutledge is any one of us who has to pick up the pieces after personal devastation, anyone with the courage to face his demons."[50] In the novels, the state of Rutledge's mind is consistently described as shell shock, though the authors claimed that his symptoms were typical of Post-Traumatic Stress Disorder (PTSD). The exploding shell that half buried Rutledge is a reminder of the literal understanding of shell shock in wartime: "before it had become apparent that shell shock was a functional disorder caused by the stress of combat, regimental medical officers were instructed to decide whether the symptoms were a result of proximity to an exploding shell (and therefore a wound) or simply the general rigours of military service (sickness)."[51] It serves, however, also as a signifier of the collective "shock" of the war upon the fighting soldiers.

When Inspector Rutledge returns to Scotland Yard from a private hospital where he was treated for shell shock, he is still suffering from claustrophobia. More importantly, he hears the voice of a Scottish soldier named Hamish McLeod, a corporal in Rutledge's unit who refused to obey the order to take a group of soldiers over No Man's Land to destroy an enemy machine-gun position. According to Rutledge, Hamish had simply exhausted his capacity to endure. He was arrested, court-martialled, and sentenced to death. There was no chance for mercy, since the attack in which Hamish had refused to participate turned out to be a success. The firing squad consisted of reluctant men who fired wide and only wounded the corporal. Rutledge shoots him, a scene peculiarly reminiscent of the coup-de-grace scene in Joseph Losey's *King and Country* (based on James Lansdale Hodson's *Return to the Wood* and John Wilson's *Hamp).* This act of killing a fellow-soldier discloses the origins of Rutledge's disturbed psyche in the aftermath of war: "The fallen man never spoke, and yet inside Rutledge's skull Hamish was screaming, *End it! For pity's sake!* The pistol roared, the smell of powder and blood enveloping Rutledge. The pleading eyes widened and then went dark, still, empty. Accusing."[52] Despite the authors' assertion that Rutledge suffers from what today is defined as PTSD, there is actually no mention of auditory hallucinations among the symptoms typical of this kind of psychological disorder. This voice therefore becomes the signifier of individual guilt, the burden that Rutledge is doomed to carry: "the most intriguing concept was someone who had worked as a policeman, then gone off to war and returned to pick up the threads of his job. How does killing affect a man who hunts killers? What strengths or weaknesses come out of the trenches? How had war changed him psychologically? Has he learned skills beyond those he'd possessed in 1914? Is he more empathetic, or more callous?"[53]

The crimes are constructed in such a way as to remind Rutledge of his war past. In *Test of Wills*, he is forced to interrogate a witness who is far more severely shell-shocked than himself, a former RFC pilot and decorated war hero. In *A False Mirror*, he defends a man with whom he had fought in the trenches. The pattern is repeated in each novel, creating reasons for Rutledge never to forget Hamish's death. The depersonalized voice of a dead soldier is an impossible voice, because it takes its beginning from an absence that lies at the heart of traumatic guilt. The impossibility of this voice-construct perfectly epitomizes the nature of the traumatic experience. The entire series thus foregrounds the quest for personal absolution. Self-expatiation is the condition of life, and the failure of the quest will end with death; in the inspector's own words, "it was a question of survival."[54] Rutledge knows that as long as he hears Hamish's voice he can live, but the day he sees his face in front of him he will have to alleviate his guilt by giving his own life.

Airth has stated in an interview that his first novel in the John Madden trilogy was inspired by a question: "how would the police have dealt with the problem posed by serial killers before they were recognized as such; before the very concept of forensic psychology had been developed?"[55] A series of brutal murders makes a perplexing case for Scotland Yard, forcing the policemen to consider—through reluctantly—different ways of solving the mystery: "The new scientific approach to crime detection was slowly gaining ground, though not without meeting resistance. Juries remained suspicious of forensic evidence. Even judges were inclined to give it little weight in their summing up."[56] The ritual nature of the murders, its overt sexual meaning, though lacking evidence of rape, the intricacy of the attacks pointing to deliberate planning, yet obviously an outcome of a disturbed psyche, together demand "calling in an expert in the field of psychology."[57] The decision to include psychological profiling was, in the author's words, deliberate: "for that purpose I created the character of a Viennese psycho-analyst, Dr. Franz Weiss, who appears in the first two books."[58] The character serves as a bridge between the historical past (Freudian psychoanalysis) and the present (criminal profiling). The title of the novel derives from Dr. Weiss's diagnosis that, "the sexual instinct flows like a river through our lives and if, for many, it is a broad sunlit stream, for others it can be a source of pain and anguish. A river of darkness."[59]

The manner in which the murders were executed is of particular interest. The murderer planned his attacks in every detail, stalking the victim and then retreating to a self-made shelter, usually in the nearby forest. Madden discovers one such place and is stunned that, with its duckboards and tin roof, it appears to be a reconstruction of a dugout. On the basis of witness testimony, Madden concludes that the murderer charged into the house of the intended victim as if he was taking part in an infantry assault, and killed with the bayonet fixed to his rifle: "The correct method, as taught by the army, is a short stabbing thrust followed by a half-twist to break the friction as the weapon is withdrawn ... whoever killed them was an expert in the use of the weapon."[60] The military guise under which the murders were committed, as well as the fact that the murderer started his killing spree while serving on the Western Front, is explained by Dr. Weiss, who sees the connection between war and the sexual undertones of the murders:

"we see a very definite connection to his time in uniform. When it comes to injuries wrought to the human psyche, there is no need to look further than the experience of the common soldier in the trenches."[61] The sexual overtones of the killings is made apparent through the psychoanalytical meaning of the bayonet, for as Dave Grossman has stated, "Thrusting the sexual appendage (the penis) deep into the body of the victim can be perversely linked to thrusting the killing appendage (a bayonet or knife) deep into the body of the victim."[62] According to Weiss, the murderer is "a psychopath, an extreme case. One who has lost touch with reality. He does not see his victims as human beings, but as objects of gratification."[63]

Airth emphasizes the murderer's exceptional war service, for which he received two decorations.[64] He had joined the army well before the outbreak of the war and achieved the rank of sergeant major. One witness who had known him in the battalion said that the moment he saw him he knew "[the man] was a killer. Eyes like stones." During the war he was both respected and feared by the soldiers for his "almost suicidal bravery." He volunteered for patrols and trench raids, and "he never failed to present himself, rifle in hand, ready on the fire step to repel an enemy attack, at the ritual stand-to just before dawn."[65] He appeared totally unaffected by the suffering and death around him. He killed without remorse and he witnessed his soldiers' deaths without pity. This is a portrait of a psychopath as an extremely efficient soldier. As Grossman points out, "the negative connotations associated with the term 'psychopath' are inappropriate [for the fighting men] since this behaviour is a generally desirable one for soldiers in combat."[66] Of course, this does not mean that all soldiers are, or should be, psychopaths. Yet, in Airth's novel only the psychopath is not traumatized by the war; others, like John Madden, are doomed to carry their mental scars. Lack of empathy allows one to kill the enemy effectively, yet the perfect soldier can become a perfect murderer in times of peace. In contrast, the lack of emotional distance to killing in wartime safeguards the humanity of man but creates psychological casualties.

The basic aim of popular literature is to provide entertainment for the readers, yet there is a general consensus among scholars that this type of literature fulfills a very important social function. William W. Stowe has written that, "popular art ... is a vehicle by which a society teaches and perpetuates its values. It is a bearer of culture ... as a bearer of knowledge and tradition which human beings require in order to interact with their environment."[67] Ben Elton, Anne Perry, Jacqueline Winspear, Caroline and Charles Todd, and Rennie Airth are novelists who, by situating their mysteries during or immediately after the Great War, have testified to the continuing need to remember a conflict that took place a century ago. Historical detective fiction may promote an interest in the past which is an end valuable in itself: "it is highly likely that mass-market popular historical narratives are shaping popular historical awareness to a much greater extent than the histories produced by professional historians."[68]

More importantly, an analysis of these novels offers valuable insight into the intricacies of the contemporary post-memory historical consciousness, unveiling diverse ideological perspectives. The detectives are characters whose purpose is to convey the so-called "truth" of the Great War, and it is significant that this truth varies depending on the author, ranging from an affirmation of the conflict of 1914–18 as a just war by Anne Perry to a reassertion of the war as a futile tragedy by Ben Elton. This, in turn, opens the way for a discussion of the manner in which the Great War is remembered today in popular culture. There is the additional layer of interpretation created by the juxtaposition of murder (in peacetime) and legitimate killing (in wartime) that allows for a discussion of the ethics of war. The conflation of detective fiction and the war narrative is a means of upholding an interest in a past conflict; it may serve the purpose of conveying historical knowledge and understanding, but it challenges this knowledge and understanding by raising, even if inadvertently, the questions of the definition of war in relation to crime and the definition of crime in relation to war.

NOTES

1. Mark Rawlinson, *Pat Barker* (New York: Palgrave Macmillan, 2010), 168.
2. Mark Salber Phillips, "History, Memory, and Historical Distance," in *Theorizing Historical Consciousness*, ed. Peter Seixas (Toronto: University of Toronto Press, 2006), 92.
3. Ibid., 98.
4. Eric Leed, "Fateful Memories: Industrialized War and Traumatic Neuroses," *Journal of Contemporary History* 35, no. 1 (2000): 87.
5. Peter Middleton and Tim Woods, *Literatures of Memory: History, Time and Space in Postwar Writing* (Manchester and New York: Manchester University Press), 1.
6. Jay Winter, "Kinship and remembrance in the aftermath of the Great War," in *War and Remembrance in the Twentieth Century*, ed. Jay Winter and Emmanuel Sivan (Cambridge: Cambridge University Press, 2000), 42–43.

7. Jacqueline Winspear, "Skylarks above No Man's Land," www.jacquelinewinspear .com/essays-skylarks.php.

8. John Scaggs, *Crime Fiction* (London: Routledge, 2005), 91.

9. Rennie Airth, "Murder Between the Wars," Ron Hogan's Beatrice: Introducing Writers to Readers Since 1995, http://beatrice.com/wordpress/2009/07/21/ rennie-airth-guest-author (accessed 25 August 2011).

10. John R. Gillis, "Memory and Identity: The History of a Relationship," in *Commemorations: The Politics of National Identity*, ed. John R. Gillis (Princeton: Princeton University Press, 1996), 3.

11. "Introduction," *Memory and Memorials: The Commemorative Century*, ed. William Kidd and Brian Murdoch (Aldershot: Ashgate, 2004), 3.

12. J. Kingston Pierce, "A Test of Todds," *January Magazine*, n.d., http:// januarymagazine.com/profiles/ctodd.html (accessed 25 August 2011).

13. Caroline and Charles Todd, *Wings of Fire* (New York: St. Martin's, 1999), 25.

14. Phillip Knightley, *The First Casualty: The War Correspondent as Hero, Propagandist and Myth-Maker from the Crimea to Iraq* (London: André Deutsch, 2003).

15. Ben Elton, *The First Casualty* (London: Black Swan, 2006), 167.

16. Ibid., 157, 152–53.

17. Scaggs, *Crime Fiction*, 125.

18. Middleton and Woods, *Literatures of Memory*, 58.

19. Scaggs, *Crime Fiction*, 60.

20. John G. Cawelti, "Canonization, Modern Literature and the Detective Story," in *Theory and Practice of Classic Detective Fiction*, ed. Jerome H. Delamater and Ruth Prigozy (Westport: Hofstra University Press, 1997), 6.

21. S.S. Van Dine, "Twenty Rules for Writing Detective Stories," *New York Magazine*, September 1928.

22. Scaggs, *Crime Fiction*, 48.

23. Ibid.

24. Middleton and Woods, *Literatures of Memory*, 82.

25. Cawelti, "Canonization, Modern Literature and the Detective Story," 8.

26. Ibid., 9.

27. Elton, *The First Casualty*, 129.

28. Anne Perry, *At Some Disputed Barricade* (London: Headline, 2007), 449.

29. Anne Perry, *We Shall Not Sleep* (London: Headline, 2008), 241.

30. Keith C. Barton and Linda S. Levstik, *Teaching History for the Common Good* (Mahwah: Lawrence Erlbaum Associates, 2004), 92.

31. Samuel Hynes, "Personal Narratives and Commemoration," in *War and Remembrance in the Twentieth Century*, 207.

32. Elton, *The First Casualty*, 12.

33. Paul Fussell, *The Great War and Modern Memory* (Oxford: Oxford University Press, 1977), 7–8.

34. Elton, *The First Casualty*, 20–22, 219.

35. Ibid., 267.

36. Anne Perry, *No Graves as Yet* (New York: Ballantine Books, 2004), 359.

37. Anne Perry, *Angels in the Gloom* (London: Headline, 2006), 374.

38. Anne Perry, *Shoulder in the Sky* (London: Headline, 2005), 112.

39. Samuel Hynes, *A War Imagined: The First World War and English Culture* (London: Bodley Head, 1990), 53.

40. Perry, *We Shall Not Sleep*, 14–15.

41. James Hayward, *Myths and Legends of the First World War* (Stroud, Gloucestershire: History Press, 2010), 87.

42. Perry, *Shoulder in the Sky*, 308–9.

43. A. St. John Adcock, *Remembrance: Soldier Poets Who Have Fallen in the War* (London: Hodder and Stoughton, 1918), 228.

44. Perry, *Shoulder in the Sky*, 108.

45. William W. Stowe, "Critical Investigations: Convention and Ideology in Detective Fiction," *Texas Studies in Literature and Language* 31 (1989): 574, 570.

46. Nyla R. Branscombe et al., "The Measurement of Collective Guilt," in *Collective Guilt: International Perspectives*, ed. Nyla R. Branscombe and Bertjan Doosje (Cambridge: Cambridge University Press, 2004), 16–17.

47. Jacqueline Winspear, *Maisie Dobbs* (London: John Murray, 2005), 258.

48. Julian Putkowski and Julian Sykes, *Shot at Dawn: Executions in World War One by Authority of the British Army Act* (Barnsley: Pen and Sword Books, 2007), 10.

49. See Bette London's "The Names of the Dead: 'Shot at Dawn' and the Politics of Remembrance" in this volume.

50. Pierce, "A Test of Todds."

51. Edgar Jones and Simon Wessely, *Shell Shock to PTSD: Military Psychiatry from 1900 to the Gulf War* (Hove: Psychology Press, 2005), 238.

52. Caroline and Charles Todd, *A Test of Wills* (New York: Harper Collins, 2007), 155–56.

53. Pierce, "A Test of Todds."

54. Todd, *A Test of Wills*, 21.

55. Airth, "Murder Between the Wars."

56. Rennie Airth, *River of Darkness* (Basingstoke: Pan Books, 1999), 32–33.

57. Ibid., 154.

58. Airth, "Murder Between the Wars."

59. Airth, *River of Darkness*, 180–81.

60. Ibid., 50.

61. Ibid., 212.

62. Dave Grossman, *On Killing: The Psychological Cost of Learning to Kill in War and Society* (New York: Back Bay Books, 1996), 137.

63. Airth, *River of Darkness*, 214.

64. Ibid., 353.
65. Ibid., 337, 403, 221.
66. Grossman, *On Killing*, 180.
67. Stowe, *Crime Fiction*, 590.
68. Gavriel D. Rosenfeld, *The World Hitler Never Made: Alternate History and the Memory of Nazism* (Cambridge: Cambridge University Press, 2005), 14.

"BACKSTABBING ARABS" AND "SHIRKING KURDS"

History, Nationalism, and Turkish Memory of the First World War

VEYSEL ŞİMŞEK

The signing of the Moudros Armistice on 30 October 1918 ended the First World War for the Ottoman Empire.* Although the war culminated in a defeat, the governing Committee of Union and Progress (CUP) had demanded and extracted tremendous sacrifices from the Ottoman armed forces and the civilian population. The Ottoman state had mobilized hundreds of thousands of conscripts to fight in the fly-infested trenches of Gallipoli, the harsh deserts of the Sinai Peninsula, the humid lowlands of Mesopotamia, and the freezing mountains of eastern Anatolia. We still lack published, comprehensive data sets and in-depth secondary studies on Ottoman troop numbers, recruitment patterns, and the ethnic composition of army units, but according to one estimate some 2.9 million Ottoman subjects, out of a population of 22 to 23 million, were put into uniform.[1] At the end of the war, half a million of these men remained on the muster rolls, only one-fifth of them combat-ready.[2] Apart from appalling military losses (770,000 dead or missing, 300,000 seriously wounded, and perhaps 500,000 deserters),[3] millions of Ottoman civilians suffered, died, or were

*I dedicate this essay to the memory of my maternal great-grandfather, İsmail Alakuştekin, an Ottoman regular soldier, and to that of my paternal grandfather, Mehmet Şimşek, an Ottoman irregular, who both served on the Caucasus front in the Great War. I am grateful to Dr. Tracy McDonald, Steve Marti, and Lisetta Sartor for their valuable feedback while I was writing this text. Any errors are solely mine.

displaced by shortages, famines, plagues, and forced deportations.[4] The war also damaged the Empire's economy and state finances.[5]

The end of the war brought the dismantling of the Ottoman Empire. The Sèvres Treaty of 1920 left the Ottoman state with a small patch of land in central Anatolia, while the victorious Allies created zones of political-economic influence in Asia Minor. With the exception of the Kingdom of Hejaz (which would be incorporated into Saudi Arabia later), the Empire's Arab provinces were carved up and governed as "mandates" by the victors. Backed by Britain, Greece invaded Western Anatolia and Eastern Thrace to annex those Ottoman lands with sizable Greek Orthodox populations. Yet a determined group of Turkish nationalists, most of them Ottoman military officers and bureaucrats who had survived the war, managed to mobilize the war-weary Muslim peoples of Anatolia through a mixture of skilful leadership, internal negotiation, and coercion: after three more years of fighting, the Turkish nationalists led by Mustafa Kemal (1881–1938) defeated the Greek army. The "National Struggle"[6] gave birth to an independent Republic of Turkey, recognized by major world powers after the Treaty of Lausanne in 1923. Mustafa Kemal and his companions' radical reform agenda then steered the country to become a full-fledged Turkish nation-state.

This essay traces and contextualizes manifestations of Turkish nationalism in selected texts describing the Ottoman Empire's experience of the First World War. Mandatory high school and university history textbooks, widely circulated academic and popular histories, the Turkish General Staff's campaign histories, and other publications published in Turkish from the 1930s to the present constitute my source base. Texts were selected according to their status as "official accounts," high circulation, and popularity among Turkish readers. Some of these sources originated from key state institutions, such as the Turkish military, the Turkish Ministry of Education, and the Turkish Historical Society (Türk Tarih Kurumu, or THA),[7] and thus represent the "authorized" story of the war. Others were national bestsellers or widely cited works by Turkish intellectuals and scholars, often repeating aspects of the same narrative. Regardless of these texts' manifold differences, they have all contributed to the *creation* and *perpetuation* of a nationalist, exclusivist, Turko-centric narrative of the Ottoman war effort, both at the institutional level and in society at large. The texts' wide circulation during the past eighty years has substantially affected ordinary Turks' view of the war and coloured their sense of national identity.

This master narrative has attributed the war's glory and sacrifice mainly to the Ottoman Empire's Turkish population. Non-Turkish people have been erased from it, making their contributions to the war (whether voluntary or involuntary) invisible.[8] The narrative also speaks of the eventual "treachery" of Arabs and Armenians, the unavoidable fall of the Empire, and the "necessary" emergence of the Republic of Turkey. Only very recently has the ongoing "Kurdish Question" led to a makeshift modification of this narrative: now, apparently, "all the Anatolian peoples," including the Kurds, made sacrifices—but in practice the "all" in fact describes the Muslim peoples only. The services rendered by Greek, Armenian, Jewish, and other non-Muslim Ottoman subjects in non-combatant labour battalions (and, on a few occasions, in combat units) remain probably the least acknowledged aspect of the war in Turkish collective memory. Non-Muslim Ottoman subjects are still not considered founding elements of the Republic, and thus have not been granted an official place of commemoration.[9] Nonetheless, changing state policies and official discourse on the Kurdish Question have affected the language used in popular and scholarly writing on the war, and thus on how it is remembered, which has conversely triggered a counter-response by radical Turkish nationalists.

One of my goals is to question the historical accuracy of this narrative by reconsidering non-Turkish subjects' roles in an essentially imperial war effort. I will then address how and why the Turkish master narrative excludes Arabs and Kurds. Finally, I will elaborate on how the politics of war memorialization and the Kurdish Question are linked in contemporary Turkey. I do not aim to glorify the blood spilled in the war by Ottoman subjects from different backgrounds, an (supposedly) eager and widespread effort in defence of the motherland and of religion. This is the discourse adopted by the Turkish state in the past two decades: the memory of Turkey's "wars of emergence" now emphasizes how different Muslim peoples fought together and thus became "one nation," thereby avoiding the constitutional recognition of non-Sunni Muslims or non-Turkish ethnocultural identities. Yet modern armed conflicts, regardless of their destructiveness, are not inevitable natural disasters; they result from decision-makers' choices in their political, social, and economic contexts. In the Ottoman case, many ordinary soldiers and their families did not endorse the war, as high desertion rates and sorrowful folk songs testify.[10]

The war and its outcomes affected the diverse peoples of the Middle East tremendously, and Turks, Arabs, Kurds, Armenians, and Greeks have remembered their war experiences in often competing national narratives. Inevitably, both the imagined and factual accounts of the war have greatly influenced subsequent political debates and the formation of national identities after the Ottoman Empire's demise. In Turkey, the state has played a crucial role in upholding its own version of the war memory through public education and days of remembrance. Furthermore, it has built and maintained most of the memorials and war cemeteries, while private-communal initiatives of commemoration have remained minimal.[11] For ordinary Anatolian peoples, accounts of first-hand experiences, folk songs, and dirges have been crucial to the intergenerational transmittal of the memory of the Great War, especially in the first few decades after the war, because of widespread illiteracy.[12] Yet despite its importance for the configuration of modern Turkish nationalism and identity, research on the politics of remembrance and the development of Turkish collective memory about the Great War is still in its early stages.[13]

How does the information about the First World War that has been taught in school, public discourse, and the popular media influence average Turks? In October 2011, the state-funded Serhat Kalkınma Ajansı (Serhat Development Agency) interviewed some two thousand people to assess ordinary Turkish citizens' "historical consciousness" and their views about the Ottoman Empire's war experience. Although the poll alone (not least due to its unsound methodology) does not yield definitive conclusions, it does provide a rare glimpse into Turkish collective memory. Almost half of the respondents "strongly" and "very strongly" considered the history taught in schools and universities reliable. Furthermore, two-thirds of the interviewees believed that "history should predominantly include themes of heroic acts" since "it generates the sense of national belonging for the new generations."[14] The survey results showed that while Turks were willing to reconcile with "historical enemies," the majority also considered Turkish nationalism a central matter of life.

THE TEXTS

Falih Rıfkı Atay, who served as a junior reserve officer in the Ottoman 4th Army headquarters and later became a prominent journalist, parliamentarian, and a member of Mustafa Kemal's "entourage" in Republican Turkey, described the fall of Jerusalem in his memoir as follows:

> Three battalions, just three battalions!
>   We cannot send even this much to the aid of Turkish soldiers bleeding for Jerusalem in the trenches of Nabi Samwil.

In that year, [however], we [had managed to] find 20,000 worthless Turks to fight in Galicia [in northeastern Romania against Russians].

We were feeding legions of Anatolian children to the scurvy and desert in distant Medina, which had [already seceded] from the motherland.

One morning when I entered the commander's room I saw his eyes tired from crying: Jerusalem was in the hands of the British.... [However], we did not leave Jerusalem like the Israelites, but as Turks. Those who descend from Nabi Samwil to the Muslim and Christian temples [of Jerusalem] will remember the last day of the Turks.... From then on, we were only thinking of Istanbul and Anatolia. To the Empire and to all its dreams, good bye to all that.[15]

Atay selectively edited his earlier writings and observations during and after the war and published them under the title *Zeytindağı* (Mount of Olives) in 1932. The book was republished multiple times, is widely read, and has been quoted ever since.[16] In addition to Atay's influential position in journalism and literature during the early republican era, the beauty and power of his prose ensured a lasting impact on generations of Turkish readers, who accepted and repeated his description of the war without questioning.

Atay did not mince words when expressing his feelings about the subjects of the Ottoman Empire: to him, the Turks were the unpaid arbiters and protectors of Arab provinces: "Commerce, culture, farms, industry, buildings, everything belong either to Arabs or other [foreign] countries." No matter how strongly the Turks thought Damascus, Aleppo, and Lebanon theirs, they were indeed foreigners in Arab lands. Atay remarked bitterly: "We [the Turks] neither colonized these lands nor turned them into a fatherland. The Ottoman Empire is the warden for the farms and streets who works for free." Still, he added, "there is no doubt that feelings of possession and domination come from the [Turkish] blood in our veins."[17]

In Atay's book, the Turks are the only ethno-cultural group with positive character traits.[18] For Atay, Jews were cunning people, waiting for their time to come in Palestine; Druze were corrupt; Maronites Islam-hating, Muslim-killing fanatics; and Armenians ungrateful to the Empire and their supposed benefactor Cemal Pasha for his magnanimity during the deportations. Lebanese Arabs were conformist, cosmopolitan degenerates.[19] Atay portrayed other Arabs as untrustworthy and greedy people, some of whom, despite their kinship to the Prophet Muhammad, would eventually become the enemies of the Turks through British gold and weapons. Arab nomads, namely Bedouins, were unreliable half-savages eager to sell themselves either for British or Ottoman gold.

Two Turkish high school textbooks from the mid-1930s echoed with Atay's words, and arguably set the tone for the following eighty years in cementing the image of the "self-sacrificing but underappreciated Turk." One of them argued that the Ottomanism of the nineteenth century, a political idea that aimed to produce one Ottoman nation out of many elements, not only prevented the creation of a "national history" of the Turks but also erased whatever remained of it.[20] The glory and the sacrifice of the First World War were attributed solely to the Turks of the Ottoman Empire, with a manifestly essentialist-nationalist approach.[21] The victory at Gallipoli was a product of Mustafa Kemal's genius because he knew "how to use the inherent high qualities of the self-sacrificing Turkish soldier and Turkish nation in the best way possible."[22] But the army was subordinated to the Germans and their war aims, for which Turkish blood was sacrificed either on faraway fronts or in "military adventures," such as the Suez or Sarıkamış campaigns, which weakened the defence of the "real" fatherland. Still, the Turkish nation, "[which] formed the backbone of the Ottoman Army," would show its worth to the world whenever led by able commanders.[23] Some sixty years later, another high school history textbook stressed the "Turkishness" of the war effort. The authors referred to Ottoman soldiers serving on the Caucasus, Iraqi, Syrian, and Palestinian fronts as "Turks," without going into detail about the diverse ethnic composition of the actual Ottoman army.[24] On some other occasions, they used the terms "Turk" and "Ottoman" interchangeably.[25]

University textbooks present a similar narrative with only minor modifications. Regarding the Ottomans' "Holy War" and the Arabs' role in the First World War, a 1982 textbook for "History of Atatürk's Principles and [Turkish] Revolution" (HAPR) classes[26] asserted that the "declaration of Holy War on November 23, 1914, however, did not produce the results desired [by the Ottoman Empire and Germany]. In Iraq and Syria, the Turkish soldier was not only martyred by the British bullet but also by the Muslim Arab's bullet."[27] The author, Hamza Eroğlu, quoted these lines almost directly (with the addition of Syria) from Fahir Armaoğlu, a major Turkish diplomatic historian.[28] Armaoğlu had been educated and then taught at the prestigious Faculty of Political Science at Ankara University, where most prominent Turkish bureaucrats received their undergraduate degrees before taking positions in the state service. He also authored a number of widely read textbooks on political-diplomatic history. To quote from the extended eleventh edition of his *Political History of the Twentieth Century*,

> The *Şeyhülislam* [the Empire's chief religious authority] had indeed invited the Muslims of Crimea, Turkistan, India, Afghanistan, and Africa to fight against the Christian nations of Britain, France, and Russia by declaring Holy Jihad. But no result came out of this. In Iraq, the Turkish soldier would be martyred not only by the British bullet but also by the Muslim Arab in the desert. Those who gave their blood and lives at Gallipoli were in fact defending their fatherland and not Islam.[29]

Armaoğlu used the word "martyr" (*şehid*), a term that had an essentially Islamic reference in a secular-nationalist context. He did not want to question Turkish soldiers' ordeal in the Great War, but at the same time he wished to underline the national character of their sacrifices, rather than any possible religious motivations. HAPR textbooks followed Armaoğlu's arguments uncritically well into the 2000s.[30]

The Turkish state's "official" account of the First World War, and more specifically the stance of its armed forces, is manifested in the studies of the Turkish General Staff (TGS). Between the mid-1960s and the mid-1990s, the TGS published multivolume histories on the Ottoman military and the First World War.[31] However, except for some scattered references, these works neither discuss nor recognize the diverse ethnic composition of the Ottoman army units. After all, the choice of title for the series was representative of the Turkish army's institutional memory of the Ottoman experience in the First World War: *Birinci Dünya Harbinde Türk Harbi* (The Turks' War in the First World War). The volume devoted to the Ottomans' political, economic, and demographic context prior to 1914 affirmed that forty-one percent of the Empire's population was Turkish, while twenty-seven percent were Arabs, and five percent Kurds.[32] Other volumes used the adjectives "Turkish" and "Ottoman" almost interchangeably, erasing any distinction between the two. At the same time, the categorical but ahistorical statements on the Arab subjects of the Empire remain, depicting them as a potentially rebellious group that "did not forget the glory of the Abbasid caliphate. Furthermore, their desires for secession were further instigated by the British, Egyptian, and Arab committees." The volume criticized the Committee of Union and Progress (CUP) leaders' pan-Turkish ideals by pointing to the "necessity" of creating a Turkish nation in Ottoman lands in the first place.[33] As elsewhere, essentialist statements underlining Turks' warrior qualities abounded: the "Turkish nation was a heroic, self-confident nation by creation," and thus "it was an absolute truth that the army drawn from such a nation would have the same qualit[ies]."[34]

Another volume on the logistics and administration of war used similar language while surveying the Empire's demography. The Turks living in Western Anatolia were "the real owners of the area, [and] constituted a coalesced and sturdy society that dominated the minorities."[35] When referring to the peoples of Eastern Anatolia, an area that now forms part of modern Turkey, the study gave population figures for resident non-Muslim ethno-religious groups such as Armenians, Greek Orthodox, Assyrians, and Jews. Kurds, along with Turks and others, were lumped into one undifferentiated group as "Muslims." "The people of Syria and Palestine lacked patriotism and martial qualities," so "the main burdens of the wars were put on the units raised from the Turkish population [of these regions]."[36]

As outlined above, textbooks, influential historical studies, and memoirs such as *Zeytindağı* compartmentalized ethno-religious groups of the Ottoman Empire based on their alleged roles during the war years, a phenomenon that popular texts on the Great War repeated. Şevket Süreyya Aydemir, author of the widely read biographies of Mustafa Kemal, İsmet İnönü, and Enver Pasha, has echoed Atay's and the TGS's works since the 1960s. In his biography of Enver Pasha, Aydemir asserted that, apart from a few individuals who sacrificed their lives, the Kurds and Arabs did not really contribute to the war effort: "if we name the war of the Ottoman Army as the 'War of the Turkish Army', it won't be an exaggeration…. The basic fact is the main burden [of conscription] was on the shoulders of Turkish-Ottomans."[37] Aydemir's book suggests that the approximately 2.5 million Ottoman soldiers mobilized between August 1914 and December 1915 were mainly drawn from a Turkish population of twelve million living in Anatolia and Thrace,[38] which had about seventeen million inhabitants in total.[39]

In his 2008 bestseller on the Gallipoli campaign, Turgut Özakman did not proffer a new paradigm or original analyses, but merely retold and further popularized the well-established narrative. In the preface, Özakman defines Gallipoli as "a resurrection, [t]he return of the Turk." Thus the ordeal at the Dardanelles became the forerunner of the "National Struggle" and of the future republic. In Özakman's account of the Ottomans' road to war, "the Balkan nations revolted and gained their independence; the

Albanians also seceded most recently. Even the Arabs were founding separatist organizations" prior to the war, allegedly supported by the British.[40]

Unlike several other texts, however, Özakman made specific references to the "Arab" units that fought at Gallipoli, notably the 72nd and 77th infantry regiments, mainly raised from the Aleppo military recruitment district.[41] In the author's portrayal of events, the cowardly soldiers of the 77th deserted their positions in the heat of battle, costing "Turkish blood." In contrast, the Turkish units always fought courageously and selflessly.[42] Özakman wrote, "What surprised the Turkish soldiers most was that the majority of these men [Arabs] deserted their comrades [Turks] in arms under enemy fire. They[43] were realizing day by day that [the Turks and Arabs] were the children of utterly different nations and lands by living together."[44]

THE "BACKSTABBING ARABS"[45]

How accurate are the assertions about the "Turkishness" of the Ottoman war effort? Are they merely nationalist myths aimed at creating new generations of Turks mindful of their ancestors' sacrifices and errors? Or are they reflections of the simple historical fact that ethnic Turks shouldered the burden of fighting while most others shirked, conspired, or rebelled?

One official Turkish military history states that only between five thousand and six thousand Arabs, out of a total of 250,000 soldiers, served on the Sinai-Palestine front between 1914 and 1918.[46] In his important survey of the Ottoman Army during the war, Edward J. Erickson affirmed that many Arabs and Kurds served in the Ottoman military, but also asserted that, "the essence of the army was Turkish. Whenever the army got right down to the terrible matter of dying in the trenches it was usually the Turkish soldiers (*Askers* in Turkish) that accomplished the deed." Because of the widespread contemporary usage of the word "Turk" for the Ottomans and the very "Turkish essence" of the Ottoman army, he reasoned, "in this book, the term *Turkish Army* is used instead of the more proper term *Ottoman Army*."[47]

Over the course of *Seferberlik*,[48] the immense hardships and Istanbul's heavy-handed administration could very well have disillusioned Arabs who had been loyal to the ideals of Ottomanism.[49] However, nationalist sentiments did not lead to mass mutinies or defections in Arab units during the war. In fact, many ordinary Arab soldiers ran away from their units not because of their political convictions but for the same reasons that their Turkish comrades did: inadequate provisioning, the harsh conditions of military service, ill-treatment by superiors, and fighting a losing war. A majority of the Arab soldiers deserted to save their lives, evade their pursuers, and take care of their families, not to take up arms against the Ottoman forces.[50]

Revisionist research on the Hashemite Revolt of 1916 demonstrated that it was neither a willing manifestation of widespread nationalist feelings nor actively supported by most notables, military and civilian bureaucrats, and ordinary subjects.[51] No military or political figure of significance joined the Arab revolt.[52] Furthermore, although Sharif Husayn's main motives appear to have been dynastic and pragmatic, he tried to legitimize his actions through the bid for Arab nationalism and independence from the "Turk." Despite their importance, these new findings have not been taken into consideration by most historical and popular narratives of the First World War in Turkey.

After the revolt had started, Sharif Husayn reinforced his forces partly with regular Arab units from Egypt and partly with Ottoman deserters and POWs. Yet Ottoman-Arab soldiers did not appear enthusiastic to switch sides after becoming POWs; between August and December 1916, out of 110 Arab officers and 2,500 Arab soldiers held in British POW camps in India, only thirty-one officers and 249 men agreed to join the Hashemite forces under British supervision.[53] Sharif Husayn needed to recruit Arab officers and soldiers, but he did not trust them fully and favoured his Hejazi men for appointments. The friction between the defected Syrians, Iraqis, and the Hejazis caused a "partisan spirit," which had a negative impact on the rebels' fighting abilities. Consequently, the British military reports in June 1917 were still vitriolic about the overall military value of Sharif Husayn's troops, complaining about their lack of discipline, resolution, and fighting spirit.[54]

To counter the perceived risk of mutiny and popular revolt, as well as to fulfill pressing military necessities, the Ottoman authorities transferred Arab formations to fronts distant from their homelands and imposed tighter controls over the Arab populations. After the Allied landings at Gallipoli, Faysal (1883–1933, Sharif Husayn's son, later king of Iraq) came to Damascus on 23 May 1915 to talk to Arab nationalists. However, unlike during his previous visit in March, he found some of the Arab units in Syria transferred elsewhere. In June 1915, the "Arab" 23rd, 25th, 27th, and 37th Divisions were removed from Syria. The Ottoman 25th Division ended up in Gallipoli and then in Galicia, while the 37th Division was sent to the Caucasus front.[55] In the meantime, Enver Pasha and Cemal Pasha sent 150

Arab officers to Gallipoli based on investigations by the Ottoman secret service, while some fifty Turkish officers were added to the cohort to calm possible suspicions.[56] However, even though Turkish leaders grew more distrustful and their rule in Arab provinces got harsher through the war, many Arab officers, some of whom might be called Arab nationalists, remained loyal to the Ottoman state and army.[57]

When tested, the broad assertions about Arabs' and Kurds' lower morale, lack of military spirit, and participation in the actual fighting contradict the available historical research. Furthermore, the customary approach in the historiography that has depicted Arabs, Kurds, and Albanians as primarily serving in irregular units, described as unruly and mercenary tribal forces, is misleading. Since the military reforms of Mahmud II (r. 1808–39), the central authority inducted non-Turkish Muslims into the regular formations whenever it had the means and opportunity to do so.[58] Especially after the 1908 revolution, the CUP vigorously pursued centralization and the standardization of governance by installing loyal, energetic administrators and military leaders, and by deploying regular army units throughout the Empire.[59] By 1914 the Ottoman state authority had already reached the plains of Mesopotamia, larger Syria, and Kurdistan, where millions of sedentary, agrarian subjects constituted easier targets for military recruiters, just as they did in the core provinces of the Southern Balkans and Anatolia.

In this historical context, the Ottoman state of 1914 could very well induct Arabs and Kurds into regular units, some of which would eventually distinguish themselves.[60] At the planning stage of the Arab Revolt, for instance, the British were expecting a large number of Arab Ottoman soldiers to change sides. Sharif Husayn claimed that a hundred thousand Arab defectors (perhaps one-third of all Ottoman effectives at the time) would join him once he raised his banner of rebellion.[61] One historian estimated that in 1915, between 100,000 and 330,000 Arabs served in the Ottoman forces.[62] During the first attack on the Suez Canal in 1915, the "Arab" 25th Division formed the first line, while the "Turkish" 10th Division was in reserve and went into battle after a bridgehead had been established on the western shore.[63] Atay's description of the campaign in *Zeytindağı* makes no reference to this unit, one of the two regular divisions in the Ottoman expeditionary force. The Ottoman 20th Division, which was originally raised from Palestine and could be considered an "Arab" unit, had a distinguished battle record in Galicia, Gallipoli, and Palestine. A number of Turkish sources have stigmatized the "Arab" 72nd and 77th regiments at Gallipoli for their allegedly poor performances on the battlefield, subtly or unsubtly linking their judgments to the units' ethnicity.[64] Yet after a detailed assessment of the units' battle records, Erickson concludes that the claims were overstated.[65] On the battlefields of Gallipoli, Arab officers fought alongside their Turkish peers without deserting or rebelling. As Mesut Uyar noted, of 589 Ottoman officers killed at Gallipoli, ninety-seven came from Arab provinces.[66]

On 31 October 1917, British forces overwhelmed the 27th Arab Division, the main unit defending the town of Beersheba. Kress von Kressenstein, the German commander of the Ottoman 8th Army, attributed the defeat partly to the unreliability of the Arab troops, a characterization repeated by Turkish secondary sources.[67] However, Colonel İsmet (later İnönü, the future "National Chief" of Turkey after the death of Mustafa Kemal Atatürk in 1938), the Turkish commander of the defending Ottoman outfit, did not refer to any weakness caused by the ethnic Arab soldiers in his battle report. Instead, he emphasized the disproportionate odds and the long front that he had to hold with his smaller force. Indeed, the British concentrated their attack on a seriously under-strength Ottoman division with two of their own (1,400 men against 24,000). It took an entire day for the British force to defeat the Arabs despite their overwhelming numbers. Erickson concluded that, "whether Anatolian or Turkish soldiers might have held back the British onslaught is problematic at best."[68] An Ottoman report compiled in September 1917 listed 16,513 Turkish and 6,023 Arab effectives defending the Palestine front.[69] Soon the British launched massive offensives against Beersheba and Gaza; they would capture Jerusalem on 9 December 1917. A British intelligence report listed the 7,500 POWs and deserters captured between 31 October and 24 November 1917 as 64 percent Turk, 27 percent Arab, and 9 percent non-Muslim. When these figures are compared to the earlier Ottoman report from September 1917 (66 percent Turk, 26 percent Arab, and 8 percent other), it becomes apparent that desertions and surrenders were not exclusive to any particular ethno-religious group during the intense fighting in Palestine.[70]

THE "SHIRKING KURDS"

The story of the Kurds has differed from that of the Arabs. After its establishment, the Turkish Republic did not inherit the Arab-populated provinces of the Ottoman Empire, and Armenians no longer existed as a sizable minority in Asia Minor after their genocide. During the early 1920s, leaders of Turkey and Greece agreed to swap their Greek Orthodox and Muslim minorities. As a result, the Kurds remained as the most populous non-Turkish yet Muslim ethnic group, concentrated in the eastern and southeastern provinces of the new Turkish Republic. Despite the Kurds' significant population numbers and demands, the Turkish state did not recognize a distinct Kurdish ethno-cultural identity until the early 1990s. Instead, it enacted various short- and long-term policies aimed at assimilating them. The results have been mixed, but in the end, millions of Kurds could not be turned into Turks.[71] From the 1950s onward, the Kurdish intelligentsia, growing in number and increasingly politicized, aligned itself with the Turkish left. The coup d'état of 1980 and the ensuing military regime did not erase Kurdish dissenters' political consciousness; it actually radicalized some of them to take up arms against Turkish security forces. The late 1980s and 1990s witnessed widespread violence in Eastern Anatolia, where thousands of Turkish soldiers, Kurdish militants, and civilians died in fighting. The Turkish state also exiled hundreds of thousands of Kurdish villagers from their rural homes.

Given this suppression of the Kurdish identity, it is unsurprising that Kurds and their war experiences rarely appear in Turkish accounts of the Great War. In some cases, the Kurds were completely omitted from the master narrative, and broad terms such as "Ottoman" and "Turkish" were used liberally to denote the Kurds alongside other peoples of the Empire. When Kurds' contributions to the Ottoman war effort were not fully excluded, they were sidelined. In later accounts such as Özakman's, Kurds were still not recognized as a distinct group and lumped together with other Anatolian peoples to be ultimately denoted as "Turks." Thus Armaoğlu, Aydemir, Özakman, and many others basically repeated the popular, legal, and institutional assertion that the term "Turk" referred to a non-ethnic, superordinate national identity around which "Turkish citizenship" had been created.[72]

In the past two decades, the Turkish state has gradually changed its long-established stance toward the Kurds. High-level state officials have accepted the existence of Kurdish people in their statements, and some have even recognized the unlawful acts perpetrated by security forces in the 1980s and 1990s. In 2006, the Turkish Public Broadcasting Agency established a television channel broadcasting in Kurdish, and a Department of Eastern Languages and Literatures was founded in 2011 in one of the new state universities to teach, among other languages, Kurdish. There are several major reasons for this change in policy: the Kurdish movement gradually radicalized since the mid-1980s, and the limited but costly war put a heavy strain on state finances and ravaged the Eastern Anatolian countryside. Moreover, Turkey's European Union membership bid required policy changes in the interior. Besides, the governing Islamic party, AKP (Justice and Development Party), has also been trying to court religiously conservative Kurdish voters.

In this new political context, the First World War has increasingly been presented as a unifying historical experience for citizens of Turkey from different ethno-cultural backgrounds. Politicians and public figures of various political affiliations have increasingly referred to Kurds as the Turks' "brothers in arms" in *Seferberlik* without much inhibition. During the 2011 parliamentary elections, the prime minister, Recep Tayyip Erdoğan, stated at a political rally in Diyarbakır, the largest city of the Kurdish provinces: "Aren't Kurds, Turks, Lazes, Circassians, Arabs, and Roma lying next to each other at Gallipoli? Aren't our martyrs lying together at Sarıkamış? Didn't we—Turks, Kurds, Arabs—win the great victory altogether at Kut'ül-Amare? We fought the War of National Liberation together, we founded the Republic altogether."[73]

The Kurds, previously invisible to the Turkish state and society, thus burst into recognition between 2000 and 2010, a new reality that has frustrated radical Turkish nationalists. In 2009 Gökçe Fırat (Çulhaoğlu), the leader of the Ulusal Party (National Party), put forward a radical thesis in an editorial entitled "Were There [any] Kurds at Gallipoli?" in *Türk Solu* (*Turkish Left*), a weekly newspaper. Gökçe Fırat strove to "correct" the Turkish memory of the war, and the Kurds' contribution.[74] Basing his argument on the number of soldiers killed and their home provinces, he argued that Kurdish participation was insignificant not only at Gallipoli but also during the National Struggle against the Greeks.[75] According to his calculations, only four percent of the Ottoman soldiers who lost their lives in the Gallipoli campaign came from eastern and southeastern Anatolia, which were and are predominantly Kurdish-populated.[76]

Osman Pamukoğlu, leader of HEPAR (Rights and Equality Party), repeated similar arguments about the Kurds the same year.[77] Pamukoğlu is a highly decorated retired Turkish general who served in internal security operations in the east during the 1990s.[78] While Pamukoğlu's party and Gökçe Fırat's supporters do not have a significant hold on the Turkish political scene,[79] their belligerent stance against the Kurds and their aggressive tone do seem to appeal to many Turkish citizens with more mainstream nationalist views.[80]

Gökçe Fırat's assertions about the Gallipoli campaign are problematic and disregard the Kurds' overall role in the Great War. Even if one determines the magnitude of sacrifice solely by counting the number of fallen soldiers, one should take into account the demographic composition of the former Ottoman provinces and the number of recruits they provided to assess which community paid the heavier "blood tax." Gökçe Fırat's essay lacked such a discussion, or any reference to Kurdish civilian suffering and contributions. Second, using the casualty figures from only one particular front can be misleading: not every Ottoman soldier was sent to the Dardanelles, so the Gallipoli campaign alone cannot be used to "calculate" the Kurds' part in the Great War. Finally, we still lack the complete quantitative studies on the origins and service records of the Ottoman conscripts that would permit drawing the kind of decisive conclusions that Gökçe Fırat does.[81]

Extant estimates suggest that Kurds may have constituted ten to fifteen percent of Anatolian and Thracian Muslims,[82] which seems disproportionate to the percentage of Kurdish battle deaths (four percent) given by Gökçe Fırat.[83] However, we have concrete evidence that the units comprising Kurdish troops fought elsewhere, generally in the Caucasus, Iraq, and later in Syria.[84] The peacetime recruitment districts of the Ottoman XI Corps (with the 18th, 33rd, and 34th Divisions attached) were densely populated with Kurds, such as Muş, Mamüretü'l-Aziz, and Van.[85] These units sustained devastating casualties during the disastrous offensives in the winter of 1914–15.[86] The 35th Division, raised in multi-ethnic but Kurdish-dominated northern Iraq, continuously battled against the British in Mesopotamia, while the 36th Division, raised from the same region, served in the major campaigns of the Caucasus front.[87] Mehmed Emin Zeki, an Ottoman Kurdish staff officer who held various posts during the war, indicated that the Ottoman XI and XII Corps (with the 35th and 36th Divisions attached) mainly included Kurds at the outbreak of the war. He also remarked that in addition to the regular formations, 135 irregular Kurdish cavalry squadrons joined the war on the Ottoman side. The TGS's history corroborates Zeki's point, listing four reserve cavalry divisions mainly drawn from Kurdish-dominated areas.[88] Eastern Anatolia, where hundreds of thousands of Kurds lived, became the battleground for the Russian and Ottoman armies that lived off the land. It is impossible to determine the exact death toll, but the Kurdish civilian population was certainly greatly affected by shortages, famines, diseases, dislocations, and forced deportations, the latter part of the CUP's Turkification policies.[89]

CONCLUSION

The problematic relationship between modern Turkey and its Ottoman heritage is evident in the Turkish memory of the Ottoman Empire's First World War. Written from a nationalistic perspective, most Turkish narratives have selectively appropriated, distorted, or ignored the precise Ottoman experience of war. According to the stories they tell, Ottoman soldiers' victories and suffering were associated with their (assumed) Turkishness. The fact that the Ottoman army was a multi-ethnic (and to a certain extent multi-religious) force has been continually overlooked throughout the decades. In other cases, contributions of various ethno-religious groups other than Turkish Muslims were minimized or simply omitted from the master narrative. Finally, the alleged wartime "betrayals" of "subject nations," such as Arabs and Armenians, supposedly pointed to the "necessity" and "inevitability" of a Turkish nation-state after the fall of the Ottoman Empire.

Turkish state institutions and generations of Turkish historians and intellectuals have been instrumental in perpetuating this memory of the war, which was closely tied to the Turkish nation-state and its nation-building project. As is often pointed out, the establishment of modern Turkey marked a sharp break with the Ottoman Empire. The new republic persistently tried to distance itself from its "dark Ottoman past," which was "non-Turkish," "non-secular," and "non-progressive."[90] As a result, the contributions (willing or unwilling) of the Arabs to the Great War have been left out of history textbooks and historical bestsellers, which has influenced how Turks remember the war. Sharif Husayn's "Great Arab Revolt" did not, in fact, have a great military impact or boost support from ordinary Arab subjects. However, the prestigious Hashemites, descendants of the Prophet Muhammad's tribe and Ottoman vassals for several centuries, chose to rebel against the central authority during the war. The new Turkish Republic then used the alleged failure of the declaration of Holy War, along with the "Arab betrayal," to justify the primacy of national interests and the national identity of the Turks, and to cut past and potential future ties with Arab peoples. The historical contact with Arabs, their culture, and even their religion allegedly had negative effects on the Turks, who gradually forgot about their national essence and (supposed) nationhood. Therefore, future intimacy with the Arabs became irreconcilable with the establishment of a secular modern Turkish national identity. In the end, Arabs became one of the "others" of Turkish nationalism and national identity.[91]

Distancing itself from Arab peoples and their quarrels with Britain and France after the First World War brought Turkey international recognition for its national sovereignty, a compromise that the founders of the republic were eager to make.[92] Estranged from the Arabs, the Turkish state could implement and legitimize its pro-Western commitments and policies toward Israel and Arab countries during the 1950s in the context of the Cold War. From the 1960s to the 1990s, this detachment again helped the Turkish state conduct its cautious, non-interventionist foreign policies toward the larger Middle East, a geography that became ever more volatile with Arab–Israeli conflicts and the rise of anticolonial nationalist movements.[93]

In the 1920s, the Turkish state made the decision to turn Kurds into Turks, a policy whose roots can be traced to CUP rule during the First World War.[94] According to Turkish state discourse, the Kurdish Question had so far been merely "an issue of political reaction, tribal resistance or regional backwardness, but never an ethno-political question." Those subjects resisting Turkish state policies "were not Kurds with an ethno-political cause, but simply Kurdish tribes, Kurdish bandits, Kurdish sheikhs—all the evils of Turkey's pre-modern past."[95] Ultimately, the policy failed and the repressive state measures led to prolonged fighting between Turkish security forces and armed rebels in the Kurdish provinces. Yet in the past thirty years, shifts in state policy and discourse have affected the Turkish public and its memory of the war in various ways.

The Turkish state and Turkish society, for both of whom nationalism has been a central ideology, have given different responses to Kurdish political demands. Since the 1920s, the state's policies have varied, including forced deportations, assimilationism and "civilizing mission(s)," and recently the superficial recognition of a distinct Kurdish cultural identity. In light of statements by high-ranking government officials, the writings of popular journalists, and rising communal tensions, Yeğen has held that, in the past decade, some Turks have realized that most Kurds will not consent to assimilation into Turkishness. Turkey's efforts to become a member of the EU, the establishment of an autonomous Kurdish region in northern Iraq, and, more recently, the creation of one in northern Syria have further underlined the existence of the Kurds and their demands; at the same time, they have also heightened the disappointment of the Turkish state and of some Turkish citizens.

As the Kurdish Question intensified after the 1980s, the participation of different ethnicities in the Great War was highlighted to underline how the different *Muslim* peoples (to the exclusion of non-Muslims) of Anatolia consented to become one nation by having bonded by "fire and blood" during the *Seferberlik*. Consequently, the Kurdish subjects of the Ottoman Empire were finally included in the long list of ethnic groups that participated in the war effort. Yet responding to these recent developments in Turkey and to Kurds' increasing visibility, radical Turkish nationalists from both right and left have begun to deny Kurdish participation in Turkey's "wars of emergence." Aiming to create a yet another memory of the First World War, the nationalists have adopted a novel political stance that signifies the "abandonment" of the Kurds, who are now no longer entitled to their part of the "Turkish nation." Instead of reintegrating the Kurds into the republic within a democratic framework, the nationalists refuse the Kurds as part of the Turkish body politic altogether. In July 2010 a poll conducted with about ten thousand interviewees throughout Turkey showed that between forty-seven and fifty-seven percent of those who defined themselves as Turks did not want Kurdish neighbours, business partners, or sons- and daughters-in-law.[96] The looming question is how many Turks with mainstream views would support the idea of completely breaking the cultural, social, and political ties with the Kurds, which could drastically reshape the main narrative of memory of the First World War in Turkey for the coming years.

APPENDIX: Ethnic Compositions and War Records of Selected Ottoman Units[a]

Unit	Ethnic Composition (excluding non-Muslim servicemen)	Service Record	Recruitment District
18th, 33rd, 34th Divisions, XI Corps[b]	Kurdish, Turkish	Caucasus	Eastern and southeastern Anatolia
35th Division, XII Corps, 1914[c]	Kurdish, Turkish, Arab	Iraq	Northern Iraq
36th Division, XII Corps, 1914[d]	Kurdish, Turkish, Arab	Caucasus	Northern Iraq
37th Division[e]	Arab	Caucasus (Iran)	Central Iraq
38th Division[f]	Arab	Iraq	Southern Iraq
51st Division[g]	Turkish, Kurdish	Iraq	
53rd Division[h]	Turkish, Arab	Palestine	
141st Regiment[i]	Arab	Iraq	

142nd Regiment[j]	Arab	Iraq	
20th Division[k]	Arab	Gallipoli, Galicia, Palestine	Palestine
72nd Regiment, 19th Division[l]	Arab	Gallipoli	Syria
77th Regiment, 19th Division[m]	Arab, Turkish	Gallipoli	Syria
23rd Division[n]	Arab	Suez, Palestine	Syria
25th Division[o]	Arab	Suez, Gallipoli	Syria
27th Division[p]	Arab	Palestine	Syria
12th Depot Regiment[q]	Arab	Palestine	
1st, 2nd, 3rd, 4th Reserve Cavalry Divisions[r]	Kurdish	Caucasus	Eastern and Southeastern Anatolia

[a] The list is compiled from secondary sources that indicated the ethnicity of Ottoman army units and their recruitment districts. I do not claim it to be exhaustive. Furthermore, the table mainly reflects the ethnic make-up of the units earlier in the war. Due to attrition, replacements, and transfers, the ethnic composition of the Ottoman units must have changed throughout the conflict, something that must still be studied in depth. In its peacetime organization, the Ottoman army had thirty-six infantry divisions, which increased to sixty-two over the course of the First World War. During the war, a typical Ottoman division at its full strength had between ten thousand and twelve thousand men, organized into three regiments. However, Ottoman army units often found themselves under-strength; it was not uncommon for an outfit to be at half its strength on paper, or even less, especially toward the end of war. Erickson, *Ottoman*, 64, 101, 168–70.

[b] TGS, *Türk*, vol. 10, pp. 92–93, 617 (Appendix 12); Jwaideh, *Kurdish*, 125. See Dündar, *Modern*, 459–60 (Appendix 10 A–B) for an ethnographic map of eastern Anatolia.

[c] TGS, *Türk*, vol. 10, p. 617 (Appendix 12); Erickson, *Ottoman*, 63; Jwaideh, *Kurdish*, 125; Tauber, *The Arab Movements*, 59.

[d] TGS, *Türk*, vol. 10, p. 617 (Appendix 12); Erickson, *Ottoman*, 67; Jwaideh, *Kurdish*, 125; Tauber, *The Arab Movements*, 59. According to the British *and* the Turkish state's statistics, the Kurdish population of Musul Province changed between fifty-six and sixty-five percent between 1914 and 1947, making Kurds the predominant population in the region. Fuat Dündar, "Statisquo: British Use of Statistics in the Iraqi Kurdish Question (1919–1932)," 45, online working paper, http://www.brandeis.edu/crown/publications/cp/CP7.pdf.

[e] Tauber also asserts that the Ottoman 42th, 43rd, and 44th divisions were "entirely Syrian." TGS, *Türk*, vol. 10, p. 617 (Appendix 12); Tauber, *The Arab Movements*, 59; Erickson, *Ordered*, 105.

[f] TGS, *Türk*, vol. 10, p. 617 (Appendix 12); Erickson, *Ottoman*, 62–64; Erickson, *Ordered*, 66–68.

[g] Zürcher, "Between," 240; Erickson, *Ottoman*, 64–65.

[h] As of September 1917, Arabs constituted 28.5 percent of the four-thousand-strong division. Erickson, *Ottoman*, 101.

[i] Zürcher, "Between," 240; Erickson, *Ottoman*, 64–65. Zürcher appears to have made a mistake by using the term "division" instead of "regiment," however.

[j] Zürcher, "Between," 240; Erickson, *Ottoman*, 64–65.

[k] Turkish General Staff, *Türk*, vol. 10, p. 617 (Appendix 12); Erickson, *Ottoman*, 135.

[l] Tamari, *The Year*, 13; Erickson, *Ottoman*, 36–38.
[m] Tamari, *The Year*, 13; Erickson, *Ottoman*, 24, 32–33, 36, 39.
[n] Erickson, *Ordered*, 69–70, 176, 216 n. 8; Erickson, *Ottoman*, 95, 124; Tauber, *The Arab Movements*, 59, 65–66.
[o] TGS, *Türk*, vol. 10, p. 617 (Appendix 12); Üzen, "Birinci," 252–55, 281; Tauber, *The Arab Movements*, 59, 65–66.
[p] TGS, *Türk*, vol. 10, p. 617 (Appendix 12); Tauber, *The Arab Movements*, 59, 65–66. As of September 1917, Arabs constituted seventy-six percent of the three-thousand-strong division. Erickson, *Ottoman*, 101.
[q] Erickson, *Ottoman*, 101. "Depot battalions" were formed out of older draftees. Beşikçi, *The Ottoman Mobilization of Manpower*, 111.
[r] TGS, *Türk*, vol. 10, p. 93; Dündar, *Modern*, 459–60 (Appendix 10 A-B); Jwaideh, *Kurdish*, 125.

NOTES

1. Mehmet Beşikçi, *The Ottoman Mobilization of Manpower in the First World War* (Leiden: Brill, 2012), 108–9, 112–13; Edward J. Erickson, *Ordered to Die: A History of the Ottoman Army in the First World War* (Westport, CT: Greenwood Press, 2001), 211, 243. According to Erickson, Ottoman casualties during the war amounted to 1.72 million. Erickson also estimated that about one million Ottoman soldiers were still under arms at the end of the war, which may be an overestimate.
2. Maurice Larcher, *La Guerre Turque dans la Guerre Mondiale* (Paris: Chiron and Berger-Levrault, 1926), 540.
3. Erickson, *Ordered to Die*, 243.
4. Hikmet Özdemir, *The Ottoman Army, 1914–1918: Disease and Death on the Battlefield*, trans. Şaban Kardaş (Salt Lake City: Utah University Press, 2008); Uğur Ümit Üngör, *The Making of Modern Turkey* (Oxford: Oxford University Press, 2011), 106–22; Fuat Dündar, *Modern Türkiye'nin Şifresi* (Istanbul: İletişim Yayınları, 2008), 335–422; Rashid Khalidi, "The Arab Experience of the War," in *Facing the Armageddon: The First World War Experienced*, ed. Hugh Cecil and Peter Liddle (London: Leo Cooper, 1996), 642–55.
5. On the Ottoman war economy, see Zafer Toprak, *İttihad-Terakki ve Cihan Harbi: Savaş Ekonomisi ve Devletçilik 1914–1918* (Istanbul: Homer, 2003).
6. In Turkey, this is one of the names given to the war against Greece of 1919–22.
7. A semi-autonomous state institution founded by Mustafa Kemal Atatürk in 1931 to investigate Turkish history. It continues to publish, fund research projects, and organize conferences.
8. Erol Köroğlu has pointed out the "Turkification" of the overall war effort and the perpetuation of "anti-Arab" sentiments from the 1920s to the 1940s in Turkish popular fiction. See his "Taming the Past, Shaping the Future: The Appropriation of the Great War Experience in the Popular Fiction of the Early

Turkish Republic," in *The First World War as Remembered in the Countries of the Eastern Mediterranean*, ed. Olaf Farschid et al. (Beirut: Orient Institut Beirut, 2006), 223–30.

9. Conversely, conscription into the Ottoman army was hardly deemed a cause for celebration by Armenians or Greeks after the First World War. The contributions of non-Muslims to the war effort and their representation constitute an important topic that this study will unfortunately not be able to discuss in detail because of space constraints. Further archival research will establish definitive figures and conclusions, but available evidence suggests that Ottoman labour battalions had some hundred thousand men enrolled in their ranks at the outbreak of war. See Beşikçi, *The Ottoman Mobilization of Manpower*, 129–39. During the preparation of the current volume, Ayhan Aktar has published the memoirs, in Turkish, of Sarkis Torossian, who had served as an Armenian captain in the Ottoman army during WWI. See Yüzbaşı Sarkis Torosyan, *Çanakkale'den Filistin Cephesine*, trans. Ayhan Aktar (Istanbul: İletişim, 2012); first published as *From Dardanelles to Palestine: A True Story of Five Battle Fronts of Turkey and Her Allies and a Harem Romance, Etc.* (Boston: Meador Pub. Co., 1947). The book sparked lively public and academic debates in regard to service of non-Muslims in the Ottoman military, a subject unknown to most Turkish citizens. For a book-length response, see Y. Hakan Erdem, *Gerçek ile Kurmaca Arasında Torosyan'ın Acayip Hikâyesi* (Istanbul: Doğan Kitap, 2012). Regardless of the debate around the historical accuracy of Torossian memoir, Aktar's comprehensive introduction to the text is significant for acknowledging and reincorporating non-Muslims in the memory and history of the Ottoman army during World War I.

10. Erik J. Zürcher, "Between Death and Desertion: The Experience of the Ottoman Soldier in The First World War," *Turcica* 28 (1996): 245–46; Erickson, *Ordered*, 243; Yiğit Akın, "The Ottoman Home Front during the First World War: Everyday Politics, Society, and Culture" (Ph.D. diss., Ohio State University, 2011), 218–36; Beşikçi, *The Ottoman Mobilization of Manpower*, 247–49.

11. Klaus Kreiser, "War Memorials and Cemeteries in Turkey," in Farschid et al., *First World War*, 183–201.

12. For an excellent overview, see Akın, "The Ottoman Home Front," 180–236.

13. M. Talha Çiçek's works are informative for understanding formation of national identities and perceptions of the "Great Arab Revolt" in early republican Turkey and newly emerged Arab countries after the war. See his "Erken Cumhuriyet Dönemi Ders Kitapları Çerçevesinde Türk Ulus Kimliği İnşası ve 'Arap İhaneti,'" *Divan* 17, no. 32 (2012): 169–88, and "Şerif Hüseyin İsyanı'nın Türk ve Arap Kimlik İnşa Süreçlerindeki Etkisinin Analizi" (M.A. thesis, Sakarya Üniversitesi, 2007).

14. Hüseyin Tutar et al., *Türk Halkının Sarıkamış Algısı* (Kars: T.C. Serhat Kalkınma Ajansı, 2011), 61–62, 72, 74, 76–79, 84–85.

15. Falih Rıfkı Atay, *Zeytindağı*, 4th ed. (Istanbul: Milli Eğitim Bakanlığı, 1997), 112. This edition of five thousand was published by the Turkish Ministry of National Education.

16. Erol Köroğlu noted that Atay chose for his book the texts that emphasized the heroism of Turkish soldiers and depicted Arabs negatively. Erol Köroğlu, *Türk Edebiyatı ve Birinci Dünya Savaşı: Propogandadan Milli Kimlik İnşasına* (Istanbul: İletişim Yayınları, 2004), 337–40.

17. Atay, *Zeytindağı*, 37–39.

18. For observations to this effect in early republican Turkish fiction on the war, see Köroğlu, "Impact," 227–29.

19. Atay, *Zeytindağı*, 68–72, 41, 53–54, 63, 83–85.

20. Türk Tarihini Tetkik Cemiyeti (TTTC, later the Turkish Historical Association), *Tarih IV: Türkiye Cumhuriyeti* (Istanbul: Maarif Vekaleti [Ministry of Education], 1934), v.

21. TTTC, *Tarih III*, 308–9. The Turkish Ministry of Education printed 32,000 and 10,000 copies, respectively, of *Tarih III* and *Tarih IV* in 1932 and 1934. Compare with Turkish General Staff (TGS), *Birinci Dünya Harbinde Türk Harbi: Osmanlı İmparatorluğu'nun Siyasi ve Askeri Hazırlıkları ve Harbe Girişi*, vol. 1 (Ankara: Genelkurmay Basımevi, 1970), 156.

22. TTTC, *Tarih IV*, 23.

23. TTTC, *Tarih III: Yeni ve Yakın Zamanlar* (Istanbul: Maarif Vekaleti, 1933), 308.

24. Bahaeddin Yediyıldız et al., *Tarih 2 Ders Geçme ve Kredi Yönetmeliğini Uygulayan Ortaöğretim Kurumları için Ders Kitabı*, 2nd ed. (Milli Eğitim Bakanlığı, 1994), 73–74. The textbook had a print run of 200,000 copies. For an analysis of the theme of "Arab treachery" in early republican textbooks, also see Çiçek, "Erken," 179–85. Similarly inaccurate generalizations that minimized Arabs' involvement in the war and exaggerated the Arab Revolt's effects appear even in the most recently published Turkish history textbooks. See, for instance, Vicdan Cazgır et al., *Ortaöğretim Tarih 10*, 4th ed. (Milli Eğitim Bakanlığı, 2012), 196, 216. On the nationalist-militarist discourse and its continuity in textbooks from the 1930s onward, see Tuba Kancı and Ayşe Gül Altınay, "Educating Little Soldiers and Little Ayşes: Militarised and Gendered Citizenship in Turkish Textbooks," in *Education in "Multicultural" Societies: Turkish and Swedish Perspectives*, ed. M. Carlson et al. (London: I.B. Tauris, 2007), 51–70.

25. Yediyıldız et al., *Tarih 2*, 73.

26. After the coup d'état of 1980, the military regime brought Turkish universities under strict state control via persecutions and expulsions. Soon the state made HAPR courses mandatory for all undergraduates. The Turkish Ministry of Education published 150,000 copies of this HAPR book. Hamza Eroğlu, *Türk İnkılap Tarihi* (Istanbul: Milli Eğitim Basımevi, 1982). The fourth edition was available from another publisher as late as 2010.

27. Eroğlu, *Türk*, 80.

28. Compare Fahir H. Armaoğlu, *Siyasi Tarih Dersleri 1789–1919* (Ankara: Ankara Üniversitesi Siyasal Bilgiler Fakültesi Yayınları, 1961), 548, and Atay, *Zeytindağı*, 59, 64.

29. Fahir Armaoğlu, *20.yy Siyasi Tarihi*, 11th ed. (Istanbul: Alkım Yayınevi, n.d. [1990s]), 111. Compare it to the 1934 textbook: "Indian, Algerian, and Tunisian Muslim soldiers attacked the [Ottoman] caliph's dominions and assaulted his armies without any religious [concerns]." TTTC, *Tarih IV*, 309. For a repetition of the same argument, see the more recent and immensely popular Turgut Özakman, *Diriliş: Çanakkale 1915* (Istanbul: Bilgi Yayınevi, 2008), 74–75, 83.

30. See Semih Yalçın et al., *Türk İnkılap Tarihi ve Atatürk İlkeleri*, 3rd ed. (Ankara: Siyasal Kitabevi, 2004), 82–95. On the origins of Arab nationalism and the story of the Arab Revolt from the Turkish nationalist perspective, see Yusuf Hikmet Bayur, *Türk İnkılabı Tarihi*, vol. 2, part 3 (Ankara: Türk Tarih Kurumu, 1951), 191–231. The book was published by the THA as part of a multivolume history that can be considered the "official" account of the Turkish Republic's emergence.

31. Turkish General Staff (TGS), *Birinci Dünya Harbi'nde Türk Harbi*, 10 vols. (Ankara: Genelkurmay Basımevi, 1967–96).

32. TGS, *Birinci*, vol. 1, p. 129.

33. Ibid., 156.

34. For the quote and other references to the "warrior essence" of the Turks, see TGS, *Birinci*, vol. 1, p. 183; also see the history textbook by Enver Ziya Karal, *Türkiye Cumhuriyeti Tarihi* [History of the Turkish Republic] *(1918–1965)* (Istanbul: Milli Eğitim Basımevi, 1973), 208–9. Karal also authored the standard account of the later history of the Ottoman Empire, first published by the Turkish Historical Association in the 1940s.

35. The original description in Turkish is wordier and generally more grandiose. TGS, *Türk Silahlı Kuvvetleri Tarihi, Osmanlı Devri, Birinci Dünya Harbi İdari Faaliyetler ve Lojistik*, vol. 10 (Ankara: Genel Kurmay Basımevi, 1985), 20.

36. By contrast, the authors did not mind making a brief reference to the Kurds when discussing the demography of Mesopotamia under Ottoman rule, probably because Mesopotamia is not a part of modern Turkey in which TGS authors supposed no Kurd existed. TGS, *Türk*, vol. 10, pp. 25, 29, 33.

37. Şevket Süreyya Aydemir, *Makedonya'dan Ortaasya'ya Enver Paşa: 1914–1922*, vol. 3 (Istanbul: Remzi Kitabevi, 1985), 29. Compare the phrase "War of the Turkish Army" to the title of the TGS's multivolume history of the First World War cited above.

38. Aydemir, *Enver*, vol. 3, pp. 29, 175–76.

39. Beşikci, *The Ottoman Mobilization of Manpower*, 108, n. 61.

40. Özakman, *Diriliş*, 26, 67

41. TGS, *Türk*, vol. 10, p. 617; Edward J. Erickson, *Ottoman Army Effectiveness in The First World War* (London: Routledge, 2007), 22, 24.

42. Özakman, *Diriliş*, 282–83, 296–97.
43. It is unclear whether Özakman solely referred to the Turks, or to the Arabs and Turks together.
44. Özakman, *Diriliş*, 297. See also Özakman, *Diriliş*, 132, 336, 547–48.
45. Celal Bayar, a prominent statesman of the early Republic and the third president of Turkey, once stated, "[The early Republican leaders] were not disposed to re-establish a close relationship with a nation [the Arabs], which had stabbed the Turkish nation in the back." Yücel Bozdağlıoğlu, *Turkish Foreign Policy and Turkish Identity: A Constructivist Approach* (New York: Routledge, 2003), 114. Similar utterances can be heard in common Turkish parlance referring to the Arab Revolt of 1916, to Arabs' alleged treachery during *Seferberlik*, and to their essential backwardness as a people.
46. TGS, *Birinci Dünya Harbi'nde Türk Harbi, Sina-Filistin Cephesi*, vol. 4, part 1 (Ankara: Genelkurmay Basımevi, 1979), 83, in Beşikçi, *The Ottoman Mobilization of Manpower*, 253, n. 22. However, this dismissive depiction of Arab participation was contradicted by the data provided by another TGS study, Hüseyin Hüsnü Emir [Erkilet], *Yıldırım* (Ankara: Genelkurmay Basım Evi, 2002), reprint of the May 1921 edition, 346, in Erickson, *Ottoman*, 101.
47. Erickson, *Ordered*, xv–xvi, 16. Erickson appears to have adjusted his position and tone in his later work, *The Ottoman Army's Effectiveness in the First World War*.
48. Ordinary Turks, Kurds, and Arabs dubbed the war experience *Seferberlik*, or "the Mobilization."
49. See, for instance, Salim Tamari, *The Year of the Locust: A Soldier's Diary and the Erasure of Palestine's Ottoman Past* (Berkeley: University of California Press, 2011), 133, 137–38, 155.
50. Erickson, *Ottoman*, 120; Eliezer Tauber, *The Arab Movements in The First World War* (London: Frank Cass, 1993), 111. Regardless of their ethnic background, all Ottoman conscripts could face beatings, insufficient rations, and harsh living conditions. Yet during their interrogations, several Muslim Arab and non-Muslim prisoners claimed incessant subjection to various forms of discrimination and ill-treatment by the Turkish officers and soldiers. For a brief assessment based on Turkish archives and interrogations of the Ottoman POWs by the British, see Beşikçi, *The Ottoman Mobilization of Manpower*, 257–68. Last, if they were fighting, marching, or stationed near their homelands, the Ottoman troops might have been more likely to desert their units.
51. On the changing historiography on the emergence of Arab nationalism and the Arab Revolt, see the essays in Rashid Khalidi, Lisa Anderson, Muhammad Muslih, and Reeva S. Simon, eds., *The Origins of Arab Nationalism* (New York: Columbia University Press, 1991); and Ernest C. Dawn, "From Ottomanism to Arabism: The Origins of an Ideology," in *From Ottomanism to Arabism: Essays on*

the Origins of Arab Nationalism (Urbana: University of Illinois Press, 1973). For a thorough critique of popular perceptions of Hashemite intentions and the nature of the Arab Revolt, see Efraim Karsh and Inari Karsh, "Myth in the Desert, or Not the Great Arab Revolt," *Middle Eastern Studies* 33, no. 2 (1997): 267–312.

52. David Fromkin, *A Peace to End All Peace* (New York: Henry Holt, 2001), 219.
53. Tauber, *The Arab Movements*, 104–8, 117–21.
54. Karsh, "Myth," 282–83, 293, 299–300, 305–6.
55. Dawn, "The Amir," 27–31; Tauber, *The Arab Movements*, 65–66.
56. İsmet Üzen, "Birinci Dünya Savaşında Kanal Seferleri (1915-1916)" (Ph.D. diss., İstanbul Üniversitesi, 2007), 279–83; Tauber, *The Arab Movements*, 66.
57. Karsh, "Myth," 282–83, 289–93; Dawn, "From Ottomanism," 155–57; Üzen, "Birinci," 283; Erickson, 100–101.
58. Helmuth von Moltke, *Türkiye Mektupları*, trans. Hayrullah Örs (Istanbul: Remzi Kitabevi, 1969), 256, 261, 271, 276; Tobias Heinzelmann, *Cihaddan Vatan Savunmasına, Osmanlı İmparatorluğu'nda Genel Askerlik Yükümlülüğü 1826–1856*, trans. Türkis Noyan (Istanbul: Kitap Yayınevi, 2008), 171–205; Tobias Heinzelmann, "Changing Recruiting Strategies in the Ottoman Army, 1839–1856," in *The Crimean War, 1853–1856*, ed. Jerzy W. Borejsza (Warsaw: Wydawnictwo Neriton, 2011), 23, 37–38.
59. Şükrü Hanioğlu, *A Brief History of the Late Ottoman Empire* (Princeton: Princeton University Press, 2008), 87–88, 164–67.
60. Tamari, *The Year*, 12–13.
61. Fromkin, *A Peace*, 219.
62. Tauber, *The Arab Movements*, 59. Tauber's designations for Arab and partly Arab divisions must be read with caution and cross-checked with other sources, as some divisions were recruited from populations that were not entirely Arab.
63. Üzen, "Birinci," 152–53, 157–59, 226–27; Erickson, *Ordered*, 70–71. Compare with Atay's account of a purely "Turkish" attack on the Suez Canal, where Arab soldiers were missing from the narrative. Atay, *Zeytindağı*, 128–31.
64. Erickson, *Ottoman*, 109, 135. For a recent study that repeated this view, see Sean McMeekin, *The Berlin Baghdad Express: The Ottoman Empire and Germany's Bid for World Power* (Cambridge: Harvard University Press, 2010), 189. Also see Özakman, 282–83, 296–97.
65. Erickson, *Ottoman*, 22, 24, 36. Moreover, Mesut Uyar opened the "Arabness" of the 77th Regiment to question, since Aleppo Province, the unit's recruitment district, had a considerable Turkish-speaking population. Mesut Uyar, "Ottoman Arab Officers between Nationalism and Loyalty during the First World War," *War in History* 20, no. 4 (2013): 538–39.
66. TGS, *Türk*, vol. 10, p. 657; Uyar, "Brothers in Arms: Turkish Officers in the Çanakkale (Dardanelles) Campaign," paper presented at "Gallipoli

in Retrospect: Ninety Years On," Onsekiz Mart University International Conference, Çanakkale," 21–23 April 2005, p. 22.

67. The TGS quoted von Kressenstein's essentialist statements about the traits of races at length. See TGS, *Birinci*, vol. 1, pp. 183–84.

68. Erickson, *Ottoman*, 108–12.

69. The 24th Division with 3,200 effectives could not report and was not included in the calculation. Erickson, *Ottoman*, 100–101.

70. Erickson, *Ottoman*, 120–21.

71. For overviews of these policies and the Kurdish responses, see Mesut Yeğen, ed., "'Müstakbel Türk'ten 'Sözde Vatandaşa': Cumhuriyet ve Kürtler," in *Müstakbel Türk'ten Sözde Vatandaşa* (Istanbul: İletişim Yayınları, 2006), 47–88; and Üngör, *Making*, 170–217.

72. For a critique of the ethnicist and exclusivist aspects of the term "Turk/ Turkish," see Mesut Yeğen, "Yahudi-Kürtler ya da Türklüğün Yeni Hudutları," in *Müstakbel*, 99–114.

73. "Recep Tayyip Erdoğan's speech in Diyarbakır, 1 June 2011," AKP website, http://www.akparti.org.tr/site/haberler/1-haziran-diyarbakir-mitingi-konusmasinin-tam-metni/8230 (accessed 6 March 2015). Note the similarities between Erdoğan's and Özakman's emphases on the superordinate "Anatolian" identity in their discourses, even though the men hailed from different ends of the political spectrum. Many Turkish and Kurdish intellectuals and politicians consider recent attempts at recognition and reconciliation superficial, as the AKP's statements and promises have not translated into any concrete legal or institutional framework. For an assessment of the Kurdish Question in Turkey and the deficiencies in the AKP's current policies, see Johanna Nykänen, "Identity, Narrative and Frames: Assessing Turkey's Kurdish Initiatives," *Insight Turkey* 15, no. 2 (2013): 85–101.

74. The essay was also appended in Gökçe Fırat, *İstila: Kürt Sorununda Gizlenen Gerçekler ve Kürt İstilası* [Invasion: The Concealed Truths about the Kurdish Question and the Kurdish Invasion] (Istanbul: İleri Yayınları, 2007).

75. It appears that Gökçe Fırat used the casualty lists published by the Ministry of National Defence (T.C. Milli Savunma Bakanlığı, *Şehitlerimiz* [Our Martyrs], 5 vols. (Ankara: Kozan Ofset Matbaa, 1998). These lists were extracted from the ministry's own vast archive, situated in Lodumlu, Ankara.

76. Gökçe Fırat, "Kürtler Çanakkale'de var mıydı?", *Türk Solu*, 15 June 2009. A number of articles published in *Türk Solu* are clearly racist in tone and argument. Among the contributors to the newspaper have been high-ranking retired Turkish civil servants, scholars, and artists.

77. Balçiçek Pamir, "Osman Pamukoğlu İkiyüzlü Değil," *Haberturk*, http://www.haberturk.com/polemik/haber/174421-osman-pamukogluikiyuzlu-degil (accessed 6 March 2015).

78. For his biography, see HEPAR's official website, http://hepar.org.tr/osman
    -pamukoglu (accessed 6 March 2015).
79. During the 2011 elections, HEPAR won some 123,000 votes, significantly less
    than one percent of the total electorate.
80. According to the Serhat Development Agency's poll cited above, 16 and
    19.9 percent, respectively, of the interviewees "strongly" or "very strongly" dis-
    agreed with the idea that soldiers from the "whole Muslim geography" fought
    together at Gallipoli and Sarıkamış. Hüseyin Tutar et al., *Türk*, 93, 122.
81. *Şehitlerimiz* identified approximately 130,000 battle deaths between 1877 and
    1974 in the armies of the Ottoman Empire and the Republic of Turkey, which is
    apparently a low estimate. Several theses from Turkish universities cataloguing
    the death toll in select Ottoman provinces support this point. See, for instance,
    Gülseren Çınar, "Balkan Savaşları'ndan Milli Mücadeleye Şehit Olan Konyalılar
    Üzerine Bir Sosyal Tarih Araştırması" (M.A. thesis, Selçuk Üniversitesi, 2009).
82. Ahmed Emin Yalman, *Turkey in the World War* (New Haven: Yale University
    Press, 1930), 79; Erickson, *Ordered*, 16.
83. Gökçe Fırat estimated the total battle deaths at Gallipoli at about 48,000, which
    he distributed among the provinces of modern Turkey. In an earlier TGS pub-
    lication, however, the total number of Ottoman battle deaths at Gallipoli was
    given as 56,495. TGS, *Türk*, vol. 10, p. 657. The difference of 8,500 was probably
    undocumented, or indicated deaths of soldiers from outside modern Turkey,
    some of whom were possibly not ethnic Turks.
84. Kamal Madhar Ahmed, *Kurdistan During the First World War*, trans. Ali
    Maher Ibrahim (London: Saqi Books, 1994), 90–92, 98, 103–5. Ahmed noted
    high casualties and large-scale desertions among the Kurdish troops, espe-
    cially in irregular cavalry formations.
85. Dündar, *Modern*, 459–60.
86. Ahmed, *Kurdistan*, 90–92. From December 1914 to March 1915, the number
    of XI Corps' riflemen fell from 22,254 to 4,206 due to fighting and attrition.
    Erickson, *Ordered*, 57, 64.
87. For the battle records of the two divisions, see Erickson, *Ordered*, 68, 104, 106–
    7, 111–15, 121, 125, 135, 149–50, 152.
88. Wadie Jwaideh, *Kurdish National Movement: Its Origins and Development*
    (Syracuse: Syracuse University Press, 2006), 125. Jwaideh appears to have
    made a mistake by using the term "army" instead of "corps," however. Four
    reserve cavalry divisions attached to the IX and XI Corps were created and
    stationed in areas where Kurds predominated, such as Hınıs, Karaköse, Erciş,
    and Viranşehir. TGS, *Türk*, vol. 10, pp. 93, 600; Dündar, *Modern*, 459–60. Yet
    Zeki's assertion that most officers and soldiers in the IX and X Corps were
    Kurds is debatable. There were Kurds living in those corps' recruitment dis-
    tricts (areas around Erzurum, Erzincan, and Sivas), but they were probably

not the dominant ethnic group. In addition, most Ottoman war memoirs agree that irregular Kurdish cavalry lacked discipline during military operations.

89. Jwaideh, *Kurdish National Movement*, 125–28; Üngör, *Making*, 106–22; Dündar, *Modern*, 399–422.

90. For a succinct account of Ottoman/Turkish transformation in the nineteenth and twentieth centuries, see Engin Deniz Akarlı, "The Tangled Ends of an Empire: Ottoman Encounters with the West and Problems of Westernization— an Overview," *Comparative Studies of South Asia, Africa, and the Middle East* 26, no. 3 (2006): 353–66.

91. Tamari, *The Year*, 5; Çiçek, "Erken," 179–87; Üngör, *The Making*, 218–32.

92. Akarlı, "Tangled," 365–66.

93. For further details, see Bozdanlıoğlu, *Turkish*, 111–40.

94. Üngör, *The Making*, 106–217; Dündar, *Modern*, 399–422.

95. Mesut Yeğen, "The Kurdish Question in Turkish State Discourse," *Journal of Contemporary History* 34, no. 4 (1999): 555.

96. In 2010, 76.7 percent of the interviewees defined themselves as Turks and 14.7 percent defined themselves as Zaza and Kurdish. The same study concluded that a much lower percentage (22 to 24 percent) of Kurds did not want Turkish neighbours, business partners, or in-laws. Konda, *Biz Kimiz [20]10: Kürt Meselesinde Algı ve Beklentiler Araştırması Bulgular Raporu Mayıs 2011* (Konda Araştırma ve Danışmanlık, 2011), 13–46.

MEN OF SUVLA
Empire, Masculinities, and Gallipoli's Legacy in Ireland and Newfoundland

JANE McGAUGHEY

There is a smell that lingers over the gullies, cliffs, and sandy beaches on the Turkish peninsula just west of Çanakkale.* Despite the abundance of poppies in the tall fields, the overwhelming aroma at Gallipoli, fittingly, is that of rosemary, the herb of remembrance. With this familiar perfume in the air, Gallipoli stands as a battlefield of the Great War particularly connected to commemoration, memorials, and memories. If gravesites are monuments that denote the personal sacrifice of individuals, then cenotaphs and war memorials are collective symbols speaking for communities as a whole.[1] At the tip of the peninsula, the Helles Memorial stands as an enormous marker to the unknown dead, recounting ships of the line, regiments, divisions, and the individual names of the fallen. At Chanuk Bair, the view down to Anzac Cove and the Aegean can mist over in a matter of minutes. There, a huge statue of Mustafa Kemal Atatürk, the future president of Turkey who became a hero at Gallipoli, stands bare metres away from the New Zealand obelisk, denoting the location's importance to both nations. Veysel Şimşek has argued in this volume that the Turkish state has played a crucial role in

* The author thanks the Deputy Keeper of the Records for permission to publish material from the Public Record Office of Northern Ireland, and Captain R.H. Lowry for permission to publish from the Montgomery Papers. Extracts from the papers of John McIlwain are published with the permission of Mrs. Hazel McIlwain. Every effort has been made to trace the copyright holders of materials at the Imperial War Museum, and both the author and the museum would be grateful for any information that might help to trace those whose identities or addresses are not currently known.

forming its nation's modes of remembrance, allowing memories from the war to transfer from one generation to the other. And yet, this is not a universal pattern. When one looks up the beaches to Suvla Bay, two curiosities stand out, notable for their omission rather than their presence: the Irish plinth and the Newfoundland caribou.

Ceremonies at Green Hill Cemetery in 2010, marking the ninety-fifth anniversary of the battle, brought together various dignitaries from around the world. The President of Ireland, Mary McAleese, dedicated a memorial plinth to the 10th (Irish) Division, while HRH The Duke of Gloucester, president of the Somme Association, planted four myrtle trees—symbols of love and immortality—to honour Ireland's four ancient provinces from which men had enlisted to fight in that nation's first volunteer division in the Great War. It has only been within the past two decades that the Republic of Ireland has begun openly to incorporate memories of the Great War within its national consciousness, reflecting the selective amnesia that pervaded the country for eighty years regarding Irishmen fighting in British uniform; no doubt, the success of both the 1998 Good Friday Peace Agreement and the visit of Queen Elizabeth II to the republic in May 2011 were catalysts for change in the island's historical narrative. The trees, still only saplings, are just to the right of the cemetery wall; the memorial unveiled by President McAleese, however, is missing. While it was on site for the dedication ceremony, the plinth has since become figuratively trapped in the bureaucratic processes of war commemoration. The Irish government holds that the monument will return in time, following final approval from the official bodies responsible for the conservation and management of the battlefield.[2] Nevertheless, given the lengthy wait for any official recognition of the 10th (Irish) Division at home or abroad, the plinth's absence is both ironic and unfortunate.

This is not the only "missing monument" at Gallipoli, however. In the decade following the Armistice, Newfoundland's *Veteran Magazine*, the mouthpiece of the Great War Veterans' Association of Newfoundland, chronicled the splendid upkeep at Gallipoli of "the thirty-two most beautiful cemeteries in the world."[3] It was presumed that, in due course, the dominion would erect a monument and those visiting the peninsula would "learn the stories of the heroes and how it was the young Newfoundlander came to lie in a grave in the Farland."[4] Suvla Bay is the only theatre of the Great War for Newfoundlanders not to be marked by the "Trail of the Caribou." Statues of a rampant caribou, the symbol of the Royal Newfoundland Regiment,[5] can be found at all of Newfoundland's key battle sites in France and Belgium, most notably at Beaumont Hamel, the scene of the regiment's virtual destruction on the opening day of the Somme, 1 July 1916. However, Newfoundland's first significant victory of the war, the appropriately named Caribou Hill at Suvla,[6] has no symbolic representation linking that battlefield to the others along the Western Front, or to the province's memorial park in St John's. Despite the desires of Lieutenant-Colonel Padre Tom Nangle, the officer-priest put in charge of Newfoundland commemorations abroad after the Armistice, and fundraising efforts within the community of ex-servicemen, Gallipoli's inclusion in the Trail of the Caribou was never realized.[7]

The 10th (Irish) Division and the Newfoundland Regiment share the distinction of being imperial troops from the North Atlantic world with complicated memories of the Dardanelles campaign and equally complex histories of remembrance.[8] When writing about the different nationalities that fought at Gallipoli, Jenny Macleod has noted that there is "nothing inevitable about the way in which an event is remembered in any given country, or indeed whether it is remembered at all."[9] Kimberly Lamay's chapter in this volume notes the relative lack of remembrance given to the last American doughboy, Frank Buckles, in comparison to other western nations as the final veterans of the Great War died. The importance given to a battle in a nation's history and mythology comes from making a choice to give it significance and cultural weight. Gallipoli matters more in some countries than others—Australia and New Zealand come to mind immediately—however, that was not because of historical determinism, but through the choices made by individuals and collective communities in how they applied historical memory. The following argument centres on the shared connections between warfare, masculinities, and imperialism witnessed and experienced by soldiers from Ireland and Newfoundland in the final six months of the Gallipoli campaign. In a way, the "missing monuments" stand as ironic codas to the regions' relationships with the British Empire and the notion of imperial warfare.

Like other countries that fought in the Great War, Ireland and Newfoundland formed part of a colony-to-nation motif, although they experienced different relations with Britain. Tensions existed from time to time with the Imperial government in Newfoundland, but Newfoundlanders continually saw the empire and their place within it in a positive light; Ireland's experiences with colonialism and imperialism were much more complicated and contested, to say the least.[10] The two countries form an interesting site for comparison, given the strong presence of the Irish Diaspora in Newfoundland culture;[11] this phenomenon of dispersal and settlement was not confined to political and social aspects of life, but also had cultural and militaristic elements that connected people across time and space. The Irish Military Diaspora was a paradigm that had existed, in one form or another, for over three hundred years prior to the outbreak of the Great War. Simply put, the Irish Military Diaspora was the historic mobilization of Irishmen fighting in "foreign" wars (i.e., not on the island of Ireland) who went into battle either to change Ireland's future or as a broader reflection of Irish-related ideals and identities as descendants of the diaspora. It comprised varying interpretations of manly heroism, loyalty, Irishness, and the control of national futures through force of arms. The military aspect of the diaspora was a tradition visible in the Thirty Years War, the War of the Spanish Succession, the American Revolution, the Napoleonic Wars, the American Civil War, the Canadian Red River Rebellion, and the Second South African War at the turn of the century. Soldiers could be either of Irish birth or extraction, but no matter where they went to war, they were reflections of an Irish connection; quite often, this presence abroad also ran in concert with the larger aims of the British Empire in terms of both military action and colonial administration.[12] Military units from Ireland and Newfoundland were part of the Great War's incarnation of the Irish Military Diaspora, alongside those from Britain, Canada, India, Australia, New Zealand, and South Africa. The service of Ireland and Newfoundland at Gallipoli and, later, at the Somme, continued to highlight connections between these two lands that dated back for centuries.

The Irish Diaspora has had a strong presence in the former Dominion of Newfoundland and Labrador since the late 1500s, mainly due to the famous fishing trade of the north Atlantic. Tim Pat Coogan once wrote that "[o]utside Ireland itself, there is probably no more Irish place in the world than Newfoundland."[13] Newfoundland journals such as the *Newfoundland Quarterly* regularly reported on Irish affairs; an article by the Reverend John L. Slattery in December 1915 proudly noted Ireland's strong record in the war thus far and that many in Newfoundland had a "special interest" in Ireland's achievements in battle.[14] Although Newfoundland did not share in the large numbers of Irish Protestant immigrants who dispersed to the rest of British North America, it did become a hotbed of Orangeism, which, of course, came into conflict with Roman Catholicism. By 1920 one-third of all the adult Protestant males in Newfoundland were part of the Orange Order, including those of English and Scottish heritage, as well as those of Irish descent; the comparative figure for Northern Ireland at the same time was one-fifth, making Newfoundland the country with the greatest number of Orangemen per capita in the world.[15]

The one area, however, where there was major cleavage between Irish and Newfoundland society during the Great War was in Newfoundland's willingness, even eagerness, to proclaim itself a British colony and dominion, and to fight for recognition within the imperial family of nations. "We feel a keen interest in everything British," wrote Annie M. Warne in *Among the Deep Sea Fishers*, a popular wartime journal. "Our loyalty has been fired anew," she continued, "by the need to defend what we, as a British nation, possess. The far-flung border line of our Empire has not always received the attention and the consideration to which it was entitled."[16]

At the same time as this pro-imperialist sentiment on one side of the pond, Ireland had been arming itself for a civil war between unionists and nationalists over the proposed Third Home Rule Bill, which granted Ireland a separate parliament in Dublin. Tens of thousands of guns and millions of rounds of ammunition had been smuggled into the north by militant unionists,[17] while nationalists and republicans welcomed the reintroduction of the gun into Irish politics. After the Larne gun-running episode had armed the Protestants of the north in 1914, Pádraic Pearse, the future leader of the Easter Rising, wrote that he was "glad that the Orangemen are armed, for it is a goodly thing to see arms in Irish hands.... We must accustom ourselves to the thought of arms, to the sight of arms, to the use of arms. We may make mistakes in the beginning and shoot the wrong people; but bloodshed is a cleansing and a sanctifying thing."[18]

That said, prior to the Easter Rising in 1916, many Irish politicians were keen to use the war effort as a means of uniting a people on the brink of internecine conflict. This was a period when unity between Irish Protestants and Catholics was politicized and publicly promoted, both in Ireland and abroad. Numerous times, the record of Irish enlistment and that of the wider Irish Diaspora was referenced in public speeches in order to provide a sense of cohesion and depth to the image of Irishmen in uniform. Lieutenant Willie Redmond, MP, of the 16th (Irish) Division went to great lengths in a speech at Bray, County Wicklow, to demonstrate that Ireland was doing just as much for the imperial war effort as any other part of the empire. Canada, Australia, "and every other portion of the British Empire had done magnificently in rallying to the standard of freedom and of liberty," Redmond contended, and he was proud that, "thousands upon thousands amongst the Canadians, Australians, New Zealanders, and South Africans were Irishmen either by birth or extraction."[19] These claims were dismissed in

Belfast's overtly unionist *Northern Whig* as misplaced Catholic-nationalist propaganda, countering that "these patriotic Colonials of Irish birth or parentage are almost to a man Protestants and Unionists." The *Whig*'s article continued that Sam Hughes—one of Canada's most infamous Orangemen in uniform—was responsible for clearing out the Canadian Orange Lodges, and that, of all the men Redmond claimed were fighting for Ireland, "a great majority are staunchly opposed to Home Rule."[20]

Politics aside, it is clear that Gallipoli, of all the battlefields in the Great War, is the most representative of the Irish Diaspora at work. Thousands of the men who fought there for the British Empire were, as Redmond proposed, of either Irish birth or heritage. Captain David Fallon, MC, author of *The Big Fight (Gallipoli to the Somme)*, fought with the ANZACs, but was a County Mayo man who had joined the British Army in 1904 and saw service in China and India before eventually arriving in Australia.[21] Tombstones in the cemeteries on the peninsula also point to the dispersal of Irishmen around the world, with men born in Derry fighting with the Australians, and members of the Inniskilling Fusiliers coming from South Africa.[22]

Unlike some of the irreverence toward British authority that heralded the presence of the ANZACs, the experiences of the Newfoundland Regiment at Gallipoli were "cloaked in heroic rhetoric that espoused the paramountcy of the colony's imperial ties and the majesty of the Empire."[23] This can be seen in the profile of Private Michael P. Murphy, of Harbour Grace, in the *Commercial Annual* in 1918. The brief biography recorded that three Murphy brothers, all Catholics, had served in the Newfoundland Regiment, one of them dying at Lemnos. Their great-grandfather had emigrated from Ireland in the mid-nineteenth century; he had been of the "fighting stock from the County of Cork in Old Ireland, and it is no wonder that the three 'boys' rallied to the Standard when fighting was to be done in the cause of King, Country, Freedom and the Empire."[24] There was no separation here between an Irish Catholic background and a loyal imperial identity.

While this profile of Private Murphy came at the war's end, after the Easter Rising had occurred and forever altered the course of Irish history, Newfoundland papers before 1916 had noted Ireland's place within the sisterhood of empire. At the outbreak of war, the *Harbour Grace Standard and Conception Bay Advertiser* proposed that Ireland had shown its imperial loyalty "gloriously" and that Newfoundland would soon follow suit.[25] Over a year later, it paraphrased Irish Parliamentary Party leader John

Redmond in noting that Ireland, "for the first time in history is eager to do her full duty to the Empire, which no longer stands for oppression, but for independence of Belgium, Serbia and the small nations of Europe, and for the freedom of the world."[26] Gallipoli proved to be the site where the first major contingent of Irish volunteers—the 10th (Irish) Division—made those sentiments a reality.

Despite having enjoyed the lion's share—such as it has been—of academic interest in the Irish at Gallipoli, the 10th (Irish) Division were not the first Irishmen to take part in the Dardanelles campaign. More men of Irish heritage across the diaspora fought together here than in any other theatre of the war, coming from Ireland, Britain, Australia, New Zealand, South Africa, Newfoundland, Canada, and India;[27] more control was given to Irish officers than anywhere on the Western Front, including General Sir Alexander Godley, who was in charge of the New Zealand Division, and Lieutenant-General Sir Bryan Mahon of the 10th (Irish) Division. On 25 April 1915, Irishmen as part of the 29th Division and the ANZACs attacked the Gallipoli Peninsula. The Munster, Dublin, and Inniskilling Fusiliers landed at X and V Beaches. With the age-old reputation for Irish bellicosity still in its heyday, these men were put in the front lines. The Irish Military Diaspora—to its equal fame and detriment—has always been fuelled by the global belief in the warlike attitude and "natural aggression" of the Irish.[28]

In reviewing Irish participation in the attack, however, national identity was not presented by officers and propagandists as a monolithic structure, but a combination of various influences and categories, so that the men could be both imperial and Irish figures. Major-General Weston congratulated the Dublin Fusiliers on an action "done by men of real and true British fighting blood.... Well done, the Dubs!"[29] For Weston, the highest praise he could bestow was to transform the Irishmen into genuine British soldiers. The same event received a different spin from S. Parnell Kerr, author of *What the Irish Regiments Have Done* (1916). Kerr argued that, if any detractors of Irishmen in khaki spoke "slightingly of the services Irish soldiers have rendered to the Empire in this great crisis of her fate, let the sacrifice of the Dublins and Munsters on V Beach on this spring morning of 1915 be their answer, and shame them forever into silence."[30]

One of the reasons we can look back to Gallipoli as a triumph of Irishness under fire is because, unlike the Somme, it has not been claimed solely by Orange or Green factions. Ironically, because of this lack of politicization, Gallipoli has not only been one of the most Irish of the war's campaigns, but one of the most forgotten. Gallipoli was the first major engagement for Irish

troops in the war, as volunteer divisions intended for the Western Front—
the 36th (Ulster) and 16th (Irish) Divisions, respectively—were mired in
sectarian wrangling about the appropriate names, insignia, and composition of their soldiers.[31] Instead, Gallipoli was given to the men of the 10th
(Irish) Division, a mix of Irish Catholics and Protestants from the north
and the south who became the first Irishmen of Kitchener's New Army
to reach the front lines. As with other comments about Irish participation in the war, however, there were sectarian disagreements as to the true
make-up of the division. Major-General Hugh de Fellenberg Montgomery
surmised that the 10th was the division "which the Nationalists always talk
about as if it consisted exclusively of R. C. Home Rulers, who were sent
to Shuvla [sic] Bay and other dangerous places while the Ulster Division
was kept in safety."[32] In fact, Montgomery's numbers, obtained from a
chaplain in the division, showed that Protestants in the 10th (Irish) out-
numbered Catholics by nearly one-third.[33] Regardless of religious factors,
being in the 10th (Irish) gave these soldiers earlier opportunities to make
a difference in the war than soldiers bound for the Western Front—either
in securing Home Rule for Ireland, or by cementing the British connection—and also chances to explore new places and have new adventures.
In the weeks leading up to Suvla Bay, the 10th Division was "somewhere
in the South of England, trained to the highest point, like a lean and eager
greyhound, awaiting the order for the front."[34] According to a report from
a "general officer" in the *Irish Independent*, he had "as yet seen nothing better than those that have come from Ireland."[35] In his 1918 history of the
division, *The Tenth (Irish) Division at Gallipoli*, Bryan Cooper pined that
Ireland was "a land of long and bitter memories, and those memories make
it extremely difficult for Irishmen to unite for any common purpose. Many
have believed it impossible, and would have prophesied that the attempt
to create an Irish Division composed of men of every class, creed and political opinion would be foredoomed to failure. And yet it succeeded."[36]
Despite the romantic tones within Cooper's history, this nostalgia for a lost
moment of camaraderie and pan-Irish brotherhood was a defining feature
in Irishmen's memoirs of their time at Gallipoli.

Newspaper reports of the 10th (Irish) Division's efforts at Suvla were
decidedly positive; in addition to wartime censorship, the reality of the true
cost of the Great War still had not been fully realized by much of the reading public on either side of the Atlantic ocean. The *Irish Times* of Dublin
wrote at the end of August that the Dublin Fusiliers had been involved in
"gallant deeds" at the front. "All through the war it has been the same," the

article read, "no odds have been too great for them and no task too difficult. They have won right through, and their spirit and their morale are as
good today as they were twelve months ago."[37] The *Irish Independent* put
off rumours of disaster, proposing that it "would be better for the public to
suspend judgment until the facts are fully ascertained. The casualty lists,
at any rate, show that the Irish troops fought bravely and suffered heavily."[38] Instead, the Irish press focused on the romantic rhetoric that, prior to
the Somme's catastrophes, still featured quite heavily in newspaper reports
from the front. "The gallantry and dash of the troops in the fighting was
beyond all praise,"[39] the *Independent* contended, and that the Irishmen
at Scimitar Hill were involved in "a stirring bayonet attack."[40] Reports in
Newfoundland months later similarly focused on the "splendid spirit" that
existed "between Catholic and Protestant Irishmen fighting side by side for
one great cause."[41] However, in quoting from a letter of one of the 10th's officers, the picture presented in the *Harbour Grace Standard and Conception
Bay Advertiser* seemed a bit more realistic by the year's end: "Suffice it to say
that the Tenth Irish Division paid a very heavy toll, and I am sure poor old
Dublin has been weeping of late. There is no back or front about this show.
We are all in it. No football behind the firing line, the same as one hears of
from France. I have my hair fairly well standing on end all day from shell
fire and all night from rifle fire."[42]

It was in the personal notations and memoirs of the soldiers themselves
that the true picture of Suvla Bay became clear. The analysis of Irish participation at Suvla was decidedly mixed: one Australian officer proposed
that the "Empire can do with a heap more of 'freshies' of the Irish brand,"[43]
and General Sir Alexander Godley, then leading the Kiwis at Chanuk Bair,
felt great pride as a fellow Irishman in the achievements of the Connaught
Rangers, remarking that, "as an Irishman who has served in two Irish
Regiments, it gives me the greatest pride and pleasure that the Regiment
should have provided such gallant deeds."[44] There were also decidedly
less flattering portrayals that implied inexperience and flawed leadership.
Corporal Albert Kingston of the 53rd Division Signals noted that the dead
of the 10th Division were all around him after the first landing. "Talk of
green troops, of course," he wrote in his memoir.[45] Similar sentiments were
noted by H.F. Kemball, who felt assaulted by the "nauseating smells of
dead and decomposing bodies of Australians, New Zealanders, Connaught
Rangers etc."[46] Captain Guy Nightingale was quite bleak in his outlook,
writing to his mother that there was "no doubt about it, we've played all our
cards on this new landing and failed. The opportunity has been lost and if

there had been any troops other than only those who took part in it, I think they would have done it … you can see from our last attempt to advance, how hopeless it is."[47] Colonel J. Coke wrote home to his wife that the

> accounts of the 10th Div. are not by any means good (but for good-
> ness' sake don't <u>breathe</u> it to anybody)—it is said that their failure (from
> what reason is not known) to continue their advance from the Suvla
> side a few weeks ago spoilt all chance of what wd. have been a great
> success. There were only 3 Turkish Regts in front of 'em! If they had
> gone on & supported the Australians we should have been right across
> the peninsula east of Achi Baba & had 'em cut off…. The 10th has now
> gone up to S.—a new name for them is "the submerged tenth" which is
> distinctly clever.[48]

In answer to these criticisms, Bryan Cooper—the divisional historian and a veteran of the 5th Connaught Rangers—noted that the 10th (Irish) had been "shattered, the work of a year had been destroyed in a week, and nothing material gained. Yet," he continued, "it was not in vain. It is no new thing for the sons of Ireland to perish in a forlorn hope and a fruitless strug-gle; they go forth to battle only to fall, yet there springs from their graves a glorious memory for the example of future generations."[49] This was the Irish Military Diaspora set into words, envisioned as a tragic yet inspiring phe-nomenon that did not depend upon victory in battle in order to exist. Like Irish-themed engagements around the world in centuries past, failure was just as powerful as success in representing the concept of Irishmen in battle.

As the Irish division left Suvla for Salonika, the Newfoundlanders arrived.[50] Gallipoli also proved to be the Newfoundland Regiment's intro-duction to combat in the Great War. In his analysis of the Newfoundlanders' time at Suvla, Lackenbauer noted that it was a markedly different theatre compared to what the Irish or ANZACs had first encountered. Unlike the ANZACs' tragic slaughter on the beaches in April, or the 10th (Irish) Division's questionable performance, the Newfoundlanders, representing Britain's oldest colony, experienced Gallipoli as "a baptism of fire that began to cultivate a sense of national identity through military valour."[51] The First Battalion of the regiment, the famous "First Five Hundred," was also known as the "Blue Puttees" because a shortage of khaki material for their uniforms meant that their leggings matched the Aegean rather than Gallipoli's scrubby hills. They arrived in the Dardanelles in September 1915; by the time they withdrew in January 1916, only 117 of the colony's 1,100 soldiers remained unscathed.[52] When war broke out, the total population of Newfoundland was only around 250,000 citizens, making its contribution to the imperial contingent that much more of a cost at home. On 4 August 1914, there were only a handful of trained men, with many of the original First Five Hundred coming from the various cadet organizations, including the Catholic Cadet Corps, the Methodist Guards, the Anglican Church Lads Brigade, and the Newfoundland Highlanders of the Presbyterian Church.[53] Their duty, as voiced in the recruiting posters around the island, was simple: "At this very moment the Empire is engaged in the greatest War in the history of the world. In this crisis your Country calls on her young men to rally round Her Flag and enlist in the ranks of Her Army. If every patriotic young man answers Her Call, Great Britain and the Empire will emerge stronger and more united than ever.... Men of the Ancient and Loyal colony, Show Your Loyalty. NOW."[54]

However, as with the contentions regarding the religious composition of the Irish divisions raised for the war effort, Newfoundland—as part of the Irish Diaspora—showed similar difficulties with perceived sectarian bias in the ranks. Charges of "Protestant bigotry" were reported because the regiment had promoted more Protestants than Roman Catholics to officer status. Despite the dominion's history of tension between Orange and Green elements, the press argued that, "Our Roman Catholic fellow countrymen have come forward heartily in response to the call of God, Humanity and Empire.... It will be a great mistake to let sectarian feeling arise, or to do anything to affect injurious the efficiency of the force. The best men should be chosen irrespective of denomination." To further this position, the *Harbour Grace Standard* pointed out that the main things for an officer "besides knowledge and intelligence are bravery, manliness, and the refinement that is inbred; and it is unreasonable and insulting to suppose that our Roman Catholic boys do not possess both the natural and the acquired social qualifications to entitle them to more places of rank in the Regiment than has been accorded them."[55] Newfoundlanders, like other communities of the Irish Diaspora, were very aware of the political and sectarian tensions in Ireland immediately prior to and after the declaration of war, and they were not the Irish characteristics they, as part of the wider Irish world, wished to emulate. In the end, the organizers of the Newfoundland contingent "could not foresee to what extent denominational differences would largely be forgotten once the men, united by their communal way of life, were away from the sectarian restrictions that had separated them in the homeland."[56]

After a period of training at Edinburgh Castle, the Newfoundlanders left Britain for Egypt, arriving 1 September 1915, just as the 10th (Irish) Division was reeling from the cost of Suvla. Here in Alexandria, the Newfoundlanders "underwent a further hardening process—if indeed such were not redundant for a body of men already blest with a splendid physique, born of healthful toil in forest and fishery which a year's rigorous military training had brought to the peak of condition."[57] In his history of the regiment, Nicholson shows a high appreciation for the physical condition of the Newfoundland men, citing them as a pinnacle of imperial manliness, presumably in comparison not only with the Canadians but also all other troops fighting under the auspices of the British Empire. This highlights again the awareness among both contemporary sources and the regimental historiography of the men's omission from many of the war's accolades and the hierarchy of imperial masculinities that defined prowess in battle.

Captain W.G. Wallace, a stretcher-bearer with the 3rd Londons, referred to the Newfoundlanders in this pre-battle period as "grand fellows," whom Kitchener had "fitted out in style."[58] Some colonial troops certainly seemed aware—to a certain extent—of the Newfoundland Regiment's reputation for bellicosity. Australian troops previously had been condescending to the smaller colony, but after a "memorable clash in an Egyptian bar some of the Australians were overheard warning one another: 'Keep away from the guys with the goat on their cap; they're a bunch of savages!'"[59] In this instance, a reputation for savagery was far preferable to neglect and dismissal. In fact, as Nicholson points out, "a mutual liking and respect for fellow 'colonials'"[60] soon grew between the two groups of soldiers; it was easier for Newfoundlanders to socialize with Aussies than Canadians, as the former had no annexationist designs on St John's. It is also notable that the fraternization between ANZACs and the Newfoundland Regiment brought together two of the more notable descendents of the Irish Diaspora in a single theatre of battle.

Arriving in the *Prince Abbas*, the Newfoundlanders were the only non-regular battalion in a division of veteran troops, which might account for some of the less-than-generous comments made about their initial comportment under fire. R.E. Atkinson, a cyclist with the 29th Division recorded that the Newfoundlanders were attached to his division "for Discip." He also thought that they were "very nervous of shells" soon after their arrival in the line.[61] Lieutenant King-Wilson, a Canadian surgeon at Suvla, was frankly baffled by the Newfoundland Regiment under fire. After the evacuation of Suvla and their re-assignment to Cape Helles in late December 1915, King-Wilson wrote that he had "witnessed a curious sight. The Newfoundland Regiment, moving down to the Beach.... Luck seemed to be with the men of the 'Old Dominion' and group after group disappeared over the crest of the cliff.... The shells had missed them in marvellous fashion, always exploding in ... the wrong place. But the very last group literally ran into a shell, which, bursting in their midst, killed or wounded every one, and they fell like a child's house of cards."[62] In this instance, the men of the regiment were recognized as both colonials from the "Old Dominion" and, simultaneously, green soldiers. For both the Irish and the Newfoundlanders, the phrase "baptism of fire" took on a very literal meaning during their time at Gallipoli.

In terms of day-to-day events, the Newfoundland Regiment seemed to have experienced the triumphs and catastrophes of Gallipoli just like all the other troops from across the empire; however, the predominant feeling was one of boredom rather than adventure. The one exception to this monotony was, of course, the regiment's exploits at Caribou Hill. The Turks had established themselves on a slight rise that aided their sniping positions, about 150 yards in front of the trenches. Lieutenant J.J. Donnelly was chosen to lead the expedition to push back the Turks and recapture the area for the British.[63] Donnelly and his group of Newfoundlanders not only gained the objective, but held it a further forty-eight hours until reinforcements arrived. Unlike the tedium associated with the rest of the Gallipoli campaign, with its digging and swatting and sniping, the victory at Caribou Hill "marked the beginning of the heroic exploits that were to bring worldwide renown to Newfoundland through the Newfoundland Regiment."[64]

Portrayals of warrior masculinities occurred for both Irishmen and Newfoundlanders during their time at Gallipoli in ways that blended cultural observance with the harsher realities of warfare. As John Tosh has argued, "empire was a man's business,"[65] from which follows the conclusion that defending the empire was the ultimate test for soldier heroes, even if an individual's personal politics were of a more nationalist nature. The men who had been sent to the Dardanelles had been told that they were natural warriors, "well worth looking at, tall and slim, with the lean strength that told of work outdoors, and of perfect physical condition."[66] Both nations saw their contribution to the war effort as part of a wider colonial experience, in line with both the expanse of British imperialism and the connections of the Irish Diaspora. Many of the memoirs written by Irishmen and Newfoundlanders note "an egalitarianism and a relaxed attitude out of the line" that echoed the lack of deference many in the war associated with the ANZACs.[67] These feelings also undermined the reports in the press of a sectarian tension that had haunted the recruiting process. David Fallon, who had journeyed from Ireland to Australia as part of the British Army, felt that he was "lucky in having a keen love of athletics and a pride of achievement in many branches of sport. There's nothing like such a disposition to keep a boy clean and straight." This particular Irishman went to great lengths in his memoir to note the kinship of colonial manhoods, with Australians—and Irish-Australians—standing as the equals of their North American counterparts. They were brothers "in every degree of character to the American and Canadian miners, ranchers, trappers, cowboys; they are big, lean, brave, boyishly chivalrous men, shy of women but adoring them, willing to play romping dog any old time to win the smile of a child or the pat of its little hand."[68] For Fallon, the war was fought to defend these women and children who were the focus of men's gentler aspects, even as their martial skill gave them currency in the rigorous world of masculine adventure.[69]

Oliver Hogue echoed this in his own characterizations of Irish-Australian soldiers. Father Michael "Mike" Bergin, a chaplain assigned to the 5th Australian Light Horse, was "a good sport, a good priest, brave as a lion, and with wounded soldiers gentle as a nurse. His only fault was that he always wanted to be right up in the firing line, for he dearly loved a 'scrap'— being Irish."[70] Irish Protestants also were prominent in Hogue's vision of the Gallipoli front lines, visible in his account of the death of Lieutenant Digges La Touche, a Trinity College scholar in the 13th Battalion, Australian Imperial Force (AIF), whose "fiery orations" had inspired the men to "patriotic self-sacrifice and zeal for Empire." La Touche was an "uncompromising Unionist" and an "electric Irishman" who was killed "in the first minute of his first battle."[71] According to Hogue,

> For ten months he had pleaded with Church and State to let him serve as a soldier of the king. For ten weeks he wore the uniform of an officer of the Australian Imperial Force. For ten hours he did duty in the trenches. For ten brief seconds he knew the wild exultation of the charge. Then there passed away a great-hearted Britisher, strong of soul and clear of vision, who counted it a great privilege to fight and die for his king and country.[72]

The connections between Irishmen and Australians at Gallipoli were also the source for some interesting insights regarding physical bodies.

Recovering in a hospital on Lemnos, "Juvenis" recalled that, "Here and there the bronzed Australian orderlies, in their usual charming deficiency of clothing, were fetching and carrying medical stores among the tents."[73] His thoughts were not too far from those of John McIlwain of the 10th (Irish) Division. On a break from the front lines in the late summer, McIlwain sat on a cliff overlooking the sea, writing in his journal. He noted the number of broken and wounded bodies going past him on stretchers, and then jotted down that he could not help but notice the "magnificent physique and condition of the almost naked young Anzacs."[74] McIlwain's brief yet perceptive comment about the ANZACs carried none of the political or sectarian overtones that often appeared in Irish war journals and memoirs; instead, it was a simple enjoyment of men displaying vigour and vitality in the face of death. These two passages together underlined the importance of whole, healthy men in a setting where so many male bodies were being torn apart. Juxtaposing those observances with an obvious approval for the ANZACs' bodies emphasized Juvenis's and McIlwain's horror of one and enjoyment of the other. Physical fitness had the potential to remind soldiers how beautiful the male body could be when in prime condition and not being cut down by shrapnel or a sniper's bullets. An intimacy with violence on a daily basis shaped men's ideas about physical expressions of masculinity, not necessarily in a homoerotic manner, but certainly in terms of valuing male bodies—their own and those around them—as repositories of strength and as potent reminders of the physical cost of war. Three weeks later, after the attack on Scimitar Hill, McIlwain faced the anger of the ANZACs he had once admired, as they were livid that the Irishmen had "lost the trench." He ended his observances at Suvla reflecting that receiving this castigation from fellow imperial soldiers made it "the most awful night of my life."[75]

According to the press in Ireland, the men of the Irish division had borne "themselves as Irishmen should do in the face of danger" and had set a new example of heroism for all the other soldiers in the field.[76] The Newfoundland newspapers were not far behind in terms of setting their own standards of masculinity. The colony's desire to join the fight at Suvla was summed up in a simple headline: "Wanted: MEN."[77] They had already received tremendous accolades from their commanding officers and the governor of Newfoundland. In his parting tribute to the regiment in 1914, the Canadian Lieutenant-Colonel Clegg believed that the Newfoundlanders were "not surpassed by any unit in the camp for all round smartness on parade, steadiness in the ranks and general intelligence, while their physical fitness appears to be excellent."[78] His successor, Lieutenant-Colonel R. de

H. Burton wrote to Governor Sir Walter Davidson that the men's good conduct was a source of "great satisfaction. The men are also very fit and their healthy, fresh and vigorous appearance as compared with the men of other Units around has been remarked on."[79] Governor Davidson, meanwhile, wrote in his papers that Newfoundland was a poor colony financially, but rich in "fine, stalwart men" who, when the time came to be soldiers, "will play their part too like men."[80] Like the two colonels, he also thought the dominion's soldiers were of "fine physique, rather short in stature but thick set and enduring; they are also handy men and very hardy and accustomed to hard work."[81] The press argued that both the Newfoundlanders and the Irish in the trenches at Suvla were "brave men, true men, all of them. They could work and they could play, yes, and they could give their lives" as well as any other men from the British Empire.[82]

Tension mingled with a sense of impending action at the time of the final evacuation from Gallipoli. Lieutenant A.N. Anderson of Ballynahinch, County Down, serving with the Royal Irish Rifles, noted that a "retirement in face of an enemy on land where you have plenty of room is a very difficult and critical operation but under the circumstances here, where one is bang up against your enemy, and where you have absolutely no room to sling a cat … you can imagine what a difficult anxious job it is."[83] Even in this most stressful of times, David Fallon, the Irish captain assigned to the 1st Division of the AIF, commented on the irascible sense of humour that even the worst of fighting conditions could not destroy: "One dug-out showed a placard announcing: 'Anzac Villa—To Let for the Season. Beautiful Sandy Beach all to Yourself. Splendid sea view. Home comforts. Lots of pleasure and excitement.'"[84] Oliver Hogue, the Australian journalist who wrote about many Irishmen in the ANZAC contingent, described the absolute secrecy necessary for the evacuation's success. "One single traitor could have queered the whole pitch," he emphasized, but "British, Indians, New Zealanders and Australians were loyal to the core."[85] This was an operation in which everyone had a vested interest; it was also yet another instance when Newfoundlanders were left out of the list of imperial nations fighting at Gallipoli. Historians have been able to fill in the gap left by primary sources, noting that Newfoundlanders were assigned to the rearguard during the Suvla departure, and that it was a complete success in which the Newfoundlanders "played a respectable part."[86] After a brief return to Cape Helles, men from the regiment were among the last to set foot on Turkish soil before beating a final retreat to Mudros and Alexandria. Six months later, the Newfoundland Regiment went over the top at the Somme.

Gallipoli was an awakening to the realities and casualties of war, which became even more visible after Ireland and Newfoundland had each suffered on the Western Front in the summer of 1916. Lackenbauer has described how the collective memory of the Dardanelles Campaign was created in Newfoundland through a mixture of newspaper reports and "unofficial histories" of war memoirs, veterans' magazines, and flutterings of amateur attempts at poetry.[87] Similar cultural and literary tropes were used in Ireland to remember the campaign, particularly in the years between 1916 and 1919, the most notable of which was Bryan Cooper's official history of the 10th (Irish) Division. However, the overwhelming weight of what occurred in France on 1 July 1916 eradicated the longevity of both countries' first experiences in the Great War. On that summer morning, the 36th (Ulster) Division went over the top at Thiepval and became Protestant Ulster's legendary sacrifice that demonstrated its loyalty to the empire and reaffirmed the union with Great Britain.[88] The later efforts in September of that year by the 16th (Irish) Division in the final weeks of the Somme engagement further removed Ireland's focus from the Dardanelles and the events of 1915, not to mention the domestic repercussions of the Easter Rising in April of 1916. Less than five years after the Somme, Ireland had been partitioned and the "great amnesia" regarding Irish nationalists in British uniforms became the normative stance toward the Great War for much of the island—a fact that was, no doubt, aided and abetted by the Orange Order's triumphalist appropriation of the Somme as unionism's new Battle of the Boyne.

Only a short distance down the line from the 36th Ulsters, the Newfoundland Regiment attained their place in the legends of the Great War through their actions at Beaumont Hamel. At 9:15 a.m., 780 Newfoundlanders advanced through lines of barbed wire and trenches before entering "no man's land."[89] Most of these men were dead or wounded before reaching their own front line; not a single Newfoundlander fired a shot, let alone inflicted a casualty.[90] The Newfoundland Regiment incurred an infamous casualty rate of over ninety percent on 1 July 1916, with only sixty-eight men answering roll call the following morning. From that moment on, the Somme battlefield was the primary place for Newfoundland's national mythology, attaining the same aura that Anzac Cove had done for Australia and New Zealand, and what Vimy Ridge would bring to the Canadian Corps in 1917. Memorial Day in Newfoundland was set on the anniversary of Beaumont Hamel and became a time when civilians were urged to "hold fast to those principles of truth, honesty, purity and manhood" displayed by the regiment.[91]

However, it is this very forgetting of Suvla Bay, either as an intention or a coincidence, that unites Ireland and Newfoundland as North Atlantic members of the British Empire and Irish Diaspora who, in the end, were left out of the collective memory of the Dardanelles. Lackenbauer cites the importance of Newfoundland's presence at Suvla as a foundation for the regiment's masculine construction at Beaumont Hamel as disciplined and battle-hardened troops. But because Newfoundlanders were not present for the initial landing at Suvla in August, for them the "blood that was spilled was not shed in a united colonial thrust during a major Allied offensive."[92] Similarly, the 10th (Irish) Division's distant geographic location in the Mediterranean for most of the war enabled their virtual omission from the histories of the conflict and, closer to home, the commemorations that occurred immediately after the Armistice. During the 1919 Peace Day celebrations in Belfast to celebrate the signing of the Versailles Treaty, nationalist veterans decried the preferential treatment Ulster's population bestowed upon the Protestant 36th Division—but their protest was framed as a competition between the 36th and 16th Divisions.[93] The 10th Division was forgotten before it even had a chance to be remembered.

Men of Irish descent fought throughout the Gallipoli campaign, participating in the first landings in April at Cape Helles and Anzac Cove, as well as at Suvla Bay. They were not only from Ireland, but Britain, South Africa, India, Australia, New Zealand, and Newfoundland. A high price was paid by these sister nations of the empire; however, Newfoundland and Ireland—at least the unionist community in the north of Ireland—did not conform to Eric Hobsbawm's argument that many colonies and dominions developed a brand of anti-imperial nationalism after the war.[94] In 1923, the Reverend E.C. Earp promoted the idea of the Newfoundland ex-serviceman as "the country's greatest asset" and a man who was "in very truth an Empire builder."[95] Newfoundland's unveiling of Beaumont Hamel Memorial Park at the Somme in 1925 was an event steeped in the glories of empire, with the caribou statue draped in an enormous Union flag and Field Marshal Lord Haig as the guest of honour. The dominion's focus on imperialism was also visible in the growth of the Orange Order, with a membership that had quadrupled in the first twenty years of the century.[96] The Battle of the Somme had claimed a disproportionate number of Ulstermen and Newfoundlanders on 1 July 1916; however, there was no correspondingly uniform impact upon lodge membership. Of course, the difference between Newfoundland Orangeism and the type found in Northern Ireland was that the order in Newfoundland was never dominated by Irish Protestants, but was instead a reflection of Britishness on "the Rock."[97] In fact, it was an Orange prime minister, Sir Richard Squires, who worked with Lieutenant-Colonel Padre Tom Nangle to create the "Trail of the Caribou," the collection of bronze statues that have signified Newfoundland sacrifice in the Great War for nearly a century.

But Gallipoli remained unremembered and indistinct in the war memories of both Ireland and Newfoundland until very recently. Because Gallipoli occurred in the first two years of the war, before the Easter Rising of 1916 or the schism of the Irish Conscription Crisis in 1918, that country's reaction to 1915 was far different from what was expressed by the time of the Armistice. Similarly, because the Newfoundland Regiment's experiences at Suvla occurred in that brief time before its devastation at Beaumont Hamel, its distance—both as a cultural memory and a geographic location—enabled its omission from the "Trail of the Caribou" and the refashioning of Newfoundland's legends of the war. Neither country dwelt on images of wartime masculinities fashioned in the Dardanelles, focusing instead—if at all—on the mythic manliness of France and Flanders as expressions of imperial bravery and sacrifice.

Antlered statues and commemorated plinths do not have the power to rewrite history, and their absence from Suvla Bay is hardly a conspiracy of silence in today's information age and ever-growing popular interest in the Great War. But it is fascinating that, in an empire supposedly anchored in the plurality of identities, the most imperial of engagements in terms of composition was, for these two nations, the easiest to forget.

NOTES

1. P. Whitney Lackenbauer, "War, Memory, and the Newfoundland Regiment at Gallipoli," *Newfoundland Studies* 15, no. 2 (1999): 176–214.
2. Linda Farrell, Secretariat, Government of Ireland, email message to the author, 27 September 2011.
3. E. Ashmead Bartlett, CBE, "Great Deeds in Gallipoli," *Veteran Magazine* 7, no. 4 (December 1928): 22–24.
4. Dan Carroll, "In Memory of Private Michael John Blyde," *Newfoundland Quarterly* 15, no. 3 (December 1915), 9.
5. The Newfoundland Regiment did not receive the "Royal" designation until the beginning of 1918, following the recommendation of Field Marshal Sir Douglas Haig to King George V. Haig cited the "bravery and resolute determination" of the regiment at recent engagements in Cambrai and Ypres, and felt that the

"Royal" title for the regiment would not only honour the men, but the colony as a whole. The king granted Haig's request on 25 January 1918. See National Archives (Kew), WO/32/5012, memorandum from Field Marshal Sir D. Haig, KT, GCB, GCVO, KCIE, Commander-in-Chief, British Armies in France to the Secretary, War Office, London, 15 January 1918; letter from B.B. Cubitt, Assistant Secretary to the War Office, to Field Marshal Sir D. Haig, 25 January 1918.

6. Gary Browne and Darrin McGrath, *Soldier Priest in the Killing Fields of Europe: Padre Thomas Nangle, Chaplain to the Newfoundland Regiment WWI* (St. John's: DRC Publishing, 2006), 75.

7. "Trail of the Caribou," *Veteran Magazine* 2, no. 1 (April 1922): 12.

8. The focus of this chapter is a comparison of Ireland's and Newfoundland's roles within the Irish Diaspora as geographically small, transatlantic nations with powerful war histories. Numerous countries are part of the wider Irish Diaspora in both the northern and southern hemispheres, including Canada, the United States, Argentina, Barbados, New Zealand, Australia, India, South Africa, and continental Europe. It is beyond the scope of this article to provide a comparison of Irish identities and imperial masculinities for all of the Irish diasporic nations that fought in the Great War, although this is a fascinating area of research that deserves greater exploration. See Jeff Kildea, *Anzacs and Ireland* (Cork: Cork University Press, 2007), and Keith Jeffery, *Ireland and the Great War* (Cambridge: Cambridge University Press, 2000).

9. Jenny Macleod, *Battle of the Nations: Remembering Gallipoli. The Trevor Reese Memorial Lecture 2005*, series edited by Carl Bridge and Catherine Kevin (London: Menzies Centre for Australian Studies, 2005), 22.

10. James K. Hiller, "Status without Stature: Newfoundland, 1869–1949," in *Canada and the British Empire*, ed. Philip Buckner (Oxford: Oxford University Press, 2008), 133; Jim Smyth, *The Men of No Property: Irish Radicals and Popular Politics in the Late Eighteenth Century* (Dublin: Gill and Macmillan, 1992), 82; Donald Harman Akenson, *The Irish Diaspora: A Primer* (Toronto: P.D. Meany, 1996), 141–51.

11. Gearóid Ó'hAllmhuráin, "Soundscape of the Wintermen: Irish Traditional Music in Newfoundland," *Canadian Journal of Irish Studies: Revue canadienne d'études irlandaises* 34, no. 2 (2008): 33–46.

12. Akenson, *The Irish Diaspora*, 143.

13. Tim Pat Coogan, *Wherever the Green Is Worn: The Story of the Irish Diaspora* (New York: Palgrave, 2000), 415.

14. The Rev. John L. Slattery, "Ireland and the War," *Newfoundland Quarterly* 15, no. 3 (December 1915): 26.

15. David Wilson, "Introduction," in *The Orange Order in Canada*, ed. David A. Wilson (Dublin: Four Courts Press, 2007), 14.

16. Annie M. Warne, "Britain's Oldest Colony—Labrador," *Among the Deep Sea Fishers* 15, no. 1 (April 1917): 11.

17. A.T.Q. Stewart, *The Ulster Crisis* (Belfast: Blackstaff Press, 1967), 184–212.

18. Pádraic H. Pearse, *Collected Works: Political Writings and Speeches* (Dublin: Phoenix, 1924), 98–99.

19. *Irish Independent*, 30 July 1915. Similar sentiments were recorded by the Reverend Slattery as having been stated by Willie Redmond's brother, John, the leader of the Irish Parliamentary Party. The latter held that in the "portion of Irishmen who are serving gallantly in the Canadian, Australian and New Zealand Forces, you will find the Irish race unlike anything that ever existed in history before." See Slattery, "Ireland and the War," 26.

20. *Northern Whig*, 27 August 1915; Public Record Office of Northern Ireland (hereafter PRONI) D627/429/4, Montgomery Papers, letter from Hugh de F. Montgomery to Mr. Coote re: religious affiliations of the 10th (Irish) Division, 25 March 1916. For more on Sam Hughes and his role in the Canadian military, see Tim Cook, *The Madman and the Butcher* (Toronto: Allen Lane, 2010), and Ronald Haycock, *Sam Hughes: The Public Career of a Controversial Canadian, 1885–1916* (Ottawa: National Museums Canada, 1986).

21. Captain David Fallon, MC, *The Big Fight (Gallipoli to the Somme)* (London: Cassel, 1918), 1–4.

22. Trooper Henry George McNeill of the Australian Light Horse was from Londonderry, but served with the ANZACs and is buried in Ari Burnu Cemetery. See the Commonwealth War Graves Commission database: http://www.cwgc.org/search-for-war-dead/casualty/621645/McNEILL,%20 HENRY%20GEORGE (accessed 19 June 2012); Private Alfred Christopher Harrison fought with the Royal Inniskilling Fusiliers, but was from Durban, Natal, South Africa, and is buried in Twelve Tree Copse Cemetery. See the CWGC database: http://www.cwgc.org/search-for-war-dead/casualty/603069/ HARRISON,%20ALFRED%20CHRISTOPHER (accessed 19 June 2012).

23. Lackenbauer, "War, Memory and the Newfoundland Regiment at Gallipoli," 191.

24. "805 Private M.P. Murphy," *Commercial Annual* 27 (Christmas 1918), 47.

25. *Harbour Grace Standard and Conception Bay Advertiser*, 7 August 1914.

26. Ibid., 10 December 1915.

27. Canadians, though few in number, were present at Gallipoli as part of the medical corps. Major Norman King-Wilson was a surgeon with the Canadians, but served at Gallipoli as a temporary lieutenant in the British Army. He landed at Suvla Bay with the 88th Field Ambulance, 88th Brigade, 29th Division, and remained on site until the final evacuation of Cape Helles in January 1916. See Imperial War Museum (hereafter IWM) P232, Papers of Lieutenant N. King-Wilson, "Jottings of an M.O."

28. Joanna Bourke, "Effeminacy, Ethnicity and the End of Trauma: The Sufferings of 'Shell-Shocked' Men in Great Britain and Ireland, 1914–39," *Journal of Contemporary History* 35, no. 1 (2000): 61.

29. Weston quoted in S. Parnell Kerr, *What the Irish Regiments Have Done* (London: Unwin, 1917), 149. Weston's quotation was also made into a recruitment poster later in 1915.

30. Ibid., 144.

31. Tim Bowman, *Carson's Army: The Ulster Volunteer Force, 1910–22* (Manchester: Manchester University Press, 2007), 166–68.

32. PRONI, D627/428/4, Montgomery Papers, letter from Hugh de Fellenberg Montgomery to Mr. Coote, 25 March 1916.

33. PRONI, D627/429/8, Montgomery Papers, 10th (Irish) Division Religious Census November 1915. According to the figures collected from the 29th, 30th, and 31st Brigades, the division had a total of 13,608 men—8,734 Protestants and 4,874 Roman Catholics, a difference of 3,860 men. Within the Protestant numbers, the largest denomination was Anglican (7,208), followed by Presbyterians (1,112) and Wesleyans (414). It should be noted, however, that this information was recorded in November 1915 when the division had been moved to Salonika, some three months after they had fought at Suvla.

34. *Irish Independent*, 1 July 1915.

35. Ibid.

36. Bryan Cooper, *The Tenth (Irish) Division in Gallipoli* (Dublin: Irish Academic Press, 1993 [first published 1918]), 137.

37. *Irish Times*, 26 August 1915.

38. *Irish Independent*, 27 August 1915.

39. Ibid.

40. Ibid., 28 August 1915.

41. *Harbour Grace Standard and Conception Bay Advertiser*, 10 December 1915.

42. Ibid.

43. Jeremy Stanley, *Ireland's Forgotten 10th: A Brief History of the 10th (Irish) Division 1914–1918 Turkey, Macedonia and Palestine* (Ballycastle and Coleraine: Impact Printing, 2003), 35.

44. Godley quoted in Tom Johnstone, *Orange, Green and Khaki: Story of the Irish Regiments in the Great War, 1914–18* (Dublin: Gill & Macmillan, 1991), 145.

45. IWM, 88/27/1, A.H. Kingston Papers, memoir, 7.

46. IWM, 91/42/1, H.F. Kemball Papers, "The experiences of a Territorial Officer in 1915," 2.

47. IWM, P216, 1915 Letters of Captain G.W. Nightingale, letter to his mother, 25 August 1915, 5.

48. IWM, 91/10/1, Private Papers of Colonel J. d'E.F. Coke, CMG, CVO, CBE, letter to his wife, October 1915, 2–3. Emphasis as in original.

49. Cooper, *The Tenth (Irish) Division in Gallipoli*, 179–80.

50. *Free Press*, 28 September 1915.

51. Lackenbauer, "War, Memory, and the Newfoundland Regiment at Gallipoli," 176.

52. Macleod, *Battle of the Nations*, 5. These numbers are slightly contested in Harding's article, wherein he posits that of 930 men there were 760 casualties, and "170 soldiers remained to answer the roll call." See Harding, "Glorious Tragedy," 5.
53. W. David Parsons, "Newfoundland and the Great War," in *Canada and the Great War: Western Front Association Papers*, ed. Briton C. Busch (Montreal: McGill-Queen's University Press, 2003), 148.
54. Library and Archives Canada (hereafter LAC), RG38, vol. 437, M-43-A, Royal Newfoundland Regiment—General—1915.
55. *Harbour Grace Standard and Conception Bay Advertiser*, 29 October 1915.
56. G.W.L. Nicholson, *The Fighting Newfoundlander: A History of the Royal Newfoundland Regiment* (St. John's: Government of Newfoundland, 1964), 177.
57. Nicholson, *The Fighting Newfoundlander*, 161.
58. IWM, 86/9/1, Papers of Captain W.G. Wallace, *Memoirs of 1914/1918*, 27.
59. Nicholson, *The Fighting Newfoundlander*, 162.
60. Nicholson, *The Fighting Newfoundlander*, 162.
61. IWM, 95/1/1, R.E. Atkinson Papers, diary entries, 22–23 September 1915.
62. IWM, P232, Papers of N. King-Wilson, "Jottings of an M.O.," 45.
63. Anonymous, "Triumph of the Newfoundland Regiment," *Newfoundland Quarterly* 15, no. 4 (April 1916): 2.
64. Tait, "With the Regiment at Gallipoli," 42–43.
65. John Tosh, *Manliness and Masculinities in Nineteenth-Century Britain* (Harlow: Pearson Education, 2005), 193.
66. Duley, *A Pair of Grey Socks*, 1.
67. Macleod, *Battle of the Nations*, 6.
68. Fallon, *The Big Fight*, 3, 6.
69. Tosh, *Manliness and Masculinities*, 202–3.
70. Hogue, *Trooper Bluegum*, 180.
71. Ibid., 222, 219.
72. Ibid., 220.
73. Juvenis, *Suvla Bay and After*, 96.
74. IWM, 96/29/1, Papers of J. McIlwain, diary entry, 7 August 1915.
75. Ibid., 27 August 1915.
76. *Irish Independent*, 25 August 1915.
77. *Harbour Grace Standard and Conception Bay Advertiser*, 8 October 1915.
78. Lt. Col. Clegg quoted in Nicholson, *The Fighting Newfoundlander*, 125.
79. LAC, RG38, vol. 437, M-43-A, Royal Newfoundland Regiment—General—1915, letter from R. de H. Burton to Sir W.E. Davidson, KCMG, Governor of Newfoundland, 27 January 1915.
80. LAC, RG38, vol. 437, M-43-A, Royal Newfoundland Regiment—General—1915, letter from Sir W.E. Davidson to the Lord Provost of the City of Edinburgh, 5 April 1915.

81. Davidson quoted in Nicholson, *The Fighting Newfoundlander*, 118.

82. Comrade, "A Night on Gallipoli," *The Veteran Magazine* 1, no. 2 (April 1921), 9.

83. PRONI, D961/8, Correspondence relating to Lt. A.N. Anderson's military service 1915–20, "Evacuation of Gallipoli," 18 December 1915, 1.

84. Fallon, *The Big Fight*, 88.

85. Oliver Hogue, *Trooper Bluegum at the Dardanelles* (London: Andrew Melrose, 1916), 274.

86. Lackenbauer, "War, Memory, and the Newfoundland Regiment at Gallipoli," 180.

87. Lackenbauer, "War, Memory, and the Newfoundland Regiment at Gallipoli," 190–94.

88. For more on the Somme's importance to Ulster soldiering masculinities, see Jane G.V. McGaughey, *Ulster's Men: Protestant Unionist Masculinities and Militarization in the North of Ireland, 1912–1923* (Montreal: McGill-Queen's University Press, 2012), 83–108.

89. Nicholson, *The Fighting Newfoundlander*, 274.

90. Harding, "Glorious Tragedy," 7.

91. Ibid., 12. Ironically, after Confederation with Canada in 1949, Newfoundland's Memorial Day on 1 July also became their national holiday, reflecting the 1867 creation of the British North America Act.

92. Lackenbauer, "War, Memory, and the Newfoundland Regiment at Gallipoli," 195.

93. *Irish Independent*, 11 August 1919.

94. Eric J. Hobsbawm, *Nations and Nationalisms since 1870: Programme, Myth and Reality* (New York: Cambridge University Press, 1990), 136–39.

95. Rev. E.C. Earp, "The Ex-Service Man as Citizen," *The Veteran Magazine* 3, no. 2 (April 1923): 19.

96. Eric Kaufman, "The Orange Order in Ontario, Newfoundland, Scotland, and Northern Ireland: a macro-social analysis," in Wilson, *The Orange Order in Canada*, 54.

97. After 1920, the Orange Order also was no longer dominated by Irish immigrants in Canada, with many members coming from English, Scottish, German, and Mohawk backgrounds. That said, the majority of participants were still of Irish heritage. See Cecil J. Houston and William J. Smyth, "The Faded Sash: The Decline of the Orange Order in Canada, 1920–2005," in Wilson, *The Orange Order in Canada*, 175.

HISTORY TRUMPS MEMORY
The Strange Case of Sir Richard Turner

WILLIAM F. STEWART

The death of John Babcock in 2010, the last surviving veteran of the Canadian Expeditionary Force (CEF), leaves no living memory of the Canadian military experience of the First World War. Historians of the CEF are no longer able to test their assertions against the memory of any living participants; they must rely on documents, memoirs, and oral records as the basic building blocks for their narratives and analysis. Whilst this can carry the benefits of a detached objectivity, it also bears the risk of subordinating memory to "history," as we lose touch with the context and texture of the times. The memories of veterans themselves, however, can be problematic, as they evolve over time and may reflect the current popular discourse, and as a result, become a less reliable reflection of their original opinion. Further, historians may ignore their initial views if these memories contradict this popular discourse. This is particularly the case with military leaders whose reputations rise and fall because of new insights into strategy, new information, revised assessments of their decisions, and judgments made in the light of current values about the cost and futility of war. In making these judgments about military leadership, a key consideration has to be the recollections of those they led. The officers and men of a military leader provide an invaluable perspective for any assessment of that leader. Hence, it is important to look beyond loyalty, at how the men and officers experienced and remembered this leadership as a crucial part of an assessment.

The purpose of this chapter is to look at how historians ignored the recollections of dozens of veterans in revising the reputation of the controversial Canadian general Sir Richard Turner. During the war and immediately after, Turner's officers, staff, and soldiers held him in high regard. As "history" replaced memory, accelerating from the 1960s, Turner's reputation deteriorated to the point that historians regarded him as the worst Canadian commander of the First World War and deeply compromised by his political connections, a view that is arguably inaccurate or exaggerated given new evidence.[1] To his troops, however, Turner was "every inch a soldier," and was highly regarded for his competence, courage, approachability, and leadership. This paper examines how Turner's reputation diminished as judgments based on participants' recollections shifted to those relying on documentary sources, and a key part of his leadership skill set became less appreciated.

The chapter will provide a concise outline of Turner's career to establish a context for the analysis. It will then establish the contemporary view of Turner as expressed in letters, diaries, and histories from the war and immediate postwar period. The paper restricts "memory" to those reflections recorded in diaries, letters, and articles written during the war and the immediate postwar period. Memory is volatile, plastic, and conditioned and shaped by outside influences as it undergoes constant change, revision, and reinvention. To minimize these changes to memory, the paper's focus represents the most authentic version of the opinion of Turner, meaning those memories closest to the period. This will help delineate the baseline of how contemporaries viewed Turner, or the "remembered" version of his leadership. The paper then defines the revised, modern, or "history" version, which varies considerably from the "memory" one and questions the completeness of those historical judgments given the absence of how contemporaries viewed Turner in this popular narrative. The paper also examines the factors underpinning why Turner's reputation has declined so precipitously. It concludes with three observations arising from this study relevant to all historians dealing with military reputations and the shift from dependence on memory to other sources.

Richard Ernest William Turner was born in 1871 to a wealthy Quebec City merchant and prominent provincial Liberal. He had a conventional upbringing and education ending at high school. He joined his father's wholesale grocery and lumber firm in 1891, and rose to become a partner after the Boer War. His military career commenced in 1892, when he joined the longstanding militia cavalry regiment in Quebec City, the Queen's Own Canadian Hussars, as a second lieutenant. He was an able junior officer and reached the rank of major in 1900. He reverted in rank to serve in the Second Canadian Contingent in the Boer War. There he won considerable distinction, with a Distinguished Service Order, a Victoria Cross, and two serious wounds. His success in the Boer war made his career as an officer and a figure of national renown. Following his recovery and return to Canada, Turner commanded his cavalry regiment and a militia cavalry brigade until his retirement in 1912.

In 1914, he was an obvious selection to lead the 3rd Brigade of the 1st Division because of his prewar record of command, awards for courage, and active service in the Boer War. At the Battle of Second Ypres in April 1915, he performed bravely but made a serious error amidst the confusion, chaos, and unprecedented conditions of the battle that grievously affected his later reputation and his relationship with the British commander of the 1st Division, Lieutenant-General Edwin Alderson. Turner's conduct of the battle was conditioned by commanding a division-sized line, oriented at right angles, with unprepared defences on most of the front, poor to non-existent communications, no artillery support, and the equivalent of two brigades to control.[2] No British or Canadian commander on the Western Front faced the extreme challenges that Turner confronted, and despite this Turner and his brigade performed surprisingly well in their first action. His conduct of the Battle of Festubert a month later showed an improvement in his command, but resulted in further alienation between Turner and Alderson over the poor planning and staff work of the division.[3]

Over Alderson's objections, Sam Hughes, the minister of militia and defence, selected Turner to command the 2nd Division in August 1915. He commanded the 2nd Division at the defeat at St. Eloi Craters, and historians have sharply criticized Turner for his conduct of the battle. As the divisional commander, Turner bears responsibility but not culpability for the battle, as he took all the reasonable steps available to salvage an unwinnable engagement.[4] For instance, the Germans concentrated three times the artillery firepower on St. Eloi than did the Canadians in the successful attack at Mount Sorrel on 13 June 1916—in which the Canadian artillery commander claimed more shells were fired than was required.[5] Alderson wanted to remove him, but owing to the political intervention of Max Aitken, Hughes's "personal representative" in England, and the Commander-in-Chief of the British Expeditionary Force General Douglas Haig's low regard for Alderson, Turner retained his position and Alderson was transferred. Turner led the 2nd Division at the Battle of Courcelette on 15 September 1916, where it won the major Canadian victory at the Somme. Turner also led the division in two less successful operations at the battles of Thiepval and Ancre Heights.[6]

In reaction to the abysmal Canadian administration and training situation in England, the prime minister, Sir Robert Borden, formed a new Ministry of Overseas Military Forces of Canada (OMFC). In November 1916 the new minister, Sir George Perley, selected Turner to command the Canadian forces in England to reform the system. Turner was instrumental in transforming a chaotic and dysfunctional administration into a far more effective and efficient machine. Turner remained in this position until retiring in 1919. He held no further military positions, but did play a critical role in unifying the multiple veterans' organizations into what became the Royal Canadian Legion in 1926. He led the initiative in part because of his popularity with men and officers of the CEF. He died in 1961.

Turner's subordinates, both officers and men, extolled his competence, approachability, and courage. Memoirs, diaries, and contemporary letters rarely mention senior officers, but a surprising number of Turner's subordinates refer to him and do so in a positive light. Senior officers in the First World War were typically remote figures, both physically and psychologically, from the frontline fighters. This was the result of army policy restricting division commanders to their headquarters during battles, the difficulty of reaching the frontlines, and a neglect of proper man-management.[7] Only a few individuals were able to stamp their character on their formations, and Turner was one of these exceptions.

One example of how Turner was viewed is D.E. Macintyre on the event of Turner's transfer to England to command Canadian forces: "certainly [he] is the right man in the right place. Unfortunately, it is a great loss for us, everyone was his friend out here. He is not only a capable soldier but an absolutely honest and fearless man and should go far."[8] Another is Private Fraser, writing in his diary about the contempt the men felt toward their officers: "One officer I can single out as a decided exception. He is General Turner, V.C."[9] A further example: "Gen Turner the great Canadian General, was here today. He is very popular as [he] is every inch a fighting man."[10] Finally, Andrew Macphail, the Canadian literary figure and doctor: "From all of us he won instant devotion, even from myself who am not disposed to yield devotion upon first demand."[11] The regimental histories published before the Second World War were also commendatory, with two containing forwards written by Turner, indicating the esteem with which he was held.[12] A typical description of Turner is in the history of the 24th Battalion in Turner's 2nd Division: "it is certain that the units of the division regretted his departure profoundly."[13]

During the war and immediately post-war, Turner had a distinguished reputation, much like Douglas Haig.[14] As to be expected during the war, works like J.A. Currie's *The Red Watch* and Aitken's *Canada in Flanders* lauded Turner with descriptions such as: "All I can say is that no braver, better, truer man than General Turner, V.C., ever lived."[15] As Hodd discusses in his chapter in this volume, "Too Close to History," Aitken's intent was that *Canada in Flanders* be a reliable narrative—source material for future historians but not necessarily history. These works would not highlight high-command blunders unless the errors were blatant and had resulted in the officer's removal, so it is not surprising Turner was portrayed positively. Immediately after the war, accounts were either laudatory, triumphal commentary devoid of significant criticisms of leaders, or detailed regimental histories where battles of reputation were irrelevant. Authors would pass over failures like St. Eloi quickly, as in Harwood Steele's *Canadians in France*, or explain them away: "But the blame for these misfortunes cannot well be laid at anyone's door."[16] As a result, Turner's reputation matched and may have even surpassed Currie's in the immediate postwar period. Certainly in 1921, Currie believed "the clouds which had enshrouded his name" prevented his selection as president of the largest of the postwar veterans' groups.[17]

A conventional discourse shapes Turner's current reputation. Scholars acknowledge Turner's courage, but as Greenhous states, "Brave men do not necessarily make good generals,"[18] suggesting that Turner's bravery somehow detracted from his ability to command. Historians portray Turner as an incompetent field commander, whose failures at Second Ypres, St. Eloi Craters, and on the Somme were inexcusable.[19] Further, both Turner's promotion to command at the division level and his retention after St. Eloi were the result of blatant political meddling.[20] This conventional treatment characterizes Turner's appointment to command in England as a means of removing a politically powerful but incapable officer, after his failures at St. Eloi and the Somme.[21] It is also suggested that the commander of the Canadian Corps, Lieutenant-General Sir Julian Byng, played a crucial role in ridding the corps of this supposedly incompetent general. The evidence does not support this view, as Perley offered the post to Currie on Byng's recommendation.[22] When Currie refused the post, Turner was the logical choice.[23]

Scholars following the conventional narrative will grudgingly admit Turner performed well in command in England, but will credit the first minister of the OMFC, Sir George Perley, as the one most responsible for the success.[24] Desmond Morton, in *When Your Number's Up*, did observe correctly that Perley left Turner to make the military decisions.[25] While in England and after Currie had received command of the Canadian Corps in June 1917, historians tend to blame Turner for the disputes that periodically broke out between Currie and him.[26] Examination of Turner's command files, heretofore not reviewed, indicate the conflict with Currie was the inevitable outcome of institutional imperatives and Currie's challenging personality, and not the result of obstructionist jealousy by Turner. Turner demonstrated considerable forbearance in the face of Currie's prickly and unsympathetic behaviour.[27]

As Veysel Şimşek argues in his chapter in this volume, the standard Turkish Great War narrative ignores or discounts elements of the history that do not fit the conventional discourse; aspects of Turner's career are likewise overlooked. Missing from the conventional narrative is Turner's strong nationalism, manifested by his drive to Canadianize staff positions in the Canadian Corps, his advocacy for the Canadian Air Force, and his crucial role in the formation of what became the Royal Canadian Legion.[28] Also, absent is the respect his officers and men had for him during the war and immediately after.

Why are these specific aspects of Turner's career missing in the modern narrative? Three reasons can be posited: the metrics by which we assess leaders have changed in the last hundred years, Turner's affable temperament masked his incompetence and resulted in an unduly favourable opinion on the part of his officers and men, or later historians have ignored or overlooked this aspect of Turner's reputation. The modern conception of what makes a leader admirable has evolved from what held force in the early part of the twentieth century. Historians no longer hold leaders like Alexander the Great and Hernán Cortés in the same regard as they once did because of these evolving standards. In Turner's case, however, the values for which he was extolled—courage, competence, and approachability—are still respected for the most part today.

A second alternative was that Turner, like the commander portrayed in Sassoon's "The General," was popular but incompetent.

> "GOOD-MORNING; good-morning!" the General said
> When we met him last week on our way to the line.
> Now the soldiers he smiled at are most of 'em dead,
> And we're cursing his staff for incompetent swine.

"He's a cheery old card," grunted Harry to Jack
As they slogged up to Arras with rifle and pack.
.   .   .   .
But he did for them both by his plan of attack.[29]

The poem describes a "cheery old card" whose poor staff work and faulty planning result in the deaths of Harry and Jack, the two protagonists. Based on the evidence of diaries and letters, those best able to evaluate Turner, the soldiers and officers at the front, continued to respect him throughout the war. It was improbable that an affable but incompetent officer would continue to garner respect over the long term, especially in battle conditions. As David Englander writes, "Inefficiency and incompetence were not easily concealed from men who rapidly became keen judges of the officer performance."[30] Raw courage and popularity could not maintain a senior officer's reputation in the face of evident incompetence.

The most likely explanation is historians have missed or overlooked this aspect of Turner's character. With most of the focus on sources hostile to Turner, such as Currie's papers, and official documents, which do not expose this part of Turner's reputation, most scholars working on the First World War do not engage with evidence that highlights how Turner was viewed during the war. Further, historians easily dismiss the wartime works and regimental histories written between the wars as poor histories and not worthy of consideration. As a result, writers lose the memory of Turner's repute.

Turner's reputation, like Haig's, has suffered a steady deterioration since the immediate postwar period. Contrast this with the steady rise of Currie's stature, in part because of a better appreciation of Currie's accomplishments and contributions. In the 1920s, without detailed academic or official histories, the rumours of Currie's poor standing with the men of the Corps affected the narrative. During the war, Currie did not garner much affection from his troops and his troops did not regard him as a heroic leader.[31] Currie's victory at his libel trial in 1928 lifted the pall from his reputation and allowed both officers and rank-and-file to rally around him.[32] In 1928 Currie sued and won a libel suit against a Port Hope newspaper over accusations that Currie had unnecessarily ordered a costly attack on Mons on the last day of the war.

The major inflection point for Turner's reputation was the publication of the long-delayed first volume of Duguid's Canadian official history of the Great War.[33] Based on official documents and meticulous research,

Duguid placed veiled criticisms of Turner's conduct of the battle at Second Ypres in the text, while highlighting Currie's performance. Duguid did not believe the full story could be told while Turner was alive. Having served with the Canadian Corps, Duguid accepted wholeheartedly Currie's view of Turner as a bungler. The British official history volumes covering Turner's battles were published before the Canadian ones, and were circumspect in the treatment of all Canadian officers. J.E. Edmonds, the British Official Historian, was extremely critical of the Canadian documentation—the war diaries—related to the battle and believed them to be concoctions to mask serious errors made by Canadian commanders.[34] Edmonds's bias rankled Duguid and Canadian senior officers, and resulted in Edmonds producing three drafts before a version satisfied the Canadians. In this last draft, criticisms of Canadian officers are almost entirely absent.[35]

After a long hiatus, the dust settled from the Second World War, and with the fiftieth anniversary of the battles looming, historians returned to the First World War with a deluge of books. Identifying a hero to rally around, writers elevated Currie to his rightful place as the dominant Canadian leader in the First World War. However, in the process it was apparently necessary to break down Turner's reputation. These histories, such as Swettenham's *To Seize the Victory* and Goodspeed's *The Road Past Vimy*, focused on the operations of the Canadian Corps with an emphasis on the later part of the war.[36] They established the primary contours of the standard narrative of Currie as the superlative commander of the Canadian Corps at odds with the politicians and the incompetent political general Richard Turner. The tide against Turner was running so strong that even as enthusiastic a supporter during the war as D.E. Macintyre, quoted earlier, only mentions Turner in his book on Vimy in a perfunctory listing of attendees to the 1936 Vimy Pilgrimage.[37] In the wake of Duguid's failure to publish only a single volume of the projected eight, G.W.L. Nicholson's one-volume official history published in 1962 had to cover the entire Canadian war effort.[38] Nicholson had to be frugal with his coverage, and his treatment of Turner was neutral, while burying few criticisms in footnotes. Nicholson did not explicitly condemn Turner for his battlefield failings, but neither did he praise Turner's contributions in England.

With the opening of the British and Canadian First World War archival holdings, there was greater academic interest in delving deeper into the First World War, and another flood of books emerged, starting in the 1980s, which further established the emerging dominant narrative. Varying significantly in quality, these works again concentrated on the combat operations of the Canadian Corps.[39] The 1970s and especially the 1980s saw increased academic interest in Canadian Great War participation. Works such as Hyatt's biography of Hughes, Haycock's on Currie, Desmond Morton's multiple works, and Harris's on the Canadian staff provided broad coverage, and were based on under-utilized primary documentation to reveal aspects of the war previously hidden.[40] This trend culminated in Tim Cook's two award-winning books on the Canadian Corps, which covered not only the battles but also the experiences of the soldiers at the front and away from the battle.[41] Nevertheless, in all these works the standard narrative persisted to at least some degree.

Turner participated in four battles or campaigns, including Second Ypres, Festubert, St. Eloi Craters, and the Somme.[42] The only battle that has received book-length treatment is Second Ypres, which has a plethora, even a surplus, of books on the topic.[43] They vary greatly in value, tend to follow the same course, and reuse the same material. Greenfield's *Baptism of Fire* has the merit of injecting some of the German side of the battle into his account. These books are almost uniformly negative about Turner's performance, with only Iarocci adopting a more balanced tone. Cassar's *Hell in Flanders* illustrates this perspective with the comment, "Personally fearless, he was unsuited for command in the field."[44]

Turner's major failure as a division commander at St. Eloi Craters is the subject of a master's thesis by Thomas Leppard, articles by Cook and Copp, and a chapter by Campbell.[45] Other than Copp's article, historians condemn Turner's performance, with Desmond Morton portraying it as the "first and the worst Canadian setback of the war."[46] The view of the majority of historians writing on the battle is best exemplified by Dancocks: "The operation was ineptly conducted by the divisional commander, Major-General Richard Turner, who had done so poorly at Second Ypres as a brigadier."[47]

The Somme is a topic that appears never to lose its allure, and historians are still vigorously disputing the campaign in Britain. Despite the Somme being the first major engagement of the Canadian Corps, there are no monographs published on Canadian participation in the battle other than a short work by Christie.[48] All the standard Canadian Corps histories and one article by Campbell cover the battle. Campbell's "The Forgotten Victory" provides a rare, positive appraisal of Turner.[49]

Thomas Leppard is the de facto Turner authority, as he is the only one to have produced works focused on him, including a biographical article and a master's thesis on St. Eloi. In his article, Leppard makes the case that historians have treated Turner as a "peripheral figure," but "he deserves better."[50] Leppard returns repeatedly to the claim that Turner owed his success, including his early rise in the military, to political influence—to his being a Tory party hack. This is an example of how the standard narrative continues to shape Turner's reputation without evaluating its veracity. Turner's family was a strong supporter of the Liberal Party, and the available evidence indicates he was either politically neutral or leaned Liberal.[51] Even Sir George Perley, a former Conservative party whip, thought Turner was a Liberal.[52] Leppard also states that Turner never learned to command, but the article completely ignores his achievements at Courcelette, which in any account of Turner's life should receive equivalent coverage as his failure at St. Eloi. As a result, Leppard's works embody many of the core aspects of the standard narrative.

How can we reconcile the consistently positive image and reputation presented by letters and diaries written during the war and the postwar memoirs and regimental histories of officers and men who served under Turner, with the almost wholly negative view of Turner propagated by later historians? This discrepancy could have been the result of the memoirists and regimental historians pulling their punches out of fear of the considerable power that Duguid, the Canadian official historian, believed Turner still wielded. In addition, regimental historians' access to the official documents in the interwar period was predicated on not critiquing superior officers; as a result, these historians would avoid discussing officer failures.[53] For instance, the regimental history of the 15th Battalion delicately dealt with the issue of its commanding officer fleeing the battlefield at Second Ypres by describing him as collecting stragglers and stating that his return to Canada was because of a touch of gas.[54] As a result, it could be argued that more professional historians having full access to the documentary evidence can draw conclusions that are more informed and justly condemn Turner. It is highly improbable, however, that the admiration for Turner expressed in diaries, memoirs, and regimental histories was the result of fear or the avoidance of unpalatable truths. Consistently, Turner was one of the few senior officers mentioned in these works, and inevitably in a positive light. Were Turner as incompetent as claimed, it would have been apparent to his officers and men, who would have suffered because of his incapability.[55] In this case, there would be no need to mention Turner at all, because, while the regimental histories would not criticize superiors, there was no requirement that they should praise them either. As Tim Cook illustrates in his article "Literary Memorials," the histories were of varying quality, but historians should not dismiss them. Cook argues that these histories, once their limitations are understood, "give a special insight into their battalions otherwise unavailable."[56] As he points out, Fetherstonhaugh's history of the 13th Battalion won the prize for English history in 1926. These positive statements about Turner were spontaneous, and resulted from the deep and lasting imprint Turner made on his subordinates.

Why then did Turner's reputation falter? Six factors can be adduced to having contributed to his declining reputation. Like all standard narratives, this one is not wholly fallacious, as there are legitimate reasons to criticize Turner for his conduct and actions, but much of the criticism is exaggerated or incorrect. It is not that Turner made mistakes but that the focus is almost entirely on the failures, rather than both the successes and errors. Where the narrative fails is in seldom acknowledging Turner's strengths and contributions, other than Turner's courage, while focusing entirely on his failures.

Second, the prism of Currie's papers has conditioned much of the history focused at the senior command and political levels of the CEF. Currie presciently donated forty-four volumes of personal and official papers, letters, and a full diary that provide a rich level of detail. In addition, Currie's first biographer, H.M. Urquhart, circulated a questionnaire to Currie's subordinates, superiors, and associates, and their responses furnish another source of anecdote and information. The relatively abundant supply of Currie's thoughts, fears, and hopes has moulded the definition of the relationship between Currie, Turner, and the administration in England. It has also affected the perception of Turner, as Currie's negative views of Turner have dominated the discussion. Turner's meagre personal papers forced historians to rely on easily accessible official documents and unfriendly sources, and thus Turner's perspective on these issues was not examined.[57] As a result, historians have accepted Currie's view that he was at war with the authorities in England, and this assertion has gone effectively unchallenged other than in a few works like Morton's *A Peculiar Form of Politics*. Hodd's chapter in this volume discusses a similar situation in relation to Currie and his disputes with Aitken and Roberts regarding *Canada in Flanders*.

Third, Turner's battles with A.F. Duguid are well known and documented.[58] Turner feuded repeatedly with Duguid over Duguid's portrayal of the 3rd Brigade, and by extension Turner, in the Battle of Second Ypres. Turner's defence of his actions in the battle is dubious and at times obviously self-serving, such as the claim that the 3rd Brigade did the majority of the fighting in the battle. Thus, it has had to affect how historians consider Turner in his other actions.

Fourth, Canadian historiography on the Canadian Corps has more than a tinge of Whig history underlying it, unlike the unfavourable view of the war in the United States as described by Kimberly J. Lamay Licursi's chapter, in this volume, on state war histories. As Jonathan Vance put it, "Dominated by the successful defence of Ypres in 1915, the capture of Vimy Ridge in 1917, and the triumphant Hundred Days that preceded the Armistice of 1918, it gave short shrift to the failures and disappointments of the war."[59] The failure at St. Eloi disrupts and tarnishes the story of steady progress, and Turner is the ready scapegoat for the failure. The factors outside Turner's control are ignored or minimized, and are dismissed with the facile comment that a better general would have found a way to overcome these disadvantages.

The fifth factor is that Turner's close association with Sam Hughes, Garnet Hughes, Max Aitken, and other members of the Hughes faction has influenced historians' opinion of Turner. The interventions of Hughes and Beaverbrook were instrumental in his initial promotion and retention after St. Eloi, which suggests a strong tie to the Conservative party. In the twenty-first century, historians regard such overt political interventions in military appointments as corrupt and unacceptable, which influences the perception of Turner. Further, for the most part, other than Winter and Hyatt's biography and Cook's partial exculpation of Hughes in *The Madman and the Butcher*, historians treat Hughes most unfavourably.[60] Therefore, it is not difficult to see how this connection with the Hughes faction would taint Turner, as well.

Currie's reputation has followed a different trajectory, from being a butcher and "guts and gaiters" during and shortly after the war to his redemption at the 1928 Coburg libel trial.[61] He has since steadily risen in reputation and now stands quite legitimately as Canada's finest operational commander of the First World War. In fact, his statue is prominently located amongst the Valiants Memorial next to the National War Memorial in Ottawa. In order to build up a reputation, it is often useful to have a foil against whom the protagonist struggles. The primary antagonist for the first half of the war was the flawed minister of militia and defence, Sir Sam Hughes. With the resignation of Hughes in 1916, it was necessary to establish a new counterweight or foil, and Turner fits the role the best. To build up Currie's reputation, it helped to denigrate Turner's. An interesting example of this process was the disparagement of General Sir Archibald Murray, Field Marshal Edmund Allenby's predecessor in command in the Middle East during the First World War, in order to elevate Allenby's reputation.[62]

Three observations arise from this chapter that should be relevant to any historical evaluation of military reputation. First, it is necessary to appreciate contemporary recollections and not dismiss them as "blind loyalty," and to engage with these important sources in the narrative and analysis. Engagement with these sources must be balanced with an understanding of the limitations of the participants' knowledge. This does not mean that recollections are to be accepted uncritically, and may mean we arrive at a different conclusion based on the totality of evidence now available. We have the benefits of hindsight and perspective—we know how it ends. Ignoring the contemporary memory, however, means losing that "living in the moment experience," and this weakens the analysis and may lead to unbalanced judgments.

Historians often have to deal with the challenge of a lack of evidence from one participant or group in regard to an issue or event. There are practical constraints on how much time can be devoted to research or the information that is available, and as a result the analysis and narratives are necessarily constrained by limits on the perspectives we can integrate. It is therefore necessary to acknowledge the point of view adopted, and the limitations of the evidence, if the "other side of the hill" is not part of the analysis. The reader needs to be explicitly informed when the analysis is limited to one viewpoint, and as such is a preliminary finding subject to change.

The final issue is ascribing conflict wholly to personality without considering the institutional imperatives. Organizations, regardless of time, place, or sector, have their own set of imperatives that drive actors' behaviours. When these actors clash, it is often assumed that the underlying motivations are personal, when a significant factor may be different institutional agendas at play because of organizational differences in decision horizon, criteria, success metrics, reporting structure, and culture. Personalities can ameliorate or exacerbate the inherent conflict, but these tensions exist beyond the character of the actors. It is therefore critical to understand these underlying motive forces before ascribing blame entirely to the actors.

The strange case of Sir Richard Turner is an exemplary example of the consequences of a revision of reputation uninformed by the collected memory of his comrades, a key measure of his leadership qualities. Contemporary recollections can be fallible like all sources, but also provide an invaluable window into the views, attitudes, and atmosphere of the times, as well as a necessary perspective for a proper analysis. In Turner's case, ignoring his key leadership qualities defined by the regard of his officers and men has undermined his reputation.

NOTES

1. For a perspective on Turner and his competence, see William Stewart, "'Every Inch a Soldier': New Perspectives on the Military Career of a Controversial Canadian General, Sir Richard Turner" (Ph.D. diss., University of Birmingham, 2012).

2. Library and Archives Canada (hereafter LAC): RG24, vol. 1739, f. DHS 3–17 (vol. 1), Duguid to Edmonds, 18 May 1925. For an analysis of Turner's performance at Second Ypres, see Stewart, "'Every Inch a Soldier,'" 70–77.

3. Tim Cook, *At the Sharp End: Canadians Fighting the Great War, 1914–1916* (Toronto: Viking Canada, 2007), 190. For an analysis of how Turner conducted Festubert, see Stewart, "'Every Inch a Soldier,'" 77–79.

4. The conduct of St. Eloi is discussed in detail in Stewart, "'Every Inch a Soldier,'" 120–31.

5. LAC: RG9 III vol. 4957, War Diary GOCRA, June 1916, "Report on Operations of Artillery of Canadian Corps—June 2nd to June 14th 1916."

6. For more on Turner's performance on the Somme, see Stewart, "'Every Inch a Soldier,'" 159–88.

7. G.D. Sheffield, *Leadership in the Trenches: Officer-Man Relations, Morale, and Discipline in the British Army in the Era of the First World War* (New York: St. Martin's Press, 2000), 98; LAC: RG9 III vol. 4098, f. 42/1, Confidential Order, Chief of General Staff, GHQ to Second Army C.B. 888, 3 October 1915.

8. LAC: D.E. Macintyre Fonds, MG30 E241 vol. 1, Macintyre Diary, 26 November 1916.

9. Donald Fraser and Reginald H. Roy, *The Journal of Private Fraser, 1914–1918: Canadian Expeditionary Force* (Victoria: Sono Nis Press, 1985), 75.

10. Leslie M. Frost, Cecil Frost, and Rae Bruce Fleming, *The Wartime Letters of Leslie and Cecil Frost, 1915–1919* (Waterloo: Wilfrid Laurier University Press, 2007), 118.

11. LAC: Andrew Macphail Fonds, MG30 D150, vol. 4, diary, 17 August 1915.

12. R.C. Fetherstonhaugh, *The Royal Montreal Regiment: 14th Battalion, C.E.F. 1914–1925* (Gazette Printing, 1927); Kim Beattie, *48th Highlanders of Canada, 1891–1928* (Canada: The Highlanders, 1932).

13. R.C. Fetherstonhaugh, *The 24th Battalion, C.E.F., Victoria Rifles of Canada, 1914–1919* (Montreal: Gazette Print, 1930), 109.

14. Gary Sheffield, *The Chief: Douglas Haig and the British Army* (Aurum Press, 2011), 340.

15. John Allister Currie, *"The Red Watch"; with the First Canadian Division in Flanders* (London: Constable and Company, 1916), 95; Max Aitken [Lord Beaverbrook], *Canada in Flanders* (London: Hodder and Stoughton, 1916).

16. Harwood Steele, *Canadians in France, 1915–1918* (Toronto: Copp Clark, 1920); S.J. Duncan-Clark, W.R. Plewman, and W. Stewart Wallace, *Pictorial*

History of the Great War (John A. Hertel, 1919), 78. Harwood Steele was Sam Steele's son.

17. LAC: MG28 I298, vol. 73, R.B. Maxwell to Turner, undated [1921?].

18. Brereton Greenhous, *Canada and the Battle of Vimy Ridge, 9–12 April 1917* (Ottawa: Department of National Defence, Directorate of History, 1992), 27; George H. Cassar, *Hell in Flanders Fields: Canadians at the Second Battle of Ypres* (Toronto: Dundurn Press, 2010), 61.

19. Nathan M. Greenfield, *Baptism of Fire: The Second Battle of Ypres and the Forging of Canada, April 1915* (Toronto: HarperCollins Publishers, 2007), 197; C. Wesley Gustavson, "Missing the Boat? Colonel A.F. Duguid and the Canadian Official History of The First World War" (M.A. thesis, University of Calgary, 1999), 59; Robert Craig Brown, *Robert Laird Borden: A Biography*, vol. 2 (Toronto: Macmillan, 1980), 63; Daniel G. Dancocks, *Gallant Canadians: The Story of the Tenth Canadian Infantry Battalion, 1914–1919* (Calgary: Calgary Highlanders Regimental Funds Foundation, 1990), 81.

20. J.L. Granatstein, *Canada's Army: Waging War and Keeping the Peace* (Toronto: University of Toronto Press, 2002), 81; Daniel G. Dancocks, *Sir Arthur Currie: A Biography* (Toronto: Methuen, 1985), 60; Thomas P. Leppard, "Richard Turner and the Battle of St. Eloi" (M.A. thesis, University of Calgary, 1994), 11; Tim Cook, "Documenting War and Forging Reputations: Sir Max Aitken and the Canadian War Records Office in the First World War," *War in History* 10, no. 3 (2003): 278.

21. Patrick Brennan and Thomas Leppard, "How the Lessons Were Learned: Senior Commanders and the Moulding of the Canadian Corps after the Somme," in *Canadian Military History since the 17th Century: Proceedings of the Canadian Military History Conference, Ottawa, 5–9 May 2000*, ed. Yves Tremblay (Ottawa: Department of National Defence, Directorate of History and Heritage, 2001), 138; Cassar, *Hell in Flanders*, 321; Granatstein, *Canada's Army*, 86.

22. McGill University Archives: Urquhart Fonds, MG4027 C1, GHP Memorandum, 3.

23. For more on how Turner was selected, see Stewart, "'Every Inch a Soldier,'" 228–32.

24. Patrick Brennan, "Julian Byng and Leadership in the Canadian Corps," in *Vimy Ridge: A Canadian Reassessment*, ed. Geoffrey Hayes, Andrew Iarocci, and Mike Bechthold (Waterloo: Wilfrid Laurier University Press, 2007), 89; Dancocks, *Sir Arthur Currie*, 81; Desmond Morton, "Exerting Control: The Development of Canadian Authority over the Canadian Expeditionary Force, 1914–1919," in *Men at War*, ed. Timothy Travers and Christon Archer (Precedent, 1982), 12; A.M.J. Hyatt, *General Sir Arthur Currie: A Military Biography* (Toronto: University of Toronto Press, 1987), 62.

25. Desmond Morton, *When Your Number's Up: The Canadian Soldier in the First World War* (Toronto: Random House of Canada, 1993), 92.

26. George F.G. Stanley, *Canada's Soldiers: The Military History of an Unmilitary People*, 3rd ed. (Toronto: Macmillan, 1974), 312.

27. For a detailed examination of the sometimes contentious Turner–Currie relationship, see Stewart, "'Every Inch a Soldier,'" 290–340.

28. William Stewart, "'Every Inch a Soldier,'" 255–56, 371–79; William Stewart, "Missed Opportunity: Currie, Turner, and the Abortive Birth of the Canadian Air Force in the Great War," *Royal Canadian Air Force Journal* 1, no. 3 (2012).

29. Siegfried Sassoon, *Counter-Attack and Other Poems* (New York: E.P. Dutton, 1918).

30. David Englander, "Discipline and Morale in the British Army, 1917–1918," in *State, Society, and Mobilization in Europe During the First World War*, ed. John Horne (Cambridge: Cambridge University Press, 1997), 129.

31. Hyatt, *General Sir Arthur Currie*, 53; Tim Cook, *The Madman and the Butcher* (Toronto: Allen Lane, 2010), 210.

32. For details on the trial, see Cook, *The Madman and the Butcher*, 336–59; Robert Scott Demill, "The 1928 Coburg Libel Trial of Sir Arthur Currie and the Port Hope Evening Guide: The Rehabilitation of the Reputation of a Corps Commander" (M.A. thesis, University of Ottawa, 1989), Barbara M. Wilson, "The Road to the Coburg Court Room: New Material from the Archives of the Canadian War Museum on the Sir Arthur Currie–Sir Sam Hughes Dispute, 1918–19," *Canadian Military History* 10, no. 3 (2001).

33. A. Fortescue Duguid, *The Canadian Forces in the Great War 1914–1919*, vol. 1 (Ottawa: Ministry of National Defence, 1938).

34. LAC: RG24 vol. 1739, DHS 3–17 (vol 1), Edmonds to Duguid, 18 March 1925.

35. Tim Cook, *Clio's Warriors: Canadian Historians and the Writing of the World Wars* (Vancouver: UBC Press, 2006), 88; Timothy Travers, "Currie and 1st Canadian Division at Second Ypres—Controversy, Criticism and Official History," *Canadian Military History* 5, no. 2 (1996); Timothy Travers, "Allies in Conflict: The British and Canadian Official Historians and the Real Story of Second Ypres (1915)," *Journal of Contemporary History* 24 (1989).

36. John Alexander Swettenham, *To Seize the Victory: The Canadian Corps in The First World War* (Toronto: Ryerson Press, 1965); D.J. Goodspeed, *The Road Past Vimy: The Canadian Corps 1914–1918* (Toronto: General Paperbacks, 1969).

37. D.E. Macintyre, *Canada at Vimy* (Toronto: P. Martin Associates, 1967).

38. G.W.L. Nicholson, *Canadian Expeditionary Force, 1914–1919* (Ottawa: R. Duhamel, Queen's Printer, 1964).

39. René Chartrand, *Canadian Military Heritage*, vol. III (Ottawa: Department of National Defence, Directorate of History and Heritage, 2000); Bill Freeman and Richard Nielsen, *Far from Home: Canadians in the First World War* (Toronto: McGraw-Hill Ryerson, 1999); J.L. Granatstein, *Canada's Army*; J.L. Granatstein, *Canada and the Two World Wars* (Toronto: Key Porter Books, 2003); Norman Hillmer and J.L. Granatstein, *Empire to Umpire: Canada and*

the World to the 1990s (Toronto: Copp Clark Longman, 1994); J.K. Marteinson, *We Stand on Guard: An Illustrated History of the Canadian Army* (Montreal: Ovale Publications, 1992); Stanley, *Canada's Soldiers: The Military History of an Unmilitary People*.

40. Ronald Haycock, *Sam Hughes: The Public Career of a Controversial Canadian, 1885–1916* (Waterloo: Wilfrid Laurier University Press, 1986); Hyatt, *General Sir Arthur Currie*; Desmond Morton, *A Peculiar Kind of Politics* (Toronto: University of Toronto Press, 1982); Morton, *When Your Number's Up*; Stephen John Harris, *Canadian Brass: The Making of a Professional Army, 1860–1939* (Toronto: University of Toronto Press, 1988).

41. Cook, *At the Sharp End*; Tim Cook, *Shock Troops: Canadians Fighting the Great War, 1917–1918* (Toronto: Viking Canada, 2008).

42. The 2nd Division was attacked during Mount Sorrel, but the engagement and participation of the division was relatively minor.

43. *Germany's Western Front: Translations from the German Official History of the Great War, Volume II: 1915* (Waterloo: Wilfrid Laurier University Press, 2009); George Cassar, *Beyond Courage: The Canadians at the Second Battle of Ypres* (Oberon Press, 1985); Cassar, *Hell in Flanders*; Daniel G. Dancocks, *Welcome to Flanders Fields: The First Canadian Battle of the Great War: Ypres, 1915* (Toronto: McClelland and Stewart, 1989); John Dixon, *Magnificent but Not War: The Battle for Ypres, 1915* (Barnsley: Leo Cooper, 2003); Greenfield, *Baptism of Fire*; James L. McWilliams, *Gas!: The Battle for Ypres, 1915* (St. Catharines: Vanwell, 1985); Ulrich Trumpener, "The Road to Ypres: The Beginnings of Gas Warfare in The First World War," *Journal of Modern History* 47, no. 3 (1975); N.M. Christie, *The Canadians in the Second Battle of Ypres, April 22nd–26th, 1915: A Social History and Battlefield Tour*, rev. ed. (Ottawa: CEF Books, 2005).

44. Cassar, *Hell in Flanders*.

45. Tim Cook, "The Blind Leading the Blind—the Battle of the St. Eloi Craters," *Canadian Military History* 5, no. 2 (1996); Leppard, "Battle of St. Eloi"; David Campbell, "'A Leap in the Dark'—Intelligence and the Struggle for the St. Eloi Craters: Reassessing the Role of Major-General Richard Turner," *Great War Commands: Historical Perspectives on Canadian Army Leadership 1914–1918*, ed. Andrew B. Godefroy (Kingston: Canadian Defence Academy Press, 2010); Andrew B. Godefroy, "Engineer Operations at St. Eloi Craters," *Ubique!: Canadian Military Engineers: A Century of Service* 56 (1996); James Aylmer Lowthorpe Haldane, *A Soldier's Saga: The Autobiography of General Sir Aylmer Haldane* (Edinburgh: W. Blackwood, 1948); Terry Copp, "Slaughter at St. Eloi," *Legion Magazine* 55 (2004).

46. Morton, *A Peculiar Kind of Politics*, 72.

47. Dancocks, *Gallant Canadians*, 81.

48. N.M. Christie, *The Canadians on the Somme, September to November, 1916: A Social History and Battlefield Tour*, rev. ed. (Ottawa: CEF Books, 2007).

49. David Campbell, "A Forgotten Victory: Courcelette, 15 September 1916," *Canadian Military History* 16, no. 2 (2007).

50. Thomas P. Leppard, "The Dashing Subaltern—Sir Richard Turner in Retrospect," *Canadian Military History* 6, no. 2 (1997): 21.

51. Diana Bouchard, interview, 10 April 2012. For a more in-depth discussion of Turner's political affiliation, see Stewart, "'Every Inch a Soldier,'" 27–29.

52. LAC: Sir George Perley Fonds, MG27 II D12, vol. 4–7, f. 7/2, Perley to Borden, 22 November 1916.

53. For an excellent study on interwar regimental histories, see Tim Cook, "'Literary Memorials': The Great War Regimental Histories, 1919–1939," *Journal of the Canadian Historical Association / Revue de la Société historique du Canada* 13, no. 1 (2002): 179–84.

54. Beattie, *48th Highlanders*, 78, 84.

55. Englander, "Discipline and Morale in the British Army, 1917–1918," 129.

56. Cook, "'Literary Memorials,'" 178.

57. For the most part, historians have not reviewed the files of Turner's command in England. A query to LAC regarding the number of demands since 1993 for a selection of five volumes in the ministerial series and five more in Turner's command series, likely be of interest to historians, revealed that the Series A volumes were requested on average fourteen times since 1993, while only volume 806 in the Turner series had been viewed, and that just six times. LAC: RG 9 III A1 and B1 circulation statistics, 12 February 2011.

58. Cook, *Clio's Warriors*, 10; Gustavson, "Missing the Boat?"; Travers, "Allies in Conflict"; Travers, "Currie and 1st Canadian Division."

59. Jonathan F. Vance, *Death So Noble: Memory, Meaning, and the First World War* (Vancouver: UBC Press, 1997), 11.

60. Cook, *The Madman and the Butcher*; Charles F. Winter, *Lieutenant-General the Hon. Sir Sam Hughes, K.C.B., M.P., Canada's War Minister, 1911–1916: Recollections of Service as Military Secretary at Headquarters, Canadian Militia Prior to and During the Early Stages of the Great War* (Toronto: Macmillan, 1931).

61. Cook, *The Madman and the Butcher*, 261.

62. Matthew Dominic Hughes, "General Allenby and the Campaign of the Egyptian Expeditionary Force, June 1917–November 1919" (Ph.D. diss., King's College, 2000), 12.

SECTION TWO

REDISCOVERING AND REWRITING MEMORY

THE NAMES OF THE DEAD
"Shot at Dawn" and
the Politics of Remembrance

BETTE LONDON

When in February 2007 Private Harry Farr, executed for cowardice in October 1916, became the first of the newly pardoned shot-at-dawn soldiers to be officially recognized in a ceremony of remembrance, his ninety-three-year-old daughter, Gertrude ("Gertie") Harris, remarked, "I cannot believe that his name is now going to be remembered for future years, proving that he wasn't a coward but a very brave soldier."[1] At the ceremony in Wealdstone honouring Farr, a temporary plaque was unveiled bearing Farr's name and that of James Swaine, another executed soldier. The plaque had been added to the town's war memorial in anticipation of the permanent entering of the names later that year. This addition of names was one of many such ceremonies that followed the British government's announcement in August 2006 of its intention to seek posthumous pardons for some three hundred soldiers executed for desertion, cowardice, and other military offences during the First World War, but it was by no means the first such act of belated remembrance.[2] Over the preceding decade, in the wake of intensive lobbying by advocates for pardons, many local communities struggled with how to remember their own forgotten war dead, and many local memorials were "corrected." As early as June 1997, for example, the market town of Crook in County Durham voted to add the name of Lance Sergeant Joseph William Stones, shot for cowardice in 1917, to the roll of honour on the town's cenotaph—an occasion touted by the Shot at Dawn movement as its first formal victory and testimony to the popularity of a cause that had so quickly captured the public's imagination.

The soldiers shot at dawn were, of course, only a tiny percentage of the British war casualties. They were also only a fraction of the total number of soldiers sentenced to death by military tribunals; almost ninety percent of those who received the death penalty had their sentences commuted. Under military law, a number of offences carried capital penalties, but the vast majority of executions were for soldiers convicted of desertion.[3] In public perception, however, all of these soldiers tended to be branded cowards, regardless of the actual charges for which they were convicted. Apologists for the system have argued that the executions were necessary to maintain morale and discipline and that those actually executed tended to be the most egregious cases—serial offenders, men who deserted without even seeing action, men with long histories of disciplinary problems. The facts turn out to be more various. Many executed soldiers, for example, had otherwise unimpeachable records, and, in some cases, histories of long service. While some clearly fled in the face of the enemy, with no intention of ever returning to duty, others were found dazed and confused not far from the line of battle, or, after brief absences, returned voluntarily to their units. Desertion, indeed, covered a multitude of practices, with absences ranging from days and months to mere hours. Large numbers of the soldiers upon whom death sentences were executed claimed, in their defence, mental or physical incapacity. While today many of these men would be recognized as suffering from battle fatigue or PTSD, shell shock, as the condition was then designated, was imperfectly understood and unevenly diagnosed, its symptoms often not credited or recognized. With notable exceptions, the condition elicited little sympathy from military and medical authorities or from the general public.

By the 1990s, public sentiment on this issue had shifted dramatically, and Harry Farr could become a popular icon in part because of the compelling evidence in his case that he was suffering from shell shock. Indeed, as the most recognizable face of the pardons movement and the subject of a much-publicized independent lawsuit, Farr was the figure who garnered the most national attention, and the ceremony in his honour was the first to follow the official conferral of pardons in November 2006.[4] His daughter's remarks on this occasion point to the almost talismanic power accorded to the act of naming: to be named is to be remembered, and to be remembered is to have the stigma of execution lifted, to have the taint of cowardice rewritten as bravery. Her comments, moreover, underline the gap between private memory—where presumably the name has never been forgotten— and public remembrance. Hence the importance of not merely naming the dead, but inscribing the names in the public record and having these acts of inclusion publicly witnessed. But her comments also suggest that the presence of the name is itself an act of witnessing; remembrance will be achieved, the name implies, even when no one is left who can remember the individual, even perhaps if no one reads it.[5] At stake is the issue of posterity. As Daniel Sherman has argued in his study of commemorative monuments in France, "by virtue of their inscription the names constitute themselves as part of a signifying process that seeks to transcend memory and its limitations by assigning it, in its constructed 'collective' form, a historical role." The names "stake a community's claim to a place in history, representing its loss as its most essential link to the nation."[6] What does it mean, then, *not* to have one's name remembered, as was the case with the executed soldiers? And how are we to understand the belated acts of remembrance that have erupted in the last two decades, much of it fuelled by popular sentiment? As a site over which the dictates of memory would repeatedly be contested, the plight of the shot-at-dawn soldiers has served over the years as a barometer for changing attitudes to the administration of the war and to the understanding of the exorbitant sacrifice it exacted. As a limit case, this essay argues, the spectre of shot-at-dawn soldiers—in its wartime context and in its turn-of-the millennium resurrection—exposes the fault lines in the culture of remembrance, laying bare the contradictions that continue to underwrite the practices of commemoration.

The absence of names on memorials and books of remembrance was not merely an omission but an active act of erasure—an act, as it were of unremembrance. It produced an enforced anonymity in an era Thomas Laqueur has characterized as one of "commemorative hyper-nominalism"—a time when "the state poured enormous human, financial, administrative, artistic, and diplomatic resources into preserving and remembering the names of individual common soldiers."[7] This anonymity, moreover, carried through to the late twentieth century. As Anthony Babington, the first author to be granted access to the sealed court martial records, noted of these soldiers in 1983, "They are the unremembered"—a position he both confirms and corrects in his own decision, out of deference to the soldiers' families, not to name them, even as he recounts their histories in *For the Sake of Example*: "They are the central figures in this grim story but throughout the following pages they must remain anonymous."[8] On the home front, this anonymity had surrounded the soldiers from the time of their trials, and it was enforced by the government's decision in 1919 to seal the court martial records for a hundred years—scaled back to seventy-five after the "leaking" of the names in Julian Putkowski and Julian Sykes's *Shot at Dawn* (1989) rendered further secrecy superfluous. Even Ernest Thurtle, MP for Shoreditch, who championed the executed soldiers throughout the 1920s in his campaign to abolish the death penalty for wartime military offences, deliberately suppressed the names of the "unfortunate victims" when he published his exposé, *Shootings at Dawn*, in 1929.[9]

In the immediate postwar context, the anonymity of the executed soldiers takes on particular significance because it stands in stark contrast to what Laqueur has called "a new era of remembrance"—"the era of the common soldier's name or its self-conscious and sacralized oblivion."[10] "The First World War, in short," he has argued, "witnessed the most dramatic explosion of names on a landscape in world history."[11] In the official structures of mourning, moreover, names took on an almost sacred aura—so much so that name-bearing plaques were sometimes buried in consecrated ground when in the course of time a memorial site came to be demolished.[12] "Their Name Liveth For Evermore," Kipling's choice of inscription for Lutyens's Stone of Remembrance, became a grieving nation's mantra—the afterlife of the name, as it proliferated on local monuments, a testimony to and consolation for the life sacrificed. For the soldiers shot at dawn, however, the only place their name would appear to live was in the overseas military cemeteries, where they were afforded the same burial rites as other soldiers.[13]

Back at home, however, far from living for evermore, the names of these fallen soldiers were systematically wiped out, as if they never existed. They were not, for the most part, included on local war memorials or in books of remembrance in villages, townships, parish churches, schools, and workplaces.[14] They were not included in national monuments, such as the Canadian Book of Remembrance in the Peace Tower on Ottawa's Parliament Hill, or the Scottish National War Memorial at Castle Rock, Edinburgh. Although their families were informed of their deaths at the time of their occurrence, their names were excluded from official casualty lists, and their deaths, by and large, went unrecorded in regimental histories. After the war, when the army compiled its comprehensive list of men who died in active service, *Soldiers Died in the Great War, 1914–1919*, published between 1920 and 1921 in eighty parts, the names of the executed soldiers did not appear.[15] These men were casualties of war, then, but not named as such. The consequences of this namelessness were far-reaching. The soldiers' deaths were not commemorated in the local press, nor were *in memoriam* notices published. Indeed, if a death was publicly noted, it was almost always a sign that the circumstances of the death had not been disclosed. Arguing late in the war against a proposal to spare the families knowledge of their relative's execution, Lord Derby, secretary of state for war, went so far as to suggest "that such a deception in the past had resulted in the production of memorial cards, and other such methods of marking the honourable passing of a loved one"—practices he clearly deemed inappropriate in these cases.[16] Death plaques and memorial certificates were not offered to the families of executed soldiers, and medals they had earned were forfeited, although this was not the case for soldiers convicted of identical crimes whose death sentences were subsequently commuted.[17] On a private level, then, families were left without tokens and keepsakes to display as testimony to their loss and evidence of a loved one's service; and they were left without a place to go—a name to visit on a local monument— where their loss could be acknowledged publicly. They were left, in other words, without "sites to which memory could attach itself."[18] This state of oblivion also had more material consequences: the monthly service allowance a soldier's family received was suspended, and widows of executed soldiers were routinely denied pensions and child support benefits.[19] Given that all but three of the executed soldiers were privates or non-commissioned officers, the financial impact was dramatic, a pension often being all that kept a family from abject poverty.

These soldiers thus could be seen as the ultimate version of "the missing," but unlike those remembered on the Menin Gate, these were soldiers to whom the fortune of war denied not "the known and honoured *burial* given to their comrades in death," but the known and honoured *remembrance*.[20] Pushed to the logical extreme, for a culture that equated death and remembrance, one might argue, if these men are not remembered, they are not dead; they do not belong, as the *Daily Mail* intimated in its account of Harry Farr's reinstatement, to the ranks of war casualties, "Soldiers Shot at Dawn Finally Join the Ranks of the Fallen."[21] If the case of the shot-at-dawn soldiers has been difficult to put to rest, then, it may well be because the dead still occupy some limbo. Indeed, the ambiguities surrounding the executed soldiers' deaths have rendered the deaths themselves ambiguous and the dead soldiers ghostly, accounting in part for the way their stories have haunted the British imagination.[22] As Andrew Mackinlay noted, in urging the case for pardons to the House of Commons in October 1993, "The demand for this remedy is like a cry from the grave."[23]

Significantly, the last phase of the pardons campaign reached its culmination at the moment when the last Great War veterans were dying. As

John Reid noted in 1998, when he offered, in lieu of actual pardons, to add these soldiers' names to war memorials and rolls of honour, "There remain only a very few of our fellow countrymen who have any real understanding or memory of life and death in the trenches and on the battlefields of the first world war."[24] There were few, in other words, in a position to understand or judge what these soldiers went through. Whether those few would approve or disapprove of recognition for the executed soldiers—and, over the years, the presumed response of the Great War veterans has been passionately invoked by both sides of the controversy—remembrance, it would appear, could be achieved only in the absence of living memory. Indeed, not only were those veterans dying off, so were the wives and children (and nieces and nephews) of the executed men, lending a certain urgency to the inscription ceremonies.

In the media coverage of the Shot at Dawn movement, these living relatives have figured prominently. When Sykes and Putkowski first published *Shot at Dawn* in 1989, the decision to name names was attended by a certain amount of controversy, as the book stood to be the first intimation some family members would receive of a relative's execution. In the event, the book—and the formal Shot at Dawn campaign, founded by John Hipkin in 1990, that followed close upon it—prompted many relatives of executed soldiers to go public with their stories, breaking a silence in which their own families had often collaborated. The disclosure of names, in fact, unleashed not only a flood of stories about forgotten soldiers but also an outpouring of testimonials from the executed men's relatives and descendants, attesting to lives derailed by shame and outrage, and exposing what Michèle Barrett has called "the personal and human consequences of war."[25] And the public proved as hungry for these stories of continuing family trauma as for the soldiers' stories of battle fatigue and fatal lapses. The youthful faces of long-forgotten soldiers, then, captured in faded photographs reproduced in the media's "shot at dawn" stories were regularly accompanied by videos and photographic images of the aging faces and bodies of the executed soldiers' present-day advocates. The parade of images of Gertrude Harris—eighty-seven and wheelchair-bound, participating for the first time in a wreath-laying ceremony at the Cenotaph in November 2000; ninety-one and accompanied by her daughter, standing outside the High Court where a request to seek a conditional pardon for Harry Farr had been filed; ninety-three and flanked by children, grandchildren, and great-grandchildren at the ceremony honoring her father in Wealdstone in February 2007—stands as a visible reminder of the years that have elapsed since such gestures would have been timely. Few remain, in fact, who can claim such close descent to an executed soldier, and the relatives taking up the cause, themselves no longer young, most frequently belong to the next generation, typically great-nieces and great-nephews of childless soldiers or more distant cousins. Their presence at memorial ceremonies speaks to the years this solace was denied them, and it invokes the mourners *not* there beside them—the executed men's widows, sweethearts, siblings, friends, and children.

For the rest of the nation, there would most likely have been a long history of communal remembrance, much of it centred on the village or township where the family resided. In his study of British First World War memorials, Derek Boorman recounts the experience of a woman who, like Gertrude Harris, lost a father to the war when she was a young child; the story is instructive for its contrast to Harris's experience and that of other relatives of shot-at-dawn soldiers: "Mrs. Hilda Jones (née Coombes), now approaching 80, can remember her father's name being engraved on the war memorial at Shipton-under-Whychwood in Oxfordshire. She sat by the stone-mason's side, proud of the engraved name but barely realising the full implication of what was happening ... Hilda and another little girl whose father had died in the war, unveiled the memorial when the ceremony was held in 1921."[26] Such participation by children was not unusual. As Catherine Moriarty has demonstrated, "The young, whose memories would be most easily impressed and whose loss was possibly the most inexplicable," were often the focus of memorial ceremonies, with "[m]edal-bedecked children who had lost their fathers" a common choice to perform the unveilings.[27] For Gertrude Harris, in her eighties and into her nineties, there was no such memory for her to claim. And the little girl who was three years old when her father was shot was a woman of eighty-seven when she was invited to unveil the statue of Herbert Burden at the Shot at Dawn Memorial at the National Arboretum in June 2001. It would be another five and a half years before she would finally see her own father's name engraved on a memorial plaque on a local war memorial. As with other "shot at dawn" families, then, the loss of a father, son, husband, or brother was compounded by the loss of the memory of his memorialization. If, as Moriarty has argued, these memorial services functioned to sanctify personal loss, transforming private sorrow into civic pride, this transformation could not be accomplished for mourners like Harris; indeed, like Harris, many of the aggrieved did not learn of the circumstances of their relative's death until well into adulthood, and private grief, like public remembrance, could only be fully experienced belatedly.[28] Tom Stones, for example, was fifty-five in 1996, when he first learned of his great-uncle's existence and of the circumstances of his death—all mention of Joseph "Willie" Stones having been systematic-ally expunged from his family's records. As he explained in November 2000, when families of executed soldiers were first allowed to join the annual Cenotaph ceremony, "This is the first time any of these families have been able to honour their relatives with the rest of the nation."[29]

Stones did not live to see his great-uncle pardoned, and Gertrude Harris was too ill in November 2006 to attend the first Cenotaph ceremony following the institution of pardons; as her daughter explained, however, "The engraving ceremony is what she is really looking forward to so hope-fully it will spur her on to get better."[30] In this respect, Hilda Jones's story is also instructive for the emphasis it puts on the materiality of inscription—what it means to see the name of a loved one actually being etched by the stonemason. Maya Lin, who credits Great War memorials as one of the inspirations for her Vietnam War Memorial, makes a similar observation about the other monument that inspired her: "Any undergraduate who was at Yale when I started there in 1977–78 saw one or two men always etching out the names of the alumni from Yale or of the Yale students who had been killed in Vietnam. As you walked through the hall to and from classes, you'd register that there were these two men etching in the names. And you'd unconsciously register the time it was taking to etch in each name, and the time somebody had lost. It was always *there*. It was ever-present." As Lin elaborates, this inscribing of names has a visceral element: "Also, you couldn't *not* touch the names."[31] These comments help to explain why the adding of names to memorial sites has acquired so much symbolic force in the Shot at Dawn campaign, and why for so many the pardons would not be complete without an act of inscription to follow. For just as John Reid's 1998 compromise that stopped short of pardoning the victims was deemed insufficient, the granting of pardons without the adding of names to public monuments and documents was judged to be similarly inadequate. In the months and years following the government's historic decision, then, the question of how and where to name these dead continued to be fought out in local venues. In Shoreham, for example, where a contentious struggle in 1999–2000 ended with Thomas Highgate, the first British soldier to be shot at dawn, being denied a place on the town memorial, the situation remains unresolved today, despite the continuing and vociferous efforts of his great nephew, Terence Highgate, and despite the fact that when the ori-ginal memorial plaque was replaced in 2000, a space was left for Highgate's

television drama starring Daniel Day-Lewis, and later, after being adopted in the Irish secondary school curriculum, adapted for the stage by Alan Stanford for the Second Age Theatre Company (2005). Other notable treatments included Reginald Hill's *The Wood Beyond* (1997), part of his popular Dalziel and Pasco detective series, adapted the following year for Season 3 of the BBC television series. Elsewhere, "shot at dawn" characters figured prominently in genre fiction and young adult literature, but also, at least episodically, in almost all of the imaginative work written about the First World War, so much so that when Cathryn Corns and John Hughes-Wilson published *Blindfold and Alone* in 2001, they could lament, "Every modern author or screenplay about the Great War appears to feel the need [to] include an obligatory execution scene in the interests of dramatic licence."[45]

No single work, however, reached as far into the culture as Michael Morpurgo's *Private Peaceful*. Constructed as a monologue produced over a long night's vigil, the novel tells the story of a young soldier on the eve of what is eventually revealed to be his brother's execution, his prior life revealed in a set of vivid flashbacks. The 2003 novel, marketed for children ten years and up, was the first work Morpurgo published after being named Children's Laureate, and it quickly became something of a sensation, garnering enthusiastic reviews and coveted prizes, and enjoying a parallel life as a hugely successful stage drama.[46] In the stage adaptation, the narrator himself turns out to be the soldier about to be executed. *Private Peaceful* proved successful as a crossover commodity, appealing to adults and children. First performed in August 2004 at the Bristol Old Vic, the play enjoyed sellouts at the Edinburgh Festival Fringe and London's West End, with a UK tour in 2005 and a second London stint in 2006. It had also been performed, in collaboration with the *a capella* group Coope, Boyes and Simpson, as *Private Peaceful: The Concert*, and in June 2006 was released as a CD. By the time the government reached its decision about pardons, then, *Private Peaceful* had become a familiar icon for the shot-at-dawn soldier—highly sympathetic and thoroughly respectable. Indeed, *Private Peaceful* was already becoming entrenched in the English school curriculum, required reading in many classrooms.

Morpurgo, who was driven to write the novel after a journey to Ypres in which he visited execution sites and viewed the cells in Poperinghe, where the condemned prisoners spent their last hours, happened upon the grave of a Private Peaceful in a military cemetery and knew he had found the name for his title character.[47] The character he created, however, was entirely imaginary. Morpurgo himself described the real Private Peaceful, who was not shot at dawn, as the true Unknown Soldier, and in adopting the name for his creation transformed *his* Private Peaceful into a kind of First World War Everyman, the ultimate figure of sacrifice. Presenting Private Peaceful in a manner calculated to evoke empathetic identification, Morpurgo lifted the figure of the shot-at-dawn soldier out of the messiness of history, making it safe for consumption by audiences of all ages. The success of *Private Peaceful*, in all its manifestations, might be seen as symptomatic of a broader shift in public perception. Fueled by a barrage of media representations over several decades, the dominant view of the war in the public arena had become one of a war of futility—an unmitigated tragedy whose victims were, above all, the common soldiers senselessly slaughtered by inept and unfeeling generals. These perceptions were heightened by a surge in battlefield tourism, where the sheer scale of loss was visibly imprinted on the visitor and where execution sites and graves of shot-at-dawn soldiers had become regular features of the itinerary. In this climate, the shot-at-dawn soldier could become the ultimate figure for the horrors of the war—the stand-in for all the war's victims.

When in June 2006, then, one of the relatives of an executed soldier told a reporter, "There should be a statue in London of the soldiers who were shot at dawn rather than the one of General Haig," the comment was not entirely fanciful.[48] Eight years earlier, as the eightieth anniversary of the Armistice was approaching, *The Express* ran a cover story, "Why Do We Let This Man Cast a Shadow Over Our War Dead?," calling for the statue of Field Marshal Haig in London to be dismantled and replaced by a memorial to "one of the ordinary soldiers whose lives were lost in that great conflict … not of the general who, often needlessly, dispatched them to their deaths." In a follow-up story, the *Express* noted the chorus of voices joining the protest, including Julian Putkowski, who commented, "I would like to see the statue melted down and the metal used to mint medals for the families of those executed as deserters and mutineers, even though they were shell-shocked and burnt out."[49] Both stories circulated on the Shot at Dawn website. If in 2006 the moment was ripe for the government to take action, it was in part because the rhetoric of the pardons campaign had so successfully infiltrated public consciousness as to make such a reversal thinkable. As early as 1993, Andrew Mackinlay, the MP for Thurrock who spearheaded the pardons campaign in Parliament, was announcing "overwhelming public support for it." "[W]e now know," he proclaimed, "that, in a sense, the soldiers have already been pardoned by the highest court in the land—British public opinion."[50] It was a statement he would repeat over the years with increasing evidence to back him. By the end of the campaign, so effectively had a single narrative come to dominate the public discourse on the subject that when Haig's son rose to defend his father's role in authorizing the executions, offering his demurral from the general enthusiasm for the impending pardons—"many were rogues, persistent deserters and criminals, or they were guilty of cowardice. They had to be made an example of"[51] —his rhetoric sounded distinctly outdated, even churlish. For much of the rest of the public, by contrast, the shot-at-dawn soldier had been effectively evacuated of controversy. The once scandalous figure of the coward or deserter—a person no one talked about—had become a household name, had become in fact Private Peaceful. If it was in this context that the executed soldiers could be pardoned, it was also on these terms that they could now be named—named because they had become effectively nameless.

If the belated naming of the dead on war memorials marked a certain end to the legacy of shame and silence, the resolution, then, was not without its ironies. For one thing, when new names were added to memorials and books of remembrance, their addition was far from seamless: the names appear out of order, often with obvious discrepancies in the size or style of the lettering, differences in materials, and an absence of weathering. They thus testify to the fact that their presence is an afterthought, reminding us that they were once missing and that an exclusion of so many years cannot simply be repaired by the stroke of a chisel. There is, in addition, a certain irony to winning this specific form of recognition at a time when, in many instances, the names on public monuments were becoming no more than that: names without faces or stories attached to them. Many local memorials were suffering from neglect and disrepair, the brass in need of polishing or the stone so weathered as to render the inscriptions nearly illegible.[52] When Shoreham first debated adding Highgate's name to its memorial, it was because the plaque had become so worn as to require replacement. Village memorials, moreover, were no longer the hub of community life or the site of collective mourning as they were in the 1920s, when the unveiling of war memorials was a nearly daily occurrence. The spectacle of towns adding names to monuments, with their accompanying unveiling ceremonies, now appears distinctly anachronistic.

In recalling these earlier times, however, the "shot at dawn" cases, with their long contentious history, recall the forgotten histories of the monuments they modify, reminding us that the existing monuments were themselves the product of often fierce debate, persistent negotiation, and hard-won compromise over competing understandings of remembrance.[53] The absences their names repair, then, speak to other absences—some accidental omissions corrected in the past, others the results of deliberate decisions.[54] They thus invite interrogation into the other war dead excluded, or unevenly represented, on existing monuments—nurses, VADs, munitions workers, colonial soldiers and labourers, conscientious objectors—and other casualties such as Barrett highlights, "survivors" of the war who disappeared into another kind of oblivion.[55] In *The Missing of the Somme*, Geoff Dyer observes, "By the mid-thirties the public construction of memory was complete. Since then only a few memorials have been built: addenda to the text of memory."[56] As self-conscious addenda to this text, the "shot at dawn" inscriptions, and the campaign that preceded them, call into question the project's completeness. As belated acts of remembrance, moreover, they expose the paradoxes they share with the larger memorial project in which they participate.

Against the enforced anonymity of official erasure, to insist on a shot-at-dawn soldier being named, as their advocates demanded, is to insist on the fact that the life in question had meaning. At the same time, to do so is to choose for that soldier an alternative anonymity: to become merely one of the nameless names, to become just like all the others. It is the absence of a name, as the "shot at dawn" controversies remind us, that requires a narrative. To be included, to have one's name recorded, is no longer to be a name with a story attached to it. The plight of the executed soldiers has been marked by prohibitions on naming, remembering, and honouring, by the prohibition on telling men's "shot at dawn" stories; it is against this context that the breaking of the silence achieves its full meaning, and that the naming becomes an event in its own right, independent of what the name signifies. To a large extent, in the immediate postwar context these soldiers were "remembered" only when their stories were not known or deliberately repressed, as on the gravestones in the military cemeteries. The Shot at Dawn Pardons Campaign, launched in 1990, worked to put these names in the public consciousness, with its almost compulsive retelling of the men's stories; retelling their "offences," it refused the shame attached to them, insisting that these men be known not in spite of the circumstances of their deaths but because of them. So successful was this publicity effort that for a brief period the names at the centre of the campaign became among the best known of the war's casualties: Harry Farr, for example, celebrated for being "Shell Shocked and Shot," was the subject of folk ballads, the inspiration for amateur poetics, and the one-time "owner" of a MySpace page.[57] Redacted in the tabloid press, circulated on the Internet, and broadcast on radio and television documentaries, the stories of shot-at-dawn soldiers passed into common parlance. There is perhaps a final irony: if the granting of pardons and the restoring of names to memorials and books of remembrance does indeed bring closure to this contentious subject, it may well be that what remembrance has earned these soldiers is the right to be forgotten, in effect, to have their names inscribed without "Shot at Dawn" beside it.

NOTES

1. "Recognition at Last for Pardoned Soldiers," *Northern Echo*, 19 February 2007.
2. Parliament approved the conditional pardons on 6 November 2006 with section 359 of the Armed Forces Act, which came into effect on royal assent on 8 November 2006. The exact number of cases covered in the Act was not specified in the legislation; the government indicated that the pardons would apply to soldiers in the Indian Army not included in publicly available statistics of British wartime executions. The figures most generally used in discussions of the executions indicate a total of 346 executions, forty of which were for murder and not included in the pardons. For discrepancies in the records, see Gerard Oram, *Military Executions during World War I* (Houndmills: Palgrave Macmillan, 2003), 3.
3. Corns and Hughes-Wilson list the breakdown of executions by charge as follows: Mutiny (3); Desertion (266); Cowardice (18); Disobedience of a lawful order (5); Sleeping at post (2); Striking a superior officer (6); Casting away arms (2); Quitting post (7); Murder (37). Cathryn Corns and John Hughes-Wilson, *Blindfold and Alone: British Military Executions in the Great War* (London: Cassell, 2001), 103–4.
4. Even many of those generally critical of the pardons movement have acknowledged that Farr's case might be a convincing instance of injustice. When Des Browne announced the government's decision to seek pardons, there was some speculation that he was prompted by concern that the High Court was about to decide in Farr's favour and that this could unleash a spate of requests to hear other individual cases. In the event, Farr's pardon was folded into the blanket decision.
5. In *At the Going Down of the Sun: British First World War Memorials* (York: William Sessions, 1988), Derek Boorman records numerous instances of rolls of honour being inserted into caskets, sealed, and buried in the foundations of monuments.
6. Daniel J. Sherman, "Art, Commerce, and the Production of Memory in France after World War I," in *Commemorations: The Politics of National Identity*, ed. John R. Gillis (Princeton: Princeton University Press, 1994), 207.

7. Thomas Laqueur, "Memory and Naming in the Great War," in *Commemorations*, 160, 155.

8. Anthony Babington, *For the Sake of Example: Capital Courts-Martial, 1914–1920* (New York: St. Martin's Press, 1983), xi, xii. Although Babington highlights his own concern for the families as his primary reason for suppressing the names, several sources suggest that Babington was allowed access to the files on the condition that the soldiers remained anonymous.

9. Ernest Thurtle, *Shootings at Dawn: The Army Death Penalty at Work* (London: Victoria House Printing, 1929), 3.

10. Laqueur, "Memory and Naming in the Great War," 152.

11. Thomas Laqueur, in "Grounds for Remembering," *Doreen B. Townsend Center Occasional Papers* 3 (1995), 1.

12. The Church of the Transfiguration in Albert Avenue, Hull, for example, when it was slated for demolition, removed several brass plaques to individual soldiers and offered them to near relatives. Boorman notes, "Any unclaimed plaques would be buried in consecrated ground." Boorman, *At the Going Down of the Sun*, 5.

13. In 1922, the Imperial War Graves Commission announced that it had decided to erect "headstones, of the usual pattern, over their graves without any reference to the manner of their death, or if their graves are not known, to commemorate them in the same way as other officers and men whose graves are unrecorded." Quoted in Corns and Hughes-Wilson, *Blindfold and Alone*, 259.

14. There are significant exceptions, although it is not always clear when names do appear on memorials and rolls of honour whether the local community, or even the family, was aware of the circumstances of the death. In a few instances, the question was openly debated, as in the case of a deserter's inclusion on a parish roll of honour in Newport, South Wales in 1921. Robert Lortimer, one of the architects of the Imperial War Graves Commission, records the incident in a letter: "The ex-servicemen have created a disturbance and wish to insist on this man's name going on otherwise they say they will wreck the memorial. On the other hand a number of parents whose sons have been killed say that if this man's name goes on the memorial they will not permit their sons' names to go on—so there you are, a fine kettle of fish you will agree!" CWGC Archives, Item WG1606, quoted in Sonia Batten, "Exploring a Language of Grief in First World War Headstone Inscriptions," in *Contested Objects: Material Memories of the Great War*, ed. Nicholas J. Saunders and Paul Cornish (London: Routledge, 2009), 166–67.

15. Putkowski and Sykes note that fourteen of the men executed by firing squad appear in *Soldiers Died in the Great War*, "with two regiments listing all men who were executed, suggesting that some regiments were either unaware of the exclusion directive, or that they preferred to ignore its existence." Julian

Putkowski and Julian Sykes, *Shot at Dawn: Executions in World War One by authority of the British Army Act* (London: Leo Cooper, 1992), 26. *The British Jewry Book of Honour*, rev. ed. (1922), also records the names of all the executed Jewish soldiers.

16. War Cabinet Meeting no. 279, 21 November 1917 (WO32/4675). Lord Derby's response of 7 January 1918 paraphrased in Putkowski and Sykes, *Shot at Dawn*, 224.

17. In Canada, relatives did receive memorial plaques. In New Zealand in 2005, war medals, certificates, and medallions were distributed to the families of the five executed soldiers formally pardoned in 2000.

18. Catherine Moriarty, "Private Grief and Public Remembrance," in *War and Memory in the Twentieth Century*, ed. Martin Evans and Kenneth Lunn (Oxford: Berg, 1997), 126.

19. The question of pensions for an executed soldier's dependents was the subject of considerable debate and controversy, and remained an unresolved issue for much of the war. The policy, moreover, was not consistently implemented.

20. At the Menin Gate Memorial to the Missing, the inscription reads: "Here are recorded names of officers and men who fell in Ypres Salient but to whom the fortune of war denied the known and honoured burial given to their comrades in death." The words were written by Rudyard Kipling.

21. *Daily Mail*, 18 February 2007. As Michèle Barrett points out, the converse was also true—with devastating effects for some ex-soldiers: if one isn't dead, one can't be remembered. Thus she notes, "Had these men died, they would have been commemorated, as individuals, by name, on one of the memorials on the western front or at Gallipoli." Michèle Barrett, *Casualty Figures: How Five Men Survived the First World War* (London: Verso, 2007), 156.

22. The official records for these deaths were rife with inconsistencies, with different causes of death frequently recorded on different documents for the same individual. These notations ranged from the bluntly factual "Executed by firing squad," to the charitably deceptive "Died in action," to the more waffling "Died of wounds" or "Died at service," to, finally, the starkly uncompromising "Died." While specific rules governed these usages, actual practice was far from consistent.

23. Hansard, HC Deb, 19 October 1993, vol. 230, c160.

24. Hansard, HC Deb, 24 July 1998, vol. 316, c1374. Reid acknowledged that, "In a sense, those who were executed were as much victims of the war as the soldiers and airmen who were killed in action," and he called on the Members of Parliament "to join [him] in recognising those who were executed for what they were—the victims, with millions of others, of a cataclysmic and ghastly war." He went on to express the "hope that others outside the House will recognise all that, and that they will consider allowing the missing names to be added to books of remembrance and war memorials throughout the land."

25. Barrett, *Casualty Figures*, 158.

26. Boorman, *At the Going Down of the Sun*, 52.

27. Moriarty, "Private Grief," 135, 136.

28. Gertrude Harris was forty when she learned the circumstances of her father's death, and she kept the secret for another forty years before sharing it with her children. Although Harris maintains that her mother never believed in her husband's cowardice, the rest of his family disowned him, and shame kept her silent.

29. *The Northern Echo*, 11 November 2000. Beginning in 1998, Shot at Dawn families were allowed to participate in a separate remembrance ceremony on the Saturday before Remembrance Day. In 2000, they were allowed to participate in the regular Cenotaph march-past ceremony, along with other "civilians" who were included for the first time: members of the Army Pigeon Service, entertainers, and merchant mariners. One condition of their marching imposed on them by the Royal British Legion was that they change the name of their campaign from Shot at Dawn to First World War Pardon Association. It was not until 2003 that they were permitted to march under the "Shot at Dawn" banner. Tom Stones died in April 2001 at the age of sixty.

30. *The Northern Echo*, 26 December 2006.

31. Maya Lin, in "Grounds for Remembering," *Doreen B. Townsend Center Occasional Papers* 3 (1995), 8.

32. "Shot at Dawn, Pardoned 90 Years On," BBC News Online, 16 August 2006, http://news.bbc.co.uk/2/hi/uk_news/england/4798025.stm. The decision in Shoreham was especially controversial since, in a referendum conducted in 2000, a majority of the citizens had voted to include Highgate on the monument. Their voice was overruled because of objections from the British Legion, which continues to block emendation of the monument. Highgate, whose family left Shoreham soon after his birth, is memorialized on a monument in Sidcup, along with his two brothers who also died in the war.

33. Catherine Moriarty, "'The Returned Soldiers' Bug': Making the Shrine of Remembrance, Melbourne," in *Contested Objects*, ed. Saunders and Cornish, 156.

34. Hansard, HC Deb, 3 March 2009, c820–830. After learning of the omission, Iddon campaigned to press the authorities in Bolton to add Smith's name to their book of remembrance, and was able to announce at the debate an imminent positive decision (c823).

35. Thomas Laqueur, in "Grounds for Remembering," 5.

36. For an interesting discussion of some of these issues, see Jonathan Black, "'Thanks for the Memory': War memorials, spectatorship and the trajectories of commemoration 1919–2000," in *Matters of Conflict*, ed. Nicholas J. Saunders (London: Routledge, 2004), 134–48.

37. Lin, in "Grounds for Remembering," 9.

38. Bob Bushaway, "Name Upon Name: The Great War and Remembrance," in *Myths of the English*, ed. Roy Porter (Cambridge: Polity Press, 1993), 139.

39. Matt Roper, "Heroes Not Cowards," *Daily Mirror*, 22 June 2006.

40. Stephen Moss, "End of Shame," *Guardian*, 19 August 2006, 27. "But fighting to clear his name has, she says, made him come alive for her. 'It's made him more real, more of a person for me, whereas when I was a little girl I would say to my friends 'My dad died in the war' but it didn't mean anything to me because I never knew him. All this has given me a father. I didn't have one before, did I?'"

41. Roper, "Heroes Not Cowards"; Ann Gripper, Damien Fletcher, and Clare Raymond, "Heroes Not Deserters," *Daily Mirror*, 17 August 2006.

42. In *Shootings at Dawn*, Thurtle reports how one of his efforts to provide details of the executions to the House of Commons was met by a member with the cry, "More sob stuff." "I am well content," he went on, "that the men (particularly ex-Service men) and women of this country should decide whether these stories of military executions are 'sob stuff,' or damning evidence against an injustice which cries aloud for remedy" (3). In the current media representations the terms had become interchangeable.

43. Quoted in *Daily Telegraph*, 5 January 2001. Contemporaneous articles in the Belfast *News Letter* and the *Toronto Star* made specific appeals to sponsor Northern Irish and Canadian executed soldiers. For further discussion of the Shot at Dawn Memorial, see Black, "Thanks for the Memory."

44. "Shot at dawn" literature began to appear soon after the war, with A.P. Herbert's *The Secret Battle* (1919), loosely based on the execution of Sub-Lieutenant Edwin Dyett, one of three officers executed, and C.E. Montague's *Rough Justice* (1926). In 1955, J.L. Hodson published *Return to the Woods*, a novel containing a "shot at dawn" episode. John Wilson adapted this episode for his play *For King and Country* (1964), first published in 1966 under the title *Hamp*, and Joseph Losey directed a movie based on Wilson's screenplay, *For King & Country* (1964).

45. Corns and Hughes-Wilson, *Blindfold and Alone*, 20–21.

46. *Private Peaceful* was the winner of the Red House Children's Book Award in 2004, a finalist for the Carnegie Prize, and the 2005 Blue Peter Book of the Year (nominated for The Book I Couldn't Put Down category).

47. Morpurgo's discovery was not entirely accidental. Piet Chielins, a strong pardons advocate and, with Julian Putkowski, author of *Unquiet Graves,* a guide to the execution sites and graves of soldiers shot at dawn, called Morpurgo's attention to the executed soldiers during a visit to the In Flanders Fields Museum.

48. Nora High, quoted in "Heroes Not Cowards: A Pardon for the Lost Boys," *Daily Mirror*, 22 June 2006.

49. "News Clips," *The Express*, 6 November 1998.

50. Hansard, HC Deb 19 October 1993 vol. 230, cc. 160.

51. Quoted in *The Northern Echo*, 5 September 2006.

52. Boorman notes that "many such memorials are in poor condition or have been destroyed completely. Shelters in Memorial Gardens have been demolished by vandals, crosses in remote villages have been pushed over, there are countless instances of memorials being defaced by graffiti, bronze name plaques have been stolen, carved inscriptions have almost disappeared over the years, churches have been deconsecrated and their memorials lost, and schools and factories have been demolished with similar results." *At the Going Down of the Sun*, 1.

53. See especially Alex King, *Memorials of the Great War in Britain: The Symbolism and Politics of Remembrance* (Oxford: Berg, 1998).

54. Boorman notes that, "It was not impossible for a man's name to appear amongst the list of the fallen when he had, in fact, survived the war, and it was quite common for names to be omitted and added at a later, sometimes much later date.... It is usually very easy to see where names have originally been omitted because they then appear out of the normal order." *At the Going Down of the Sun*, 2.

55. Barrett, *Casualty Figures*.

56. Geoff Dyer, *The Missing of the Somme* (New York: Vintage, 2011 [1994]), 11.

57. See "The Tuesday Poem," *The Northern Echo*, 12 September 2006, for Yorkshire poet Tom Ward's "A Pardon for Harry"; see also "Private Harry Farr." The Harry Farr MySpace page has since been closed, though the Internet Archive and Open Library's WayBackMachine has archived some of the information: https://web.archive.org/web/20150124025639/https://myspace.com/private harryfarr.

LOYALTY AND SUBMISSION
Contested Discourses on
Aboriginal War Service, 1914–1939

BRIAN MACDOWALL

In a 1919 retrospective essay on Aboriginal participation in the Great War, Deputy Superintendent General of the Department of Indian Affairs (DIA) Duncan Campbell Scott remarked, "Nothing in the war has more genuine interest than the actions of the Canadian Indians in energetically espousing the cause of Great Britain and her Allies and spontaneously enlisting in the Expeditionary Force." Scott continued with a celebration of Aboriginal participation in the war by presenting evidence of the high number of Aboriginal volunteers who served with the Canadian Expeditionary Force (CEF), noted the large band donations to patriotic funds, and lauded the contributions of Aboriginal women on the home front. Scott concluded his essay with a comment on the changes to come, particularly that, "These men who have been broadened by contact with the outside world and its affairs, who have mingled with the men of other races, and who have witnessed the many wonders and advantages of civilization, will not be content to return to their old Indian mode of life."[1] Scott's essay represents an important part of a broader memorialization campaign launched by officials in the Canadian government during and after the war. This campaign was facilitated by publicized discourses in daily newspapers, popular magazines, and public DIA reports, and represented a sustained effort at memory construction during the interwar period.

This study assesses the production, transmission, and reproduction of narratives of Aboriginal war service, focusing on how the DIA represented the narrative of loyalty in media outlets and how this narrative was challenged by alternative remembrances. Annual reports of the Department of Indian Affairs, Scott's 1919 essay, and three key DIA files provide the evidence for this study.[2] The files contain over two hundred clippings from newspapers across Canada from 1914 to 1939; they represent a sample of the recurrent themes being replicated in newspapers across Canada during and after the war, and provide an accurate picture of what the DIA was articulating in the public realm. For the discussion of alternative remembrance, this study relies on internal correspondence between Aboriginal peoples and DIA headquarters, Indian agents' reports, and Aboriginal Soldier Settlement and pension case files. Though much of the sentiment regarding Aboriginal participation in the war was framed through discourses produced by colonialist officials, many Aboriginal veterans publicly contested the official memory of the war, challenging the colonialist vision of loyalty and subservience.

This study's argument is presented in three parts. Part one assesses the production of wartime narratives, the establishment of official discourses by the DIA in Ottawa, and the thematic content of the public memories of Aboriginal peoples and the Great War. Part two discusses the consolidation of the DIA's centrally directed commemoration efforts and the use of state means to reinforce these narratives, as well as the shift in thematic content toward a discussion of race, progress, and modernization. In part three, this study advances an alternative remembrance, focusing on the discourses produced by Aboriginal participants as they provide a corrective to the myth advanced by Scott. This paper contends that during and after the First World War, Canada's officials projected hegemonic narratives of Aboriginal colonial subservience and loyalty. The two concepts were intertwined; subservience implied a specific interpretation of the historical legacies of Aboriginal military relationships with the Crown, while loyalty was framed as an indicator of an uncritical acceptance of the Canadian state, assimilation, and the position of Aboriginal peoples in the socio-economic order. The loyalty discourse served to obscure wartime and postwar Aboriginal dissent and to consolidate DIA jurisdiction as the supreme authority for adjudicating Aboriginal community and individual needs. By disentangling the colonialist elements from this narrative, the roles of the Canadian government and public as critical arbiters of collective commemorations can be reassessed.

The field of war and memory has yet to be fruitfully applied to the topic of Aboriginal peoples and the First World War. Using the framework established by Paul Fussell and Jay Winter, this study uses the historiography

on memory to reinterpret the statements espoused by Canadian government bureaucrats and to delineate the relationship between war, modernity, and colonialism. Much of the literature on the Great War and memory
has emphasized the relationship between wartime and postwar literary
tradition and modernity; as Fussell notes, though the war ended in 1918,
its diction "resides everywhere just below the surface of modern experience." Yet the primary and secondary recollections, observes Fussell, are
inherently distorted, for "what possible good could result from telling the
truth?"[3] Winter's reappraisal challenges Fussell's conclusions, emphasizing
the postwar discursive reliance on "'traditional' forms in social and cultural
life, in art, poetry, and ritual" that helped explain the enormity of loss both
in the elite and popular realms—a continuity of cultural habit that only rup-
tured after the Second World War.[4] The question of modernity and remembrance has been successfully addressed in the Canadian context; accepting
that a number of dominant themes came to shape a war myth in Canada,
Jonathan Vance's *Death So Noble* asserts that "[Canada's War Myth] contained no explicit wish to return to the past, but instead looked to the past
as a source of examples for the future."[5] Vance's deft negotiation of the relationship between Fussell's and Winter's differing opinions on cultural continuity and modernity provide a nuance that this study seeks to emulate;
as with the general interpretation of the war as a catalyst for the future,
Canadian officials understood the war to signify a specific path forward
for Aboriginal peoples, a future of prosperity and modernity. In this way,
discourses on Aboriginal loyalty were fashioned to espouse a specific vision
of Canada's colonialist future predicated on the integration of Aboriginal
peoples into the wage economy and structural changes to the social, cultural, and economic activities on reserve. In this way, the DIA memorialization process can be understood as a component of the larger production of
the war myth, particularly in the linkages between history and modernity,
and the transmission of a new vision of colonialism.

Aboriginal participation in the First World War has received increased
attention in recent years, with scholars addressing the role of Aboriginal
communities overseas and on the home front, in national and local settings.[6] Many of these studies replicate the language of Scott's 1919 essay,
celebrating the patriotic responses of Aboriginal men and women to the
war effort while decrying the lack of historiographic and popular attention of these contributions. The replication of discourses on loyalty serves
the historiographic purpose; in celebrating the willing contributions of
Aboriginal soldiers, these studies seek to insert Aboriginal peoples into the

narratives on Canada and the First World War. Because the volume of records produced by the DIA vastly exceeded the number of sources produced by Aboriginal communities relating to the war, many of these studies have framed their work according to the words and actions of Indian Agents, missionaries, and DIA personnel in Ottawa. Unfortunately, these sources offer a biased and distorted view of the responses of Aboriginal peoples to the war. DIA officials adhered to a single vision of their mandate, believing in the eradication of Aboriginal cultural and social traditions and the instilling of Anglo-Saxon customs and values on Aboriginal communities. The way that DIA officials discussed the war often promoted evidence of racial progress, emphasizing how individuals or communities who participated loyally and unquestioningly accepted their subservient place within the racial hierarchy of the state. To date, few historians have systematically analyzed these recurrent themes, and have been far too generous in replicating the loyalty myth to serve recuperative historiographic purposes. This produces misunderstandings, as it implies that all Aboriginal communities responded in the same fashion to the challenges of the war. Discussing the discursive nature of DIA remembrance can reveal the discordant experiences of Aboriginal peoples during and after the war.

Recognition of the active, voluntary, and participatory role of Aboriginal communities in Canada's war effort is important. Despite remaining wards of the government, and at times being actively discouraged from enlisting by DIA and Department of Militia and Defence officials, as many as four thousand Aboriginal soldiers served with the CEF, or almost one-third of the men of military age. A number of soldiers won acclaim, including famed snipers Francis Pegahmagabow and Henry "Ducky" Norwest, the long-distance runner Tom Longboat, and the Military Cross–winning brothers Charles Smith and Alexander Smith Jr. At least seventeen Aboriginal men served as officers in the CEF.[7] Communities and individuals contributed liberally to war funds, offering significant donations to the Red Cross and Patriotic Funds, as well as purchasing government-issued bonds. By the end of the war, more than $45,000 had been donated to charitable funds.[8] On the home front, women participated by forming Red Cross societies, knitting woolen goods for men overseas, and hosting patriotic events to raise donations. Particularly in western Canada, intensive farming efforts—collectively known as the Campaign for Greater Production—increased crop yields and integrated farmers into the war economy.[9] The historiography that discusses Aboriginal peoples and the war emphasizes these contributions, but often uncritically replicates Scott's proscriptive characterization of Aboriginal peoples' loyalty, patriotism, and enthusiasm for the war effort without challenging the discursive themes so dominant in Scott's essay. Using a broader, more representative set of sources provides a way to extend analysis beyond the themes offered by government officials and deconstruct the hegemonic narratives of loyalty.

The reality of the war was far from the cohesive narrative espoused by Scott, and substantially more complex than the historiography describes. While many Aboriginal communities hosted recruitment functions and actively participated in wartime patriotic work, other communities used the recruitment processes to address grievances with the government.[10] A number of enlistees deserted from their units, particularly in Quebec, where cross-border reserves and family networks aided escape networks; some were treated leniently while others were prosecuted and incarcerated—a varying system of punishment that depended on location, circumstance, and community solidarity.[11] At the very least, the desertion rates challenge the notion that Aboriginal communities were unwavering in their sub-servient loyalty. Food regulations, regulations against idleness, censorship, and questionable recruiting tactics applied to Aboriginal communities as much as to the rest of Canada.[12] The prohibition on alcohol consumption was upheld even for Aboriginal soldiers serving overseas, confirming that, even while in uniform, these men were seen as Indians first and soldiers second.[13] The generous donations of bands and individuals to support war funds were often given with the expectation that financial donations would serve in lieu of enlistments, and DIA officials patronizingly rejected some donations over questions of interest rates and administration of funds. For example, the Walpole Band attempted to invest $10,000 in band funds toward the Liberty Loans, a gesture both of "patriotic desire" and the extra percentage point offered compared with the DIA trust fund, but Scott blocked the investment, writing in the margins of the letter, "this won't help any."[14] Some communities were wracked by serious divisions between those who supported the war effort and those who suggested a more ambiva-lent path. In light of the tensions between enlistment and desertion, spon-taneous patriotism and authoritarian regulation, the war experiences of Aboriginal peoples were more heterogeneous than has been explained by other historians. For some Aboriginal participants, the war represented pre-cisely the moment of transfiguration that Scott promoted. For others, the war represented an intensification of the patterns of state surveillance and moral regulation—an amplification of the DIA's assimilationist administra-tion. Inherent in the design of the DIA's loyalty discourse was the silencing of alternative memories and narratives of the war—a suppression of the memory of the war's darker side.

As early as 1916, Scott campaigned to include Aboriginal peoples in the public discourses of military participation. The DIA's annual reports persistently lauded the high rate of Aboriginal enlistments, large financial contributions to the Red Cross, Belgian Relief, the Canadian Patriotic Fund, and other charitable programs, and the informal contributions of Aboriginal women to fundraising and cottage-craft production. Scott's production of a discourse on loyalty served two purposes. First, it aligned discourses on Aboriginal peoples in a broader framework, asserting that Aboriginal peoples' contributions were at least equal to those of non-Aboriginal Canadians. Second, it justified the DIA's administrative regime, generating political capital for Scott's authoritarian version of colonial administration and concomitant budgetary allowance, as well as proving his personal contribution to the war effort.

Scott took an active role in promoting these contributions in public fora; for example, on 31 May 1916 he contacted J. Hector B. Charlesworth, editor of *Saturday Night*, with an account of military activities of the community of Cape Croker, Ontario, and a photograph of men "wearing the King's Uniform." Scott asked Charlesworth to "find space in 'Saturday Night' to reproduce the picture and print the enclosed account of the Cape Croker Indian soldiers." [15] In the account, Scott extolled the military service of Aboriginal men, writing, "True to the brave spirit of their race the Canadian Indians have made a ready response to the call to arms … fighting in the trenches, for the cause of justice and in support of British principles." In this sense, Scott directly contacted public sources to convey his message of loyalty through enlistments and actively promoted his colonialist message by fashioning commemorative discourse.

Initiative did not always come from Scott and the DIA; on 30 October 1916, Scott was contacted by the editor of the *The Civilian* for a short piece on DIA civil servants and their contributions to the war effort. Scott's response noted DIA employees' service, but focused much of the narrative on Aboriginal loyalty through enlistment, donations, and gendered work. [16] Even in media narratives that did not feature his own writing, Scott and his employees performed a central role in controlling the sources of information. For a *Victoria Daily Times* column from 1916, Scott dictated information to the reporter, emphasizing patriotic enlistments and large financial donations from Aboriginal peoples across Canada. [17] In the article "Red Men on the Firing Line," E.W. Thompson makes no reference to personal correspondence with Scott, yet summarizes the large numbers of Aboriginal enlistments, financial donations, and women's work. This represented more than a replication of the positive narrative of wartime unity, but rather an exact reproduction of the DIA's reports. Thompson notes that his information for the article was gleaned exclusively from the DIA's 1916 *Annual Report*.[18] Even in the absence of direct correspondence, Scott's specific message of Aboriginal participation was replicated in media outlets across the dominion. Because these replications were so repetitive, the discourses produced a hegemonic interpretation of Aboriginal peoples in the war.

Though general in tone, wartime narratives of Aboriginal participation in the war often contained a number of devices to emphasize the key themes of Aboriginal patriotic volunteerism. Media reports often used the spectre of community enlistments to emphasize the large numbers of Aboriginal men in the CEF. This narrative device is typified by a 1917 article in which the author reported that when Okanagan Indians were told to report for conscription registration, all available men were already away fighting.[19] Mention of the many conditional responses from band councils—that their donations or enlistments were predicated upon the expectation of greater inclusion in socio-economic matters after the war—were absent. Moreover, the problems of Aboriginal desertion, as well as numerous band council resolutions in opposition to recruitment, were similarly subsumed in the predominant pronouncements of patriotism and unquestioned loyalty.

In addition to anecdotes of community enlistments, the public narratives of Aboriginal participation often contained individual examples of discursively constructed parochial "Indians" and the lengths to which they strove to enlist. A December 1917 article included stories of Joe Delaronde and Simon Oombash, both Aboriginal men who had "never been out of the woods," yet strove to serve the king.[20] The parochial device was replicated at length in general publications and DIA Reports. The stories of young men from remote areas striving to enlist served to demonstrate the strong bonds of loyalty felt by these young men toward the Crown, and highlight the ways in which the war was inspiring great social and racial changes across the dominion.

The public narratives similarly emphasized the specialized role of Aboriginal men in the CEF, noting that their cultural and racialized skills in hunting, tracking, and scouting made them natural snipers. A Winnipeg article from October 1918 remarked, "Indians, the cables tell us, are being used with great success in scouting work on the western front."[21] DIA annual reports and newspaper articles alike made reference to Aboriginal soldiers' specialized roles, often in tandem with tales of the men who had "never been out of the woods," yet found their modern calling with the CEF. As a modification to the noble savage trope, this theme emphasized the civilizing aspect of the war; the old modes of life offered a base set of skills that could be molded through military training to become excellent soldiers. The subject matter of some of these articles is not factually incorrect. A number of Aboriginal soldiers won acclaim as snipers. Because some had experience hunting and trapping prior to the war, their knowledge sets were easily transferred into a military setting. Yet the discourses on racialized skills did not infer the same reasonable conclusions. This narrative device reimagined Aboriginal peoples across Canada into a single racial classification, subsuming cultural differences and historically divergent experiences. Moreover, the typology employed in this device undermined the great variety of wartime experiences of Aboriginal servicemen. The assumption that all Aboriginal soldiers were snipers and scouts obscured the many Aboriginal soldiers who served with distinction in pioneer battalions, forestry drafts, and the like.

Lastly, the newspaper articles often replicated gendered language in discursive descriptions of Aboriginal soldiers, noting their masculine characteristics while in service. A *Winnipeg Telegram* article from April 1917 noted the enlistment of Aboriginal men from across the Prairies and concluded, "These young men truly represent the best physical type of manhood."[22] The focus on masculinity also served as a platform to promote a crude version of racial equality, such as the *Daily News-Chronicle* article that noted, "A Man is a man 'over there' … He is a man whatever the uniform."[23] Yet the language of masculine individualism also maintained a racialized boundary of behaviour, that access to manliness was reserved for Aboriginal men who were loyal patriotic subscribers to the War effort, and that this masculinity could only be accessed through active service in France. This theme of masculine equality provides two intersecting interpretations; racial distinction was upheld in the dominion, but spatial regard for race contained ostensible limits. Alternately, perhaps the transition to manliness through military service overseas would precipitate greater equality upon return. Either way, those who served domestically, or could not serve, were denied access to a wholesome masculinity and full equality.

The four thematic elements to wartime memorialization reinforced parameters of behaviour for both Aboriginal and non-Aboriginal communities during the war. Discussions of masculinity, parochialism, and loyalty served as much to reinforce the necessity for non-Aboriginal men to enlist as they did to promote successful assimilationist narratives. Particularly in the individualist and parochial sentiments, the DIA sought to relay the importance of the war in drawing out the least-assimilated Indians and integrating them within national institutions. Wartime themes are also interesting for what they omitted, even within the framework of subservient loyalty.

Particularly after 1916, Scott directed institutional memorialization during the war by directly and indirectly managing information released to the press and replicated in the articles. Beyond serving motivational, gendered, and assimilationist purposes, these narratives confirmed the competency of the DIA in administering its subject population at a time when internal debate cast doubt on its efficacy in managing reserve economies, manpower allotments, and discipline on and off reserve. This in turn compelled the DIA to enhance its commemoration project in the postwar period through a consolidated narrative. The wartime discourse that emphasized unity across racial boundaries was used to consolidate an image of the war in which the sacrifices of the nation were necessary. The construction of an image of Indian soldiers and communities standing together to aid the British Empire helped subvert the realities of war, in which harsh measures of social control sought to curb dissonant behaviour and obscure the fact that Aboriginal peoples stood to gain little from victory.

In the postwar period, the maintenance of the loyalty discourse took on greater importance. Though the crises of recruitment, economic mobilization, and wartime regional dissent had passed, the period following armistice provided scarce relief for the government and peoples of Canada. A deadly influenza outbreak killed fifty thousand Canadians, and as many as forty million people worldwide. Demobilization riots highlighted the troubles of demobilizing the more than 400,000 Canadian soldiers requiring transport home.[24] Domestically, economic fluctuations erased families' wartime wage gains, and farmers were hard-hit as crop prices plummeted. Labour strife accentuated the sense of upheaval, particularly with the Winnipeg General Strike's bloody conclusion.

The administration of veterans represented a tacit recognition by government agencies that something was owed to the men and women who had served with the CEF, as well as an attempt to curb radicalism among returned soldiers. Pension rates for disabled men were negotiated and renegotiated, offering a small measure of relief to those who could not return to work because of their injuries. Retraining schemes were established to reintegrate disabled soldiers into the workforce with new skills.

For soldiers who escaped injury, a soldier settlement program provided government loans to purchase land and farming equipment to resettle successful applicants and their families onto farming tracts, trading swords for ploughshares. Pensions, retraining schemes, and soldier settlement—the core of Canadian governmental veterans administration—proved problematic. Pension payments were penurious, and the qualification system was extremely strict. Many pension claims were rejected on the grounds that the injuries could not be confirmed as war-related, with a demanding burden of proof to confirm otherwise.[25] Retraining schemes were equally challenging, for the options available to disabled veterans were extremely limited and the programs themselves were strict. Moreover, the slight economic boom in 1918–19 meant that few returned soldiers sought retraining when easy employment was still available without it. Soldier Settlement was a disaster, as loans were granted when the inflation of farming goods peaked, and matured as crop prices started to bottom out. Frustrated by such inadequate programs, many returned soldiers began to organize associations. The largest of these, the Great War Veterans' Association, agitated for changes to the administrative regime governing veterans' programs.

Aboriginal veterans suffered many of the same problems as non-Aboriginal returned soldiers. Though Aboriginal veterans technically qualified for almost all of the same benefits as non-Aboriginal veterans, many of the programs were administered through the DIA instead of the Department of Soldiers' Civil Re-Establishment (DSCR) or the Department of Pensions and National Health. As an extension of the expanded jurisdiction that the DIA had won during the war, and following the legacy of separate administration for Aboriginal peoples, few government officials challenged the DIA's veterans' programs. The DIA administered its own version of Soldier Settlement for Aboriginal applicants, in part because of the problems of land ownership as defined under the Indian Act. Loans and land allotment to Aboriginal soldier settlers were often significantly smaller than to non-Aboriginal settlers, and the application process was tightly controlled.[26] Disability retraining programs were run through DSCR channels, but the DIA channelled Aboriginal applicants and made suggestions on what represented appropriate training for the veterans. When disabled veteran Joseph Ackabe requested retraining as a tailor, his Indian Agent W.R. Brown wrote DIA Headquarters to report, "I hardly think that a tailoring job would suit this man as he has always been used to outside work. Should think that a railway job such as a watchman or jump man would be more in his line or could he be pleased as teamster on one of the

Western reserves."[27] The DIA vision of retraining conflicted with applicants' expressed desires, often ignoring or adjusting the applicants' qualifications to reflect the inferior socio-economic position of reserve economies. As with retraining, pensions were similarly run through the veterans' bureaucracy; the Board of Pension Commissioners adjudicated Aboriginal pension claims somewhat independent of the DIA, though the DIA was given the results of the claims and could oversee the monthly payments to ensure pension funds were not being "misused" by pensioners or their families.[28] Pension allowances were often lower for Aboriginal veterans compared to non-Aboriginal pensioners. Until 1936, Aboriginal veterans were denied access to War Veterans' Allowance funds or Last Post funds, evidence of disparate treatment between Aboriginal and non-Aboriginal veterans. Against this backdrop of discord and mistreatment, the DIA struggled to maintain the narrative of progress. The purported loyalty and patriotism of Aboriginal soldiers and communities that helped contribute to victory—a discourse that conveniently ignored the inequalities and discord of wartime realities—could be undercut easily in light of the treatment of Aboriginal veterans. A strengthened discourse on loyalty and modernity was employed with the specific purpose of undercutting the counter-narratives of discontent articulated by Aboriginal veterans and their communities.

In the immediate aftermath of the war, Scott's 1919 essay cemented departmental sentiments about crafting discourses on loyalty. The liberal modernity espoused near the end of his piece, that by participating in the war the Indians of Canada were poised to transition to a state of civilized assimilation, remained a cornerstone of postwar remembrance discourses. Yet Scott's vision of modernity was at odds with the broader modernist sentiments that espoused urbanism, consumerism, and industrialism, or the more abstract reconceptualization of time and space. Rather, this vision extended so far as to represent the abolishment of "Indianness" through voluntary enfranchisement, a transition to either commercial farming or insertion in the wage economy, and the wholesale adoption of Anglo-Saxon cultural and social norms. Scott was envisaging a reform that simultaneously harkened back to the longer processes of assimilation and integration that had been cornerstones of colonialist policy since at least the 1830s, and imagining created environments and commodified time-space that had been features of modernist sentiment through the nineteenth century.[29] A *Brantford Expositor* article from January 1919 replicated the modernizing sentiment. The author notes organized resistance to the proposed forced enfranchisement of Aboriginal peoples, but concludes that when bands of restraint are removed, "the remnants of the once numerically great race will step out into freedom." As for political agitation on the Six Nations reserve regarding proposed changes to the system of band council election, the author is dismissive: "Come what may of the agitation, the six nations Indians have played a noble part in the war."[30] The *Belleville Intelligencer* article also echoed Scott's liberal tone, noting that Aboriginal participation in the war was leading to "opportunities and … wealth."[31]

Scott ensured that this sort of celebratory reportage was replicated across the Dominion, and public ceremonies of remembrance featured prominently in postwar public narratives of Aboriginal peoples and the war. A July 1919 article presented the story of a gathering at Mount Elgin, Ontario. The author noted "Anxious Moments" in relation to Aboriginal chiefs' concern over land allotments and the Soldier Settlement Act, but reinforced the unwavering loyalty of Six Nations peoples to the Crown during and after the war. This article reinforced the point by quoting a speech by Chief Scobie in recognition of the three thousand Indian soldiers: "There's the flag that knows no colour line, it is the flag Indians will respect, love, and honour."[32] As with the notion that wearing the uniform produced a singular masculine identity, Scobie's assertion contains an important corollary to loyalty; implying that other symbols, or perhaps an absence of national symbols, strengthened "colour lines" meant that this submerging notion of loyalty and due deference to the flag offered a modern future free from racial boundaries. The *Charlottetown Guardian* reported in July 1922 a "Grand Celebration at Lennox Island Yesterday." The article noted the "Unveiling of Magnificent Monument Erected in Memory of Fallen Indian Soldiers" and declared the monument an "inspiration" for future generations of Lennox Island Indians.[33] Postwar media, framed according to Scott's 1919 essay, focused on commemorative celebrations, abandoning the gendered, individualist, and parochial discursive forms of the wartime literature.

While previous literary devices had been jettisoned by the postwar period, certain themes were carried over, recast with notions of progress and modernization. As Scott had predicted a great and civilized future for Aboriginal peoples in 1919, public discourses replicated this hope. One article mentioned the high rates of enlistment and financial contributions of Aboriginal bands across Canada, and hyperbolically queried, "were there any who visioned the day when the Tepee would give way to the Skyscraper?"[34] The precise meaning of this phrase is difficult to render; the author likely did not presume to imagine skyscrapers built on reserves. More likely, the author was intimating at the longer processes of historical change, in which vestiges of Canada's colonial past were being replaced by great representations of modernity. A November 1927 article from Regina celebrated the wealth and prosperity of Indian farmers in the province, noting that the impetus for farming and prosperity germinated with wartime service, as "it remained for 4000 young braves to bring further glory to their tribes while serving in France with the Canadian Corps."[35] Modernity, in this case representing the realization of older forms of assimilationist policy and insertion of Aboriginal peoples into the socio-economic order, framed much of the postwar public discourses on commemorating Aboriginal wartime service. As Scott had predicted, postwar public commemoration imagined Aboriginal peoples across Canada as having been fundamentally changed by the experiences of the war, easily assimilated into a productive framework of socio-economic status in Canada as a result of war service and poised to grasp at a "civilized" future.

During the war, DIA officials worked with the media to construct a discourse on loyalty that served to highlight the willingness of Aboriginal men and women to contribute to the war effort. Following the war, this discourse was slightly modified to emphasize how the loyal actions of Aboriginal soldiers intimated a modernized future, in which the outdated superstitions and practices would be extinguished in favour of an assimilated and integrated relationship with non-Aboriginal society. Depictions of modernity as a place of opportunities, wealth, and skyscrapers disguised the ugly forms of colonialist administration that coloured the treatment of Aboriginal veterans, and the many harsh colonialist measures enacted throughout the interwar period.[36]

Aboriginal peoples were not passive victims in the process of discursive production. Much of the previous historiography has overlooked this point, relying on the discourses produced by colonialist agents to discuss Aboriginal military service. During and after the war, Aboriginal individuals and organizations actively sought to insert their voices into the discourses on war service and modify the message of loyalty as a method of attaining a new relationship with the Crown. Through these discourses the Aboriginal participants often asserted a message of pride in their military service, but sharply disputed a number of tenets of the DIA's discourse on loyalty. They expressed disappointment in the postwar treatment of veterans, and reflectively used the DIA's own statements to condemn the treatment of pensioners and soldier settlers.

Throughout the war, many Aboriginal communities articulated expressions of loyalty in various media. Shortly after the outbreak of hostilities, the Six Nations band council offered "a very suitable address, touching on the relations between the Six Nations and the British."[37] This statement was devised and read in accordance with the wishes of the band council. The Mohawks of the Bay of Quinte repeated this sentiment of loyalty: "We came over with the United Empire Loyalists from the United States. Our treaties are with the Crown, so, when the Crown calls, you go."[38] Mike Mountain Horse, a Blood veteran, wrote in 1923:

> The intrepid sons of great warriors of various Indian tribes manifested their belief in the cause of the Great White Father by spontaneously enlisting in the Canadian Expeditionary Force. Some 3,500 Indian lads from all parts of Canada rallied to the colors in those hectic days. And although the proportion of the aborigine was in the minority, the power of their example was strong, and they were mentioned by the Germans as enemies worthy of their opprobrium.... From the outset of this colossal struggle the Red Man demonstrated his loyalty to the British Crown in a very convincing manner.[39]

Citing the relationship between Aboriginal peoples and the Crown, Aboriginal discourses did not share the DIA's sentiment of subservience, but articulated a vision of autonomy. Noting the close alliances between Aboriginal peoples and the Crown during periods of military strife in the colonial era, Aboriginal groups framed the participation in the First World War as part of a longer historical process in which mutual allegiance should propel mutual welfare. Many statements referenced the longstanding relationship with the Crown, particularly the cooperative military activities of the War of 1812. The DIA made reference to this longer historical relationship as well, connecting the historical moments of military cooperation to the First World War as part of the narrative of subservient loyalty; as Aboriginal groups had served the Crown in the past, they were obliged to respond in the same fashion during the First World War. Yet Aboriginal discourses on military cooperation rejected this narrative. Framing participation in the war as part of a continuity of relationship, Aboriginal participants sought to situate their current conditions within historical processes. References to 1812, for example, bespoke a moment when Aboriginal groups were vital allies of the Crown, and maintained a level of autonomy and sovereignty that had been sharply reduced in the subsequent century.

Aboriginal discourses also served a more immediate purpose. Following the war, Aboriginal veterans often used the DIA's discourse on loyalty to critique their inadequate treatment. Writing to the DIA in response to news that War Veterans' Allowances would not be available, Caughnawaga veteran Angus Goodleaf proclaimed, "Do you believe yourself that is justice? I am asking for no special favours or anything like it as I simply believe we owe the Gov. nothing but they certainly owe us plenty."[40] Goodleaf's awareness of this injustice was more acute considering his personal connection to the war effort. Similarly, Mrs. Angus McAuley wrote to Superintendent General of Indian Affairs Thomas Crerar in April 1937 to ask for poverty relief, noting that, "my husband fought for this country and got all kinds of promises which were never fulfilled."[41] President of the Indian War Veterans Association William F. Powless wrote to Franklin Smoke, MP, to discuss an injustice felt keenly by members of the association: "The injustice, they believe, lies the in the fact that returned men, other than pensioners, are not entitled to relief though they are in greater need and also that the amount allowed is only about half of that allowed on the white side."[42] The disparate treatment of Aboriginal and non-Aboriginal veterans featured prominently in many discontented soldier settlers' letters, including Rama settler Ben Sawyer, who wrote "I haven't got a square food [sic] of land anyplace in the province of Ontario where I can make a shelter. Is that the way the government treats his returned men. Is it because I am an Indian not compare the same colour like my white brothers Canadians who served in active service in France. Do I entitle the same show as other boys."[43]

Collectively, Aboriginal participants in the war expressed their own vision of loyalty, patriotism, and progress. References to loyalty and patriotism did not escape many Aboriginal discourses, but these notions were used to critique the DIA's paternalistic administration and inadequate treatment of veterans. Fred Loft's attempts to generate support for a pan-Indian movement used the concept of wartime services as a platform to suggest that communities shared a common experience, and that better treatment by government officials was overdue.[44] As with the DIA's discourses, Aboriginal peoples understood their participation in the war as a transitional moment, but felt this transition should have brought greater autonomy to their communities, or at least a general improvement of their socio-economic position. Yet these expressions were often within the bureaucratic framework of the colonialist state. The deployment of discourses to challenge the exclusion of Aboriginal veterans from programs like the War Veterans' Allowance and the Last Post Fund brought tangible results; in 1936 Aboriginal veterans were finally granted access to these funds, in part because of the persistent and public critiques of the unequal treatment of Aboriginal veterans. Yet alternative discourses did not precipitate a broader reconceptualization of the relationship between Aboriginal peoples and the state. The narratives produced by the DIA through public channels were too well entrenched by the 1920s to be fractured by indigenous scripts. Loyalty, the contested watchword deployed by both DIA and Aboriginal discursive producers, was understood by the general public to imply subservience and acquiescence in the colonialist regime that dominated the interwar period. Aboriginal voices were unable to penetrate the matrix of government and media, but continued to propagate alternative memories at the community level.

Only after the Second World War did the question of Aboriginal military service begin to challenge underlying assumptions regarding the relationship between First Nations and the Crown. Though the DIA's version of Aboriginal war service commanded public interpretations of Aboriginal war service, alternative narratives were not eradicated, but persisted as a counter-narrative in the stories, remembrances, and expressions of participants and their descendants. Recent historiography has begun to uncover these alternative narratives, and popular culture has begun to present these stories to a wider public. The discourse that has coalesced public understandings of Aboriginal participation in the war as loyal subservience is finally starting to erode, almost a century after its inception.

Narratives on the connection between loyalty and modernity served as powerful cleansing agents against a backdrop of contested colonialism in the immediate postwar period. As much as the wartime discourses sought to downplay dissent by presenting a uniform image of Aboriginal loyal subservience, postwar narratives solidified the memory of Aboriginal peoples in the war as a great turning point in which the patriotic loyalty of communities and individuals would serve as a springboard toward a prosperous, assimilated future. As with the desertion and dissident crises of the war years, the postwar period brought great uncertainty both to DIA headquarters and its wards. Triumphant public proclamations of wartime loyalty and postwar modernity became a powerful colonialist tool for the DIA to justify its ongoing assimilationist efforts. The official remembrances oppressed individual memories of the war, confirming that the act of constructing official memory was inexorably linked to power relations. Alternative memories of wartime dissent or of the mistreatment of Aboriginal veterans were afforded little public space, but rather subsumed in the overarching progressive narrative—though these counter-narratives were not completely extinguished and are beginning to receive public and academic attention. In

Death So Noble, Jonathan Vance concludes, "The memory of the Great War never realized the high promise that its most vigorous proponents saw in it because it was so obviously assimilationist. It could indeed rejuvenate the country, but only if all citizens subsumed themselves within it."[45] As wards, Aboriginal peoples were not citizens. Their voices were not included in the official memory, and DIA employees who sought to realize the longstanding aims of assimilation actively silenced these voices. As sub-myths within the official Canadian war myth, remembrances of Aboriginal submissive loyalty justified colonialist policy as much as it justified the war. Loyalty and patriotism, modernity and assimilation, purchased a sustained enthusiasm for the project of enforced colonialism upon Aboriginal peoples through the interwar period.

NOTES

1. Duncan Campbell Scott, "The Canadian Indians and the Great World War," *Canada in the Great War, Vol. III: Guarding the Channel Ports* (Toronto: United Publishers, 1919), 285, 327.
2. Library and Archives of Canada (hereafter LAC), RG10, vol. 3180, file 452, 124-1, Ottawa—Correspondence and Canada Gazette Regarding the Involvement of Native Peoples in the War of 1914 (Newspaper Clippings) 1914–1916; vol. 3181, file 452-124-1A, War General Correspondence 1916–; vol. 3207, file 520, 486 pt. 1, Newspaper Clippings Concerning Indians 1919–31.
3. Paul Fussell, *The Great War and Modern Memory* (New York: Oxford University Press, 1975), 189, 182.
4. Jay Winter, *Sites of Memory, Sites of Mourning: The Great War in European Cultural History* (New York: Cambridge University Press, 1996), 5.
5. Jonathan Vance, *Death So Noble: Memory, Meaning, and the First World War* (Vancouver: UBC Press, 1997), 266.
6. See Frank Gaffen, *Forgotten Soldiers* (Penticton, BC: Theytus Books, 1985); James Dempsey, *Warriors of the King: Prairie Indians in World War One* (Regina: Canadian Plains Research Center, 1999); Adrian Hayes, *Pegahmagabow: Legendary Warrior, Forgotten Hero* (2003); James W. St.G. Walker, "Race and Recruitment in The First World War: Enlistment of Visible Minorities in the Canadian Expeditionary Force," *Canadian Historical Review* 70, no. 1 (1989). Katharine A. McGowan, "'We are wards of the Crown and cannot be regarded as full citizens of Canada': Native Peoples, the Indian Act and Canada's War Effort" (Ph.D. diss., University of Waterloo, 2011). These studies have generally adhered to what Sheffield and Lackenbauer call the "forgotten warrior" genre. See P. Whitney Lackenbauer and R. Scott Sheffield, "Moving Beyond

'Forgotten': The Historiography on Canadian Native Peoples and the World Wars," in *Aboriginal Peoples and the Canadian Military: Historical Perspectives*, ed. P. Whitney Lackenbauer and Craig Leslie Mantle (Kingston, ON: CDA Press, 2007): 209–32. One noteworthy exception is Timothy C. Winegard, *For King and Kanata: Canadian Indians in the First World War* (Winnipeg: University of Manitoba Press, 2012). Winegard's book systematically addresses the "forgotten warrior" orthodoxy by challenging a number of myths surrounding the question of Aboriginal military participation in the war.

7. Winegard, 119.

8. Canada, Sessional Papers 1927, "Annual report of the Department of Indian Affairs for the Year Ended March 31 1927" (Ottawa: King's Printer, 1927), 10.

9. The three purposes of Greater Production were stated in the DIA's Annual Report for 1919: the "establishment and operation of Government Greater Production Farms," an increased effort to encourage individual Indians to farm, and the "leasing of reserve land to whites for farming and grazing purposes, in order to assist the greater production campaign." To run this scheme, South Saskatchewan inspector of Indian agencies William M. Graham was promoted to commissioner for the Department of Indian Affairs in Manitoba, Saskatchewan, and Alberta. Canada, Sessional Papers 1919, Sessional Paper No. 27A, "Annual report of the Department of Indian Affairs for the Year Ended March 31 1919" (Ottawa: King's Printer, 1927).

10. When DIA Employee and honorary recruiting officer Charles A. Cooke visited the Gibson Reserve in April 1916, he reported that, "the treatment given them by the Government with reference to the tenure of their land appears to have no small influence in their attitude of indifference to the matter of enlisting." He noted resistance on the Parry Island Reserve, that "The Indians, particularly the old, are opposed to their young men enlisting. They claim that the Government failed to fulfill its promises made to the Indians after the war of 1812 in the matter of pensions and presents." Historical narratives worked both ways; some groups were compelled to participate in the war because of their longstanding military relationships with the Crown, while others saw historical patterns of mistreatment as reason enough to eschew military participation in the First World War. LAC, RG10, vol. 6765, file 452-7, Cooke to Scott, 6 April 1916.

11. The treatment of deserters depended on region and context. In Quebec, prior to the Military Service Act, DIA and Military Officials worked to produce "a special concession made to Indians," where those who were willing to return to their duties would be transferred to a non-combat unit, such as a railway or forestry battalion. Laurie Plume and Jim Only Chief from the Blood Reserve were arrested twice for desertion. Mississauga of the Credit Joseph Chubb Jr. was arrested for desertion and died while incarcerated. LAC, RG10, vol. 6767, file 452-16 pt. 1, Fiset to Scott, 9 February 1917.

12. One such case of questionable recruitment tactics surfaced in November 1916, when members of the Chippewa of the Saugeen band forwarded a petition to Sir Edward Grey alleging that seventeen young men from the reserve were forcibly enlisted after being threatened with fines and imprisonment. LAC, RG10, vol. 3181, file 452-124-1A, petition from the Chippewa of the Saugeen to Sir Edward Grey, 20 November 1916.

13. When asked by Kamsack, Saskatchewan district magistrate J.W. McLennan if Aboriginal soldiers were considered Indians or British subjects under the liquor prohibition in the Indian Act, Scott responded, "I beg inform you that Indians who enlist still retain their status as Indians, and are subject to the provisions of the Indian Act." LAC, RG10, vol. 3180, file 452-124-1, Scott to McLennan, 15 January 1916.

14. LAC, RG10, vol. 6770, file 452-23, Walpole Indian Agent to Scott, 30 October 1918.

15. LAC, RG10, vol. 3180, file 452-124-1, Scott to Charlesworth, 31 May 1916.

16. LAC, RG10, vol. 3181, file 452-124-1A, editor, *The Civilian*, to Scott, 30 October 1916.

17. LAC, RG10, vol. 3181, file 452-124-1A, *Victoria Daily Times*, "Indians Respond to Call to Arms," 12 June 1916.

18. LAC, RG10, vol. 3181, file 452-124-1A, E.W. Thompson, "Red Men on the Firing Ling," unidentified.

19. LAC, RG10, vol. 3181, file 452-124-1A, *Winnipeg Tribune*, "Okanagan Indians Prove their Patriotism," 24 November 1917.

20. LAC, RG10, vol. 3181, file 452-124-1A, *Port Arthur Daily News-Chronicle*, "Many Indians in the Army and Their Record is Good," 22 December 1917.

21. LAC, RG10, vol. 3181, file 452-124-1A, *Winnipeg Tribune*, "Indians in the War," 4 October 1918.

22. LAC, RG10, vol. 3181, file 452-124-1A, *Winnipeg Telegram*, "What the Indians of Canada are Doing for Their Country," 7 April 1917.

23. "Many Indians in the Army and Their Record Is Good," 22 December 1917.

24. Desmond Morton, "'Kicking and Complaining': Demobilization Riots in the Canadian Expeditionary Force, 1918–1919," *Canadian Historical Review* 61, no. 3 (1980): 334–60.

25. Section 11 of the 1919 pension bill read, "The Commission shall award pensions to or in respect of family members who have died ... when the disability or death in respect of which the application for pension is made was attributable to or was incurred or aggravated during military service." But it was revised to drop the "or was incurred or aggravated during" in 1921 during a period that Morton and Wright characterize as "tightening up." Desmond Morton and Glenn Wright, *Winning the Second Battle: Canadian Veterans and the Return to Civilian Life* (Toronto: University of Toronto Press, 1987), 157.

26. Robin Jarvis Brownlie, "Work Hard and Be Grateful: Native Soldier Settlers in Ontario after the First World War," in *On The Case: Explorations in Social History, ed.* Franca Iacovetta and Wendy Mitchinson (Toronto: University of Toronto Press, 1998), 181–203; Sarah Carter, "'An Infamous Proposal': Prairie Indian Reserve Land and Soldier Settlement after the First World War," *Manitoba History* 37 (1999): 9–21.

27. LAC, RG10, vol. 6771, file 452-32 pt. 1, W.R. Brown to Scott, 9 December 1920.

28. The system of close oversight of pensions was established between the DIA and the Board of Pension Commissioners after a number of allegations of "misconduct" by women receiving government funds was forwarded to DIA Headquarters by Moravian Agent E. Beattie. The DIA negotiated with the Pension Board to be given the opportunity to oversee the expenditure of pensions. In reality, this was done sparingly, with a 1925 list only naming fourteen accounts being actively managed by Agents across Canada. LAC, RG10, vol. 3181, file 452-124-1A, W.C. Mariott to McLean, 7 March 1925.

29. Scott's abject promotion of modernity conforms to the more theoretical historiography that has wrestled with modernity and modernism. This study uses Michael Mann's interpretation of modernity as a consolidation of abstract and diffuse power networks featuring a unity of space-time and the march of reason and progress. Similarly useful is Stephen Kern's elucidation of the changing understanding of time and space from 1880 to 1918. Michael Mann, *The Sources of Social Power vol. 1: A History of Power from the Beginning to AD 1760* (Cambridge: Cambridge University Press, 1986); Michael Mann, *The Sources of Social Power vol. 2: The Rise of Classes and Nation States 1760–1914* (Cambridge: Cambridge University Press, 1993); Stephen Kern, *The Culture of Time and Space, 1880–1918* (Cambridge: Harvard University Press, 1983).

30. LAC, RG10, vol. 3181, file 452-124-1A, *Brantford Expositor*, "Indians and the Great War," 22 January 1919.

31. LAC, RG10, vol. 3181, file 452-124-1A, *Belleville Intelligencer*, "Our Indian Brothers," undated.

32. LAC, RG10, vol. 3207, file 520,486, *St. Thomas Journal*, "Indian Chiefs Confident of the Future of Their Race," July 1919.

33. LAC, RG10, vol. 3207, file 520,486, *Charlottetown Guardian*, "Grand Celebration at Lennox Island Yesterday," 31 July 1922.

34. LAC, RG10, vol. 3207, file 520,486, "Annual Departmental Report Contains Some Interesting Figures," unidentified.

35. LAC, RG10, vol. 3207, file 520,486, *Regina Post*, "Native Indians Retain Place in Canadian Life," 5 November 1927.

36. For example, the contentious 1920 amendment to the Indian Act referred to as Bill 14 allowed for the enfranchisement of select Indians against their will. Also, changes to game laws and prosecution of violations of the Migratory Bird Conservation Act resulted in fewer commercial opportunities for northern

communities. See E. Brian Titley, *A Narrow Vision: Duncan Campbell Scott and the Administration of Indian Affairs in Canada* (Vancouver: UBC Press, 1986), 49–53.

37. LAC, RG10, vol. 3180, file 452,124-1A, signed J.S. Johnson, Deputy Speaker, Six Nations Council. Copy of the minute book of the Six Nations Council.

38. C.P. Champion, "Putting the Empire Back into Canada," *Dorchester Review* 2, no. 1 (Spring/Summer 2012).

39. Mike Mountain Horse, *My People the Bloods*, ed. Hugh A. Dempsey (Calgary: Glenbow-Alberta Institute and Blood Tribal Council, 1989), 139.

40. LAC, RG10, vol. 3181, file 452-124-1A, Goodleaf to the Secretary, Department of Indian Affairs, 2 December 1933.

41. LAC, RG10, vol. 6762, file 452-1 pt. 1–5, Mrs. Angus McAuley to Crerar, 23 April 1937.

42. LAC, RG10, vol. 6762, file 452-1 pt. 1–5, Powless to Smoke, 4 November 1932.

43. LAC, RG10, vol. 7502, file 25,024-6, Ben Sawyer, transcribed and forwarded by W.C. Mariott, Department of Soldiers Civil Re-Establishment, to J.D. McLean, 23 December 1921.

44. See Kiera L. Ladner, "Visions of Neocolonialism: Renewing the Relationship with Aboriginal Peoples," *Canadian Journal of Native Studies* 21, no. 1 (2001): 105–25; John Moses, "Aboriginal Participation in Canadian Military Service," *The Army Doctrine and Training Bulletin: Canada's Professional Journal on Army Issues* 3, no. 3 (Fall 2000): 14–18; E. Brian Titley, "The League of Indians of Canada: An Early Attempt to Create a National Native Organization," *Saskatchewan Indian Federated College Journal* 1 (1984): 53.

45. Vance, *Death So Noble*, 260.

"KITCHENER'S TOURISTS"
Voices from Great War Hospital Ships

CAROL ACTON

Recent diving expeditions to sunken wrecks of hospital ships like the *Rewa* and the *Glenart Castle* in or near the Bristol Channel, televised in the program *Deep Wreck Mysteries*, have called attention to their history, even as the expeditions themselves raise questions about the relationship between that history and its manipulation as a form of recreation.[1] Although the image of a hospital shipwreck reminds us of the dangers faced by the personnel on board and while the documentaries do include coverage of the actual sinkings and loss of life, the primary narrative of these dives is presented in the popular media as a historical mystery-crime story—Were they or were they not carrying arms? Which side, Allies or Central Powers, committed the war crime? The wrecks are also portrayed as exciting sites for diving. In particular, such programs play on the undeniable mystery and glamour surrounding sunken ships. However, this kind of interest, even when it includes mention of the individuals whose lives were lost or irrevocably changed, tends to place the politics of the event or the thrill of the dive in the foreground; moreover, they focus not on the role the ships played in the lives of medical personnel and their patients on a daily basis, but merely on their demise. The problem inherent in this kind of popular remembering is highlighted by Carpentier's assertion that, "however hard our cultures try to materialise memory by enshrining it in memorials, museums, and other sites of memory, our representations are unavoidably all we are left with."[2] While hospital ship losses are represented on memorials, the lack of a site as a place of memory that can be visited, as at Vimy Ridge, Verdun, or the Somme, means that these ships and the memory of war they carry are in danger of being lost, erased not only by their disappearance as concrete objects but by representations that concentrate on their entertainment value. Occupying no specific space during the war, ships were also sunk, dismantled, or refitted and renamed, leaving no obvious trace; with this disappearance, the experience of those on board seems also to have disappeared.[3] Where their rediscovery becomes television drama, in the case of ships like the *Rewa* and the *Glenart Castle*, the subjective memories they carry are lost in the re-remembering, and sites of suffering become sites of recreation. While memorializing necessarily rewrites all war experience, the human story carried by these ships, of their patients and the medical personnel who cared for them in this cramped and dangerous environment, is at risk of being obscured, a selective and narrowly focused popular history replacing the lived story and what it offers us in understanding the war experience. As Bette London claims in her analysis of the Shot at Dawn campaign in this volume, "to be named is to be remembered"; there is always a gap between private memory and public remembrance that we need to try to close, especially when that gap contains individual lives that have been omitted from the war story. Similarly, Alice Kelly's chapter on nurses' representations of the dead draws attention to the importance of listening to individual accounts as a way of returning the unpalatable facts behind war death to the larger memory of the war.

As Kelly's chapter shows, it is not unusual for the medical story of the First World War to be lost in the historical shuffle of writings and rewritings, histories and revisionist histories. In spite of Erich Maria Remarque's famous assertion in *All Quiet on the Western Front* that, "a hospital alone shows what war is," military history has tended to relegate the medical war to the margins, if including it at all; in fact, until very recent research such as Mark Harrison's *The Medical War*, it belonged almost entirely to the women's nursing history of the war, officially placed outside combat. Quoting Ron Eyerman, "how an event is remembered is intimately entwined with how it is represented," Carpentier stresses that the "process of memorialization also implies forgetting.... The processes of glorification of the Self and demonization of the Enemy are by default used to make sense of the loss, which also impacts on what is remembered and what is forgotten."[4] The focus in *Deep Wreck Mysteries*, which seeks to discover on which side the fault lay—were these despicable acts of German atrocity, or were the British using hospital ships for the purpose of carrying weapons?—maintains a combat focus by reinforcing binaries of Self and Other rather than considering ways of moving beyond them. The medical story represented in this discussion transcends such binaries—for example, in the inclusion in the accounts of German patients as wounded, not as Enemy Other.

In the Canadian context of what is remembered and what is forgotten, the victory at Vimy dominates the national memory of the war, while the sinking of the HS *Llandovery Castle*—with the greatest collective loss of life of medical personnel in the war—receives much less attention, perhaps because it fits less easily into the story of victory, and because, as already noted, it is the story of those whose work placed them officially outside combat.[5] In theorizing "the politics of war memory and commemoration," T.G. Ashplant, Graham Dawson, and Michael Roper argue that analyses of war memory and commemoration have tended to be "very weak on the ground of individual subjectivity, under-conceptualizing both the richness and complexity of personal memory." In addition, they emphasize the extent to which power relations play a role in remembrance, such that "the weaker and more marginalised have less access to the agencies of either state or civil society and less capacity to influence prevailing narratives or project their own narratives into wider arenas."[6] The discussion of hospital ships here fits into the larger discussion around power relations and memory central to the reclaiming that takes place in many of the chapters in this volume, and is particularly visible in Dan Bullard's discussion of Africans who fought for Germany. In reclaiming their story from that which centres on the Western Front, he illustrates the extent to which history involves a selection process that privileges some stories while excluding others. While medical personnel are not usually seen as a disenfranchised group in war memory, their position and training—whereby those they care for are situated at the forefront of their own accounts—works against their claiming a place in the larger memory of the First World War. This privileging of one narrative over another, even when it is embedded in the text that needs to be reclaimed, reflects concerns raised in other chapters in this section that deal with gaps and silences in the history of the war and work to include these in the larger narrative. Like many of these, medical narratives have, until very recently, been all but omitted from the war story; the particular experience of medical personnel on hospital ships has received almost no attention.[7] At the same time, this chapter differs from others in this section in its focus on the importance of retrieving not only the silenced voices of combatants, but those of non-combatants, as we search for a larger and more nuanced understanding of the war.

Until the publication of Stephen McGreal's 2008 book *The War on Hospital Ships*, these medical sites were almost entirely without a public voice, barely making it into military or medical histories.[8] When they do, the focus is on the logistics of transport and care, as in Harrison's chapter on hospital ships and the Gallipoli campaign.[9] While McGreal does include some first-hand accounts, much unpublished material by doctors, nurses, and orderlies who worked on them is absent from his narrative. When we retrieve their stories and foreground them in another kind of salvaging exercise that brings the human experience to the surface, we not only restore to history the lived experience of the medical personnel who worked on these ships, but also extend the narratives of the sick, wounded, and dying combatants beyond the fighting front through this transitional space of pain that remains part of their war story, and, for many of them, the place where the story ended. As Kelly concludes in her discussion of nurses' accounts of hospital deaths, "the cultural work of our research is to make public" such writings to "remind us of the traumatic effect [of such death] on those who witnessed it," and of the terrible nature of that death for those who suffered through it.

Even as *Deep Wreck Mysteries* deflects attention away from the human story of these ships, the paradox evoked in the television documentary, where the wreck is at once glamorous and a testament to the brutality of war, is often reflected in the wartime experiences themselves. Witnessing terrible suffering and being haunted by the dread of mines and torpedoes is at times juxtaposed against the excitement attending their former use as luxury liners and the opportunities they afforded medical staff for foreign adventure: travelogue and participation in terrible suffering exist alongside each other in a way that sets these narratives apart from medical accounts from other war zones.

On 19 January 1916, Nursing Sister Mary Brown, leaving the Mediterranean en route to Italy and England, refers to her hospital ship *Devenha*'s occupants as Kitchener's Tourists, but her remark seems descriptive rather than ironic.[10] This term appears to have been a common one. It occurs again in the diary of Sister Kathleen Mann, also on the *Devenha*, who wrote on 19 January 1916 that, "We have fixed on a very suitable title for us, namely 'Kitchener's Tourists' as that is what we feel like, just lounging in deck chairs on a very comfortable steamer slowly passing up the most beautiful coast line. But what we are in for we do not know. The scene will change and I feel will be a very pitiful one."[11] The idea of a Mediterranean cruise at the expense of and in the service of Lord Kitchener, and particularly Mann's reference to the "change of scene" from "beautiful" to "pitiful," alerts us to the contradictions inherent in their position and in the accounts of nurses and doctors on these ships. The term is further qualified by Brown's entry four days later, when she notes how fast they are going and later in the day realizes they are being chased by an enemy submarine. Several accounts directly address this paradoxical concept of war tourism, articulating the appeal of visiting exotic locations that would never have been accessible outside war service. Travelling to Malta as a Voluntary Aid Detachment (VAD) nurse in September 1916 on the *Britannic*, Vera Brittain voices the incongruous coming-together of ocean liner glamour and the fear of a horrible death: "The expensive equipment of our cabins was illogically reassuring; those polished tables and bevelled mirrors looked so inappropriate for the bottom of the sea … it was difficult on so warm and calm an evening to convince oneself that at any moment might come a loud explosion, followed by a cold choky death in the smooth black water." At the same time, she mentions "the feelings of terror the dark hours used to bring us" in a letter to her mother, but then contrasts this with the excitement of adventure: "But even feeling so desperately afraid could not entirely quench the thrill of passing those far, enchanted lands which to a sixteen year old Cook's tourist had seemed so inaccessible."[12] Such incongruity is partially captured in the menus from hospital ships that bear vestiges of their origins as ocean liners, and in ships' postcards made over into patient information cards. It does appear that this excitement of "adventure," particularly for women who might otherwise never have left home, seems to offer some compensation for the hard and exhausting work and the pain and death they witnessed. Yet the idea of adventure also incorporates the dangers of war. Except in rare instances toward the end of the war, when some hospitals in France were bombed, the majority of nurses were relatively safe from belligerent action if not from disease. Hospital ships were the one front where they shared the same risks as the men they worked with and their patients, bringing them much closer to full participation in the war and allowing them to transcend the limitations war service placed on their sex.

Canadian nurse May Bastedo, writing home from the *Kildonan Castle*, gives only cursory mention of her patients, but is enthused by the "wonderful trip" that has taken her "places where very few others will go" (3 November 1915). Yet in the same letter she describes their proximity to the fighting at Gallipoli: "we were there two days and of course the fighting and bombarding didn't stop because we were there, in fact one Gun boat on our bow fired the big guns across us on to the hills.... You know how I love guns well I had nervous prostration fairly."[13] Fellow nurse Ruby Peterkin likewise writes somewhat sardonically, as they are sent from place to place in confusion over where the Canadian nurses are to be disembarked, "we have just been taking a little Mediterranean cruise and taking in the places we did not visit when you and I were over here last"; but in case her parents misread her, she adds, "of course, you understand, we have been working our passage," but again says almost nothing about the patients they were bringing from Gallipoli.[14]

While Bastedo and Peterkin say little about their patients, Nursing Orderly Frederick Brittain's diary of his experience on the HS *Egypt* illustrates the tension between treating the very ill and terribly wounded, and the strikingly beautiful landscape, like Mann juxtaposing injury and travelogue. On Sunday 19 September 1915, he writes, "The man with fifteen holes in him who likes me to dress him got quite excited because he thought I was not going to. Bathed a blind man's eyes with boracic, poor fellow, he is dreading the day when his wife will know. Later on deck reading. The sea is glorious in the moonlight and beautifully calm."[15] On Monday the 20th, having weighed anchor at Gibraltar, he records, "went back across the bay, which looked very beautiful with the sun setting behind its enclosing hills and glittering on the water. Darkness fell as we passed Tarita, so did not see the sunset run 'glorious blood red reeking into Cadiz Bay.' Today's ward work consisted of dressings, pills, formentations, and atropine tablet in eyes, etc." Arriving in Malta on 16 October 1916, his short entry reads, "Passed Gozo and arrived at Malta at 8. Put in at Valetta Harbour to pick up an officer. Fine view of the town with rows of yellow houses, castles, etc. and small boats like gondolas. Attended a lecture on haemorrhage." By Wednesday the 20th, he is visiting Alexandria: "Had a free train ride. Bought presents to take home and went into the Greek Cathedral.... Afterwards we wandered miles backwards and forwards all round the native quarters. A glorious moon made the ruins and native houses with projecting triangular windows look very picturesque." Brittain's setting of injury against the scenic emphasizes the visual; his experience is made up of the incongruous juxtaposition of the ugliness of war injury with the beauty of the setting. Although he does not draw attention to it, there is a sense that his recording of both arises out of gratitude that he is in the privileged position of being able, literally, to *see* the land and seascape, when so many of those he cares for have been blinded. A month earlier, on 15 September, taking on patients he writes:

> Saw some bad cases, one poor fellow is blind and lies with his face hidden all the time, another has his leg and thigh off and has bed sores....

> Someone was calling all the time so did not get away until nearly 9 pm. On deck a little, the moon was bright, and showing a silvery sea but I was too tired to appreciate it. Saw a patient on deck reading *Is War Consistent with Christianity?* I asked him what he thought. "Absolutely not," he said and added that he had seen things he never thought it possible to see and never wished to see again.

While on the one hand Brittain notes he is too tired to appreciate the sight of the moon on the sea, his recording of it suggests its importance in the context of the blind man. In particular, the repeated emphasis on seeing or not seeing plays the natural beauty of the moon and sea off against one who cannot see and another who has seen what he "never wished to see again."

As in Brittain's diary, it is against the quasi-tourist narrative that the dark story of massive suffering stands in such stark relief. Many accounts focus almost entirely on that suffering in the face of which all other narrative is inconsequential and therefore omitted. A.J. Gilbertson, a naval surgeon on the HS *Rewa*, began his diary on 29 October 1914 by documenting his arrival at Dunkirk at 4:00 p.m. and the loading of patients "at 6.45 from trains, ambulances, all sorts and conditions ... most extraordinary wounds, 3 with bullets right through the lungs walking about ... German wounds absolutely untouched for ten days."[16] Like the other diary accounts discussed here, Gilbertson's gives the immediacy of the situation, a telling not even hours old—a memory in the present, one might say—offering a representation of war that focuses attention on the immediate lived experience. It is the human story behind the logistics and the historical-political debates that is crucial to retrieve and place in the foreground as memory becomes history.

Another individual concerned with caring for the wounded on a hospital ship at the same time as Gilbertson is Nurse Ina Humphrey, on the HS *Asturias*. On 3 September 1914, having just come from service in France, she admires the patient capacity of the ship and exclaims, "the joy of having baths again! and a real English breakfast! and a spring bed, and sheets."[17] By 7 September, however, returning from St. Nazaire with "700 wounded men and 58 officers," her tone is sombre: "receiving men straight from the trains ... many of the men not having been dressed since the first Field Dressing was applied," although on 12 September she affirms, "operating on ship. It has been splendid work—and I love it—." While Gilbertson's descriptions of wounds and hours worked indicates the condition of the patients and his responsibility through numbers, Humphrey includes her emotional response to "a very heavy 'take in' nearly 1300 men" on 29 October 1914: "All day the deck has been a living stream of suffering humanity in almost all its forms. As I looked along the deck at the crowded faces, more than ever the awful meaning of War came home to me—here were strong men in their hundreds, literally halt, maimed and blind! And for hours without ceasing the stretcher-bearers were bringing on those who were still more seriously injured." More than any account here, her diary makes us acutely conscious of the danger to the ship's crew, medical personnel, and patients. Even at this early stage of the war the possibility of sinking is very real: "One has to remember the awful possibility there is of our striking a mine. There are many about in the Channel now … it may happen we shall be called, not only to face likely danger, but to suffer it…" [her ellipses]. But her attitude is stoic: "We can have but one prayer, if this should be so, that no sick are on Board! —For the rest, there are many worse things to fear than possible death at the post of Duty—." Reading this entry, one feels that for Humphrey to verbalize her fears and respond with stoicism is a means of coping with the possibility she must face. To draw on the concept of duty usually used in the context of combat is to position herself as participating in wartime masculine ideology. At the same time, it also reflects her nurse's training—to put the needs of her patients first. She had plenty of reason to be concerned. An attempted torpedo attack on the *Asturias* on 1 February 1915 was the first recorded attack on a British hospital ship. Fortunately the torpedo missed. However, on the night of 20 March 1917, the *Asturias* was torpedoed off the Devon coast: "Among the dead were a nurse [Sister Phillips], doctor and twelve RAMC orderlies."[18]

Humphrey's diary account sets her narrative of the wounded alongside pages that log the numbers on board and the operations, thus giving some indication of the actual work. Gilbertson's diary focuses on the very concrete, providing detailed descriptions of some of the wounds he encounters; but by 31 October 1914, he is calculating the enormity of the casualties in terms of ship's capacity: "With this our 3rd trip we shall have carried just short 2000 wounded, and when one thinks that beside ourselves 'Plassey' and 'Liberty' and 2 French ships carry 800 each at least it gives one some slight idea of the slaughter, the wounded are arriving in Dunkirk at a rate of 600 per diem and that is drawing on only one small portion of front." Gilbertson's diaries are particularly important because of his role as a ship's surgeon. In contrast to doctors near the front, who were overwhelmed by numbers at dressing stations or casualty clearing stations, Gilbertson is able to provide a very concrete documenting of the patients, their wounds and condition, and of his work and sleep times, which allows us to participate in his experience through almost daily entries. Humphrey's recording of her physical and emotional response (and her logs), set alongside Gilbertson's notations of time, not only reveal the numbers of patients, but simultaneously indicate the toll that the volume of casualties took on those caring for them, part of the experience rarely acknowledged by caregivers who are primarily concerned with emphasizing the suffering of their patients over their own discomfort or exhaustion. On 4 November 1914 she writes, "at 1 am just as I got to sleep a knock came and I was asked to go to the Theatre.... A man's life saved in the nick of time, who would not be proud to be able to help any hour of the night in such a cause: even if the previous day had been almost more than one could cope with." The next day she reveals honestly the extent of her exhaustion, which the satisfaction of helping cannot overcome: "Thurs Nov 5. Up at 7.30 am not joyfully! I will pretend no longer: for my every bone aches, and my head is going round and round today: —and there must be many others feeling as I do."

The hospital ships serving the Gallipoli campaign have been noted as sites of terrible suffering, overshadowing the experiences of those on the routine transportation of wounded running between France and Belgium and Britain. Humphrey's description of taking on wounded on 12 May 1915 from the Battle of Neuve Chapelle anticipates the scenes of suffering from Gallipoli that we will see in accounts by Gilbertson and other medical personnel, and is a reminder that, for the individual soldier, significance lies in the wound and in the resources to treat it, rather than where it was received:

It was a time I shall not soon forget. The horror of it all, the great wounds and calm patience of those heroes, one could barely understand what it all meant, the very flower of English man-hood, lying in long rows: helpless and suffering. No words can ever paint a scene like that, none are strong enough, great numbers of men had come straight from the field, barely dressed but in the roughest way, Neuve Chapelle is the cause of all this. All over the ship it was the same, men not washed or barely fed, or clothed, except in the dirtiest of garments—Oh God!! one's heart [word illegible] bled for them and the pathetic gratitude of the worst cases was almost more than one could bear—We all worked and worked!

But the suffering from wounds is only part of her concern: "At a crossing like this a terrible fear comes to one now and again—if we should be mined!!!

One is thankful, oh so thankful for each safe arrival at Southampton of our laden, suffering ships." Here the enormity of what she is articulating is such that the ship itself is made a synecdoche for the mass casualties: the wounded *are* the ship.

Gilbertson's second diary runs from 5 July to 12 August 1915, when the *Rewa* was sailing between Malta and Gallipoli. On 14 July he notes: "Too tired to write had a long day only 2 hours sleep last night and started in at 5am just off to bed midnight. Operating since 5pm." He adds briefly, "wonderful stories of wounded," and at the same time, "filthy state of some wounds (maggots) Full now over 500 on board (actually 680)." The next day, he moves from the general to the particular, giving a sense of the individual human suffering behind the numbers, and the weight of that suffering that he takes on:

> Started off at 5.30 am by having to go see leg, found it gangrenous (gas) amputated through thigh at 6.30 am and have been at it ever since. We are now at Mudros … arrived here at 6.30 pm. Why we are here nobody knows, we did so hope we were on our way to England. I hate parting with those poor maimed fellows who do so long to get home. It really is heart breaking at times, the worst of all is a man gets a small wound of hand or foot and then develops gas gangrene and the limb has to come off and even then he probably dies.

While Gilbertson refers only very briefly to his emotional response to the sick and wounded, Miss A. Hills, a nurse on the HS *Syria*, sets the hardness of the work and her sadness at the patients' condition against the worth-while nature of her toil. Bringing patients from Gallipoli to Alexandria in November 1915, she records, "Our patients are splendidly brave and grate-ful. It is so sad to see some of them that I should be miserable only that I am happy in doing so much for them," and later, "we are so busy that I have lost count of the days … I have got such bad cases … The work I am doing is just what I have always wanted."[19]

Hills draws on her nurse's ideology of caring to support herself psych-ologically in these instances; for others the sense of working in a context of severe limitations on their ability to give adequate care exacts an emotional toll when they are unable to relieve suffering. This reaction is now defined as moral distress, a contributing factor in Post-Traumatic Stress Disorder: "Moral distress arises when one knows the right thing to do, but institutional constraints make it nearly impossible to pursue the right course of action."[20] Such distress, and the seeming indifference of the military administration, is clearly behind Gilbertson's angry outburst at a bureaucracy that cannot operate effectively, resulting in lives lost. On 26 July, he writes:

> I think the military are a rotten lot for many reasons, the men are the best fighters in the world but the higher ranks of officers the very rottenest and the Germans from point of view of organisation deserve to win, and we have not won yet, it is merely individual bravery and self sacrifice that saves us at all, what we hear is enough to make one turn socialist, stories such as told by Australian RAMC whom we brought from Alex[andria], lying there months doing nothing while wounded are being put on to transports 7 and 800 with 2 drs and so on.... Can't possibly enumerate the different stories I have heard from all ranks and all the while the Argon is stiff with big officers doing nothing at all but live well.

Frederick Brittain's account shows that the situation still had not been resolved by September. Docked in Alexandria harbour, he writes that, "nurses who came on board from the S.S. Carapara say their ship has accommodation for 300 yet they had brought 700 home from the Dardanelles, with patients lying on deck tables, anywhere."

The limitations of care are constantly reiterated in Mary Brown's diary of the *Devenha*, also taking patients from Gallipoli to Malta and Lemnos where her time overlaps with Gilbertson's. She conveys the immediate experience of nursing in the conditions that so angered Gilbertson on 26 July: "July 12th 1915 Very busy day trying to get around my large family ... such a crowd that they cannot get the attention they ought." On 8 August she is back at Anzac/Cape Helles, and on the 9th records: "before we got breakfast a boatload of wounded came alongside, and all day the boats were bringing them down. We dressed nearly 1000 ... we were at it all day and had no time to pay attention to the fighting ... the whole thing is too ghastly to write about." Her reference to the fighting here refers to the shells passing overhead, which she mentions on another occasion, and perhaps to stray bullets. Gilbertson's diary is more direct about the dangers. On 13 August he records: "We have to move out a little as it is too dangerous here, the Guilford Castle though further out had 3 men wounded last night"; and on 14 August: "Dressings on deck. Bullets whizzing all over nobody hit yet."

While Gilbertson makes no direct mention of his response to the medical situation in his entry of 22 August, the markers of time reveal the unspoken narrative: "Started at 11pm last night and went to bed at 3.30 up at 6.45 and have just finished at 10.30 [p.m.], we have 700 pts on board and passed 400 on to sweepers. In Theatre from 7.30 until dinner then did dressings on deck, very tired, enormous casualties." In both instances, here, what Brown and Gilbertson infer but do not describe goes some way to communicating the terrible nature of the conditions and numbers of patients.

The vantage point of the hospital ship also provides Gilbertson with immediate knowledge of the terrible conditions from which his patients have come. On about 28 August he writes: "most depressing news from shore. 3 division landed ... Welsh Territorial do badly. N.C.O.s have to shoot men to get a move on them, same old story, more men wanted. I am sorry for the new men coming into this hell." Yet, whatever the conditions aboard ship, the almost inexpressible hell of treating casualties on the beaches was documented by Medical Officer Norman Tattersall earlier that month. He comments on 6 August that he is "moderately safe" in a dugout at Anzac, but that, "the Colonel says we will be working day and night for 3 days and must expect some 30,000 casualties. I can't estimate the horror of all this now, probably I will in three days time."[21]

Tattersall's diary provides an important context for understanding the conditions of the patients on ships such as the *Devenha* and the *Rewa*, as well as the logistics involved in getting patients into the hospital ships. In an entry dated 7 August, 7:30 p.m., Tattersall records:

> For the last 36 hours have been working incessantly without any time to think—much less write. Had no time for any food yesterday—only water [he later realizes this carries dysentery] ... About 8.30 am yesterday the wounded started pouring in.... It is useless to try and describe the wounds—everywhere—everything and of all degrees of severity. All we could do was to lay them down on the beach and ... get them on board when possible. The great difficulty was getting lighters to take them away in; ... Couldn't get our wounded cleared last night, and had about 80 patients lying out in the open—blazing sun—no shade—stray bullets. They lay there in the dust all Saturday afternoon and the all night. All we could do for them was to give them water and morphia ...
>
> Have nearly 200 lying here now and will not be able to get more than half of them embarked tonight and they are continually filling up from behind.

August 9th—Monday 8pm

Have had another 24 hours of Hell. Cleared about 800 wounded from the pier since last night but cannot cope with the ever increasing stream. Have now worked 62 hours without a break, and only water and biscuits—no sleep—am getting tired. The stretcher bearers are magnificent—the wounded have to be carried down about 2 miles in the blazing heat—over rough ground—and under direct fire all the way. Many of them have been doing it for nearly 70 hours now without a break and still go on—exhausted—and bleeding feet—Sniped and cannot shoot back—they are heroes to a man.

Given these conditions, it is no wonder that on 24 August he records a visit to Brown's ship, the *Devenha*, as a relaxing break in what must have seemed an entirely different world, where he "had tea and dinner with Dr Rainey … it was glorious to have clean tables…. Came back at 9pm with presents of books, papers, cigarettes, tobacco, and chocolate for my fellow sufferers here."

In October this hell resulted in more illnesses than wounds, with Gilbertson recording "dysentery, pyrexia of a curious nature, jaundice, rheumatism, septic sores causing cellulitis, pneumonia" (16 October). What such illness actually meant is vividly and graphically evoked by Sister Mary Fitzgibbon, caring for dysentery patients on the *Essequibo*:

Most of the time we were under shell fire. The wounded were easy enough to deal with, but the sick! They were in a terrible state, all suffering from dysentery and enteric. Their insides had simply turned to water, and all they had been able to do for them on shore was tie their trousers round their legs with pieces of string … We had wounded as well, of course—because there were many wounded—but it's the sick I'll remember. I'll never forget them. Just pouring with dysentery—sick, miserable, dehydrated and in terrible pain. It was pitiful to see them, so weak, and blood and water pouring out of them.[22]

Characteristically, here, Fitzgibbon ignores her own situation under fire and places the suffering of the patients at the forefront.

By November, cold, along with wounds or illness, had become a major cause of death. The most detailed and shocked account in Gilbertson's diary comes on 19 November 1915. With the temperature between twenty-seven and twenty-nine degrees Fahrenheit, the *Rewa* is ordered to go close in to shore to take on patients suffering from exposure:

It was bitingly cold and the poor fellows many of them had not even great coats on … it was a most pitiable sight the majority could only just crawl up the ladder, dozens tried, failed and had to be carried, they came on mouths open, gasping, faces bluish grey, eyes glazed, many of those [who] could stumble had to be led as they just walked automatically, their clothes frozen stiff. I shall never forget the experience. We got them all into cots (as many as possible there were 340 we only have 214 cots) and on to mattresses, filled them up on hot soup and Bovril and piled blankets on to them, wonderful thing was only one died, heaps had frostbitten feet … at 9 pm another 306 came alongside in tug. These were put into mattresses all over place, turning patients off cots who had come round to make room for those who were worse, the whole deck below was covered, we had them packed even under cots … I was going until midnight wrapping up feet in cotton wool. The stories the men told were awful … eventually the cold became so severe that several men died in trenches … that rainstorm had washed away all equipment and food, then began the scramble to hospital.

As already noted in other accounts, the patients' predicament is made central to the narrative, while the physical and mental strain on the doctors, nurses, and orderlies is approached only obliquely. Yet, we have a glimpse of the burden they carried in Gilbertson's description and his statement, "I shall never forget the experience," echoing Humphrey on the wounded from Neuve Chapelle.

Similarly, Brown does acknowledge her own exhaustion, but immediately compares it to the plight of those much worse off, the combatants: "I am dead tired, it has been a very trying day for everyone, some of our men had no food for three days, and no proper sleep for weeks and as for a wash or change some not for 12 or 14 weeks." The use of the term "trying" implies but avoids articulating the experience she shares with her fellow medical staff, but she immediately replaces her exhaustion with the conditions from which the patients have just come. When she does have some time outside her work, she focuses not on herself but on her patients. On 24 December she writes: "We left Mudros for Alexandria about 9.30 am. It is Christmas Eve, but none of us can realise it, we managed to scrape up odds and ends for all our boys of 16, 17, 18, and 19. I have 12 in my ward under 19. I saved up my oranges and apples for days past so that I could put them in their stockings." Brown's account here exemplifies what Christine Hallett refers to as the nurse's role in "containing trauma," a responsibility taken on by nurses whereby ameliorating the suffering of the patient extends beyond medical attention to wider forms of care, particularly performing a maternal, nurturing role. Hallett writes: "Healing was seen to depend upon containment—of the physical self (by the prevention of shock or the healing of wounds), of the emotional self (by psychological reintegration) and of the moral and social self (by self-composure and the restoration of faith in one's world). Yet, containment was only possible if healers—nurses— were able to provide its preconditions. And their work could only be done if they themselves were 'contained' in an integrated state."[23] She notes that, "nurses used 'familial' relationships with patients to provide comfort while at the same time avoiding the possible dangers of crossing emotional and relational boundaries."[24] Of course, this also meant that nurses and doctors (as we see in Gilbertson's diary) carried the psychological and emotional burden of responsibility for this kind of containment, yet rarely acknowledged their own need for such support. Gilbertson's anger at the bungling of military administration that failed to provide adequate medical care for the wounded at Gallipoli, and Brown's brief references to the problems of treating huge numbers of casualties, reflect this weight of responsibility.

Brown's description of the Christmas stockings, so similar to many of the more familiar accounts by nurses on the Western Front at Christmas, who attempted to make some form of Christmas gift for their patients, offers a semblance of normalcy here, but at the same time brings home forcefully the ages of those who were bearing the burden of the disastrous Gallipoli campaign. Yet, even the idea of planning for Christmas indicates the need for nurses and their patients to avoid considering the possible fate of their hospital ship, supposedly protected by the Hague and Geneva conventions. The nurses' actions here suggest again the need for emotional control. Preparing for Christmas is a way of transferring a sense of security to their patients, even though, as we have seen in Humphrey's account, they must have been well aware of the dangers they all faced.

In this instance the ship did reach England safely, but for C.E. Dingle, a conscientious objector and member of the Friends Ambulance Unit working as a medical orderly on the *Glenart Castle*, the worst fear of everyone on those ships was about to be realized.[25] In March 1917, the *Glenart Castle* struck a mine en route from Le Havre to Southampton.[26] Dingle's understated account illustrates both the calmness of the staff and the problems of moving severely injured patients into lifeboats: "March 2. At a quarter to twelve I awoke to hear my name being shouted by Abbatt, who wanted to know whether I was closing my portholes." Initially Dingle thinks it is an exercise, but "[he] soon discovered that all the patients who could walk were leaving the ward to go on deck, and soon [he] heard that the ship had been struck aft and that [they] were in for the real thing." His tone is matter-of-fact, but vivid: "The patients were crowded all over the decks, and the whole mass of moving humanity on the ship, which now listed considerably to starboard, was lit up by a destroyer's searchlight." The control over his language in describing moving the patients reflects the controlled evacuation, reminding us that the lives of the patients were in the hands of Dingle and the other medical personnel. As with Hallett's discussion of nurses, such control is a form of containment—of one's own fears and the patients'. Since he is writing in the aftermath, his tone also conveys a sense of having overcome a potentially life-threatening situation: "It was a task of some difficulty carrying men with femur and splints down [the] ladder and impossible to do so without causing them pain. At 2.30 am we put off in ship's boat no 4 ... I shall long remember gazing at the old bus ... as she stood out of the black sea, gaunt and stricken." Dingle at once underplays his own efforts and falls back on a received image of the "stricken" ship to describe the scene, deflecting any emotion onto the ship. In the event, the *Glenart Castle* was towed to England and repaired. But in 1918 she was torpedoed in the Bristol Channel and sank rapidly. Fortunately for Dingle, he was by then back in France working on an ambulance train. Gilbertson's ship, the *Rewa*, as already noted, was torpedoed near the Bristol Channel in January 1918. Gilbertson's last entry in the diary on file is 14 December 1915, so perhaps he was not on the *Rewa* when she was sunk.[27]

While Dingle does not address the emotional toll of the event, other accounts, especially where the sinking included loss of life and the disappearance of the ship, acknowledge the impact on individuals. Nursing on Malta, Vera Brittain reported the frequent arrival of crews from torpedoed and mined ships, and her description of visiting a nursing friend from her voyage out on the *Britannic*, who had later been torpedoed on the ship, gives some idea of what that meant:

> We went to see her at Floriana Hospital ... and found her completely changed—nervous, distressed and all the time on the verge of crying. But to talk of the disaster seemed to bring her relief, and from her conversation we learnt the story of the ship's last hours.... None of the women were lost; but a number of casualties occurred among the orderlies.... The medical officers, remaining to the end, climbed down the wire ropes—which almost cut their hands to pieces—dropped

into the sea in their lifebelts, and struggled to the boats already afloat. Two of them disappeared and were never accounted for … she sank in three-quarters of an hour … and for many of the survivors, the worst part of their ordeal was the sight of her disappearance … the dreadful cry of the last siren, "All hands off the ship!" just before she sank, would haunt their nights, our friend said, for the rest of their lives.[28]

Nurse C.E. (Eve) Dodsworth's firsthand account of the sinking of the *Aragon* similarly presents the trauma of witnessing death and destruction alongside the shock of abandoning ship. Having been taken on board a destroyer from her lifeboat, what is most distressing for her is watching "men pouring down the side [of the *Aragon*] into the sea; it was simply a swarm of khaki all down the side and it seemed as if it would never clear before she went down altogether. We felt that all our friends were drowning before our eyes." One of the destroyers removing men from the *Aragon* was also hit by a torpedo, and began to sink: "The torpedo hit her in the oil bunkers, so all the men who were thrown into the sea were swimming in a pool of oil…. It was terrible to see where the ships had been, and where now there was nothing but a little floating wreckage and hundreds of swimming figures."[29]

Very little in the way of sympathy is offered to the surviving nurses. Dodsworth describes the arrival in Alexandria:

We were given a much needed meal…. As soon as we had finished we were each given a pair of pyjamas and ten grains of aspirin and sent to bed. Bed at 5pm with one's head in a whirl. Had we only been allowed to spend a normal evening, we should have had so much more chance of sleeping…. Later—We got undressed and in to bed and after some time went to sleep, but I know I kept waking in terror every time I dozed off and started to dream.[30]

Her account continued the next morning: "The other hospitals all gave the following day off as well but our matron said that after the shock we had she thought it better to start work at once and so avoid thinking about it." But work cannot prevent the persistence of a more unconscious reaction; the aftermath stayed with her during her time nursing in Alexandria: "The work was thrilling and I was glad of it. I was terribly jumpy and was sleeping very badly. A banging door would leave me shaking all over."[31] A stoic response to such an ordeal was the cultural expectation both of the time and of wartime nursing; individual emotional reactions were expected to be suppressed. Vera Brittain's account of her nursing friend shows, however, that retelling the experience could be therapeutic. The diaries and recollections discussed here offered the men and women who wrote them a space in which to process a range of unprecedented and often traumatic experiences. However, the failure to acknowledge the importance of the story at the time—the tendency, metaphorically, to prescribe aspirin and bed rest rather than admit to the enormity of the experience—may underlie the subsequent lack of attention these accounts have received.

As Dodsworth indicates in her description of how her experiences remained with her at a subconscious level, the accounts here, almost all still unpublished, need to be retrieved, and the story of the interdependent experience of nurse, doctor, orderly, and patient told. Even as memory of the First World War moves into history, and as increasing attention is paid to war experience beyond that of the combatant and the Western Front, hospital ships and the lives they saved and lost are still situated at the margins. If, to reiterate Carpentier, "our representations are unavoidably all we are left with," these firsthand accounts and what they have to tell us about war must not be ignored or subsumed by the popular entertainment of *Deep Wreck Mysteries*, but made an essential part of Great War history.

NOTES

1. *Deep Wreck Mysteries 3*: "Red Cross Outrage," a UK/Canada co-production, Mallinson Sadler Productions/Northern Sky Entertainment, 2006.
2. Nico Carpentier, *Culture, Trauma, and Conflict: Cultural Studies Perspectives on War* (Newcastle: Cambridge Scholars Publishing, 2007), 9.
3. Many hospital ships were requisitioned liners, such as the Cunard liners *Mauretania* and *Aquitania*; the Union Castle line supplied most of the hospital ships, including the *Glenart Castle* and the *Kildonan Castle*; other companies were also crucial, such as the Royal Mail Steam Packet Company, the P&O ferry service, and the British India Steam Navigating Company, which owned the *Rewa* and the *Devenha*. Hospital ships were crucial in evacuating the wounded and sick from Gallipoli and in ferrying wounded and sick between the French Channel ports and Britain. There was no stable number of hospital ships, as the same ship often went through several conversions; thus, for example, the "*Kildonan Castle* operated as a 600-bed carrier from 6 October 1915; five months later she became an armoured merchant cruiser." Stephen McGreal, *The War on Hospital Ships 1914–1918* (Barnsley: Pen and

Sword Maritime, 2008), 53. For a full historical discussion of hospital ships in the war, see McGreal.

4. Ibid.

5. For a detailed account of the sinking of the *Llandovery Castle*, see McGreal, *The War on Hospital Ships*, 198–206.

6. T.G. Ashplant, Graham Dawson, and Michael Roper, eds., *The Politics of War Memory and Commemoration* (London: Routledge, 2000), 11, 21.

7. McGreal's book focuses on the "war" on the ships, rather than on the details of life on these ships.

8. John Plumridge's book *Hospital Ships and Ambulance Trains* (London: Seeley, Service, 1975) has a chapter on First World War hospital ships.

9. Mark Harrison, *The Medical War: British Military Medicine in the First World War* (Oxford: Oxford University Press, 2010).

10. Nurse M. Brown, unpublished diary, Imperial War Museum (88/7/1). Quotations from this source appear with the kind permission of Mrs. E. Cleverly, OBE.

11. Kathleen Mann, *Women in the War Zone: Hospital Service in the First World War*, Anne Powell, ed. (Stroud: History Press, 2009), 257.

12. Vera Brittain, *Testament of Youth* (London: Virago Press, 1978), 296–97.

13. "My Trip Abroad," May Bastedo Fonds, CWM 19780041-001, George Metcalf Archival Collection © Canadian War Museum. Quotations from this source appear with permission of the Canadian War Museum, Ottawa, Canada.

14. Library and Archives Canada, Ruby Peterkin fonds, (RT630-0-X-E).

15. Frederick Brittain, unpublished diary, Imperial War Museum (99/55/1), reproduced by kind permission of the Imperial War Museum, London.

16. A.J. Gilbertson, unpublished diary, Imperial War Museum (92/46/1). Extracts reproduced by kind permission of Liz Wagstaff. The importance of returning to primary sources is exemplified in Gilbertson's diary. Both Plumridge and McGreal state that the *Rewa* began her career as a hospital ship in January 1915, and Plumridge writes that she left Gallipoli with her last load of patients on 29 April 1915. In fact, as Gilbertson's diary shows, the *Rewa* was used to transport wounded from France to Britain in 1914, and was still in Gallipoli late in 1915 taking on patients. She was sunk in January 1918.

17. Ina Humphrey, unpublished diary, Army Medical Services Museum archives (Box 25). Reproduced with kind permission of the Army Medical Services Museum, Keogh Barracks, UK.

18. McGreal, 59–60, 130.

19. Miss A. Hills, unpublished diary, Imperial War Museum (Documents 9601). Extracts are reproduced by kind permission of John D. Ferrett.

20. Janeton quoted in Judith Wilkinson, "Moral distress in Nursing Practice: Experience and Effect," *Nursing Forum* 28, no. 1 (1987–88): 16–29.

21. Norman Tattersall, unpublished diary, Imperial War Museum (98/24/1). Extracts are reproduced by kind permission of Michael Tattersall.

22. Mary Fitzgibbon in Lyn Macdonald, *Roses of No Man's Land* (London: Michael Joseph, 1980), 115–16.

23. Christine Hallett, *Containing Trauma: Nursing Work in the First World War* (Manchester: Manchester University Press, 2009), 206.

24. Hallett, 178.

25. C.E. Dingle, Unpublished Diary and Recollections, Liddle Collection, University of Leeds, (CO 024). Reproduced by kind permission of Richard Davies, Archivist, Liddle Collection.

26. See McGreal, 178.

27. For a full account of these two sinkings, see McGreal, 172–75, 177–85.

28. Brittain, *Testament of Youth*, 312–14.

29. Diary of Kit and Eve Dodsworth, in Macdonald, *Roses of No-Man's Land*, 238–39.

30. Vaughn-Phillips (nee Dodsworth) diary, Liddle Collection, University of Leeds (WO 126). Reproduced by kind permission of Richard Davies, Archivist, Liddle Collection.

31. Ibid.

THE FORGOTTEN FEW
Quebec and the Memory
of the First World War

GEOFF KEELAN

"The essence of Canada's myth of the war ... [is] a discourse that communicated the past in a pure, unambiguous, and simple fashion," writes Jonathan Vance. For English Canadians, the process of simplifying the nation's experience of the Great War helped create a strong, national myth that eventually evolved into a durable historical narrative. Vance argues that Victorian ideals shaped English Canada's attempts to justify their role in the war, regardless of the cost it incurred, and provided a moral and cultural framework that shaped the emerging historical narrative that developed in the 1920s and 1930s. The dominance of that narrative, he states, was difficult to integrate with the memory of French Canadians, who did not agree with the "proper combination of remembering and forgetting" that emerged among English-speaking Canadians.[1] The problem, Vance implies, arose out of the conflict between English Canada's majoritarian narrative of the war and an equally unambiguous French-Canadian narrative. However, this simplified division of two cultural perspectives does not adequately explain the complexity of Quebec's evolving memory of the First World War. Vance's English-Canadian myth of the Great War existed in part because it was able to produce a "pure, unambiguous and simple" narrative. The Québécois,[2] however, faced complex and competing stories about the war, some of which faded while others continued to resonate.

This chapter isolates three narratives of Quebec and the First World War. These narratives highlight how emphasis on different war experiences produced three memories that served a purpose for those who remembered them. Thus, this chapter examines both history and the historical narratives that form social memory. One such narrative is that of the veterans of the 22nd (French-Canadian) Battalion; the second formed around Henri Bourassa and his role in the war; and the third is the relatively recent resurrection, to English Canada, of Talbot Mercer Papineau as a French-Canadian hero. These stories are not memories that have survived since the First World War; rather, they represent separate remembrances[3] of the war that emerged in its aftermath. Each demonstrates how different details were, as Vance noted, important to remember or forget. Their disparate nature reveals the difficulty in "lining them up" as one coherent memory of Quebec. The events remembered by the veterans of the 22nd Battalion faded after the end of the Second World War and were forgotten by other Québécois. Henri Bourassa has been an enduring figure for both sides of Canada's linguistic divide for his role during the war—but by the 1960s seemingly for contradictory reasons. Papineau has only been vaguely remembered in the last few decades, but his tale was sensationalized by a dominant English-Canadian majority rather than those in his "native" province. These remembrances do not cover the breadth of French-Canadian narratives during the Great War, as Acadians, Franco-Ontarians, or Franco-Manitobans could attest. They demonstrate the difficulties historians must face when discussing Quebec and the Great War.

The veterans of the 22nd (French-Canadian) Battalion created a narrative of the war that was important to themselves if not their countrymen. They had not gone to war for Britain or for Empire as the English-Canadian war myths trumpet; rather, they fought for their country of Canada, for France, for their province, or for their faith. Echoing Vance's Victorian English-Canadian ideals, they developed a justification for the war based on the idea of the *survivance* of French Canada's language, religion, and culture.[4] Their memory of the Great War was the memory of a *patrie* and what they sacrificed to preserve it. It is a particular understanding of French Canada and the First World War that was a minority experience, even among their own people.

In September 1914, Dr. Arthur Mignault offered $50,000 to raise a French-Canadian battalion for the Second Division. On 15 October, fifteen thousand Montrealers gathered in Parc Sohmer to hear Sir Wilfrid Laurier and other notable French Canadians implore volunteers to join the war effort. Despite its organizers' claims of success, by 5 November there were only thirty-two officers and 891 volunteers of other ranks in the 22nd

Battalion, requiring an additional hundred men for its departure for the front on 15 May 1915.[5] It was a dubious beginning for Canada's only fully French-speaking unit, reflecting Quebec's general attitude toward the war rather than the volunteers' commitment to fight. Their abilities would be proven a year later in the fall of 1916, as the battalion fought one of its most terrible battles at the French village of Courcelette in the final days of the Somme offensive.

The second year of the war still offered Canadians the tenuous hope of a unified war effort. Canada, after the terrible casualties of the Somme, was fully exposed to the Great War's costs, even as recruiting continued to wane.[6] On 1 January 1916, Prime Minister Robert Borden declared that the Canadian army would expand to 500,000 men in uniform, doubling its previous number.[7] With conscription looming, pro-war advocates undertook some limited efforts to convince Québécois that it was in their best interest to serve the country willingly. In that spirit, Toronto businessmen began the *Bonne Entente* movement, which attempted to unify the divided country by bringing together English- and French-Canadian community leaders. Unfortunately, the effort to combat the influence of Bourassa and others opposed to the war "withered into resentment and anger."[8] Similarly the government, finally realizing that the recruitment situation in Quebec was not like the rest of Canada, appointed Colonel Arthur Mignault as the chief recruiting officer in the summer of 1916. His predecessor was a Protestant minister, Major C.A. Williams, appointed in 1914, whose efforts had been an impressive disaster. The selection of Mignault, the same who had spearheaded the 22nd Battalion's formation the year before, would be too little and too late.[9] The task of undoing the Conservative government's previous failure was daunting. Worse yet, the Judicial Committee of the Privy Council, the highest appellate court for Canada, upheld Ontario's Regulation 17 that restricted French-language schooling in 1916. According to Mason Wade, the decision caused a "passionate emotional reaction which ... always developed whenever one of the essentials of national survival [was] endangered" to sweep through Quebec.[10] The resulting furor and debate over the issue helped shift French Canadians' focus from the war overseas toward the defence of their rights at home.[11] That summer Talbot Mercer Papineau, a French-Canadian officer in the Canadian army, published a letter to his cousin Henri Bourassa attacking Bourassa's opposition to the war and imploring his French-Canadian brethren to join the fight. In this ambiguous context, the 22nd Battalion fought over the shell-torn ground at Courcelette.

At Courcelette, Major-General Richard Turner commanded the 2nd Canadian Division, tasked with advancing on the left flank of General Sir Henry Rawlinson's 4th Army as he attempted once again to break the German lines along the Somme and Ancre rivers. The 2nd Division had early successes on the morning of 15 September, and as reports came in of German disorganization, Turner received orders to seize the village of Courcelette.[12] The 22nd Battalion was chosen to attack that evening. As the assault began, two companies marched toward the village of Martinpuich and Candy Trench, with two companies following behind them in reserve. Bombarded by shells and shrapnel, the French-Canadian soldiers kept the line moving forward. By the end of the night, they had established a defensive line north of the village and captured over three hundred prisoners and a large quantity of German weapons. The soldiers of the 22nd repelled thirteen counterattacks from the Germans over the next three days. Between 15 and 18 September, the battalion suffered 207 killed and wounded. Of the twenty-two officers who entered the battle, six were killed and five wounded.[13] They were engaged in heavy fighting until 10 October, when they left the theatre. Most remember the overall failure of the Somme offensive during the summer of 1916, but for the 22nd Battalion the success at Courcelette became one of their proudest memories.

In its immediate aftermath, the battle of Courcelette was understood by its survivors and the home front as not simply a victory, but as an affirmation of French-Canadian prowess. For the veterans of the 22nd, it was where the dreadful slaughter of the Western Front was glorified and accepted as a necessary consequence. "Il a bien merité de la patrie," wrote Claudius Corneloup of the French-Canadian battalion in the Great War.[14] Corneloup, an Alsatian by birth, joined the 22nd Battalion in 1915 and published his memoir just a year after the war's end. It emphasized the glory and courage of the French-speaking soldiers who had fought in British uniform. Corneloup summed up the soldiers' perspective when he wrote of Courcelette that "le 22ième d'alors marchait vers l'immortalité,"[15] while his commanding officer, Lieutenant-Colonel Thomas-Louis Tremblay, warned that if hell were as terrible as what he had seen at Courcelette, he would not wish it upon his worst enemy.[16] The experience at Courcelette solidified the battalion as a hardened, battle-ready unit. They had survived front-line trench warfare and emerged successful. Metropolitan Quebec newspapers reflected this attitude and extolled the triumph of their French-Canadian soldiers.[17] One of Montreal's leading French-language newspapers, *La Patrie*, featured the battle on its front page with the headline "Le Grand Courage et L'Initiative de nos Canadiens Français."[18] Another, *La Presse*, proclaimed that the battle proved that, "La Province de Québec est loyale."[19] Even two years after the battle, Bishop Camille Roy would preach that at Courcelette it was "l'élan impétueux des Canadiens français, qui balayèrent tout devant eux et brisèrent comme un fétu la résistance d'un ennemi numériquement supérieur."[20] The exaggerated heroism matched the English-Canadian rhetoric present since the war's beginning. For those on the French-Canadian home front, Courcelette answered the lingering question about whether their people had the will to fight.

The accomplishments of the 22nd Battalion invigorated the martial spirit among French-speaking Canadians, but it failed to sway English-Canadian attitudes toward French Canada or French Canadians opposed to the war. English-Canadian newspapers and politicians, as they had since the start of the war, ignored or belittled Quebec's contributions and focused on the war's opponents, Henri Bourassa and his fellow *nationalistes*.[21] Their perceived lack of patriotism and the province's supposed low number of volunteers were key points of contention during the campaign for conscription the following year.[22] In contrast, the aggravating leadership of the minister of militia, Sam Hughes, and the refusal of Ontario to compromise on the issue of French-language schools, continued to sour many French Canadians to the Britannic call to arms. Equally, Courcelette had no lasting impact on the war's opponents in French Canada. A day before Courcelette, Bourassa's editorial entitled "La Réorganisation de L'Empire" claimed that Canadians were "les complices aveugles de l'impérialisme" and they were now paying for their "complaisances passées" in blood.[23] The extreme nature of his position fuelled the anger of those English Canadians who demanded total support for the war and who depicted Quebec as traitorous or, at least, unworthy. As conscription loomed, the accomplishments of the 22nd seemed less significant. Few saw the worth in acknowledging the victories of the 22nd Battalion; their part in the Great War remained an aberration in the war narrative being established by its defenders and detractors.

After the imposition of the *Military Service Act*, the cancellation of exemptions and rioting throughout the province in April 1918, French Canada was isolated from the rest of the country. Most Québécois forgot the headlines championing the courage and initiative of their home-grown volunteer soldiers. Still, the small, steady stream of recruits who volunteered for Canada's French-speaking battalions and had witnessed the horrors of the European battlefields did not simply disappear. Those who had believed in their duty to fight the war would never escape what Desmond

Morton calls a "conflict of loyalties" between fighting for their country and their provincial identity.[24]

In the years after the war, when most French Canadians remembered their oppression as a nexus for the war's most important events, the struggles of their veterans were marginalized. The majority of the province did not want to praise a conflict that had forced conscription in a British war. Still, the memoirs published by the soldiers of the 22nd Battalion continued to express a laudatory view of French Canadians' role in the conflict. An unofficial history of the battalion was published in 1919 and detailed the unit's war service; it was entitled *Les Poilus Canadiens*, a fusion of France's slang for its infantrymen and the traditional term for French Canadians.[25] Another well-received book was the "souvenirs et impressions" of Arthur Lapointe. It began with a note to the reader that despite the horrible nightmares of the war he now endured, "j'ai la consolation d'avoir été utile à mon pays, et d'avoir payé ma dette de reconnaissance à la vieille France."[26] Lapointe agreed with Claudius Corneloup's description of the 22nd soldiers who "s'interpellaient en français, se battaient à la française, c'est à dire d'un mordant irrésistible."[27] They had fought in their native tongue and for their ancient homeland. Canada was just as dear as France for the men of the 22nd Battalion. What the veterans chose to emphasize in their memoirs was the bravery and unit cohesion that carried them to the front and allowed them to endure the awful life of the trenches. As one officer reminisced fondly, the battalion's motto served them well: "on s'ostine," stolen from its British original, "what we have, we hold."[28] Even by 1941, at the twenty-fifth anniversary of Courcelette and in the midst of another world war, Thomas-Louis Tremblay, now a major-general, reminded his former comrades to "Be worthy of the 22nd!"[29] Be worthy of the battles they had won and the men who had fallen. Yet it was a memory of the war that would only last as long as its soldiers. When the final veteran's memoir was published in 1952,[30] the history of the veterans of the 22nd Battalion had been long overshadowed by the Second World War and Quebec's new inward-looking identity. Only in the halls of their successors, the Royal 22nd Regiment, the VanDoos, did their stories continue to be told.

As their forgotten history passed into forgotten memory, another French-Canadian living narrative of the war ended. On 31 August 1952, the day before his eighty-fourth birthday, Henri Bourassa passed away at home. His death ended a five-decade-long career of commenting on the politics of his country and province. Unsurprisingly, historians and other intellectuals quickly sought to define the venerable nationalist's role in shaping the turbulent, post–Second World War Canada. French and English Canadians chose to define Bourassa's influence during the First World War only so far as it reinforced their separate understandings of the war's purpose. Both simplified the substance of his critical commentary of war aims during the First World War, as well as the forces influencing Bourassa's reasoning.

Originally a Liberal MP, Bourassa split from the Laurier government over the Boer War in 1899. To him, the Boer War was not only immoral and unjust, but also Canada had no legal obligation to join.[31] This was a theme he would repeat fifteen years later. The break, writes historian Réal Belanger, incited Bourassa to work toward "a clearer understanding of Canada's relations with the Empire and the nature of the relationship between the country's English Canadian Protestant majority and its French Canadian Catholic minority."[32] Ultimately, Bourassa believed that Confederation had promised an equal relationship between two peoples, French and English, and that compact had to be upheld for Canada to reach its full potential. Working toward that compact would shape the rest of his public life. His best vehicle for it would come a decade later when he started his own newspaper, *Le Devoir*. As editor from its founding in 1910 to his resignation in 1932, Bourassa elucidated his opinion on provincial, national, and international topics to a small but influential audience.[33] Though he briefly allied with the Conservatives to overthrow former Liberal leader Sir Wilfrid Laurier in the 1911 election, and toured English Canada extensively in the years before the war, he was painted by contemporary opponents as the dire enemy of imperial Canada, the dreaded French-Canadian nationalist. His fiery attacks against the limitation of French-language schooling in Ontario through the enactment of Regulation 17 reinforced the view that he was the enemy of English Canadians as much as he was the protector of Catholic French Canada. His reputation, or his infamy, only grew during the Great War.

For contemporaries and historians, Bourassa became a villain in the patriotic war narrative that was fashioned on the slopes of Vimy Ridge and figured dominantly in the English- and French-Canadian memories of the war. As historians have noted, Bourassa, along with most Canadians, initially supported the war. In August 1914, Bourassa was in Alsace on the last leg of a trip to England and the continent aimed at connecting with European statesmen and investigating Europe's language policy toward minorities, such as the Irish, the Welsh, the Walloons, and the Alsatians. While in Europe he had witnessed German-ruled Alsatians gather to pray for France, Frenchmen unite under the *union sacrée*, and Englishmen join the side of their ancient continental enemy against a new one.[34] The elation of his escape from the continent and the powerful images he had seen were captured in the only editorial he would ever write that offered outright support for the war effort.[35] The war, he believed, was the chance for English and French Canadians to unite, as well. Still, Bourassa tempered his praise with criticism of Canada's "excessive" war effort—an action that his enemies eagerly denounced.

By the fall of 1914, his demands for a limited Canadian contribution to Britain's war had earned the disdain and contempt of English Canadians. Faced with an exaggerated imperial patriotism, Bourassa actively began to oppose the war, and in 1915 he asked, in a provocative summary of his views on the war, *Que devons-nous à l'Angleterre?*[36] The answer, he argued, was far less than what Canadians were providing. His long campaign against the war had begun in earnest.

Bourassa wrote prolifically about the war's economic costs and political consequences at home and abroad throughout the four years Canadians fought on European battlefields. He celebrated the interventions of Pope Benedict XV and American president Woodrow Wilson, who strove to end the bloodshed.[37] His French-Canadian compatriots were affected by the pressures of wartime, so when the Judicial Committee of the Privy Council ruled to uphold Regulation 17 in 1916, French Canada's apathy toward the war moved closer to outright rejection. It pushed Bourassa further to the forefront of a common cause for Canada's French-speaking peoples, as he continued to mock the politicians who supported the ruling against Canada's minority while championing the rights of the "petits peuples de l'Europe."[38]

Bourassa's defence of French Canada grew more urgent as the war continued. Prime Minister Borden's announcement that the Canadian army would grow to 500,000 soldiers, especially after the casualties of the Somme offensive in 1916 and Vimy Ridge in the spring of 1917, meant that conscription became a near certainty. By March 1917, Bourassa began his campaign against those who sought to justify conscription. He asked ominously, if the government enforced the law, did French Canadians have the right to revolt rather than submit to injustice?[39] Alarmed by the first stage of the Russian Revolution in February and angered by the American entry into the war in April, he warned Canadians of the danger of revolution among all the belligerent powers.[40] In the months before the December 1917 election over the issue, Bourassa repeatedly decried the government's position on conscription, day after day attacking the English-Canadian narrative that declared the war effort a national obligation.[41] The election split the country between the pro-conscription merger of Conservatives and Liberals, the Unionists led by Sir Robert Borden, and the pro-referendum on conscription Liberals led by Sir Wilfrid Laurier. The result was a Liberal Quebec and Unionist English Canada. Bourassa mourned the isolation of French Canada and the ultimate failure of his campaign.[42] He continued fervently to denounce his opponents until April 1918, when riots broke out across the province and military intervention in Quebec City killed some of the rioters. Appalled by the violence and exposed to new censorship laws, he withdrew from his front-line position in the debate about the war's consequences.[43]

Most Canadians remember Bourassa in the First World War as the pivotal opponent of conscription and the epitome of Quebec's resistance to the war. His evocative polemics and the eventual violence of the Easter Riots cemented the part he had been given. After the war, the dominant French-Canadian narrative focused on the English-Canadian repression that Bourassa experienced from the Great War's earliest months. It was a story in which Bourassa refused to participate. Alarmed by the violence his words had helped cause, he retreated from the fervent *nationaliste* position he had held before and during the war. An audience with Pope Pius XI and travels through Europe convinced Bourassa of the growing dangers of nationalism and confirmed his retreat from his wartime writings.[44] He was effectively replaced as the de facto leader of the French-Canadian nationalists by Abbé Lionel Groulx. Groulx filled the absence that Bourassa left among the ardent believers who saw Quebec's isolation from the other provinces imbued with a special meaning.[45] Though Bourassa was elected to the House of Commons from 1925 to 1935, he primarily discussed international or constitutional issues. With the renewed threat of conscription in the Second World War, Bourassa's powerful voice once again thrilled audiences, as he was called on by another generation of nationalists led by Maxime Raymond and André Laurendeau[46] to rally a new generation of French Canadians opposed to the military draft. It was an echo of his former role enmeshed in the politics of Canada's government policies and national purpose. By the time of his death, Bourassa had contested the will of an English-Canadian majority in Canada's last three major wars. Yet, instead of being remembered by the "traitor" label he had been branded with during the war years, or by his withdrawal after the war, a new generation of Canadian and Québécois historians emphasized very different aspects of Bourassa's long life. After his death, his role in the First World War was marginalized by both sides, though for differing reasons.

In Quebec especially, where historians had a pivotal role in shaping neo-nationalism, the historian's view of Bourassa is worth considering.[47] The two decades after his death produced brief flurries of academic interest in his career.[48] Battles over bilingualism, Quebec nationalism, and Canadian identity marked the Canada of the 1960s and kept Bourassa's ideas and legacy at the forefront of political consciousness. Bourassa's wartime career was rarely explicitly examined. Claude Ryan, editor of *Le Devoir*, offered a useful snapshot of Bourassa's historical significance on the centenary of his birth in 1968. He noted that Bourassa had been redeemed in English Canada as the prophet of an independent nation strengthened by the coexistence of its two founding peoples. To solve the "French question," the Liberal government of Prime Minister Lester B. Pearson proposed a bilingual and bicultural Canada. Quebec was no longer regarded as an intransigent minority unwelcome under the umbrella of the ambiguous British-Canadian identity forged after the First World War. The new Canada influenced historians and the public alike as they searched for new foundational myths.[49] Bourassa, whose support for a bilingual and bicultural Canada was a solution to a much different Canadian problem, was easily subsumed in the new story Canadians sought to tell about themselves.

As Canada rethought what it meant to be Canadian, Québécois were also reimagining their province and their perspective on Henri Bourassa. The province faced serious societal conflict in the aftermath of the transformative Quiet Revolution that modernized Quebec. A new historical consciousness was developing, as historians debated the legacy of New France and Confederation for the Quebec of the twentieth century. They largely skipped over Bourassa's career for direct historical study, but reflected on many of the same themes of nationalism, clericalism, and survival. Claude Ryan reminded his readers that Québécois were praising Bourassa on the anniversary of his birth as a unifying figure and the grandfather of a new Quebec nationalism.[50] The new breed of neo-nationalists, led by historians and political leaders alike, believed their province was the *only* French-Canadian minority worth protecting. For them, Bourassa's actions during the war were important as a symbol of resistance to English-Canadian domination.[51] His determination to protect all of French Canada, such as his passionate defence of Franco-Ontarians that formed the core of his wartime policy, was forgotten. The Catholic ultramontanism that influenced Bourassa's positions and was often the driving force behind his writing on domestic and international issues was now anachronistic.[52] Instead, Quebecois neo-nationalists focused on the inward-looking nationalism that had emerged from Bourassa and Quebec's war experience with the Conscription Crisis. Bourassa had played only a minor role in the emergence of neo-nationalism after the Great War; still, his opposition during the conflict (and perhaps his brief return during the Second World War) meant he was lauded as a catalyst and hero. Biographer and historian Robert Rumilly declared that, "Je connais de jeunes Canadiens français qui, lorsque la situation nationale leur paraît décourageante, se réconfortent en pensant: 'Il y a eu Bourassa!' Ainsi Bourassa, le grand Bourassa que nous venons de perdre, continue de nous protéger."[53]

On the other side of the divide, English-speaking historians focused on Bourassa's attempts to unify French and English Canada. English-Canadian historians who touched on Bourassa's influence treated him as an advocate of political or economic transformation.[54] Joseph Levitt, a prolific writer on Bourassa, argued that his political and economic ideas were far more analogous to the ideas of English-Canadian philosophers such as George Grant or Charles Taylor than those of Abbé Groulx.[55] Robert Craig Brown and Ramsay Cook used their contribution to the Canadian Centenary Series to emphasize that the crux of Bourassa's position had been that Canada was more Canadian than British.[56] Cook, who wrote extensively about "the French Canadian question" over four decades, portrayed Bourassa's role in Quebec as a visionary of a unified Canada, though tainted by his nationalism and religion.[57] Throughout his many essays on the subject, Cook did not investigate the First World War other than as the context behind problems that related to Canadian unity and the cultural and linguistic divides of the 1960s. Bourassa's role as an international commentator and instigator of the split that caused many of the unity problems raised by Cook is entirely ignored. This English-Canadian focus is equally evident in other works.[58]

The narrative of Bourassa's war, like the heroic narrative of the 22nd, became a study of which events to remember or to forget. Bourassa's war was not defined by accomplishments on the battlefield, but by the domestic struggle over cultural equality. Quebec remembers 1917 as the epiphany when they could no longer rely on Ottawa (that is, English Canada) to accommodate their right to participate in national decisions. English Canadians remember Bourassa as the primary opponent of the war in military history, but have also crafted an entire body of work that ignores the context of his views on war and peace. Instead they used him as a vehicle to debate contemporary issues about the nature of Canadian nationhood in the 1960s. Bourassa's integral role in both of these selective understandings of the war reflects how the creation of historical memory pivots so much on which aspects are emphasized over others, and the context of the present.

One final Canadian narrative of the First World War is the resurrection of Talbot Mercer Papineau as a figure of historical importance. This has largely been the preoccupation of English-Canadian journalists and filmmakers who sought to promote a constructed idea of the French-Canadian "patriot" in Canada's wartime nation-building exercise. In contrast to the other constructions in this chapter, Papineau represents a memory of Quebec during the war constructed entirely by Canada's English-speaking majority. It is a study not only of a forgotten story, but also of what Margaret MacMillan would call an "abuse of history."[59]

Papineau was French Canadian by name and birth, but was raised by his American mother, educated at Oxford, and served as an officer in the Princess Patricia's Canadian Light Infantry.[60] He was the great-grandson of Louis Joseph Papineau, the rebel of 1837 and the cousin of Henri Bourassa. In August 1914, he found himself on the far side of the country, speaking to the Canadian Club in Vancouver on the subject of nationalism in Quebec.[61] He spoke with apparent authority and publicly assured his listeners that, "as many French Canadians as English Canadians [would] take up arms in defence of the Empire."[62] Papineau enlisted as a Lieutenant later that month and was one of the first Canadians on the battlefields. He naively believed that the war held few dangers, and, like many other young soldiers, ignored the grave threat it presented.[63]

He achieved that success and was one of the first Canadians to be awarded a Military Cross in the battle of the St. Eloi in 1915, but his experience on the battlefield deeply affected him. His citation read: "For conspicuous gallantry when in charge of bomb throwers during our attack on the enemy's trenches. He shot two of the enemy himself, and then ran along the German sap throwing bombs therein."[64] After the battle, he wrote to his mother in sixteen long pages, which portrayed the trench raid in an entirely different light. He told her of the frightening violence of fighting in trenches, leaving nothing out. In one scene he described, "[the soldier next to me] jumped up to look at [no. 21 trench] and then sank back into my arms. He bled frightfully. He had been shot in the back of the head. I bound his head up as best I could. The brain matter was oozing out."[65] Faced with uncertainty about participating in such a slaughter, Papineau began to question the Canadian presence there. The rambling letter to his mother proved that, despite his medal, he was not the seasoned veteran intimated in the sanitized citation he had received. There is little fear in his words, but much confusion. He did not comprehend the purpose behind the carnage, which was far worse than anything he had expected. Six months afterward, when he understood his experience more clearly, Papineau noted that, "there should be no heroism in war. No glorification—no reward. For us it should be the simple execution of an abhorrent duty—a thing almost to be ashamed of."[66] By the summer of 1915, Papineau was the only officer of the regiment's original complement not to have been killed, wounded, or captured.[67] He struggled to understand what value lay in his military service and in Canada's participation in the war. Even as he was promoted to Captain and achieved the success that had inspired him to enlist, Papineau found his purpose and focus adrift.

By the summer of 1916, Papineau had answers to his questions about the meaning of Canadian losses on the Western Front. His accomplishments and name attracted the attention of Sir Max Aitken, and he joined the newly formed War Records Office in June after impressing Aitken at a meeting the previous year.[68] He toured the trenches extensively, retracing the steps of privates and generals as he wrote press releases detailing the triumphs of the Canadian army. Papineau began to mould the reputation of Canadians soldiers as he decided that the war was worthwhile because it was vital to the creation of a new Canadian nation. In March, he wrote a letter to Bourassa urging his fellow French Canadians to join the war effort. It was eventually published in August after being rewritten to be more digestible to the Canadian public, indicating that Papineau's true audience was not his cousin but his fellow Canadians.[69]

Papineau argued that the new Canada being forged in the trenches was worth the blood of French-Canadian soldiers. How could a nation that had been assured of its "national life" by the actions of English soldiers refuse to make sacrifices for them in their time of need? That would be a nation without pride. If Henri Bourassa "was truly a nationalist," Papineau wrote, he would "recognise this moment as [Canada's] moment of travail and tribulation." A loyal Canadian would fight for his country in this moment of national birth. In Papineau's view, Bourassa's support should stem from this patriotic impulse to defend "Canadian territory and Canadian liberties." His letter is filled with passionate phrases:

> French and English-Canadians are fighting and dying side by side. Is their sacrifice to go for nothing or will it not cement a foundation for a true Canadian nation, a Canadian nation independent in thought,

independent in action, independent even in its political organization—
but in spirit united for high international and humane purpose to the
two Motherlands of England and France?

The letter brought Papineau fame and attention across Canada and Britain,
where he was hailed as the "Soul of Canada."[70]

In the fall of 1916, Papineau enjoyed a safe administrative job and fame
at home. Through his old law partner, Andrew McMaster, Sir Wilfrid Laurier
offered him a spot to run in an election if one was forced in October.[71]
Instead, Papineau decided to return to his regiment at the front. Confiding
in his close correspondent and romantic interest Beatrice Fox, he wrote that
he could not escape the ferocity of war when so many of his friends did not
have that luxury. "By what strange law am I still here?" he asked. "What
right have I to self pleasure any longer. Should my living life not be consecrated just as their dead lives have been?"[72] Determined to return to the
Princess Pats, he accepted a place at the Canadian Corps Command School.
Papineau gave a well-publicized lecture there about the purpose of Canada's
war, but the school only reinforced his desire to serve at the front.[73] He left
the school in February 1917 and joined his regiment soon afterward as a
major in command of a company. In October, Papineau entered into the
muddy battlefield of Passchendaele alongside his fellow soldiers. Two days
later, after many close calls, an artillery shell exploded next to him. Major
Talbot Mercer Papineau was dead.

His death at Passchendale in October 1917 cut short what seemed to
many to be a promising career as a leader in the new Canada that would
emerge from the war. For English Canada, Papineau had become a symbol of
the "ideal" French Canadian who fought and died in service of the Empire.
The tributes published after his death offered testament to the burgeoning
image he had cultivated in his limited foray into Canadian public life. The
Ottawa Citizen wrote that Papineau had "resented the intolerance of certain
Anglo-Saxon elements in Canada but he also deplored the narrow obscur-
antism of many sections of Quebec."[74] The English-language *Montreal Star*
proclaimed that, "[had] Talbot Papineau been other than he was—a man
worthy of occupying an exalted place in his day and generation—he would
not have been equal to the test he has just met with undying glory."[75] *La
Presse* described Papineau's significance to the Canadians at home:

Le héros disparu comptait aussi parmi les Canadiens qui ont le plus à
cœur le problème des races et qui soupirent après le jour où Canadiens

de sang anglais et de sang français fraterniseront dans l'égalité, la justice et la paix. Malheureusement, la mort est venue le prendre au moment où il faisait les plus beaux rêves pour ses compatriotes et son pays.[76]

Mixed within the patriotism-infused obituaries was the repeated note of grief—not for the Papineau who died on the Western Front, but for an idealized Papineau that represented the coming together of French and English. Yet, after the war he drifted from national hero to historical footnote. Just as with the 22nd Battalion, Canadians in the years after the war had little room for a French-Canadian soldier, even only in name.

For decades after the war, Papineau was barely mentioned in the history of the First World War. His resurrection in the late 1970s would recast him as a symbol of the war's tragic cost and a romantic visionary who dreamed of a unified Canadian nation. He was English Canada's perfect French Canadian, though this time it was more important that he was not a separatist rather than that he was a war supporter. In the 1980s and 1990s, Canada faced two referenda on Quebec independence. Papineau and his "Canadian nation ... united for high international and humane purpose" fit the country that had been wrought by Pierre Elliott Trudeau's decade-and-a-half tenure as prime minister. Some English Canadians, enamoured with their new multicultural, peacekeeping nation, saw Papineau as an important historical precedent for their imagined future.

Papineau's rediscovery began in 1977, when Heather Robertson published *A Terrible Beauty: The Art of Canada at War*, which catalogued Canada's war artists and communicated a view of the war from the soldier's perspective.[77] One of its key features was letters from soldiers, and she used Papineau's correspondence (which had been donated to the National Archives of Canada by his mother) extensively. In 1992, Sandra Gwyn included him in her look at the personal lives of several Canadians during the First World War. The main cast of characters in her book *Tapestry of War* ranged from the soldier Papineau on the front lines to socialite Ethel Chadwick in Ottawa. Papineau became the gallant officer and love-struck gentleman, dying after guilt forced him to return to the front lines instead of a safe administrative job. Gwyn drew a strong link between Papineau and Prime Minister Trudeau. "He was the product of two cultures," she wrote, "in some ways prefiguring [Trudeau]." A few pages later, she observed that "much in the manner of Pierre Trudeau, there was little that overawed Papineau."[78] Like Trudeau, Gwyn implicitly argued, Papineau envisioned a new, stronger Canada that was independent from the colonial vestiges of its past.

In 2007, the Canadian Broadcasting Corporation aired a new documentary film from Brian and Terrence McKenna, *The Great War*, which followed a group of Canadians who would "voyage through time to understand their ancestors' experience as soldiers and nurses at the front."[79] The film mixed the "real" experiences of the ancestors with actors portraying historical figures, and, like Gwyn, traced several personal histories of the war. One such history was, again, the story of Talbot Papineau. The McKenna brothers attempted to mould a narrative for Papineau and his time with the Princess Patricia's Canadian Light Infantry that stood out from that of the normal Canadian. For the role, they cast Justin Trudeau, eldest son of former Prime Minister Trudeau. The choice seemed remarkable given the link Gwyn had made, though neither Justin Trudeau nor Brian McKenna suggested that the connection was anything more than a coincidence.[80] Intentional or not, the symbolism remains.

The filmmakers imagined Papineau as an impassioned speaker for Quebec, one who supported the cause of his nation enough to fight and die over it, yet remained true to his paternal heritage. The film, written and directed by Brian McKenna, was again an idealized English-Canadian memory of Quebec and the war. Nowhere is there a mention of the clash between imperialism and nationalism, or an explanation of Quebec's rejection of the war. Papineau is construed as an ardent Canadian nationalist who foresaw the future state of his native land. Meanwhile, the documentary made Bourassa into a stilted character, existing as a necessary starting point for the pleasing words of Papineau. It is an image of Quebec and its soldiers that is easier to understand than the complex social and political background of their wartime actions.

The memory of Talbot Papineau after his death reflected his life. Both he and his ideas were socially, politically, and physically removed from the French-speaking province that experienced the Great War. In the same way, the memory of Papineau seen in the last three decades is disconnected from the reality of Quebec today. Québécois have developed their own conception of the war, and Papineau has little relevance within it. Instead, it is among English-speaking Canadians, who faced a Quebec that was further and further separated from their national vision, where the effort to remember Papineau developed. It was satisfying for Canadian journalists in 1916, just as it was in the 1980s and 1990s, to conceive of an ideal Quebec participating in national endeavours and ultimately subservient to English Canada's vision of them. More than any other Québécois, Papineau embodied that fanciful dream—though it remains an illusionary memory of Quebec and the war.

•   •   •   •

The three narratives developed in this chapter highlight the complexity of discussing the memory of Quebec during the First World War. There are many influences on the construction of its memory, be it the memoirs of the 22nd Battalion's veterans, historians' contemporary concerns while debating Bourassa, or the romantic and ahistorical significance of Talbot Papineau. Each of these was produced by a diverse set of creators, in varied time periods and for different audiences. The differing needs of veterans seeking to tell their story, or historians seeking to understand their country, or television producers to glorify it, are reflected in which details are communicated and which events are emphasized. Equally, these three narratives depict the interplay between majority and minority memories of the war. The 22nd Battalion were a minority within and without their native province; in consequence, they have been largely absent from the historical narrative of the war. The figure of Henri Bourassa was contested by English and French Canadians for his impact on Quebec nationalism, which in turn reflects on Quebec's war experience. English Canadians rehabilitated their view of Bourassa and sought to remake him as a unifying figure that was then juxtaposed against Quebec's effort to make Bourassa a nucleus for its continuing fight against majoritarian oppression. In one, the majority minimized a minority's memory that conflicted with their own; in the other, the minority preserved a single-faceted memory of Bourassa to safeguard against it. Finally, Talbot Papineau's narrative is a constructed memory of the war that rests entirely upon an English-Canadian understanding of French Canada's war. When discussing the memory of Quebec during the Great War, it is impossible to remove it from its minority context. Whether it is accepting the majority interpretation, influenced by it, or rejecting it entirely, its memory remains one in the shadow of another.

Thus, even as Vimy Ridge is celebrated as the birthplace of the Canadian nation, Quebec remembers the First World War as part of its *raison d'être* for leaving the confederation of provinces that English Canada affirms. English-speaking Canadians have long been familiar with the idea that the First World War contributed to or even formed their modern national identity. Their discourse about nation-building either ignores the very different experience of French-speaking Canadians, or tries to incorporate it into the myth by stressing the role of the small number of French Canadians who openly supported it. Modern French-Canadian nationalism, now called Québécois nationalism, relies on the memory of another war experience, one that emphasizes discrimination against language and culture, conscription, and coercion. Curiously, Québécois understand their province's role in the Great War in exactly the same way as English Canadians—except instead of confirming the majority's national aspirations, it confirms Quebec's minority nationalism.

Roland Barthes writes that, "perhaps we have an invincible resistance to believing in the past, in History, except in the form of a myth."[81] He was writing about the significance of photography, but Barthes captures the essence of memory construction and its need for a single, powerful narrative to encapsulate it. His words suggest that myth-making is not the distortion of history so much as the necessary by-product of remembering it. The conflicting memories of Quebec during the First World War are testaments to this fact. Each narrative outlined here selected certain experiences over others, mythologizing the facts of their stories as "what happened" against what "did not happen." This chapter demonstrates that all of these memories stem from historical experiences that occurred parallel to one another. Some French Canadians willingly fought for their provincial identity in a European war. Some rejected the war outright. Others fought among the ranks of English Canadians to construct the nation that was supposedly born on the slopes of Vimy Ridge. None of these are completely true, nor are they completely false. Rather, they reveal the ambiguity of memory construction. As seen above, there are many ways in which narratives transform historical events into remembrances. They serve some contemporary purpose at the expense of individual experience. Societal memory must be useful, or, like that of the 22nd Battalion, it is discarded. Societies remember historical experiences because they have value—not simply because they occurred, but because they were meaningful. The search for that meaning guides the "remembering and forgetting" of Canada's and Quebec's complex Great War experience. Historians are lucky in that they pierce the myths of memory and explore their roots in historical events—but most do not have such luxury. For better or worse, contemporary memory shapes history, and the forgotten few that do not fit into Québécois or Canadian narratives of the Great War will remain forgotten until they are once again meaningful.

NOTES

1. Jonathan F. Vance, *Death So Noble: Memory, Meaning, and the First World War* (Vancouver: UBC Press, 1997), 8, 259.
2. The author uses Québécois to refer specifically to the people of Quebec and in reference to their memory, though sometimes "French Canadian" is also used,

as it was the term used in the context of the time. Québécois was not a popular term until the 1960s.

3. Jay Winter explicitly uses the term remembrance to refer to people or groups of people engaging in acts of remembrance together, which is not the meaning implied here. Rather, it is meant to describe remembering specific parts of the war and its major figures. For more on Winter's terminology, see Jay Winter, *Remembering War: The Great War Between Memory and History in the Twentieth Century* (New Haven: Yale University Press, 2006), 4.

4. For more on this point, see Geoff Keelan, "'Il a bien merité de la Patrie': The 22nd Battalion and the Memory of Courcelette," *Canadian Military History* 19, no. 3 (summer 2010): 32–35.

5. A.F. Duguid, *Official History of the Canadian Forces in the Great War, 1914–1919, From the Outbreak of the War to the Formation of the Canadian Corps, August 1914–September 1915*, vol. 2 (Ottawa: Department of National Defence General Staff, 1938), 344–45.

6. J.L. Granatstein and J.M. Hitsman note that enlistments slowed down by July 1916; 138,892 men had enlisted from January to June 1916, averaging around 23,000 a month, but by July it had dwindled to 7,961, and between August and December between 5,000 and 6,500 enlisted each month. J.L. Granatstein and J.M. Hitsman, *Broken Promises: A History of Conscription in Canada* (Toronto: Oxford University Press, 1977), 37, 46.

7. The reasons behind Borden's sudden announcement are unclear. It caught his Cabinet off guard, and Borden's biographer, Robert Craig Brown, does not offer any detailed explanation for it. See Robert Craig Brown, *Robert Laird Borden: A Biography, Volume II: 1914–1937* (Toronto: Macmillan, 1980), 60–61. Borden's diary, Brown's source for much of his work, offers similarly little detail. His entry is brief and uninteresting: "White Hughes and Reid came and I propounded to them proposal that force should be increased on 1st January to 500,000. They agreed." Library and Archives Canada, MG26-H, Borden Papers, diary, 30 December 1916.

8. Desmond Morton, *Fight or Pay: Soldiers' Families in the Great War* (Vancouver: UBC Press, 2004), 171.

9. Desmond Morton, *When Your Number's Up: The Canadian Soldier in the First World War* (Toronto: Random House, 1993), 55–62.

10. Mason Wade, *The French-Canadian Outlook* (Toronto: McClelland and Stewart, 1963), 53.

11. For an overview of Regulation 17, see Margaret Prang, "Clerics, Politicians and the Bilingual Schools Issue in Ontario, 1910–1917," *Canadian Historical Review* 41, no. 4 (1960): 281–307; Marilyn Barker, "The Ontario Bilingual Schools Issue: Sources of Conflict," *Canadian Historical Review* 47, no. 3 (1966): 227–48; Nelson Michaud, "Les écoles d'Ontario ou le dilemme des conservateurs québécois: confrontation des principes nationalistes et de la réalité politique," *Revue d'histoire de l'Amérique française* 49, no. 3 (1996): 395–417.

12. David Campbell, "A Forgotten Victory: Courcelette, 15 September 1916," *Canadian Military History* 16, no. 2 (spring 2007), 40.

13. This account of the battle is derived from "Story of the 22nd Battalion, September 15th, 1916, the Capture of Courcelette," *Canadian Military History* 16, no. 2 (spring 2007), 49. The account is anonymous; it was found in the George Metcalf Archival Collection without a source or date. The number of wounded is from Jean-Pierre Gagnon, *Le 22ᵉ Bataillon (canadien-français), 1914–1919: étude socio-militaire* (Ottawa: Presses de l'Université Laval, 1986), 103. Gagnon states that six officers died and five were wounded, and eighty-two men died and 114 were wounded. Other casualty numbers for officers exist in Thomas-Louis Tremblay, *Journal de Guerre (1915–1918)*, ed. Marcelle Cinq-Mars (Outremont: Athena Éditions, 2006), 166–67, who writes that seven were killed and eight wounded. Tremblay's record differs slightly from that of Joseph Chaballe, who stated that seven officers were killed and eleven wounded, which differs again from the document "Story of the 22nd Battalion." As well, they disagree on who exactly was wounded; see Joseph Chaballe, "Courcelette: Glorieux fait d'armes du 22ᵉᵐᵉ Régiment Canadien-Français," *La Canadienne: le Magazine du Canadien Français* 2, no. 3 (October 1920): 14; "Story of the 22nd Battalion," 56.

14. Claudius Corneloup, *L'Épopée du Vingt-Deuxième* (Montreal: La Presse, 1919), 150.

15. Library and Archives Canada: RG24, reel T-8653, file 649-C-1596, letter to Henri Bourassa, French version, 3.

16. As quoted in Gagnon, *Le 22ᵉ Bataillon (canadien-français)*, 104.

17. Keelan, "Il a bien merité de la Patrie," 32–35.

18. *La Patrie*, 16 September 1916.

19. *La Presse*, 18 September 1916.

20. J.A. Holland, *Les Poilus Canadiens* (1919), 29.

21. Not all nationalists rejected the war. In November 1915, Olivar Asselin joined the Canadian army with the rank of major to help recruit French-Canadian soldiers. He eventually made it to the front by 1917. See Hélène Pelletier-Baillargeon, "Asselin, Olivar," *Dictionary of Canadian Biography Online*, or Hélène Pelletier-Baillargeon, *Olivar Asselin et son temps. Volume II. Le volontaire* (Montréal: Fides, 2001).

22. When French-Canadian enlistment is compared to that of native-born, English-speaking Canadians, the gap narrows dramatically, but the aggressive "patriots" in English-speaking Canada refused to recognize the distinction. A good review of French-Canadian enlistment successes and problems can be found in Patrice A. Dutil, "Against Isolationism: Napoléon Belcourt, French Canada and 'La grande guerre,'" *Canada and the First World War: Essays in Honour of Robert Craig Brown*, ed. David Mackenzie (Toronto: University of Toronto Press, 2005), 115–20.

23. Henri Bourassa, "La Reorganisation de l'Empire," *Le Devoir*, 16 September 1916.

24. Desmond Morton, "The Limits of Loyalty: French Canadian Officers in the First World War," in *The Limits of Loyalty*, ed. E. Denton (Waterloo: Wilfrid Laurier Press, 1980), 79–98.

25. Holland, *Les Poilus Canadiens*. *Les Poilus* has no publisher listed, but Holland's other work is *Story of the Tenth Canadian Battalion 1914–1917* (London: Canadian War Records Office, 1919). It is not known if *Les Poilus* is also from the War Records Office.

26. Arthur Lapointe, *Souvenirs et impressions de ma vie de soldat, 1916–1919*, 4th ed. (St. Ulric: Le Devoir, 1944 [originally published in 1919]), 9.

27. Corneloup, *L'Épopée du Vingt-Deuxième*, 55.

28. Chaballe, "Courcelette: Glorieux fait d'armes du 22ème Régiment Canadien-Français," 15.

29. Joseph Chaballe, *25e anniversaire de la bataille de Courcelette, 1916–1941* (Montreal, 1941), 6.

30. Joseph Chaballe, *Histoire du 22e bataillon canadien-français, 1914–1919* (Montreal: Les Editions Chanteclerc, 1952).

31. James I.W. Corcoran, "Henri Bourassa et la guerre sud-africaine (suite)," *Revue d'histoire de l'Amérique française* 19, no. 1 (1965): 84.

32. Réal Belanger, "Henri Bourassa," *Dictionary of Canadian Biography Online*.

33. *McKim's Directory* lists *Le Devoir* as having 18,894 subscribers in 1915, a number that dropped to an estimated 14,000 by 1917. See *McKim's Directory of Canadian Publications, 1915* (1917). *McKim's* estimated Montreal, where *Le Devoir* was published, to have a population of 550,000. It is estimated that the city was 25.8 percent English and 63.5 percent French in 1915; see Andrew Sancton, *Governing the Island of Montreal: Language differences and metropolitan politics* (Berkeley: University of California Press, 1985), 27.

34. Robert Rumilly, *Henri Bourassa: La vie publique d'un grand Canadien* (Montréal: Éditions Chantecler, 1953), 503.

35. Henri Bourassa, "En France et en Alsace au Début de la Guerre," *Le Devoir*, 22 August 1914.

36. Henri Bourassa, *Que devons-nous à l'Angleterre? La défense nationale, la révolution impérialiste, le tribut à l'Empire* (Montreal, 1915).

37. For more on Bourassa's discussion about these issues, see Geoff Keelan, "Catholic Neutrality: The Peace of Henri Bourassa," *Journal of the Canadian Historical Association* 22, no. 1 (2012): 99–132.

38. Henri Bourassa, "Le Parlement et L'Inquité Ontarienne—I," *Le Devoir*, 16 May 1916.

39. Henri Bourassa, "Aurons-nous la Conscription?—II," *Le Devoir*, 27 March 1917.

40. See Bourassa's articles "Après la Guerre, La Révolution—I," *Le Devoir*, 23 April 1917; "Après la Guerre, La Révolution—II," *Le Devoir*, 24 April 1917; "Après la Guerre, La Révolution—III," *Le Devoir*, 25 April 1917.

41. Between 28 May and 17 December 1917, Bourassa wrote thirteen articles directly addressing conscription, most appearing in a nine-part series published from 28 May to 6 June. He also wrote an article in the *New York Evening Post* that concisely outlined his views; see Henri Bourassa, "Why Canada Should Not Adopt Conscription," *New York Evening Post*, 10 July 1917.

42. Henri Bourassa, "'L'Isolement' des Canadiens-Français—Fausses manœuvres de conciliation," *Le Devoir*, 26 December 1917.

43. André Bergevin, Cameron Nish, and Anne Bourassa, *Henri Bourassa. Biographie. Index des écrits. Index de la correspondance publique, 1895–1924* (Montreal: Éditions de l'Action nationale, 1966), L–LI.

44. Journalist Elspeth Chisholm collected a voluminous series of interviews with those who had known Bourassa. Accompanying them were notes from an interview conducted with his daughter Anne, who clarified her father's reticence to discuss French-Canadian nationalism after the war. Library and Archives Canada: MG 31, E50, vol. 3, Elspeth Chisholm Fonds, f. 30, Bourassa, Henri, Notes by Anne Bourassa. See also André Bergevin, Cameron Nish, and Anne Bourassa, *Henri Bourassa*, LIII.

45. For more on Quebec's changing nationalism of the 1920s, see Mason Wade, *The French Canadians 1760–1945* (Toronto: St. Martin's Press, 1968), 781–915; Susan Mann, *Abbé Groulx: Variations on a Nationalist Theme* (Vancouver: Copp Clark, 1973); Susan Mann, *Action Française: French Canadian Nationalism in the Twenties* (Toronto: University of Toronto Press, 1975); and Michael Oliver, *The Passionate Debate: The Social and Political Ideas of Quebec Nationalism, 1920–1945* (Montreal: Véhicule Press, 1991).

46. The provincial party created by Laurendeau and Raymond, the Bloc Populaire, had limited success. Though during the Second World War they capitalized on continuing antagonism over conscription, as well as Bourassa himself, they did not succeed at the polls. Michael Behiels has written much about the topic; see Michael D. Behiels, *Prelude to Quebec's Quiet Revolution: Liberalism versus Neo-Nationalism, 1945–1960* (Montreal: McGill-Queen's University Press, 1985), 24–32; Michael D. Behiels, "The Bloc Populaire and the Origins of French-Canadian Neo-nationalism, 1942–8," *Canadian Historical Review* 63, no. 4 (1982), 487–512.

47. The well-known debate between the Montreal and Laval schools of historians over the character of Quebec's history is explored in detail by many, notably in English in Ronald Rudin's *Making History in Twentieth Century Quebec* (Toronto: University of Toronto Press, 1997). Ramsay Cook has also examined Quebec historians' influence on Quebec nationalism, such as Maurice Séguin and Michel Brunet; see, for instance, Ramsay Cook, *Canada and the French-Canadian Question* (Toronto: Macmillan, 1966) 119–142, though Cook has many other publications that touch on the subject. French-language scholarship is just as detailed and useful, though a complete historiographical list is far beyond the scope of this chapter.

THE FORGOTTEN FEW **257**

48. For example, see Martin P. O'Connell, "Ideas of Henri Bourassa," *Canadian Journal of Economics and Political Science* 19 (August 1953): 361–76; Martin P. O'Connell, "Henri Bourassa and Canadian Nationalism," (Ph.D. diss., University of Toronto, 1954); André Laurendeau, "Henri Bourassa," in *Our Living Tradition*, ed. R.L. McDougall (Toronto: University of Toronto Press, 1962); James I.W. Corcoran, "Henri Bourassa et la guerre sud-africaine (suite)," *Revue d'histoire de l'Amérique française* 19, no. 1 (1965): 84–105; V.C. Smith, "Moral Crusader: Henri Bourassa and the Empire, 1900–1916," *Queen's Quarterly* 76, no. 4 (winter 1969): 635–47. An important non-academic contribution is Casey Murrow, *Henri Bourassa and French-Canadian Nationalism: Opposition to Empire* (Montreal: Harvest House, 1968).

49. On British-Canadian identity in the 1960s, see Phillip Buckner, *Canada and the End of Empire* (Vancouver: UBC Press, 2004); José Eduardo Igartua, *The Other Quiet Revolution: National Identities in English Canada, 1945–71* (Vancouver: UBC Press, 2006); C.P. Champion, *The Strange Demise of British Canada: The Liberals and Canadian Nationalism, 1964–1968* (Montreal: McGill-Queen's University Press, 2010). Each examined the disappearance of a British-Canadian identity and its consequences, though Champion suggests it was transforming instead of disappearing.

50. Claude Ryan, "Henri Bourassa devant l'histoire," *Le Devoir*, 31 August 1968.

51. For an excellent example of these perspectives, see *Hommage à Henri Bourassa* (Montreal: Imprimerie Populaire, 1952), a collection of tributes to Bourassa after his death. Also, Patrick Allen, ed., *La pensée de Henri Bourassa* (Montreal: L'Action nationale, 1954) is a published version of an issue of *L'Action Nationale* that reviews Bourassa's ideas.

52. For the most recent appraisal of the influence of religion on Bourassa's career, see Sylvie Lacombe, *La rencontre de deux peuples élus: comparaison des ambitions nationale et impériale au Canada entre 1896 et 1920* (Sainte-Foy: Presses de l'Université Laval, 2002), and Sylvie Lacombe, "Entre l'autorité pontificale et la liberté nationale: l'anti-impérialisme britannique d'Henri Bourassa," in *Le Devoir: Un journal indépendant (1910–1995)*, ed. Robert Comeau and Luc Desrochers (Quebec City: Presses de l'Université du Québec, 1996), 273–81. While historians like Michael Gauvreau today reveal the continuity between Bourassa's mix of Catholicism and nationalism and the Quiet Revolution, those linkages were not as clear to 1960s Quebec; see Michael Gauvreau, *The Catholic Origins of Quebec's Quiet Revolution, 1931–1970* (Montreal: McGill-Queen's University Press, 2005).

53. Rumilly, *Henri Bourassa*, 791.

54. Much of the English scholarship that emerged after Bourassa's death prominently references Elizabeth Armstrong, *Crisis of Quebec 1914–1918* (Toronto: McClelland and Stewart, 1937), which treated Bourassa purely as a political figure in a larger Canadian (not French-Canadian) context.

55. Joseph Levitt, *Henri Bourassa and the Golden Calf: The Social Program of the Nationalists of Quebec 1900–1914* (Ottawa: Les Éditions de l'Université d'Ottawa, 1972), 145.

56. Robert Craig Brown and Ramsay Cook, *Canada 1896–1921: A Nation Transformed* (Toronto: McClelland and Stewart, 1974), 274.

57. Ramsay Cook, *The Maple Leaf Forever: Essays on Nationalism and Politics in Canada* (Toronto: Macmillan, 1971), 74–75; Ramsay Cook, *Canada and the French Canadian Question*, 122. Cook is never negative toward Bourassa, but the greater thrust of his arguments regarding the problems of Canadian nationalism (and French-Canadian nationalism) is against both its existence and its justifications.

58. Though there are many examples of this, an excellent one is Joseph Levitt's chapter "Henri Bourassa: The Catholic Social Order and Canada's Mission," in *Idéologies au Canada français 1900–1929*, ed. Fernand Dumont, Jean Hamelin, Fernand Harvey, and Jean-Paul Montminy (Quebec City: Les Presses de l'Université Laval, 1974), 192–222, which ably demonstrates how easily the war can remain absent from otherwise comprehensive works, notably on 217. Jean Drolet's chapter (in French) is similarly revealing about how little attention is paid to the war: "Henri Bourassa: Une analyse de sa pensée: Idéologies au Canada français 1900–1929," 223–50.

59. Margaret MacMillan, *The Uses and Abuses of History* (Toronto: Penguin Group, 2008).

60. Much of this research draws from the author's own work; see Geoff Keelan, "Talbot Mercer Papineau: Memory, Myth and the Search for Meaning" (unpublished master's research project, University of Waterloo, 2010).

61. Sandra Gwyn, *Tapestry at War* (Toronto: Harper Collins, 1992), 98.

62. Desmond Morton and J.L. Granatstein, *Marching to Armageddon: Canadians and the Great War, 1914–1919* (Toronto: Lester and Orpen Dennys, 1989), 6.

63. Library and Archives Canada (hereafter LAC): MG30 E52, Talbot Mercer Papineau Fonds, vol. 2, Papineau to Mother, August 1914; Gwyn, *Tapestry of War*, 98.

64. LAC, Accn 92–93/166, Box 7559, Capt. Talbot Papineau File, Service Record.

65. Papineau Fonds, vol. 2, Papineau to Mother, 3 March 1915.

66. Papineau Fonds, vol. 1, Papineau to Fox, 14 August 1915.

67. Gwyn, "Papineau, Talbot Mercer," *Dictionary of Canadian Biography*.

68. Papineau Fonds, vol. 1, Papineau to Fox, 3 October 1915.

69. Papineau wrote to his former law partner Andrew McMaster several times with multiple edits of the letter. Papineau Fonds, vol. 2, McMaster to Papineau, 14 April 1916 and 11 June 1916. It is clear, despite claims to the contrary first voiced by Bourassa in his reply to Papineau's letter, that Papineau wrote it himself. He offers much of the same content in a speech to a Command School; see Papineau Fonds, vol. 3, *McGill News*, March 1920. The text of this speech is

found in the *McGill News*, which lists it as having occurred in February 1917, but Papineau's correspondence indicates it was given 20 December 1916. See vol. 2, Papineau to mother, 19 December 1916.

70. A copy of Papineau's letter to Bourassa is in Papineau Fonds, vol. 4.

71. Papineau Fonds, vol. 2, McMaster to Papineau, 15 October 1916.

72. Papineau Fonds, vol. 1, Papineau to Fox, 30 September 1916.

73. See Papineau Fonds, vol. 3, *McGill News*, March 1920.

74. *Ottawa Citizen*, 5 November 1917. The article is found in a booklet entitled "Captain Papineau's Letter to M. Henri Bourassa (editor of Le Devoir)," in Papineau Fonds, vol. 4. The obituaries referenced are from the same booklet.

75. *Toronto Star*, 5 November 1917.

76. *La Presse*, 6 November 1917.

77. Heather Robertson, *A Terrible Beauty: The Art of Canada at War* (Ottawa: National Museum of Man, 1977).

78. Gywn, *Tapestry of War*, 90, 94.

79. "The Great War," Canadian Broadcasting Corporation, http://www.cbc.ca/greatwar/ (accessed 29 June 2012).

80. Trudeau on the subject: "The choice of this particular role wasn't so much about me being able to try my hand at acting, it was much more about me being able to get into the character of this tremendous historical figure and bringing attention to Talbot Papineau's life." Lee-Anne Goodman, "Justin Trudeau makes acting debut in CBC docudrama," *Toronto Star*, 4 April 2007. McKenna answered the question as to why he cast Trudeau, stating that it was "out of desperation. Evidently, it's impossible to find a charismatic, fluently bilingual actor in his early 30s in Canada. Believe me, we looked. Then Justin's name came up." Stephen Cole, "Birth of a Nation," CBC Online, 5 April 2007, http://www.cbc.ca/arts/tv/birthofanation.html (accessed 28 June 2010).

81. Roland Barthes, *Camera Lucida: Reflections on Photography*, trans. Richard Howard (New York: Hill and Wang, 1981), 87.

"LOYAL UNTIL DEATH"
Memories of African Great War Service for Germany

DAN BULLARD

The Western Front holds a central place in the historical investigation of the Great War, yet the war's effects were felt far beyond Europe. The European colonies in Africa were an important theatre of battle, but investigations of Germany's Great War rarely reference the war in Africa. If that campaign is mentioned, it is usually represented as a front of marginal importance. While it did host fewer battles, this theatre constituted an important part of the wider German perception of the war. One memory has dominated this past: the notion of the Africans who were "loyal until death" in the service of their German colonizers. This memory was grounded in the myth that Africans selflessly devoted themselves to Germany between 1914 and 1918. This simplistic and incomplete conception conformed to interwar German forms of remembering their war in the colonies. By outlining the reality of German colonial rule and the instrumentalization of the war after 1918 in the former colonies, as well as in Germany, the notions underpinning this memory will be manifest. Tracing German memories, recollections in Africa, and African veterans' remembrances in Germany will show how a single memory became paramount. Recognizing these three perspectives and contexts is vital to understanding how African memory of the Great War was warped by the exigencies of the years between 1919 and 1943.[1]

It is difficult to grasp how African veterans reflected upon their German service, because very few records detail their memory.[2] This study attempts to recapture the story of this forgotten group and to participate in the explosion of research into such neglected aspects of German colonialism. The paucity of sources is the result of many African communities not retaining a written war memory or documenting their oral history. Consequently, the exploration of the "poetically intensified language of action, gesture, and the concrete sign" that Jean and John Comaroff employ will function as a way to recover marginal voices left out of written narratives.[3] Making use of this "language" allows a history to incorporate public event and performance in order to render a fuller image than that of written sources.

The chief problem for understanding this memory is that the documents overwhelmingly reflect German rather than African voices. Even the few African perspectives that were committed to paper are problematic, for authentic memories must be disentangled from public expressions for a targeted audience. The majority of sources that exist were created by the German government and colonial organizations. In Germany, a small African diaspora similarly had to conform to German expectations in recording their memories. Accordingly, their voices were documented in few archives, and, when they were retained, they were of a single perspective. Therefore, understanding the rare African remembrances necessitates the decoding of the circumstances faced by Africans both in the former colonies and Germany.

The collective memory of African veterans in interwar Africa and Germany is paradoxical and the product of differing contexts. The honest remembrance of the war by the former subjects of the colonial order was circumscribed by the atmosphere in Africa and Europe in which such memory might be expressed. In what had been the German colonies, Africans faced new mandate administrations under the League of Nations that structured the way the war years were remembered. In Germany, Germans co-opted African veterans' memories to advance colonial revisionism.

In order to understand how Africans remembered their war, it is essential to acknowledge the colonialism that constrained later interpretations. Germany's formal annexation of Africa began in 1884 and distinguished itself from other European colonizations by its latecomer status and the quick pace of conquest.[4] Key to this expansion was the pacification of indigenous power and assertion of white supremacy in the four colonies of Togo, Cameroon, East Africa, and Southwest Africa (SWA). German rule hardened through a series of conquests and repressions. One history counts seventy-six engagements in one colony between 1899 and 1905 alone.[5] The extremity of this violence occurred in the bloody suppressions of the Ovaherero revolt in SWA and the East African Maji Maji uprising, which resulted in perhaps 260,000 indigenous deaths.[6] Such wars saw the strengthening of the colonial military in the *Schutztruppe* (Protection Force) and the greater inclusion of indigenous allies. Incorporating locals into the *Schutztruppe* allowed the Germans to use Africans to suppress other Africans.[7] Through such measures, the system began to stabilize before war broke out in 1914.

Like the other combatants in Africa, Germany relied upon indigenous auxiliaries to supplement its forces. Such help was rendered by "askari" soldiers, as well as carriers and civilian forces. These aides to Germany enlisted for the reasons usual to auxiliaries: pay, social power, travel, glory, and the possibility of war trophies. To describe these men as mercenaries would not be entirely accurate, since early soldiers were bought as slaves, later askaris volunteered, and the war demanded impressment after 1914. As well, the various indigenous groups compelled to come together remained split by ethnic, regional, and religious divisions. Such schisms in fact solidified German control. Rifts between Africans were welcomed, since armed autochthons represented a clear threat to colonial rule. Africans with weapons challenged the binary hierarchies of colonialism since their existence as the purportedly colonized, yet armed, blurred colour lines and challenged colonial power structures. They also unseated notions of European supremacy in that their employment represented the tacit recognition that they were necessary to colonial rule. German policy reflected such tensions by treating these symbols of the contradictions of colonialism with great caution.

After events in Europe brought war to the colonies, local authorities mobilized the army, settler militia, and indigenous auxiliaries. In Togo, Cameroon, and SWA, these forces were small and poorly equipped, and the colonies were quickly captured by the Entente Powers. One surprising occurrence was the German attack upon one of their staunchest indigenous allies in early 1915. The Rehoboth Basters had long been loyal intermediaries in SWA, and had even repressed other local groups alongside the Germans. Nonetheless, they rose against the Germans when the outcome of the war looked certain.[8] Many Germans regarded this revolt as a bitter betrayal.

Although Germany quickly lost Togo, Cameroon, and SWA, East Africa held out until the end of the war under Major General Paul von Lettow-Vorbeck, whose tiny German-African force fought a guerrilla action in the jungle. At most, the German officers and non-commissioned officers numbered only two thousand. Their ability to engage increasing Allied forces, disappear into the forest, and even invade surrounding territories was largely the result of the askaris and carriers who fired the weapons and carried the loads. These key helpers of the German war were male soldiers, boy messengers, porters, and women who formed the baggage train that sustained the fighting. Not only did males engage the enemy but their families sometimes accompanied the army to clean, feed, and care for German and African alike. Consequently, the estimation of how many actually fought for Germany and who merely followed the army is problematic. Similarly, the number of askaris and carriers is difficult to determine conclusively given the erratic documentation and the transitory nature of their employment. It is estimated that eleven thousand Africans were engaged in the *Schutztruppe* between 1914 and 1918.[9] Yet, when Lettow-Vorbeck settled for an armistice in November 1918, he commanded only forty Germans and fewer than two thousand indigenous auxiliaries.[10] Because he had fought with so few and for so long, Lettow-Vorbeck was later glorified in Germany for leading its only "undefeated" force.[11]

The history of Germany's war in Africa cannot be seen merely through the triumphs of Lettow-Vorbeck's forces. Disease and the steady attrition of their carriers and askaris plagued the German colonial forces, which had to resort to the impressment of locals, some as young as nine years of age.[12] The fact that Africans were perpetually under-equipped and plagued by racial prejudices also meant that Africans were fed, supplied, and aided only after the Germans.[13] In addition, the askaris were treated as a homogeneous, expendable mass by their leaders. African troops fought in such conditions for years, away from their homes, with only the promise of payment. Deaths from disease and battle combined with the inability to care for the wounded while on the march to thin Lettow-Vorbeck's ranks and devastate the countryside.[14] Though the exact numbers are debated, historians have asserted that more than a third of the askaris and carriers deserted. After 1916, there was no battle that did not feature substantial attrition of the auxiliaries through desertion. The numbers lost were so significant that measures were instituted such as chaining auxiliaries together by *jougs* (neck chains) when not marching.[15] Desertion nevertheless continued. In 1917, there were 916 official cases of desertion in the records. Less than a year later, cases exceeded two thousand.[16] By the end of the war, more than four thousand Africans were listed as missing without explanation; a substantial number if we consider the estimated total of eleven thousand Africans who served in the German military during the war.

After the war ended, the Versailles Treaty's articles 119 through 133 removed millions of square kilometres and more than ten million indigenous subjects from German control. Ruling that its colonialism had been militaristic and barbaric, the treaty definitively ended German colonialism. The Versailles Treaty and Article 22 of the League of Nations's Covenant then established mandates to be ruled by the victors.[17] East Africa was partitioned into three territories for Portugal, Britain, and Belgium. SWA was given to South Africa to administer as a mandate. Last, both Togo and Cameroon became extensions of neighboring French and British colonies. These losses all empowered the forces of colonial revisionism in Germany.[18]

With the conclusion of the war, many of the colonial settlers, soldiers, and merchants were released from prisoner-of-war camps and repatriated to Germany. Leaving behind their occupations, homes, lands, and experiences, as well as spending years in captivity, set the stage for later agitation.[19] The loss of territories, businesses, and futures traumatized the former colonizers, who fought throughout the interwar period to revise the so-called "amputation" and "theft" of the colonies. The displaced settlers and soldiers particularly looked back upon the service of the fifty thousand "loyal until death" allies throughout the history of the colonies, and Lettow-Vorbeck's victories, as proof of both the successes of their colonial war and the lies of the Versailles Treaty.

A heady mixture of the memory of the Great War in Africa and hatred for the Versailles Treaty combined in Germany to vitalize powerful forces of interwar colonial revisionism and the colonial organizations' guiding role in the production of German memory of colonial war.[20] The litany of economic, social, and political crises in Weimar Germany encouraged the government to assist such organizations in their efforts to mobilize the public to demand the return of the colonies.[21] For the diverse groups comprising the colonial lobby, the only solution to these problems was the return of the wealth, markets, resources, and prestige of colonies. Nostalgic for the colonies, angry at Versailles, and unhappy with the interwar order, these embittered colonialists came together in lobby groups to advance the cause of colonial revisionism. For somewhat similar reasons, the National Socialists drew upon these themes and expanded colonial revisionism after 1933.[22] Both the Weimar and Nazi governments relied on Germans returned from the colonies to articulate this revisionism through their cultural products. These products established a narrative of the "loyal askari" for revisionist goals and public consumption. This myth played out in public events, exhibitions, travelling shows, film, and literature in a concerted effort to shape German frameworks of remembrance of their colonial war.

The image of the colonies as successful and fraternal adventures under-pinned such remembrances. Key to such narratives was the vast body of memoirs written by German veterans who celebrated the askari.[23] Many conceptions centred on the usual tropes of white leadership and the thousands of loyal askaris who supported the German war and showcased the achievements of colonialism.[24] Typical were the fifty-three narratives contained in Werner von Langsdorff's 1936 description of colonial war, which spoke of the "fraternity" between black and white soldiers.[25] Lettow-Vorbeck himself viewed his African troops as "faithful supporters of emperor and empire," who were sometimes more unwavering than German soldiers.[26] Similarly, the devoted askari legend could complement the "stab-in-the-back legend" by providing further proof of how Germany was victorious on the battlefield but had been betrayed. A final element of the loyal askari myth was the implication of the askaris' devotion. In portraying them this way, the many German authors could simultaneously exalt the "hard but fair" nature of their colonialism and skilful leadership in war. Through such frameworks, Germans relied upon indigenous auxiliaries for their own sense of accomplishment and triumph. This way of avoiding criticism and providing demonstrative proof of German success skilfully used the memory of the askari to buttress German claims.

Such unambiguously positive memories were not the only ways of remembering African veterans, for the tensions of the former empire brought out cracks within the dominant memory of the devoted askari. The rigorous punishment of Africans undermined claims of indigenous willingness to assist Germany. For instance, *Schutztruppe* doctor August Hauer considered corporal punishment of askaris to be essential to the "proper education of the blacks."[27] The willful forgetting of the past also highlighted tensions between colonialism and the desire to remember the glorious past. For when German veterans' recollections omitted being heckled as they walked through their former colonies in captivity, or being herded into prisoner-of-war camps, they disregarded a common experience for Germans in Africa.[28]

Germans rarely rejected the "loyal until death" myth. Some disagreed with the memory of the loyal askari by complaining about the inclusion of askaris in commemorative events.[29] In 1925, the former SWA soldier Alfred Guhlmann criticized what he labelled the *Askarikult*—the inclusion of askaris in parades and monuments—as "a tasteless and childish sentiment, an outgrowth of festival spirit, a racial-political folly, and an unsafe game with fire."[30] For Guhlmann, the askari myth could legitimate colonialism in the past and prepare for the colonial future, but his colonial memory convinced him that the militarization of the African presented too great a threat. Similarly, the proposal for a 1938 memorial in Potsdam featuring a kneeling African woman was squashed by racial prejudices, which opposed an African woman as a symbol of Germany in Africa. Some in the colonial movement opposed the image of what they labelled a "black whore" as a tribute to "Lettow's illustrious battles in East Africa."[31] Finally, some members of the public objected in 1940 to Africans wearing swastikas and being portrayed as veterans, which suggested an unpalatable equality between Africans and Germans.[32]

Similarly infrequent were German memories of African support that undercut notions of devoted sacrifice success. Charlotte and Ludwig Deppe were unusual in acknowledging the depredations of Lettow-Vorbeck's carriers and askaris that many deserted, the Deppes recognized their poor treatment and labour, considering it remarkable that Africans remained in German service.[33] The socialist newspaper *Hamburger Volkszeitung* challenged ideas of African dedication to Lettow-Vorbeck by citing their remembrance of him as "the man who weaves our death shroud."[34] Finally, the reality of the continued refusal of the government to pay the askaris' back wages definitely challenged the myth of the happy African and the benevolent colonizer. Lettow-Vorbeck and former colonial governor Adolf Friedrich zu Mecklenburg lamented the parsimony of a government that would rather betray the loyalty of the askaris and embarrass Germany than spend a few thousand marks.[35] Some proof of how Germans actually viewed the loyal askari can be seen in the continued unwillingness to honour promises to pay the wages of those who had fought for Germany.[36]

The memory of the former colonizers provides a starting point for understanding African memory, not merely because German memories are far better represented in the extant archive, but also because their memory conditioned that of the former colonized. Germany's position in Europe, its late start to colonialism, notions of colonial failure, and continual reference to European competitors shaped German remembrance of the war in the colonies. These factors all constrained the acceptable forms of memory of the colonial war in public discourse. The triumphant myth of Lettow-Vorbeck's corps and the place that the "undefeated" Germans of East Africa had in the postwar public imagination did not allow visions of failure. The very few contrary memories formed a tiny minority when compared to the massive weight of the government's and colonial organizations' emphasis on the positive aspects of the African war. Their success in communicating this memory in the public sphere meant that German recollection of the loyalty of Africans submerged contrary memories. The prevailing memory of loyal Africans was particularly evident in the small number of Germans who were allowed to remain in the new mandates. The settlers' memory reflected the hegemonic conception in Germany, and was sometimes even more radical.[37] Overall, the myth of the "loyal until death" askari was confirmed by German groups' exploitation of the memory of Africans.

As with the remembrance of the African war by the former colonizers, the ways in which Africans in the former colonies looked back upon the Great War was similarly contradictory, though for very different reasons. The colonial past and the substitution of the German colonizer for the new mandate rulers were the determining factors in conditioning interwar African memory. For the people involved in the war, their personal experience was also important to their later memories. Some positive remembrances of *Schutztruppe* service could have been the result of the veterans' past when their service accorded them greater pay and social standing.[38] Fond memories were undoubtedly linked to the ability of military service to bring significant wealth to an askari and his family. Service could also provide pleasant remembrances of youth, travel, and adventure. On the other hand, postwar life could shift such positive remembrances. The mandate administrators quickly recruited many of the former askaris and carriers to serve in the British and French colonial militaries. Thus, it is likely that many former German askaris were not keen to remember their service for the enemy fondly.

Pledges of undying devotion could be found in the former colonies, but these were considerably less evident and were often the product of local antipathy to the successor administrations.[39] For example, when the Nama people of SWA dressed in their German uniforms and called out "Our Germans have arrived!" to welcome the German navy's visit in the early 1930s, it was to embarrass the unloved South African authorities.[40] Similarly, the people of Kribi in Cameroon forgot depredations at the hands of Germans when they wore German hats and decorations for local ceremonies.[41] Germans in the colonial movement glorified tales such as that purportedly narrated by an East African askari that, "whenever they hear stories of them or if one of the brave defenders from the former German East Africa is visiting, the good Askaris will hike for miles to welcome 'their master' joyfully."[42] German missionaries also remembered the desire of indigenous helpers to "prove their thanks to the Germans, not with words but with deeds" through their wartime service.[43] Writer Hans Poeschel paraphrased East Africans' memories of the Germans with the Swahili description *Wadeutshi maneno makali roho nzuri*— possessing blunt words but a kind heart—which went to reinforce ideas of their hard but fair rule.[44]

Germans certainly celebrated manifestations of friendship by the former colonized, but whether or not these expressions of indigenous support were sincere, spontaneous, or uncoerced is a larger question.[45] There was also the ability among the African veterans to condemn German colonialism to their new administrators yet simultaneously to shout *Wadeutsche rudini!* (Germans, come back to us!) to the Germans. Some of the motives underlying such contradictions in this African fusion of past and present can be explained through the intriguing memory of the Ovaherero group of SWA.

The three-year war against the Ovaherero during German colonization and the remaining interwar German population made the collective memory of the war vital to the former colony. The Ovaherero Truppenspieler and Otruppe military organizations especially played with ideas of German authority, uniforms, and military service in order to establish tribal sovereignty and identity against South African rule. Creating a title for Chief Samuel Maherero as "Kaiser of Otruppe" and giving his officers pseudonyms like "State Secretary," "Treasurer von Ministermann," and "Adjutant Schmetterling von Preussen" further connected this postwar protonationalism to earlier warfare.[46] The Otruppe also divided into infantry and machine gun regiments as they paraded in their former uniforms. The soldiers barked German drill commands, bore sticks on their shoulders as surrogate rifles, and even marched under black-white-red imperial flags. Furthermore, when Maherero died in 1923, his committal was marked by the parading of Ovaherero, "mostly in German troopers' uniforms and hats." The mourners also displayed the explicit symbols of German rule: "the coffin was bedecked with the black-white-red flag, and numerous Ovaherero carried these colours wrapped around their arms or in their buttonholes."[47]

These performances of African memory of colonial war were multifaceted in meaning. Disappointment with mandate rule, the loss of traditional power, shrinking territories, and wider changes compelled the Ovaherero to develop new ways of dealing with transition and signifying their power.[48] Jan-Bart Gewald sees the memory of colonial war as providing a vital palliative to contemporary circumstances.[49] As other historians have observed, the Otruppe also showed how the early socialization of young Ovaherero in German service continued after 1919 and served as a way to articulate a distinct Ovaherero identity.[50] The gatherings and imitations of the Otruppe provided a means to reassert tribal authority, display

Ovaherero power, challenge South African rule, and unite dispersed groups in collective ceremonies.[51]

This imitation was not the sole preserve of the Ovaherero; other indigenous groups also mimicked their past colonizers for reasons relating to their present. Wearing the uniform of the Germans and carrying the accoutrements of war demanded respect from other indigenous groups, as well as from local whites. Germans who remained in the former colonies continually mocked such displays, perhaps because they understood their subversive potential, a counterpoint that illustrates well the hollowness of ideas about the loyal askari. Finally, these imitations give excellent examples of Homi Bhabha's mimicry of the colonizer and Michel de Certeau's cultural "poaching" of hegemonic culture by marginalized groups as a way to simulate, adapt, and thus appropriate some of the power of the hegemon.[52]

There were also voices raised in the former colonies in opposition to positive reflections of military service. Unsurprisingly, these few negative memories exist outside of official sources. The reminiscences of former carriers and askaris challenged notions of loyalty when they connected their service with the Swahili order *Ombasha, lete kiboko!* for the corporal to bring the vicious *sjambok* whip made from the skin of the hippopotamus.[53] SWA's Rehoboth Basters clearly remembered the violence resulting from their resistance to the war. Cameroon's war was often recollected with the word *Njokmansi* (to work without payment), a German forced-labour policy that induced many Cameroonians to flee.[54] The execution of the powerful Duala chief Rudolf Manga Bell was another major remembrance in Cameroon. Seeing German weakness in August 1914, he challenged the administration and was consequently hanged for treason. His execution established his heroic status as a proto-nationalist martyr who was later commemorated in memorials and other anti-German remembrances.[55] While somewhat banalized as a consequence of subsequent French rule, Togolese veterans nonetheless retained memories of lashes with the *sjambok*—"one for the Kaiser"—as punishment.[56] There were also Africans who remembered their war service for the Germans as being akin to slavery, complete with forced impressment, compulsory relocation, and copious beatings.[57]

That these memories were the leading ways of remembering the war and German service says much about the reality of African-German relations. Such unfiltered memories from the people who fought alongside Germany were also a clear challenge to German recollections. The memory of the former colonized in Africa presented a very different picture from that of the former colonizer, not least because of the need in Africa to forget the war in the face of new challenges. When mandate rule imposed new strictures upon the former colonized, their memories of German service were coloured by a changed context where this past had little purchase.

For many Africans who fought for Germany, the end of the war brought a migration on top of the trauma of defeat. Because of their military service for the enemy, some askaris were unwelcome in the mandates and joined the Germans in their repatriation. Forced to leave their homes and live in Germany, African veterans confronted the instabilities of the Weimar Republic and Third Reich.[58] The constraints of living in interwar Germany as Africans and the resulting remembrance of the war present a captivating memory. But understanding the creators of this memory is difficult; the paucity of sources on these transplanted Africans makes it challenging even to establish their number. Estimating from the existing documents, few more than a hundred African veterans lived in Germany.[59] In addition, many of these men had families, which further complicated their residence. Similarly, the number of people of African background in Germany exceeded eight hundred and some of them undoubtedly assumed the identity of the veteran as a way to foster a living. This use of memory hints at the multiple ways that this memory of the Great War was expressed, challenged, and received in Germany between 1919 and 1943.

Faced by a population unaccustomed to racial Others and with resulting difficulties finding employment, African veterans often found obtaining citizenship to be a key obstacle.[60] Their military service for Germany made their return to Africa impossible, as the mandates considered them to pose a direct danger to colonial control. Their precarious position as Africans living in Germany during times of crisis made them reliant on narratives that established claims to a secure identity. Since they were viewed as Africans with no rights in Germany, these veterans sought to emphasize their service and "Germanness" in order to survive. The Africans were not accorded the rights of citizenship, but were instead classified as "imperial dependents" or "wards of Germany."[61] On the other hand, because they had chosen to become Germans by serving in the military rather than being born into it, a reciprocal narrative developed where indigenous peoples claimed to be more German than the Germans. Many of these men and their families considered themselves to be citizens by virtue of their colonial service, military sacrifice, and present residence. But instead of being treated as Germans, they were ostracized by the majority of the population.

Despite the loyal askari myth, African veterans were still considered essentially alien and denied housing, employment, and civic rights, as the state sought to send these men back to their "homelands."[62] This rhetoric of "homelands" became more odious when veterans' families were threatened with expulsion from Germany, even though some had never been to Africa, having been born in Germany to African parents. The notion of home also stung some veterans who acknowledged this loss. One man named only as "Mambo" enlisted in 1897 to serve, and since the war "he admittedly had not again seen his home."[63] Similarly, Thomas Manga Akwa declared in 1929 that, "through my loyalty to Germany, I have lost my right of residence" in Cameroon.[64] Another Cameroonian, Louis Brody, wrote in 1921 to complain about his poor treatment by Germans. Appealing to notions of sacrifice as well as German affiliation, Brody is worth citing at length: "We therefore ask the Germans to consider that we have just as much as they have to suffer and not to condescend to us. In particular, we want to remark that we are not an immoral and savage race as we are currently called in Germany. We must also remind Germans that Lettow-Vorbeck did not fight alone in Africa but also that natives have given their lives for the German flag."[65] In a similar vein, Kwassi Bruce connected his service in Togo to collective African assistance with the statement that, "with the same understanding and with the same desire, the black sons of Germany rallied in the other colonies," arguing that people of all of the four colonies were united in their faithful Germanness and therefore deserved fair treatment.[66]

The key factor underpinning these assertions of German identity was that citizenship would grant access to employment in Germany. Their visible alterity forced veterans of African background out of many occupations. What little employment they could find was overwhelmingly in the service sector as waiters and servers, or in the entertainment sector as actors and musicians. Even positions in these circumscribed fields of employment were hard to find in the 1920s and 1930s, so veterans had to appeal to the authorities for assistance in finding work. For example, Juma bin Abdallah used his memory of the war to apply for work by stating he was "full of pride" for his service with Lettow-Vorbeck, which had earned him two decorations.[67] Bayume Mohamed Hussein relied on documents certifying him to have been an askari to open doors to employment. Drawing on his service to the Reich, Hussein ended a 1937 letter to the government with the Swahili title "Askari for the German Emperor."[68] Finally, the actor Himbo Monolulu advertised himself as "your fellow countryman from Cameroon" in his appeals for employment.[69]

Beyond the search for work, African veterans depended on their war service to gain support. Men like the mechanic and train driver Martin

Dibobe from Cameroon often used positive memories of colonial service to solicit government aid.[70] Hussein similarly utilized his colonial background to gain support from the authorities. Serving as a messenger in the *Schutztruppe*, he had lost his father and had survived several years in a prisoner-of-war camp.[71] His particular story led him to be granted a "special concession" by the state.[72] Alternately, Bruce pleaded unsuccessfully for support in 1934 by appealing to notions of sacrifice and describing how:

> My black comrades knew nothing of Sarajevo and its prelude.... For them, it was enough that the emperor had commanded and they would march with the desire to fulfill their sworn duty. On the afternoon of August 7, my company marched with drums and whistles to the railway station and loaded onto trains. One signal, the train jerked, and from hundreds of soldiers' throats roared a German song which was sung by millions of white German soldiers in the Motherland in similar circumstances: "The Watch on the Rhine!"[73]

Bruce's plea for favourable treatment during the Third Reich is evocative in its message and imagery. He linked his service to that of German soldiers, as well as common conceptions of fealty and sacrifice for the empire.

The unpaid wages from fighting in Africa remained another major issue for the African veterans in Germany, who considered full payment to be of foremost importance. They unsuccessfully lobbied the government for years. Hussein cited his service and his father's death as he stated, "I do not want much, I just want what is due to me."[74] He asked the authorities of the Foreign Office that, given his service, "will you deprive me of my proper recognition?" To reinforce his argument, he concluded by stating that he had not thought that Germans would act in this way. Failing to find help, Hussein appealed in 1937 for assistance from veterans' and colonial organizations. Describing himself as a "carrier, who carried the European's gun," he connected his loyal service to the German soldier when he asked for assistance from white veterans.[75] Similar appeals for support frequently relied on decorations awarded, such as the Honour Cross of the World War 1914–1918 and the Wound Medal. Decorations equated the Africans' courage to German veterans' bravery and further emphasized their equivalent status.

After the Nazi seizure of power in 1933, appeals for employment and support were typically focused on the two main fields of work deemed acceptable for Africans. The first was in the many colonial films featuring

Africans enacting the usual images of undying devotion to their colonizers. The burgeoning film industry and expanding audiences of the Weimar
Republic and Third Reich featured many films of tropical locales and adventures. Veterans and their families performed key roles as chiefs, warriors,
and other stereotypical African characters.[76] The movies made use of the
contrasting images of the threatening savage and the loyal askari to provide
a foil for the German adventurer and to play on the central memories of the
colonial revisionist movement.[77] For instance, popular movies like 1943's
Germanin reveled in portrayals of the selfless sacrifices of Germans and
the loyalty of Africans.[78] The large number of films that incorporated an
African character as a loyal adjunct to a German colonizer speaks to the
continuing salience of this memory.

The most important employment for African veterans, and a crucial
zone for the performance of their memory, was in travelling shows and
exhibitions. The shows were a popular entertainment that dispersed colonial memory through the more than three hundred groups that performed
colonial shows before 1940. Germans watching the wandering troupes were
enthralled by the evocative memories, performances, music, and dances,
and the enthusiasm of the performers.[79] As a result, Klaus Hildebrand estimates that 1.7 million Germans visited colonial shows between 1933 and
1938 alone.[80] One particular show, the German Africa Show, brought in
27,238 visitors over a month and a half in 1937 and close to 32,880 visitors
over a forty-day period in 1938.[81] Germans were eager consumers of such
entertainments because they conformed to their expectations for the portrayal of both Africa and Africans.

The colonial military was an integral part of these shows and their appeal
to government, colonial revisionism, and the general public. The shows all
included African performers in their colonial incarnations, wearing uniforms and serving dutifully beside (or behind) a white German. One show
described the "blacks, who fought for Germany under Lettow-Vorbeck and
who have earned numerous decorations, bring near the memory of that
time when the Negroes assisted their German masters with rare fanati-
cism."[82] Germans celebrated the performers' displays of "the good relations
between white and black in German East Africa."[83] An example of this comradeship was Hussein, who found work as a "Showcase Askari" at various
public displays where he personified the loyal askari in front of German
audiences, who delighted in the symbols of their benevolent colonialism
and effective war fighting.[84] Consequently, in their appeals for government
funding, the shows' organizers made much of the colonial background and

military awards of their performers.[85] Even Adolf Hitler's concerns in 1939 about the veteran status of the performers in the German Africa Show were assuaged by providing proof of their military service, which legitimated their performances.[86]

The image of the armed, trained, and faithful African servant of German colonization reveled in dominant representations of the colonial past. The shows often featured depictions of the colonies with palm fronds, Germanic heroes, and essentialized "natives," but also played with the image of the loyal askari as the counterpoint to the threatening savage. The askari thus functioned as a figure that illustrated how German rule could civilize the inhabitants of Africa. The positioning of the loyal servant and its opposite, the frightening Other, also made the askari more German, civilized, and acceptable to German memory. Continual references to Lettow-Vorbeck and this figure of the askari allowed the viewing public to identify the successes of colonialism and the victories of war. These performances shaped public opinion and allowed Africans in Germany to establish a space for themselves in an increasingly xenophobic society.

Particularly evocative for audiences was the emotive force of veterans recounting their service. Many colonial shows prominently featured Africans dressed in askari uniforms describing their homelands and war service. At one especially powerful 1938 event, Hussein took the stage in an askari uniform, flanked by Hitler Youth and swastika-bedecked colonial soldiers, to call for the return of Germany's colonies.[87] Similarly, a 1940 audience was positively enthralled when one performer saluted the audience with the Nazi salute and pledged the everlasting loyalty of his people.[88] Some of these men were actual veterans, but some were clearly chosen only for the colour of their skin and the effect that their racial difference, German uniforms, and exultation of Germany would have upon audiences.

However, enacting the myth of the loyal askari on German stages, screens, and other public venues was not without contestation. The very fact that Africans could only find employment and relative safety in carefully staged appearances says much about how the supposedly faithful servants of Germany were regarded.[89] But as Elisa Forgey asserts, the positive remembrance of the war provided a safe space in Germany for people of colour.[90] The veterans' role as living symbols of successful colonization and the war in Africa made them necessary for the German myth and thus guaranteed them a measure of safety.

Yet, when Germans sang songs at public events extolling the bravery and loyalty of their mixed "German-Coloured *Schutztruppe*" and their battles in Africa, they forgot or ignored the reality behind the myth. Such loyalty was performed by men, women, and sometimes children subjected to brutal conditions, such as carrying thirty-kilogram loads across swamps. Largely without medical care, sickness, death, and desertion decimated these auxiliaries' ranks. The African veterans were certainly aware of these experiences, and yet were forced to parrot the memories of the colonizer because of their precarious situation in Germany. As some of their letters to the government hint, they identified the lack of reciprocal loyalty on the part of their purportedly paternalistic colonizer. But this was the only rhetorical tool for African veterans to gain advantage when dealing with the government and colonial organizations, which were able simultaneously to celebrate the loyal askari while barring him and his family from respect, civic rights, citizenship, and employment. Last, although many of these soldiers declared themselves to be German soldiers, this identity was continuously undermined by Germans, who instead referred to them as "askari" and "Africans" who had only assisted the war effort. Such challenges negated their claims to Germanness, as well as their sacrifices. Obviously, there were strict limits to the rhetoric of the loyal askari in German discourse and practice.

It was the ability to navigate their liminal position both inside and racially outside of German society that allowed the African veterans to survive for many years. Though they likely acknowledged the cliché of the loyal askari and the falseness of the myth that they performed, they also recognized that it provided security for themselves and their families. Living for so long in interwar Germany, Hussein presents a great example of a former askari who was able to play on the contradictions in German memory. He parlayed his racial difference and the reminiscences connected with it into employment, often posing in his askari uniform, and thus survived in Germany as a result of this memory. This continued until his 1941 incarceration for "racial defilement" with his German wife. Identifying himself throughout his incarceration in Sachsenhausen concentration camp as the "servant of the famous general Lettow-Vorbeck," Hussein survived until 1944.[91]

Perhaps Hussein's fate is the tragic postscript to the African veterans' narrative. Though these men of African background used the memory of their undying loyalty to Germany to shape their interwar present, the last years of the Nazi regime removed their last refuge. For much of the 1920s and 1930s, they were successful in framing their memory in ways that Germans would comprehend and support. However, they were reliant on the state and colonial organizations for their livelihoods, since an alternative memory would put their lives and the situation of their families in jeopardy. For this reason, it would have been impossible for an African veteran to suggest that colonialism was less than successful or that the war in Africa had been replete with abuse, death, and desertion. The reality of their colonial pasts and their situation in Germany made their memories susceptible to instrumentalization, which forced their demonstrations of memory to conform to German remembrance.

As seen above, a variety of factors twisted African memory to reflect positive recollections of colonial war. For Africans in the former German colonies, such memory can be explained by a dislike for the mandate administrations and nostalgia for more familiar German rule. For Africans stranded in Germany, their public expressions of memory were molded by the interwar context. Positive remembrances were conditioned by the requirements of living in a destabilized and economically depressed nation, where the racial prejudices of colonialism continued. Such pressures might have made service in the *Schutztruppe* a comparatively benign experience. Additionally, there was perhaps a generational element, as some men undoubtedly felt nostalgia for their heady days of youth in German service. Bound together as a community and fighting an external aggressor, men would have imbibed the communal narratives usual to military service. Veterans could also have been silenced by their traumatic experience in the Great War, which made them reluctant to express their true memories publicly. Finally, some veterans must have felt a sense of honour about their service, particularly given their success in supporting the "undefeated" Lettow-Vorbeck.

When attempting to understand the positive memories of colonial service, it is surprising how rarely Africans expressed negative views. Their experiences were indeed dire, and yet this past was frequently forgotten. Anthropologist Marc Augé's observation that memory and forgetting are complementary holds true for this context, especially in the need to remember and forget in order to deal with the past.[92] It was perhaps this need to move on from the past that motivated so many African veterans to submerge negative remembrances and to consolidate around positive visions of the past. Through the "socially constitutive act" that Charles S. Maier terms all remembering, many Africans and Germans found strength and fixity in a certain vision of the colonial past.[93] Conforming to the overwhelmingly positive visions of colonial warfare advanced by the vocal and powerful colonial revisionists would allow the Africans some measure of community, safety, and economic security in Germany between 1919 and 1943. Nonetheless, Germans rarely accorded their former allies the fraternity they so often celebrated. It may be the ultimate irony that Germans' memories of their "loyal until death" African allies applied only to Africans' devotion to their German masters, and not vice versa.

It is certain that African veterans identified this hypocrisy, although they have left no sources overtly confirming this dissent. On the other hand, veterans of the German colonial military who remained in Africa were confronted by changed circumstances after 1919, which marginalized the remembrance of the German years. The African veterans in Germany, though few in number, were given a louder voice as their memories conformed to German memory and were thus collected and communicated to a greater extent than veterans in the colonies. In Germany, the private (and most accurate) memory of these veterans is exceedingly difficult to discover, as inadequate traces remain. But by acknowledging the reality of the war and recognizing the interwar perspectives of Germans, Africans, and Africans living in Germany that structured its memory, the instrumentalization of African memories of the war is manifest. The memories of African veterans of their Great War service for Germany is not only important as an under-studied field of investigation, but also to their historical lives. How Africans remembered the war was significant to their later history, as it was often used to shape nationalist narratives. These veterans wrestled with the negotiation of different power structures in diverse circumstances, and were neither collaborationist nor resistant. Instead, these men merely sought to navigate a changing world. In acknowledging this, this analysis goes beyond a recuperative insertion of marginalized perspectives into a more composite study of the interactions between African and German memories of the war. Furthermore, the reality of the wide gulf between African experiences of the war and their later memories also says much about the fractures in the collective memory of war by highlighting how a particular memory structured other remembrances. The fact that the victims of colonialism could become complicit in willful amnesia points to the entanglements of memory, but also complicates the purportedly homogeneous European history of the war. German remembrance of their war depended upon the positive memories of the former colonized for their own self-conception. In these ways, the war had continuing resonance for both Germans and Africans.

The remembrance of African veterans of the Great War formed a web that linked Germany to Africa. Even after German colonialism had ended, the military past held salience for many people in Germany and Africa. Not only was this memory of the "loyal until death" askari transnational in connecting the former German colonies and the metropole, but it continued as late as the 1940s. Reciprocally, the contemporary situation in interwar Germany and Africa continued to shape how the Great War was remembered. This fascinating intermingling of memories reveals how German and African societies dealt with the legacies of the war, how Africans and Germans confronted their globalized past, and the vivid interactions between past and present between 1919 and 1943. Finally, the manner in which the memory of the colonial war was used and abused in both Germany and its former African colonies speaks to the continuing importance of the African campaign to the wider history of the Great War.

NOTES

1. These years form the chronological limits because of the end of German colonial revisionism in 1943.
2. As a result of the lacking historical records, there are few studies of African veterans. Thomas Morlang, *Askari und Fitafita: 'farbige' Söldner in den deutschen Kolonien* (Berlin: Christoph Links Verlag, 2008), 8–9; Marianne Bechhaus-Gerst, *Treu bis in den Tod: von Deutsch-Ostafrika nach Sachsenhausen—Eine Lebensgeschichte* (Berlin: Christoph Links Verlag, 2007).
3. Jean and John Comaroff, *Of Revelation and Revolution: Christianity, Colonialism and Consciousness in South Africa*, vol. I (Chicago: University of Chicago Press, 1991), 37.
4. George Steinmetz, *The Devil's Handwriting: Precoloniality and the German Colonial State in Qingdao, Samoa and Southwest Africa* (Chicago: University of Chicago Press, 2007); Woodruff D. Smith, *The German Colonial Empire* (Chapel Hill: University of North Carolina Press, 1978).
5. Ulrich van der Heyden and Joachim Zeller, eds. *Kolonialmetropole Berlin: Eine Spurensuche* (Berlin: Berlin Edition, 2002), 38.
6. Bundesarchiv Berlin—Lichterfelde (hereafter BAB) R1001/2089 Bl.7a, Trotha, 2 October 1904; R1001 /2089, 2 November 1904, 100v; R1001 /2089. General von Trotha to Governor Theodor Leutwein, 5 November 1904, 100.
7. Bechhaus-Gerst, *Treu bis in den Tod*, 42–44.
8. The term "Basters" refers to their mixed Dutch-African background, and corresponds to the group's own term of self-identification. Bundesarchiv Freiburg—Militärarchiv (hereafter BAMA) MSG 3/1785 Mitteilungen der Arbeitsgemeinschaft kolonialer Verbände. Frankfurt am Main. 1 Jr., nr. 2/3, February/March 1925.

9. Gisela Graichen and Horst Gründer, *Deutsche Kolonien. Traum und Trauma* (Berlin: Ullstein, 2005), 351.

10. Kristen Zirkel, "Military Power in German Colonial Policy: The Schutztruppen and Their Leaders in East and Southwest Africa, 1888–1918," in *Guardians of Empire: The Armed Forces of the Colonial Powers, c. 1700–1964*, ed. David Killingray and David Omissi (Manchester: Manchester University Press, 1999), 108.

11. BAB R1001 /6694, 80456, #601. Deutsche Kolonialgesellschaft—Frauenbund, Bd. 2. Frauenbund der Deutschen Kolonialgesellschaft, *Deutsche Jugend und Deutsche Kolonien*. Ina Reck, "Wie Deutsch-Ostafrika wurde und war," 31.

12. Bechhaus-Gerst, *Treu bis in den Tod*, 30–33.

13. Morlang, *Askari und Fitafita*, 8.

14. Beyond soldiers, the war in East Africa caused an estimated half-million fatalities. Bechhaus-Gerst, *Treu bis in den Tod*, 51.

15. Graichen and Gründer, *Deutsche Kolonien*, 357, 359.

16. Bechhaus-Gerst, *Treu bis in den Tod*, 48.

17. BAB R1001 /6749 Gesellschaften 48, Akademische Kolonialbund an der Universität zu Berlin, *Die Deutsche Studentenschaft. Nachrichtenblatt der Deutschen Studentenschaft*, 20 January 1927, Folge 5, 55.

18. BAB R1001 /6735, Gesellschaften 36, Bund der Kolonialfreunde. *Der Kolonialfreund*, April/May 1929. Oberregierungsrat Dr. Dannert, "Zur Kolonialschuldlüge: Wie steht der Kampf?" R1001 /6390 Presse Ausstellung Köln. "Der Kolonialdeutsche" Deutsche Uebersee- und Kolonialzeitung, #10, 15 May 1928.

19. BAB R1001 /7036 Kriegssachen 2, 80493, #638, Kommission zur Feststellung von Rechsverletzungen. "Auszug, betreffend wirtschaftliche Schädigung von Deutschen in den Kolonien"; R1001 /7036 Kriegssachen 2, 80493, #638, Kommission zur Feststellung von Rechsverletzungen, "Auszug: aus persönlichen Berichten von Kolonial-Deutschen über Behandlung durch die Engländer nach der Gefangennahme," 14 May 1919, 97.

20. The number of members in the various colonial organizations varied, but the Nazi colonial organizations boasted more than two million supporters in 1941. BAB R1001 /6682 80455, #600 Gesellschaften 1, Die deutschen Kolonialverbände. Reichsverband der Deutschen Industrie to Auswärtiges Amt, Düring, 1 February 1930, 10; *Mitteilungen der Deutschen Kolonialgesellschaft*, #7, July 1928; *Der Kolonialdeutsche*, no. 1, 1 July 1926; Hans Zache, "Die Lehren von Bochum," 222; Graichen and Gründer, *Deutsche Kolonien*, 411.

21. BAB R1001 /7225, Propaganda 3, nr. 1, Abrechnungen der Deutschen Kolonialgesellschaft über die Ausgaben dem Propagandafonds. Abschrift. 1924, 12. BAB R1001 /9724, 85550, #913, Haushaltsüberwachungslisten "Voranschlag über die kolonialen Haushaltmittel für das Rechnungsjahr

1939"; R1001 /9699 Etats- und Rechnungswesen, Allgemeines, 85549, #912, Voranschlag für die kolonialen Haushaltsmittel, 1941–1944. Voranschlag über die kolonialen Haushaltsmittel für das Rechnungsjahr 1943.

22. Klaus Hildebrand, *Vom Reich zum Weltreich: Hitler, NSDAP und koloniale Frage 1919–1945* (München: Wilhelm Fink Verlag, 1969).

23. Charlotte und Ludwig Deppe, *Um Ostafrika: Erinnerung* (Dresden: Verlag E. Beutelspacher, 1925); August Hauer, *Kumbuke: Erlebnisse eines Arztes in Deutsch-Ostafrika* (Berlin: Dom-Verlag, 1922); Werner von Langsdorff, *Deutsche Flagge über Sand und Palmen: 53 Kolonialkrieger erzählen* (Gütersloh: Bertelsmann, 1936); Paul von Lettow-Vorbeck, *Heia Safari! Deutschlands Kampf in Ostafrika: Der deutschen Jugend unter Mitwirkung seines Mitkämpfers Hauptman von Ruckteschell* (Leipzig: Verlag von K.F. Koehler, 1920); Paul von Lettow-Vorbeck, *Meine Erinnerungen aus Ostafrika* (Leipzig: Verlag K.F. Koehler, 1920); Paul von Lettow-Vorbeck, *Was Deutschland verloren. Zwei Teile in einem Band. Zweiter Teil: Das Buch vom Raubfrieden. Die Ausführung und die Folgen des Versailler Friedensvertrages* (Berlin: National-Verlag, 1924); Balder Olden, *Kilimanscharo: Ein Roman aus Deutsch-Ost* (Berlin: Gydendal'scher Verlag, 1922); Hans Poeschel, *Deutschland muss seine Kolonien wieder haben* (Berlin: Dietrich Reimer, 1919); A. Schirge, *Mit Lettow-Vorbeck durch Ost-Afrika 1914–1919* (Berlin: Berliner evangelischen Missionsgesellschaft, 1919); Robert Unterwelz, *In Tropensonne und Urwaldnacht: Wanderungen und Erlebnisse in Deutsch-Ostafrika* (Stuttgart: Strecker und Schröder, 1923); Josef Viera, *Die Mikindani-Patrouille: Mit Lettow-Vorbeck in Deutsch-Ostafrika* (Reutlingen: Enßlin und Laiblin, 1938).

24. Josef Viera, *Maria in Petersland* (Breslau: Bergstadtverlag, 1937), 332; Hans Poeschel, *Bwana Hakimu: Richterfahrten in Deutsch-Ostafrika* (Leipzig: Koehler und Voigtländer Verlag, 1940), 28, 139–151; Rudolf Asmis, *Kalamba Na M'Putu: Koloniale Erfahrungen und Beobachtungen* (Berlin: Mittler und Sohn, 1942), 3, 10, 87–90; BAB NS43 /142. Außenpolitisches Amt der NSDAP. 3.2 Deutschland. 3.2.7. Außenpolitik. Kolonialpolitik 1942–43. Schriften über das deutsche katholische Missionswesen, insbesondere in Afrika. Kolonialpolitisches Amt (KPA) der NSDAP, Asmis to Aussenpolitische Amt der NSDAP, Frank, 15 May 1941, 2. "Aktenotiz. Betrifft: Missionsarbeit in den neuen deutschen Kolonien." 8 May 1941, 3–6.

25. BAMA RW51 /9 Deutsch-Ostafrika während des Weltkrieges. Vortrag vom Gouverneur Dr. Schnee, Gesellschaft für Erdkunde zu Berlin, 15 March 1919, 17; Jörg Lehmann, "Fraternity, Frenzy, and Genocide in German War Literature, 1906–36," in *German Colonialism and National Identity*, ed. Michael Perraudin and Jürgen Zimmerer (New York: Routledge, 2011), 117.

26. Lettow-Vorbeck, *Heia Safari!* 144, 159; BAMA N103 /102 Nachlaß von Lettow-Vorbeck. Was wir die Engländer über Ostafrika erzählten. Abhandlung von Paul von Lettow-Vorbeck. 1930, 31, 42.

27. Graichen and Gründer, *Deutsche Kolonien*, 357.

28. Stefanie Michels and Albert-Pascal Temgoua, eds. *La politique de la mémoire coloniale en Allemagne et au Cameroun* (Münster: Lit Verlag, 2005), 7.

29. BAB R1001 /1077/1 Seitz to Guhlmann, 3 June 1926; Elisa von Joeden-Forgey, "Nobody's People: Colonial Subjects, Race Power and the German State, 1884–1945" (Ph.D. diss., University of Pennsylvania, 2004), 521.

30. BAB R8023 /32 Unterstützungs- und Darlehensgesuche. 1077a, Hilfe und Unterstützung für die in Deutschland lebenden Eingeborenen der ehemaligen deutschen Schutzgebiete. 1912–28, 49. Alfred Guhlmann, früher Swakopmund, to Rostalski, Vorsitzender der Vereinigung der Deutsch-Ostafrikaner Leipzig, October 1925, 75.

31. Joachim Zeller, *Kolonialdenkmäler und Geschichtsbewusstsein: Eine Untersuchung der kolonial-deutschen Erinnerungskultur* (Frankfurt am Main: Verlag für Interkulturelle Kommunikation, 2000), 186–88.

32. BAB NS18 /519, 2 Reichspropagandaleitung 1933–45. 2.9 Veranstaltungen, Ausstellungen und Tagungen. Deutsche Afrikaschau. Verbot der Veranstaltung wegen des Auftritts von Negern. Bl. 81, Goger to Tiessler, Leiter des Reichsrings für nationalsozialistische Propaganda und Volksaufklärung, 21 April 1941; BAB R1001 /6383 Ausstellung 19/3, Koloniale Wanderausstellung Afrikaschau—Hillerkus. Goger, Gauleitung Niederdonau to Propaganda Ministerium (Thiessler), 29 June 1940.

33. Deppe, *Um Ostafrika*, 270–71.

34. Staatsarchiv der Freien und Hansestaat Hamburg 135-1 Staatliche Pressestelle I-IV /4319. *Hamburger Volkszeitung*, 2 August 1926. "Die schwarzweißrote Kolonialkriegs-Demonstration."

35. The wages were finally paid in 1964. BAMA N103 /94 Nachlass von Lettow-Vorbeck. Askari der Schutztruppe für Deutsch-Ostafrika, Soldabfindung: Diesbezügliche Bemühungen von Lettow-Vorbecks. 1920–24. Adolf Friedrich von Mecklenburg to Lettow-Vorbeck, 19 February 1921, 20; and DKG Abteilung Stuttgart, Verband der Württ. und Bad. Kolonialdeutschen to Staatspräsident von Württemberg, 21 February 1921, 21–22; and *Volk und Wehrkraft: Wehrbeilage der "Zeit,"* nr. 3, 18 January 1922, 35; Paul von Lettow-Vorbeck, "Die Löhnung unserer Askaris—eine deutsche Ehrenschuld."

36. BAMA N103 /94 Nachlass Lettow-Vorbeck, 21.

37. Brigitta Schmidt-Lauber, *Die abhängigen Herren: Deutsche Identität in Namibia* (Münster: Lit Verlag, 1993), 72, 75–76.

38. Morlang, *Askari und Fitafita*, 72–91.

39. Bundesarchiv Koblenz (BAK) NL37 /7 Nachlass Hintrager, Tagebuch der Süd- und Südwestafrika Reise 1930 (Manuskript, Maschinenschrift), 141, 143–47, 153; BAK NL1037 /2 Nachlass Hintrager. Eigene Abhandlungen, Reden und Vorträge Deutsch-Südwestafrika, 1906–41. Vortrag—DKG Berlin, 10 December 1930. "Ein Wiedersehen mit Südwestafrika," 4; Ralph A. Austen:

"'Ich bin Schwarzer Mann, aber mein Herz ist Deutsch': Germanophones and 'Germanness' in Colonial Cameroon and Tanzania," in *Die (koloniale) Begegnung: Afrikanerinnen in Deutschland 1880–1945, Deutsche in Afrika 1880–1918*, ed. Marianne Bechhaus-Gerst and Reinhard Klein-Arendt (Frankfurt am Main: Peter Lang, 2003), 28–32.

40. BAK N1101 /69 Epp Kolonialtagung Freiburg, June 1935. Epp Vortrag Breslau, 3 July 1932.

41. Richard Joseph, "The German Question in French Cameroon, 1919–1939," *Comparative Studies in Society and History* 17 (1975): 81.

42. Luise Diel, *Die Kolonien warten! Afrika im Umbruch* (Leipzig: P. List, 1939), 56–60, cited in Joachim Warmbold, *Germania in Africa, Germany's Colonial Literature* (New York: Peter Lang, 1989), 201.

43. Adolf Schirge, *Mit Lettow-Vorbeck durch Ost-Afrika 1914–1919* (Berlin: Berliner evangelischen Missionsgesellschaft, 1919), 44.

44. Hans Poeschel, *The Voice of German East Africa: The English in the Judgment of the Natives* (Berlin: August Scherl, 1928), 17, 55–56; BAMA N103 /96 Nachlass von Lettow-Vorbeck. Der Krieg in Deutsch-Ostafrika. Erlebnisse deutscher Kriegsteilnehmer. 1919–34. Lettow-Vorbeck, 28 March 1919, 1–2.

45. BAK N1101 /69 Epp Kolonialtagung Freiburg, June 1935. Epp Vortrag Breslau, 3 July 1932.

46. Jan-Bart Gewald, *"We Thought We Would Be Free"*: Socio-Cultural Aspects of Herero Life in Namibia, 1915–1940 (Köln: R. Köppe, 2000), 28, 65, 71; *Berichte der Rheinischen Missionsgesellschaft*, 1923, 80. Jahrgang, "Zum Tode des ehemaligen Oberhäuptlings Samuel Maharero," 117–18. Wolfgang Werner, "'Playing Soldiers': The Truppenspieler Movement among the Herero of Namibia, 1915 to ca. 1945," *Journal of Southern African Studies* 16, no. 3 (September 1990): 476; Jürgen Zimmerer and Joachim Zeller, *Genocide in German South-West Africa: The Colonial War (1904–1908) in Namibia and Its Aftermath* (Monmouth: Merlin, 2008), 208.

47. BAB R1001 /6732 Gesellschaften 36, Bund der Kolonialfreunde. *Der Kolonialfreunde*, no. 7, October 1923: 69. "Die Beerdigung Samuel Mahareros."

48. Werner, "'Playing Soldiers,'" 485.

49. Jan-Bart Gewald, "Flags, Funerals and Fanfares: Herero and Missionary Contestations of the Acceptable, 1900–1940," *Journal of African Cultural Studies* 15, no. 1 (June 2002): 105; Gewald, *"We Thought We Would Be Free"*, 137–38, 158, 174.

50. Jekura Kavari, Dag Henrichsen, and Larissa Förster, "Die oturupa," in *Namibia-Deutschland. Eine geteilte Geschichte*, ed. Larissa Förster, Dag Hendrichsen, and Michael Bollig (Wolfrathausen: Minerva, 2004), 159.

51. Gewald, "Flags, Funerals and Fanfares," 112–13.

52. Homi Bhabha, *The Location of Culture* (New York: Routledge, 1994), 121–31;

Michel de Certeau, *The Practice of Everyday Life* (Berkeley: University of California Press, 1984), xii–xiii, xviii, 34, 165.

53. Graichen and Gründer, *Deutsche Kolonien*, 357.

54. Stefanie Michels, "The Germans Were Brutal and Wild: Colonial Legacies," in *La politique de la mémoire coloniale en Allemagne et au Cameroun*, ed. Stefanie Michels and Albert-Pascal Temgoua (Münster: Lit Verlag, 2005), 53.

55. Ralph A. Austen and Jonathan Derrick, *Middlemen of the Cameroons Rivers: The Duala and Their Hinterland, 1600–c. 1960* (Cambridge: Cambridge University Press, 1999), 93, 132, 171.

56. Adjai Paulin Oloukpona-Yinnon, "Unbewältigte Koloniale Vergangenheit. Problematik der Aufarbeitung der deutschen Kolonialzeit in Togo," in *Rassendiskriminierung, Kolonialpolitik und ethnisch-nationale Identität*, ed. Wilfried Wagner et al. (Münster: LIT Verlag, 1992), 435.

57. Graichen and Gründer, *Deutsche Kolonien*, 356–57.

58. BAB R8023 /1077a, Hilfe und Unterstützung für die in Deutschland lebenden Eingeborenen der ehemaligen deutschen Schutzgebiete, 1922, 193.

59. Robbie Aitken, "Surviving in the Metropole: The Struggle for Work and Belonging amongst African Colonial Migrants in Weimar Germany," *Immigrants and Minorities* 28, nos. 2–3 (July–November 2010), 205; Joeden-Forgey, "Nobody's People," 555; Bechhaus-Gerst and Klein-Arendt, *Die (koloniale) Begegnung*, 42.

60. David Ciarlo, "Globalizing German Colonialism," *German History* 26, no. 2 (2008), 297–98.

61. Heyden and Zeller, *Kolonialmetropole Berlin*, 217.

62. BAB R1001 /7562 Verwaltungssachen 56, Bd. 1, 80552, #697, Verhinderung des Zuzugs von Afrikanern aus den Kolonien nach Deutschland und deren Heimschaffung. Der Präsident der deutschen Kolonial-gesellschaft to Auswärtiges Amt (koloniale Angelegenheiten), 1 December 1925, 47.

63. BAB R1001 /6383 Ausstellung 19/3, Koloniale Wanderausstellung Afrikaschau—Hillerkus. *Stassfurter Zeitung*, 29 September 1937.

64. Bechhaus-Gerst, *Treu bis in den Tod*, 75–76; BAB R1001 /4457 /7, Thomas Manga Akwa, June 1929.

65. Susann Lewerenz, *Die Deutsche Afrika-Schau (1935–1940): Rassismus, Kolonial-revisionismus und postkoloniale Auseinandersetzungen im nationalso-zialistischen Deutschland* (Frankfurt am Main: Peter Lang, 2006), 47; *BZ am Mittag*, Jahrgang 44/118, 24 May 1921; Aitken, "From Cameroon to Germany and Back via Moscow and Paris," 599.

66. BAB R1001 /7562, Zuzug von Eingeborenen aus den Schutzgebieten und deren Heimschaffung, August 1899 bis April 1939, Bl. 95, Kwassi Bruce, 1934.

67. BAB R1001 /6383 Ausstellung 19/3, Koloniale Wanderausstellung Afrikaschau—Hillerkus. *Stassfurter Zeitung*, 29 September 1937.

68. BAB R1001 /1105, Zuzug von Afrikanern aus Deutsch-Ostafrika nach

Deutschland und deren Rückkehr, Bl. 152; Bechhaus-Gerst, *Treu bis in den Tod*, 98.

69. Bechhaus-Gerst, *Treu bis in den Tod*, 64.

70. BAB R1001 /7220 Propaganda 1, 8/9, Koloniale Propaganda im Inlande, Bl. 132, Aktenvermerk, "Kungebung der Treue zu Deutschland," 13 June 1919; Adolf Rüger, "Imperialismus, Sozialreformismus und antikoloniale demokratische Alternative. Zielvorstellungen von Afrikanern in Deutschland im Jahre 1919," *Zeitschrift für Geschichts-wissenschaft* 23 (1975): 1296.

71. Bechhaus-Gerst, *Treu bis in den Tod*, 29.

72. BAB R1001 /5148 2.5.17 Staatsangehörigkeit, 80321, #466, Reichsangehörigkeitsverhältnisse, Naturalisationen, Deutsch-Ostafrika, 1924–41. Gunzert, Konzept, "Bescheinigung," 25 March 1935, 105.

73. BAB R1001 /7562, Zuzug von Eingeborenen aus den Schutzgebieten und deren Heimschaffung, August 1899 bis April 1939, Bl. 95, Kwassi Bruce, 1934.

74. Bechhaus-Gerst, *Treu bis in den Tod*, 54–57.

75. Bechhaus-Gerst considers this to be a misleading description that ignores the danger of carrying weapons, and therefore does insufficient justice to Hussein's bravery. Ibid., 33.

76. Marie Nejar, *Mach nicht so traurige Augen, weil du ein Negerlein bist: Meine Jugend im Dritten Reich* (Hamburg: Rowohlt Taschenbuch Verlag, 2007), 101, 112. Bechhaus-Gerst, *Treu bis in den Tod*, 114.

77. Jörg Schöning, ed. *Triviale Tropen: exotische Reise- und Abenteuerfilme aus Deutschland 1919–1939* (München: edition Text + Kritik, 1997), 7.

78. Wolfgang Uwe Eckart, *Medizin und Kolonialimperialismus* (Paderborn: Schöningh, 1997), 514; Sabine Hake, "Mapping the Native Body: On Africa and Colonial Film during the Third Reich," in *The Imperialist Imagination: German Colonialism and Its Legacy*, ed. Sara Friedrichsmeyer, Sara Lennox, and Susanne Zantop (Ann Arbor: University of Michigan Press, 1998), 166, 171.

79. BAB R1001 /6383 Ausstellung 19/3, "Koloniale Wanderausstellung Afrikaschau—Hillerkus." *Bremer Zeitung*, November 1937, 28.

80. Hildebrand, *Vom Reich zum Weltreich*, 428.

81. BAB R1001 /6383 Ausstellung 19, no. 3, "Koloniale Wanderausstellung Afrikaschau—Hillerkus." Deutsche Afrika-Schau, Monatsbericht, 5 October 1937; R1001 /6383 Ausstellung 19/3, "Koloniale Wanderausstellung Afrikaschau—Hillerkus," Die Deutsche Arbeitsfront der Deutsche Handel to Die Afrika-Schau, 18 May 1938, 94.

82. BAB R1001 /6383 Afrikaschau von Adolf Hillerkus, Bd. 2. Stock to Auswärtiges Amt, 9 November 1937.

83. BAB R1001 /6383 Afrikaschau von Adolf Hillerkus, Bd. 2. Friedrich von Lindequist to KPA der NSDAP, 20 May 1939; Elisa Forgey, "'Die große Negertrommel der kolonialen Werbung': Die Deutsche Afrika-Schau 1935–1943," *Werkstatt Geschichte* 9, no. 3 (1994): 31; R1001 /6383 Ausstellung

19, no. 3, "Koloniale Wanderausstellung Afrikaschau—Hillerkus," Lindequist to KPA, 20 May 1939, 4.

84. Bechhaus-Gerst, *Treu bis in den Tod*, 83.

85. BAB R1001 /6382 Ausstellungen 19 no. 3, Koloniale-Wanderausstellungen Afrikaschau—Hillerkus. Alfred Schneider to Kulturreferenten der Landesstelle Berlin des Propaganda-Ministeriums, 11 December 1936.

86. BAB R1001 /6383 Ausstellung 19/3, Koloniale Wanderausstellung Afrikaschau—Hillerkus. Deutsche Gesellschaft für Eingeborenenkunde to Auswärtiges Amt (Pol. X), 16 May 1939.

87. Bechhaus-Gerst, *Treu bis in den Tod*, 89–91.

88. BAB NS 18/519, 2 Reichspropagandaleitung 1933–45. 2.9 Veranstaltungen, Ausstellungen und Tagungen. Deutsche Afrikaschau. Verbot der Veranstaltung wegen des Auftritts von Negern. 42, Stellungnahme der KdF-Dienststelle Tulln, Kreisgeschäftsführer Dubitsch to Gaustabamtsleiter der Gauleitung Niederdonau, Wien, 29 July 1940.

89. BAB R8023 /1077a, Hilfe und Unterstützung für die in Deutschland lebenden Eingeborenen der ehemaligen deutschen Schutzgebiete, 1922, 193.

90. Forgey, "'Die grosse Negertrommel der kolonialen Werbung,'" 25–26, 29.

91. Bechhaus-Gerst, *Treu bis in den Tod*, 83, 139–50; Heyden and Zeller, *Kolonialmetropole Berlin*, 181.

92. Marc Augé, *Les formes de l'oubli* (Paris: Payot, 2001), 112, 119.

93. Charles S. Maier, *The Unmasterable Past: History, Holocaust, and German National Identity* (Cambridge: Harvard University Press, 1988), 169; Cathy Caruth, *Trauma: Explorations in Memory* (Baltimore: Johns Hopkins University Press, 1995), 7.

THE ENEMY AT HOME
Defining Enemy Aliens in Ontario during the Great War

MARY G. CHAKTSIRIS

"I am surprised that I am looked down on as an Outlaw because there is War in Germany ... so if I am not worth to be a Canadian citizen I don't know how is so....[sic]" —C.J. Jacobson of Hearst, Ontario, in a letter to the Attorney General, late 1914[1]

Declarations of war in early August 1914 identified countries as enemies or allies of the British Empire, and therefore the Dominion of Canada. For immigrants and naturalized Canadians of foreign birth, an association with a newly identified enemy nation could have consequences. The presence of foreign nationals in Canada sharpened the reality that ideas of "the enemy" were not abstract; instead, Canadians believed enemies were present in their provinces and their cities, their neighbourhoods and their shops. Those identified as enemy aliens could experience surveillance, fines, and even imprisonment. However, internment remains separated from broader national narratives about Canada and the First World War despite Canada's active internment operations.

Recent interest in the Great War has taken the form of a cultural fear that the war will be, or has been, forgotten. Answers to this perceived forgetfulness reinforced narratives of the war as a source of national pride for Canada. While these narratives have become important, they over-simplify the complexities present in the war and the war effort. As James Wood reminds us, "the Canadian response to the First World War reflects all the diversity of the nation itself."[2] In his work on internment and Canada during the First World War, Bohdan Kordan writes, "There is no denying the importance of such momentous events in the life and history of a people. Victories and heroes are essential in shaping historical identity. But the magnitude of these achievements, while giving them force and effect, also tends to obscure the complex nature of the nation-building process, detracting as it does from other routine albeit no less important aspects of the larger struggle for national affirmation."[3] Although internment is not necessarily ignored in Canadian narratives of the Great War, it is often relegated to the margins.

Internment presents challenges to national histories of the First World War in Canada. The scope of national histories are necessarily broad; yet focusing more closely on internment operations within the province of Ontario allows for internment to be addressed in local contexts. As you will see in the examples below, local contexts and community relationships—in short, ideas about belonging—played vital roles in defining and persecuting enemy aliens in Ontario during the First World War. In Ontario, enemy aliens were both suspected and defended by members of their communities. The experiences of enemy aliens in Ontario, as related in materials found in RCMP files at Library and Archives Canada and in files of the Attorney General at the Archives of Ontario, illustrate how communities both came together and came apart during times of war. The complex wartime experiences that emerge from these files raise questions about the Great War as a unified moment of pride for the Canadian nation.

If the Great War was the birth of a Canadian nation, what kind of nation was it? This chapter grapples with the issue of internment, and the complications that the surveillance and incarceration of enemy aliens in Ontario raises within Canadian national narratives of the Great War. Evidence from authorities demonstrates that there was little reason to suspect those classified as alien enemies even during the war years, yet Ontarians actively watched and reported on their neighbours during the war. A single and unified narrative of Canadian history leaves little room for the experiences of those suspected as enemies during the war or the experiences of those who feared the presence of enemies at home.

IDENTIFYING ENEMY ALIENS

Enemy aliens were defined as foreign nationals from territories in the German Empire or under the rule of the Austro-Hungarian Monarchy. Those classified as enemy aliens were primarily of German origin, followed by those from the Austro-Hungarian Empire, then from the Turkish Empire, and Bulgaria.[4] According to the 1920 final report of Sir William Dillon Otter, officer commanding of internment operations for the Department of Justice, 8,579 enemy aliens were incarcerated in Canada between 1914 and 1920. Of those interned, only 3,138 were found eligible by the report to be classified as "prisoners of war," with the rest identified not as "enemy aliens" but as civilians. Another eighty thousand categorized as "enemy aliens" were issued identity papers and required to carry them at all times or risk arrest, fines, or imprisonment.[5] A proclamation issued on 14 August 1914 specified, "that all persons in Canada of German or Austro-Hungarian nationality, so long as they quietly pursue their ordinary avocations, be allowed to continue to enjoy the protection of the law and be accorded the respect and consideration due to peaceful and law-abiding citizens."[6]

Despite this protection afforded by the law, many were suspected under new wartime legislation. For example, Paul Myler of the Canadian Westinghouse Company in Hamilton, Ontario, replied to inquiries from authorities about Theodore A. Altenberg, a former employee in their drafting departments. Myler wrote that the reason for Altenberg's dismissal was anti-German attitudes in the workplace: "Altenberg was a very proficient and highly educated draftsman. The other boys in the Engineering and Drafting Departments, however, being all British, made it so uncomfortable for Altenberg that Mr. Hart found it wise to dispense with his services."[7] Hart, chief engineer, stated he later received a letter from Altenberg of his arrest upon attempting to leave Canada and his internment in Kingston.

The fear that enemy aliens posed real security threats from within Canada was widespread across the country.[8] A July 1915 investigation launched in Regina reported that, "apprehension has arisen that various attempts may be made by alien enemies to burn un-cut and stacked grain, and later on to set fire to elevators."[9] Grain elevators in the western provinces were placed under guard in order to ensure that enemy nationals in Canada would not interrupt the vital grain supply to imperial troops in Europe.[10] Military officials reported that rumours of attempted train wrecks and bridge explosions were "fabrication(s) manufactured out of whole cloth";[11] however, the movements and activities of foreign nationals and naturalized British subjects continued to raise suspicion. Crown Attorney A.J. Wilkes wrote to the Attorney General's office complaining of the "large foreign element in Branford."[12] Fears about enemies at home persisted throughout the war,[13] and these fears resulted in consequences for those in Ontario identified as enemy aliens: men were dismissed from work, reported to authorities, and sometimes separated from their families.

A primary means of justifying the war was to degrade the enemy, and propagandist constructions of the German enemy and their allies presented them as the antithesis of Canadian and imperial soldiers.[14] A dichotomy between good and evil, between civilized and uncivilized, was presented as an integral part of the war effort in Canada and in the British Empire more broadly. For example, Canadian recruitment posters directly appealed to men about their service in defence of the enemy by asking, "If you were a German aged 18–50 you would be fighting for the Kaiser—what are you doing for the King?" Another asked, "What would happen to the Empire and Canada if every man stayed at home?" Yet another appealed to the women of Canada: "You have read what the Germans have done in Belgium. Have you thought what they would do if they invaded this country?"[15] Many of these calls to action appealed to the duty of men to defend their nation, and their families, from the ever-encroaching reach of an uncivilized enemy that many believed posed a threat even at home.

Canadian experiences of internment are underrepresented in the current historiography of Canada and the Great War, an underrepresentation that may stem from its treatment by military history, which highlights the war and its place in the building of the nation. In his *Military History of Canada*, Desmond Morton barely mentions internment in the context of the First World War, and in *Marching to Armageddon: Canadians and the Great War 1914–1919*, written with J.L. Granatstein, internment is reduced to a small part of Canada's journey toward nationhood.[16] Tim Cook's extensive overview of the political and personal debates surrounding the creation of Canada's official military history also demonstrates that preserving the legacy of the Canadian Expeditionary Force and presenting the war as an outstanding event for future Canadians is also an outcome of military histories.[17]

Bohdan Kordan's *Prisoners of War: Internment in Canada during the Great War* addresses the uncomfortable placement of internment in national narratives. He argues that the threats posed by enemy aliens were real, and that "their 'threat' was to the historical enterprise of nation-building and ... to the commitment of a nation being called upon to participate in the struggle ahead." Officers of the Crown were less concerned with political rhetoric or opinionated talk of war than "those aliens designated by law as the enemy whose foreign appearance, demeanour, and sullen look were grounds alone for suspicion and arrest."[18] In her research on Stanley Barracks in Toronto, the site of an internment receiving station, Aldona Sendzikas writes, "suspicions were raised over the loyalty of German-Canadians and other immigrants from nations now at war with Britain and her colonies. Anyone receiving mail from any of these nations, or even speaking with a German accent, was likely to become the target of the wartime fears and anxieties of his or her neighbours."[19]

Though Kordan and Sendzikas acknowledge the social factors that influenced internment in Canada during the First World War, little attention is paid to the community surveillance and prejudice that initially brought many of these men to the attention of the authorities. Similarly, literature on the internment of Ukrainian-Canadian communities during the war often focuses on the movement publicly to redress World War One internment operations, which received the recognition of the federal government in 2008.[20] This focus, however, overlooks the broader systemic issues that address internment as a process of identification—identification of enemy and of ally—that targeted foreign enemy nationals as identified by civilians and authorities.

Internment, while perhaps not purposely written out of the official national histories of the war, is generally not considered part of them. Internment fits uneasily into current national narratives of Canada and the Great War, and it finds limited place in military histories, which present the war as a moment of national pride. This anthology reflects on the nature of the study and commemoration of the Great War as it moves from lived memory to historical record. This research on internment explores not only how enemy aliens were identified in Ontario during the Great War, but also how communities came together, and came apart, during a time of national crisis.

SOCIAL CONSTRUCTIONS OF ENEMY ALIENS: WATCHING THE ENEMY IN ONTARIO

Robert Rutherdale explains that, "all enemy aliens lived under shadows others cast, viewed as peoples of divided loyalties and uncertain intentions."[21] Evidence of these perceived uncertain intentions are contained within letters written to authorities that demonstrate the willingness of Ontarians to notice, and report upon, the actions of their neighbours. On 25 September 1914, an anonymous letter alerted authorities to a big tall German living at 534 Adelaide St. West. As a neighbour living only a few doors from him I have noticed him acting suspiciously he has only been here about 8 weeks and he seems more like a spy then any body I ever seen…. he is a [German] reservist he talks 6 languages French English German Italian. Latin, Russian he has all kinds of cooks. He wears a blue coat with big brass buttons on it like a uniform. I would advise you to investigate immediately —from an English citizen.[22]

Another letter on 3 April 1915 reported a customer's suspicions about a German salesman at Levy's Shoe Store on Yonge Street, indicating that he "seems to be a clever man and it seems advisable to report him to you so that you can make sure he has registered."[23] The chief constable at Toronto wrote to an interned alien enemy, Alexander Pysanuk, accusing him of "keeping a bookstore where the foreign element hold meetings … I am credibly informed that in these meetings they are … agitating the foreign element against the British and the Allies winning the war."[24]

Some enemy aliens were accused of planning attacks in Canada. Kurt Guillaune, a German, was arrested in March 1916 and identified by the Toronto police as "a most determined enemy."[25] The vice-president of the Niagara Suspension Bridge Co. urged authorities to keep Guillaune confined, as he "plans mischief to the bridges." A former employee in a drafting room in Montreal, Guillaune was arrested with plans of CPR bridges, pro-German literature, and "drawings of the chief girders showing where bombs could be planted and exploded to do the most damage."[26] When a Mrs. Fairbrother was granted a visa to visit Guillaune at Exhibition Camp despite warnings of his being "a very dangerous man," authorities instructed that their meeting be closely watched.[27] Reporting on their meeting at the camp, the officer commanding wrote, "they look to be a pretty 'smooth' pair. They both appear to be well educated and to understand one another. My experience with this class of Germans is that they are all dangerous."[28] The police magistrate in Haileybury, Ontario, expressed suspicions about the Austrian and German men employed in the town mines: "From what [we] have seen of the German method of making war," he wrote to the Attorney General in Toronto, "I would not be surprised at anything they might do … with this class of men employed in the mines they have a great chance of obtaining explosives … I do not want to appear alarmist but I do feel there are sufficient grounds to warrant these people being looked after."[29] Though no evidence came to light either during or after the war connecting foreign nationals in Canada to enemy activity, men from now-classified enemy countries remained suspected and in some cases incarcerated during the war.

Those persons attempting to leave Canada, and whose departure might assist the enemy, were to be arrested and detained, along with "all subjects of the German Empire or of the Austro-Hungarian Monarchy in Canada engaged or attempting to engage in espionage or acts of a hostile nature, or giving or attempting to give information to the enemy, or assisting or attempting to assist the enemy, or who are on reasonable ground suspected of doing or attempting to do any of the said acts."[30] Foreign nationals were required to submit to an undertaking to report to the authorities on a weekly or monthly basis, and to promise they "will carefully observe the laws of the United Kingdom of Great Britain and Ireland and of Canada ... will strictly abstain from communicating to anyone whomsoever any information respecting the existing war or the movements of troops ... [and] will do no act that might be of injury to the Dominion of Canada...."[31] Internment in Toronto lasted only until 1916, with other camps closing in 1917 due to rising wartime labour shortages.[32] Some of the released interned men found work in Toronto, where they faced discrimination from soldiers' groups, specifically the Great War Veterans' Association (GWVA), for securing employment when returned soldiers often could not.[33]

While letters reporting on suspicious neighbours were written to authorities, letters were also sent in support of those under suspicion or already jailed. The Canadian Pacific Railway Company (CPR) requested the release of George Nicoloff, their employee, who was interned in August 1916 for attempting to return to Toronto from the United States. The CPR wrote seven months after Nicoloff's arrest, promising him employment should authorities release him to return to Toronto.[34] Other letters pointed to alternative motives behind the internment of those suspected to be "enemy aliens." Writing to Col. Elliot, commanding officer of Exhibition Camp in Toronto, Mrs. J. Dooner of Toronto explained the arrest of her two boarders "was purely spiteful work." She explained, "perhaps you have been informed previous to their arrest they had a few words with their boss ... and would not go back to work under his conditions, and he, their boss, to have revenge had them arrested and made false reports of them."[35] The president of the Hamilton Auto Transport Co. wrote to authorities on behalf of Oskar Menzel, pledging himself "to become responsible for [Menzel's] good behaviour."[36] Letters encouraging the release of prisoners related also to the increasing wartime labour shortages, as the government looked to enemy aliens as available and affordable sources of labour.[37]

Though authorities feared foreign nationals in Canada would continue returning to Europe to serve with enemy armies, authorities questioned the reports they received about enemy alien threats, and often concluded that suspicions were unfounded. They spoke to former employers and neighbours in order to determine the validity of reports accusing enemy aliens of unlawful activities during wartime. In the case of Private L.H. Stayzer, authorities concluded that he had been born in Canada (although his grandfather was of German origin), had a number of friends who were Canadian-born, and was well spoken of by his former employer. The Defence Intelligence Officer (DIO) concluded, "the report about Stayzer emanated from a man called Middleton in North Toronto, who himself has an unsavoury reputation."[38] Constables in Toronto also investigated accusations that Louis Gurofsky, owner of a shipping agency, sold cross-Atlantic tickets to Austrians. Constables reported, "there is no sign in his window advertising the sale of tickets to Austrians. The letter was possibly written by one of Gurofsky's Jewish competitors in the same business for the purpose of injuring his."[39] Officially, those accused were suspected of unlawfully aiding the enemy from Canada. However, as evidenced above, men were often singled out for suspicion or excluded from employment based on factors that coupled wartime suspicion and pre-existing negative sentiments toward foreigners.

RESPONDING TO CLASSIFICATIONS: RESPONSES TO LABELS OF "ENEMY"

Many of those accused did not accept their new enemy classification, or incarceration, without comment. Russell of Burks Falls, Ontario, wrote to the Attorney General stating, "I am now branded with something akin to the historic mark of Cain, and as such driven from Winnipeg to Toronto my livelihood made unpleasant." He continued:

The people here seemed in a panic far more so than the people of England, where Zepplins [sic] fly overhead; and stamped me at once as a German spy, and tried to confirm it by the most diabolical concoctions ... That I mailed many letters on the midnight trains. That I was seen helping the local Germans to have some mysterious boxes from the Railway station etc ... After such insinuating remarks I am thankful that the platoon of Soldiers acted their part nobly, and did not attempt to wreck my shack.[40]

Officials were also unsatisfied with their duties to report upon and fine men classified as enemy aliens under the law. W.J. White, a police magistrate in Bracebridge, Ontario, wrote to the Office of the Attorney General of the arrest and charges applied to a number of Austrians for refusing to register as enemy aliens in 1918. White sought the authority to remove the fines he had imposed on two of those brought before him, Mike Gamper and Mile Penguri, of $75 or six weeks in jail. White confessed, "I now find these men have families here and have bought property which they are struggling to pay for and are unable to pay the fine and to Gaol them would entail a great hardship on their families ... I feel that I have made a mistake in these cases and would ask your permission to release these men from any further penalty except the costs." The Office of the Attorney General replied that an application must be made to the Dominion, and not the province, as the provisions of the act under which the men were convicted was under the authority of the Department of Justice in Ottawa.[41]

The suspicion of enemy aliens during the war was, even at the time, often viewed to be unfounded. In response to rumours that the German Club in Toronto was taking lists of men returning to Germany to enter into service, the chief constable replied "that certain members of this department are keeping close watch on the movements of the Germans but thus far nothing has transpired that would cause the least suspicion."[42] Authorities complained that some reports of suspicious activities did not seem very suspicious at all. R.O. Kilgour wrote to the Crown attorney in Mount Forest, Ontario, about "a family by the name of Wagner," who allegedly communicated with relatives in German and participated in pro-German talk. Kilgour asserted, "All I have got is heresay.... I consider it in the best interest of all Royal Britishers to assist in stopping such talk...." As the Wagners were clients of Kilgour, he "didn't want to be mixed up" with a possible investigation of their pro-German position. Writing to the Attorney General in Toronto, the Crown attorney at Owen Sound admitted that, though they submitted the letter to the Attorney Generals' Office, "the whole matter appears to me to be so far, very vague."[43]

The case of John Balasz, arrested by military authorities at Sault Ste. Marie for receiving a crate of pigeons mistakenly identified as homing pigeons, reached the attention of General Otter and Chief Commissioner of Police A.P. Sherwood. Sherwood wrote that Balasz's "apprehension was not justified and his detention for this period of time is absolutely inexcusable. The man had resided there for years, was a hardworking individual … the importation of pigeons under the circumstances disclosed could not, by a person of reasonable mind, be looked upon as for sinister purposes."[44] Balasz's employer, Algoma Steel Limited, wrote that they were of "the firm opinion that he is being detained under an unjust suspicion" after living in Canada for seventeen years and working at Algoma Steel for six.[45] Orders for Balasz's release and the return of his pigeons, issued on 16 August 1916, also ordered a report from the officer who arrested him and reminded military authorities that, "the parole and internment of enemy aliens are matters for the police alone."[46] Balasz's experience illustrates the central role of prejudice in the suspicion and arrest of enemy aliens in Ontario during the Great War. His status as a well-established and employed resident of Sault Ste. Marie was not enough to protect him from the blind suspicion of Ontarians under wartime conditions.

The status of enemy alien, though legally defined, was socially malleable and a defining feature of wartime experiences for many enemy aliens was how well they assimilated into Canadian society. Those singled out as foreigners by dress, accent, or occupation were more at risk in regard to the negative consequences of their new status as enemy aliens than foreign nationals. However, is there room in a unified, nation-building narrative of Canada and the Great War to accommodate the experiences of discomfort, surveillance, and incarceration of those labelled outsiders by legal declarations of war?

LITTLE ROOM FOR "ENEMIES" IN NATIONAL NARRATIVES

As surmised by Tim Cook, "the Great War has come to be considered something more than a war."[47] Canada was a relatively small nation of seven million people at the outbreak of the war, and roughly 430,000 women and men served overseas during the conflict. At war's end, 138,000 veterans returned wounded, some for life, and more than 61,000 were killed.[48] Canadians immediately began the process of coming to terms with the conflict and what it meant in regard to their present circumstances. In the process of this coming-to-terms, Canadians constructed a "preferred version of the war"[49] that rejected the cynicism and perceived doom of anti-war literature to embrace the position of the Great War as an important victory against an uncivilized, dangerous, and devious enemy. The inclusion, exclusion, or forgetfulness of narratives about the war are no "accidents" of history; they are instead deliberate choices about what to include and what to exclude in order to present the past in a certain light.

In 2008 the Canadian government responded to movements by the Ukrainian Civil Liberties Association, among others, to acknowledge the unjust conditions of internment during the Great War. A $10-million endowment was established to commemorate and educate Canadians about Canada's first national internment operations.[50] However, the view that the Great War played an important role in the creation of Canada as a nation remains firmly in place and supported by contemporary commemorations. For example, in 2010 Prime Minister Stephen Harper spoke about the death of John Babcock, Canada's proclaimed last living veteran of the First World War, paying tribute to "Canada's last living link to the Great War, which in so many ways marked our coming of age as a nation."[51] On 4 August 2014, Stephen Harper again spoke of the Great War to mark the 100th anniversary of its outbreak. Harper referenced Canada as a country united because "amid the appalling loss, by any measure, Canada as a truly independent country was forged in the fires of the First World War."[52]

The idea of the Great War as a moment of great importance to the nation is popular among politicians, educators, and the public. Part of the effectiveness of this narrative stems from its strong public support. The 2013 Speech from the Throne reminded Canadians that, "As we look confidently to the future, we draw great strength from our past. Beginning with our Aboriginal peoples, Canada's story is one of risk, sacrifice, and rugged determination. From the founding of New France, to the fight for Canada in the War of 1812; from the visionary achievement of Confederation, to our victory at Vimy Ridge, Canadians have repeatedly triumphed over long odds to forge a great country, united and free."[53] This narrative of Canadian history—one of a progression from colony to nation through key events including the First World War—is presented publicly through government commemorations, veterans' movements, and school curricula. The place of the Great War in Canada's history also holds a privileged place in media coverage and community commemorations—a tradition that Jonathan Vance argues started shortly after the conflict ended.[54]

The treatment and suspicion of foreign nationals in Ontario during the Great War complicates these ideas about the place of the Great War in Canada's national histories. What the incorporation of internment might mean for national narratives is a question that remains open for debate; this chapter illustrates reactions to perceived enemies in Ontario as a starting point for that discussion. The development of the nation is not the war's only legacy, for "we should also contemplate the thousands more who survived the battle broken in body and spirit. Consider the families who cared for them, often getting by on a meager disability pension."[55] We should also contemplate the thousands of foreign nationals, some of whom were naturalized British subjects, whose lives and livelihoods were interrupted during the course of the Great War due to wartime suspicion regarding their behaviour. While not completely ignored in the existing literature, experiences of enemy aliens have been marginalized in favour of populist national narratives of a unified country at war that relegate internment to their footnotes.

NOTES

1. Archives of Ontario (hereafter AO), Attorney General Central Registry Criminal and Civil Files, 1914–1919, Creator Code 1581, C.J. Jacobson, Heart: Query re: his right to obtain naturalization papers, 1914.
2. James Wood, *Militia Myths: Ideas of the Canadian Citizen Soldier, 1896–1921* (Vancouver: UBC Press, 2010), 210.
3. Bohdan Kordan, *Enemy Aliens, Prisoners of War* (Montreal: McGill-Queen's University Press, 2002), 4. For more on minority experiences of recruitment in Ontario during the Great War, see James Walker, "Race and Recruitment in World War 1: Enlistment of Visual Minorities in the Canadian Expeditionary Force," *Canadian Historical Review* 70, no. 1 (1989): 1–26. Avery also acknowledges that though there were few instances of sabotage or espionage, enemy aliens were subject to intense Anglo-Canadian hostility during the war. Donald Avery, "Ethnic and Class Relations in Western Canada," in *Canada and the First World War: Essays in Honour of Robert Craig Brown*, ed. David Mackenzie, 272–99 (Toronto: University of Toronto Press, 2005), 276.
4. Avery, "Ethnic and Class Relations in Western Canada," 276.
5. Lubomyr Luciuk, *In Fear of the Barbed Wire Fence: Canada's First National Internment Operations and the Ukrainian Canadians, 1914–1920* (Kingston, ON: Kashtan Press, 2001), 6.
6. LAC RG24, v. 4276, 34-1-3, vol. 1, Proclamation, Ottawa, 15 August 1914.
7. LAC RG24, v. 4250, file 34-1-3, vol. 13, Paul Myler, Canadian Westinghouse Company, Hamilton, to General W.A. Logie, 4 February 1918.
8. This fear also built on pre-existing nativism about foreigners and especially about foreign labour. For more on the climate of nativism in Canada, particularly in reference to East Asian communities, see W. Peter Ward, *White Canada Forever: Popular Attitudes and Public Policy Toward Orientals in British*

Columbia (Montreal: McGill-Queen's University Press, 2002). The internment of defined enemy aliens occurred across the British Empire. For North American and Australian contexts, see Kay Saunders and Roger Daniels, eds., *Alien Justice: Wartime Internment in Australia and North America.* On enemy aliens in Britain, see Panikos Panayi, *Prisoners of Britain: German Civilian and Combatant Internees during the First World War* (Manchester: Manchester University Press, 2012).

9. LAC, RG18 Series A, Comptroller's Office, v. 492, Investigation concerning enemy aliens entering Canada and an alleged scheme on the part of Germans to burn crops, 1915.

10. Ibid.

11. "Blowing Up of C.P.R. Bridge There Absolutely Denied by Officials," *Toronto Star*, 14 August 1914.

12. AO, Attorney General Central Registry Criminal and Civil Files 1914–1919, Creation Code: 1411, A.J. Wilkes, Crown Attorney, Brantford: Request for release of Alex Pysanuk alleged to be an Alien Enemy, 1918.

13. Adam Crerar, "Ontario and the Great War," in *Canada and the First World War: Essays in Honour of Robert Craig Brown*, ed. David MacKenzie (Toronto: University of Toronto Press, 2005), 230–71.

14. Peter Webb, "'A Righteous Cause': War Propaganda and Canadian Fiction, 1915–1921," *British Journal of Canadian Studies* 24, no. 1 (2011): 32–33. For more on the importance of the enemy in warfare, see Robert W. Rieber and Robert J. Kelly, "Substance and Shadow: Images of the Enemy," in *The Psychology of War and Peace: The Image of the Enemy*, ed. Robert W. Reiber (New York: Plenum Press, 1991), 3–40. Robert Rutherdale also discusses the demonization of alien enemies in his *Hometown Horizons: Local Responses to Canada's Great War* (Vancouver: UBC Press, 2004).

15. Canadian War Museum, "If You Were a German Aged 18–50 You Would Be Fighting for the Kaiser! What Are You Doing for the King?" Artifact Number 19820376-010; Canadian War Museum, "4 Questions to Men Who Have Not Enlisted," Artifact Number 19820376-014; Archives of Ontario War Poster Collection, "To the Women of Canada," Digital Image Number 10016138. For more on war posters, see Marc Choko, *Canadian War Posters* (Ottawa: Canada Communication Group, 1994); Jeffrey A. Keshen, *Propaganda and Censorship during Canada's Great War* (Edmonton: University of Alberta Press, 1996); James Pearl, ed., *Picture This: The First World War Posters and Visual Culture* (Lincoln: University of Nebraska Press, 2010); Jim Aulich and John Hewitt, *Sedition or Instruction? First World War Posters in Britain and Europe* (Manchester: Manchester University Press, 2007); James Aulich, *War Posters: Weapons of Mass Communication* (New York: Imperial War Museum, 2007).

16. There is only one brief reference to internment and the Great War, though there are two further references to internment during the Second World War.

Desmond Morton, *A Military History of Canada* (Toronto: Hurtig, 2007), 153, 181, 188. Morton deals with internment extensively in his work on Sir William Otter, commander of Interment Operations and Desmond Morton's own grandfather. Morton concedes, "the pro-allied majority in Canada might be exasperated that some of their neighbours were thinking and very occasionally expressing unpatriotic thoughts but it appears obvious that the Germans and Austrians in Canada posed no significant military threat." Desmond Morton, "Sir William Otter and Internment Operations in Canada during the First World War," *Canadian Historical Review* 55, no. 1 (1974): 36. Desmond Morton and J.L. Granatstein, *Marching as to Armageddon: Canadians and the Great War 1914–1919* (Toronto: Lester and Orpen Dennys, 1989).

17. Tim Cook, Clio's Warriors: Canadian Historians and the Writings of the World Wars (Vancouver: UBC Press, 2006), 19.

18. Bohdan Kordan, *Enemy Aliens, Prisoners of War: Internment in Canada during the Great War* (Montreal: McGill-Queen's University Press, 2002), 20–21.

19. Aldona Senzikas, *Stanley Barracks: Toronto's Military Legacy* (Toronto: Natural Heritage Books, 2011), 107.

20. Other selected internment literature: Bohdan S. Kordan and Craig Mahosky, *A Bare and Impolitic Right: Internment and Ukrainian-Canadian Redress* (Kingston: McGill-Queen's University Press, 2004); Lubomyr Luciuk, *A Time for Atonement: Canada's First National Internment Operations and the Ukrainian Canadians 1914–1920* (Kingston: Limestone Press, 1988); Bohdan S. Kordan and Peter Melnycky, *In the Shadow of the Rockies: Diary of the Castle 1915–1917* (Edmonton: Canadian Institute of Ukrainian Studies Press, 1991); Lubomyr Y. Luciuk, *Without Just Cause: Canada's First National Internment Operations and the Ukrainian Canadians, 1914–1920* (Kingston: Kashtan Press, 2006); Lubomyr Y. Luciuk and Borys Sydoruk, *"In My Charge": Canadian Internment Camp Photographs of Sergeant William Buck* (Kingston: Kashtan Press, 1997). For a full listing of internment literature on First World War Canada, specifically in reference to the Ukrainian experience, see the reference listing available on the website of the Canadian First World War Internment Recognition Fund. More details on the nature of redress in Canada are available in Jennifer Henderson and Pauline Wakeham, *Reconciling Canada: Critical Perspectives on the Culture of Redress* (Toronto: University of Toronto Press, 2012).

21. Rutherdale, *Hometown Horizons*, 152

22. LAC, RG24, v. 4250, file 34-1-3, vol. 14, Letter 25 September 1914, Toronto, likely sent to Military District No. 2 Headquarters, 135 College Street.

23. LAC, RG24, v. 4278, file 34-1-3, vol. 6, European War German, Austrian Prisoners of War etc., Services.

24. AO, Attorney General Central Registry Criminal and Civil Files 1914–1919, Creation Code: 1411, A.J. Wilkes, Crown Attorney, Brantford: Request for release of Alex Pysanuk alleged to be an Alien Enemy, 1918.

25. LAC RG24, v. 4250, file 34-1-3, vol. 12, Vice-President Niagara Falls Suspension Bridge Co. to Lieut. A.F. Coventry, Exhibition Camp, 17 April 1916.

26. Ibid.

27. LAC RG24, v. 4250, file 34-1-3, vol. 12, Lieut. D.I.O. to Officer i/c Prisoners of War, Stanley Barracks, Toronto, 25 April 1916.

28. LAC RG24, v. 4250, file 34-1-3, vol. 12, Vice-President Niagara Falls Suspension Bridge Co. to Lieut. A.F. Coventry, Exhibition Camp, 17 April 1916.

29. AO, Attorney General Central Registry Criminal and Civil Files 1914–1919, Creation Code: 726, S. Atkinson, Police Magistrate, Haileybury: Query re: arrest of enemy aliens in the Timmins and Cobalt areas, 1915.

30. LAC RG24, v. 4276, 34-1-3, vol. 1, Proclamation, Ottawa, 15 August 1914.

31. LAC, RG24, v. 4276, file 34-1-3 vol. 1, Undertaking of John Paul Henry Hoffmann, Toronto. For more on the process of undertakings in Toronto, see Sendzikas, *Stanley Barracks*, 107–8.

32. Sendzikas, *Stanley Barracks*, 113. For more on labour movements during the war years, see Craig Heron, *The Workers Revolt in Canada, 1917-1925* (Toronto: University of Toronto Press, 1988).

33. Tensions between the GWVA and alien communities in Toronto are discussed in Nathan Smith, "Fighting the Alien Problem in a British Country: Returned Soldiers and Anti-Alien Activism in Wartime Canada, 1915-1929," in *Other Combatants, Other Fronts: Competing Histories of the First World War*, ed. James Kitchen, Alisa Miller, and Laura Rowe, 285–310 (Newcastle: Cambridge Scholars Publishing, 2011) and briefly in Crerar, "Ontario and the Great War," 25–26.

34. LAC RG24, v. 4250, file 34-1-3, vol. 13, CPR to General W.A. Logie, Exhibition Camp, 6 April 1917.

35. LAC, RG24, v. 4277, file 34-1-3, vol. 4, European War German, Austrian Prisoners of War etc., Services.

36. LAC RG24, v. 4276, 34-1-3, vol. 1, C.F. Whitton, Prest. of Auto Transport Co Hamilton, to M. Elliot, Militia and Defence, Toronto, 4 September 1914.

37. For a detailed account of enemy alien labour and the associated ideas of "otherness," see "War, Patriotism, and Internment: The Debate over Otherness," in Bohdan Kordan, *Enemy Aliens, Prisoners of War: Internment in Canada during the Great War* (Montreal: McGill-Queen's University Press, 2002).

38. LAC RG24, v. 4250, file 34-1-3, vol. 12, DIO Military District no. 2 to Officer Commanding, 170th O-S. Battalion, 25 April 1916.

39. LAC RG24, v. 4276, 34-1-3, vol. 1, Chief Constable Toronto to Lieut. Col. Elliot, Military Headquarters, Toronto, 29 August 1914.

40. AO, Attorney General Central Registry Criminal and Civil Files 1914–1919, Creation Code: 491, Luke Russell, Burks Falls: Complaint of his being persecuted for allegedly being a German Spy, 1916.

41. AO, Attorney General Central Registry Criminal and Civil Files 1914–1919, Creation Code: 1406, W.J. White, Police Magistrate, Bracebridge: Request for

permission to remit fines imposed on certain Austrians for failing to register as enemy aliens, 1918.

42. LAC RG24, v. 4276, 34-1-3, vol. 1, Chief Constable to Col. H.M. Elliot, A.A.G., 2nd Division, Toronto, 13 August 1914.

43. AO, Attorney General Central Registry Criminal and Civil Files 19141919, Creation Code: 826, T.H. Dye, Crown Attorney, Owen Sound: Request for Investigation into alleged seditious utterances by Germans near Mount Forest, 1915.

44. LAC RG24, v. 4250, file 34-1-3, vol. 13, Memorandum for The Chief of the General Staff, Canadian Militia, Chief Commissioner of Police, Canada, 1 August 1916.

45. LAC RG24, v. 4250, file 34-1-3, vol. 13, McFadden & McMillan to A.P. Sherwood, Chief Commissioner of Police, Ottawa, 27 July 1916.

46. LAC RG24, v. 4250, file 34-1-3, vol. 13, Brig. Gen, Commanding Military District No 2 to Militia Council, Ottawa, 16 August 1916.

47. Tim Cook, *At the Sharp End: Canadians Fighting the Great War 1914–1916,* vol. 1 (Toronto: Viking Canada, 2007), 3.

48. Ibid., 2–3.

49. Jonathan Vance, *Death So Noble: Memory, Meaning, and the First World War* (Vancouver: UBC Press, 1997), 179.

50. The Canadian First World War Internment Recognition Fund, with funds endowed by the federal government, works to "support projects that commemorate and recognize the experiences of all of the ethno-cultural communities affected by Canada's first national internment operations of 1914–1920." This fund seeks to combat the marginalization of internment in the overarching "preferred" narrative of the Great War, and is itself part of a larger movement to redress internment and its place in history. See internmentcanada.ca.

51. Nicolas van Rijn, "Canada's Last First World War Vet, John Babcock, Dies," *Toronto Star,* 19 February 2010.

52. Lee-Anne Goodman, "'Canada Forged in the Fires of First World War': Stephen Harper Marks Anniversary of Historic Conflict," *National Post,* 4 August 2014.

53. Government of Canada, Full Speech from the Throne, 16 October 2013, http://www.speech.gc.ca/eng/full-speech (accessed 24 June 2015).

54. As Vance illustrates, the myth of the Great War as a valiant sacrifice constructed in the 1920s grew out of movements by "'average Canadians' to come to terms with the loss of life and, for some, a fundamentally altered sense of self." Vance, *Death So Noble,* 7.

55. Geoffrey Hayes, Andrew Iarocci, and Mike Bechthold, "Afterthoughts," in *Vimy Ridge: A Canadian Reassessment,* ed. Geoffrey Hayes, Andrew Iarocci, and Mike Bechthold (Waterloo: Wilfrid Laurier University Press, 2007), 316.

SECTION THREE

SEEING AND
FEELING MEMORY

THE BATTLES OF CORONEL AND FALKLAND ISLANDS (1927) AND THE STRUGGLE FOR THE CINEMATIC IMAGE OF THE GREAT WAR

MARK CONNELLY

From its humble beginnings as a circus attraction, cinema rapidly grew in influence and status and made a massive breakthrough into mainstream culture during the Great War, when all the combatant states deployed it as a motivational tool on the home front and as a medium for influencing neutrals. By the 1920s cinema was regarded as a potent mass communicator capable of shaping the opinions of vast numbers of people. At the same time, many states came to fear the power of American cinema, believing it was undermining national cultures. These fears intensified when Hollywood embarked upon a series of lavish productions set during the Great War. According to many in Britain and France, as well as in their empires, this appeared to be an attempt to rewrite the history of the conflict in favour of the US by portraying it as the decisive player.

Unsurprisingly, this created controversy in Britain and France and served to politicize the role of cinema in society further, and in particular public discourse placed a huge onus on war films to carry and reflect certain national values. With the war having placed such a strain on the British people and the bonds of empire, the British government was anxious to use film as an imperial solvent deployed to reinforce a common culture and identity. It was in this atmosphere that British Instructional Films produced a series of battle reconstructions, culminating in 1927 with *The Battles of Coronel and Falkland Islands*. The film constitutes a multi-faceted text, for it not only reflects the cultural currents mentioned above, but also realignments in British international and economic relations in the 1920s, domestic and foreign debate about the nature of the war and how it should be remembered, the public image of the Royal Navy, as well as the Senior Service's views on publicity, and, finally, the public's perception of a tiny outpost of the British Empire.

Before embarking on an analysis of *The Battles of Coronel and Falkland Islands* as a text, it is first necessary to establish the nature of the British film industry in the 1920s, its relationship with the state and its perceived role in the empire. The first point to note is the atrophy, by the early 1920s, of the British film industry. Although highly active in advancing the film business in the years before the war, the British had lost their way by the 1920s. With the end of the war it was soon realized that Britain had been overtaken decisively by other filmmaking nations, the US being the obvious production giant. British silent cinema rapidly came to be seen as uncompetitive in the world market due to its inability to appeal to mass audiences and lack of imagination when it came to finding a national expression. By the mid-twenties a revival was under way driven by a number of factors: first, the emergence of a new generation of filmmakers, including Alfred Hitchcock, Herbert Wilcox, Adrian Brunel, and Michael Balcon, all of whom were open admirers of foreign cinema and consciously sought to incorporate the best overseas elements. Film was gaining respectability as an art form, a development epitomized by the establishment, in 1925, of the London Film Society, with its determination to intellectualize cinematic art. At the same time, British filmmakers were moving toward a national cinematic voice by revealing a marked talent for innovative and artistic documentary films. Finally, the Cinematograph Act of 1927 brought a measure of protection, which allowed the whole to coalesce.[1]

The Cinematograph Act of 1927 was a remarkable piece of legislation given Britain's long-standing commitment to free trade, for it introduced protection into the British film industry by stipulating that a set number of films exhibited in British cinemas each year had to be domestic products. The fact that the Cinematograph Act, or "Quota Act" as it was often called, came before protective measures for other aspects of the British economy perhaps reveals the intensity of the cultural fears regarding cinema's influence. It was a measure many were prepared to support; an editorial in *The Times* stated, "Only by creating a centre, a home for the industrial art of the cinema, will it be possible by study and experiment to try out the economic, aesthetic and technical issues and the social, political and moral values implicit in them.... To place the industry on a footing of equality with its foreign competitors we must contribute something of our own.... There can be no national tradition of the film until there is an ideological nucleus."[2] The undoubted target of the Act was Hollywood and the desire to fight off encroaching American cultural imperialism. The sensitivity over Americanization was one largely driven by the middle class intelligentsia— but it was also rather vague as to what constituted Americanization and how it manifested itself.[3] The popularity of American cinema in Britain certainly provoked a good deal of class snobbery, for it was believed that the working classes were particularly susceptible to a mass-produced culture of little depth or value. Economic and moral arguments were also intermixed, with American dominance being attributed to the enormous reserves of capital its industries could draw upon due to wartime profiteering, while Europeans were fighting and dying.[4] But in trying to curb American influence, the Act threw up a significant issue regarding Britishness and its precise definition. In the end, this definition was left deliberately vague, partly in response to the dominions, the leaders of which argued that British should be a synonym for imperial production.[5] Despite these grey areas, the Act certainly stimulated expansion and production in Britain, but not necessarily, as many feared, at the expense of quality.[6]

Given the haziness over what actually constituted British production, the Act put the onus on the British industry to produce films likely to find favour across the empire. One company determined to live up to this expectation was British Instructional Films (BIF). Founded in 1919 by H.B. Woolfe, the company quickly gained a reputation as a maker of high-quality scientific, educational and industrial documentary films. Realizing that there was a public appetite for information about the war, Woolfe commenced on a series of documentaries about the conflict. The first, *The Battle of Jutland*, appeared in 1921 and was a great critical success. Devised in collaboration with the eminent military historian Sir George Aston, the film utilized wartime footage alongside maps and models to follow each twist and turn of the action. Painstaking freeze-frame animation was used, requiring three million tiny movements of the models to create the overall effect.[7] Significantly, the film was exhibited in the United States, where it was very definitely perceived to be a piece of British propaganda aimed at winning the struggle for the meaning of the battle.[8]

Emboldened by the success of *The Battle of Jutland*, BIF replicated the format two years later with *Armageddon*, a documentary outlining the success of the Egyptian Expeditionary Force and lionizing Allenby's role in the defeat of the Ottoman Empire. Showing a good eye for publicity, BIF's distributor and exhibitor secured the attendance of Victoria Cross holders from the campaign at the premiere, along with the presence of Princess Mary.[9] As might be expected, the film aroused great interest in Australia due to the role of ANZAC forces in the campaign. The Adelaide *Register* referred to it as "a magnificent war film" and noted "the pictures of the light horse men on the march are themselves well worth seeing, fine men on fine horses, a credit to their country."[10] Similar sentiments were expressed by the Adelaide *Advertiser*, which judged it "a picture every Australian should see … it [is] a lasting record of the valor of the Australian soldiers."[11] The success of *Armageddon* encouraged Woolfe to be much more ambitious in his next project. He opted to produce a re-enactment of the famous 1918 raid on Zeebrugge, but added specially reenacted reconstructions to the list of effects. *Zeebrugge* (1924) therefore featured a mix of archival footage, model work, and a dramatic reenactment of the storming of the Mole involving hundreds of extras. Anxious to ensure authenticity, Woolfe was successful in seconding a representative from the Admiralty for advice and assistance on points of detail.[12]

Prior to its release, the film was boosted by the dramatic interpretation of the raid in the Admiralty Theatre of the Wembley Empire Exhibition, which proved extremely successful.[13] This whetted the public's appetite before it was formally premiered in London's West End. Woolfe achieved the greatest coup of his career to this point by persuading the king and queen to attend the gala premiere, the first time a British monarch had ever attended a public screening, thus revealing the importance of the production to the image of British cinema and the determination to maintain control over the (celluloid) history of the war. The *Film Renter*, an influential British trade paper, was deeply impressed by both the product and the royal presence at the premiere: "one felt proud of the fact that a British company had re-created this wonderful adventure so that millions could see it again on screen."[14] Once again, a success was achieved across the empire. The *Toronto Daily Star* called it "the marvellous reproduction of one of the greatest exploits in world history," while the Hobart *Mercury* believed it was the duty of "every British citizen" to see it, and in the process illustrated the ambiguity over the boundaries of Britishness. The New Zealand *Evening Post* averred that, "there is no other picture with which it can be compared or likened to."[15]

Riding high on the prestige of *Zeebrugge*, BIF's next project was an even more ambitious reconstruction. *Ypres* (1925) was directed by Walter Summers, himself a former officer who had served on the Western Front, and told the story of the salient by reconstructing a series of famous incidents. A huge success across the empire, the film's impact was reinforced by an ironic tribute from the Irish Republican Army in the Irish Free State. Deeply fearful of the film's power, the IRA launched a campaign against it, causing disruption at cinemas attempting to show the film as well as confiscating and burning copies.[16] Serving as an icon of the Great War for virtually every part of the empire, in many ways it was unsurprising that a film about Ypres should have aroused such interest. However, *Ypres* succeeded on its own merits. Cinemagoers were stunned by its sense of realism and atmosphere, and the way it balanced drama, pathos, and humour. As with *Zeebrugge*, part of the film's appeal lay in its claim to authenticity, having been made with the assistance, and blessing, of the War Office. The film broke all box-office records in Britain and evoked a remarkable degree of engagement in the dominions.[17] An equally emotive subject was chosen for the next project, the Retreat from Mons. Such was BIF's standing by this point that Woolfe even managed to persuade Lieutenant-General Sir Horace Smith-Dorrien to appear in the film, alongside a host of fellow veterans, recreating his part as II Corps commander.[18] Released in 1926, *Mons* proved yet another success, and once again raised the ire of the IRA as copies of it were destroyed across the Free State.[19]

Having established a profile with a clutch of well-received, well-made reconstructions of Great War battles, a number of threads now started to come together for BIF. Its relationship with the government, and in particular the Admiralty and War Office, was firmly founded; it had a team of innovative and imaginative filmmakers; and it was keen to remain in the export market and ensure distribution of its films across the world. This combination situated it perfectly to exploit the Quota Act in letter and spirit by making films celebrating British and imperial sentiments. Confident, at the very least, of a good domestic market for its products, BIF unveiled its most ambitious project to date in the autumn of 1926. A gala dinner was held to announce that *The Battles of Coronel and Falkland Islands* was entering production, and was very clearly to be used as a platform to deliver a number of messages. First, the ambition and scale of the film was stressed, thus revealing the ability of the British film industry to deliver quality and quantity. Charles Tennyson, deputy director of the Federation of British Industry, was present, and underlined this message, stating that his organization gave full backing to the project. Tennyson's presence serves to reinforce the extraordinary significance attached to cinema, and the belief in its potential to become a staple of the British economy alongside its traditional sectors such as mineral extraction and textiles. This message was aimed not just at a British and imperial audience, but very firmly at the Americans, too. It deeply impressed the many journalists present, and they reported it to their readers.[20] George Atkinson, the influential film critic of the *Daily Express* and champion of British cinema, was especially pleased by this emphasis and believed it would counterbalance the pernicious influence of American blockbuster war movies.[21] The desire was picked up in the US and reported in the *New York Times* under the headline, "John Bull has high hopes for his new pictures."[22] The desire to make a double-statement to the Americans— that Britain could not only make good films, but good *war* films, too—was even more intense by this point due to widespread debate about the message of *The Big Parade*. Although a box-office success across the world, many read it as a glorification of America's role in the war, and, conversely, a belittling of the other combatants.[23] *The Battles of Coronel and Falkland Islands* was therefore conceived as a project that would put the record straight.

The second main message of the launch was the collaboration of the Admiralty and Navy League. This was an important part of BIF's appeal to the public, for it emphasized the quasi-official nature of the film and allowed the BIF to claim it was producing an authentic account of events rather than a sentimentalized Hollywood version. Rear-Admiral Luce, a veteran of the battle, spoke in support of the project, and was followed by H.M. Denny, president of the Navy League, who gave his organization's blessing. Perhaps most significant was the announcement that two men with direct experience of the Navy had been appointed to write the scenario in Captain F.C. Bowen and F.W. Engholm.[24] Finally, the desire to ensure authenticity meant active collaboration with the Germans, which in turn meant an alleged insistence on impartiality. BIF's press release referred to its desire to ensure input from German veterans and to portray the brilliance of the German admiral, Graf von Spee, who was finally defeated off the Falkland Islands in December 1914. Further, German actors would be cast in the leading German parts.[25] Such a decision reflected a number of interlocking themes. The need to establish a separate British cinema culture, and one that took ownership of the war-film genre in particular, made the emphasis on documentary reality and impartiality a deliberate alternative to the supposedly self-serving, melodramatic Hollywood efforts. At the same time, the need to counter Hollywood led many European filmmakers to the conclusion that collaboration was the only way to equalize American economies of scale and technical excellence. This strand of thought was particularly strong in Britain and Germany, and led to exchanges of personnel and joint projects by the mid-twenties.[26] On a higher level, this was also a period in which Western European relations were thawing, and Britain and France were enjoying a much better relationship with Germany in which all three nations sought to put the war behind them and guarantee the stability of Europe. With its premiere in 1927, *The Battles of Coronel and Falkland Islands* can be viewed as a cinematic adjunct to the Locarno Treaty, signed between the Western European former belligerents, and the subsequent "Locarno honeymoon" period.[27]

BIF certainly achieved its aim through the gala launch, as journals across the empire and the US noted the instigation of the project. Public interest in the unfolding production was kept high through regular press bulletins. The dual commitment to quality and authenticity was enhanced when it was announced that Walter Summers, the director, was off to Malta to shoot sequences with the Mediterranean Fleet, and that he had been granted access to naval facilities at Portsmouth, Devonport, and Weymouth. Back in the studio, huge tanks were built to hold equally vast models of the ships, and a special license was granted to buy eight tons of explosives for the special effects. By the completion of the production, over forty thousand naval personnel had been involved and four thousand others directly employed.[28] This cleverly managed campaign culminated in a well-staged national premiere at the prestigious New Gallery Cinema, Regent Street, in London's West End, and was preceded by a private showing for the king and queen at Balmoral. BIF ensured that the press was kept well informed of the royal showing and must have been immensely gratified by the royal response, especially the King's admission that he could not tell the difference between footage shot with the fleet from that reconstructed in the studio. The king's knowledge of naval affairs being well known, such an accolade added greatly to BIF's claims of realism and authenticity.[29] The official premiere on 16 September was equally effective. A special score had been composed based on traditional sea shanties, a bugler was employed, and the Cinema's full special-effects team deployed to replicate bells and buzzers, the crash of the sea, the crunch of shovelling coal, the noise of the engine rooms, and, of course, the gunfire.[30] Crowds gathered to see the specially invited guests enter the Cinema, which included a broad selection of British and German naval officers, as well as Admiral Phillimore, who commanded HMS *Inflexible* in the battle. Phillimore addressed the audience before the film commenced and continued the theme of Anglo-German harmony by stating that both navies retained the utmost respect for each other, and that mutual gallantry was shown throughout the battle.[31] In making his speech, Phillimore provided the audience with a final signal as to how the film was to be viewed and interpreted, which was entirely in keeping with BIF's overall aim.

The film lived up to expectations and provided BIF with its last great success of the silent era. Before exploring the responses of audiences and critics, it is worth sketching out the structure and form of *The Battles of Coronel and Falkland Islands*. The film opens with the British Admiral Cradock searching for Admiral von Spee's squadron, which has been wreaking havoc on British trade in the Pacific. When von Spee is sighted at the Coronel bank off Chile, Cradock valiantly offers battle even though he knows his ships are no match for the enemy, and gallantly goes down with his men. News of the defeat reaches Admiral "Jackie" Fisher at the Admiralty, and he decides on an immediate repost in the form of a force led by two new battlecruisers, HMS *Inflexible* and HMS *Invincible* under Admiral Sir Doveton Sturdee. Back in the Pacific, von Spee puts into the port of Valparaiso and is entertained to lunch by the German community. A boorish and drunken German toasts "Damnation to the Royal Navy," but von Spee refuses it and instead raises his glass "in honour of a very gallant enemy." In Britain, frantic preparations are made for the dispatch of the two battlecruisers, and thanks to the dedication of the dockyard workers the ships depart on schedule. Having considered his options, von Spee decides to assault the Falkland Islands, anxious to acquire its coal stocks and destroy its wireless equipment. Aware of the danger, the Falkland Islands Defence Force prepares itself, and the islanders keep watch for any signs of the German fleet. Thanks to the speed of the British response, Sturdee has reached the islands, but when the German ships are spotted, they are still coaling in Stanley harbour. The alarm is sounded and the British ships rapidly put out to sea. At this point von Spee imitates the actions of Cradock by gallantly and fatalistically accepting battle, knowing that this time he is hopelessly outclassed. Nonetheless, the German ships fight heroically and when the final ship is sinking its few remaining survivors defiantly keep the Imperial German Navy ensign aloft. The Royal Navy crews are deeply impressed by the behaviour of their enemies and view them with respect. Back in London, Fisher is informed of the victory and is quietly satisfied that a task has been well done, and the film ends. The narrative therefore falls into three sections: a long prologue telling the story of a British defeat, a shorter middle section in which the Germans and British plan their next moves, and the final chapter ending in an honourable British victory.

The impact of the film was remarkable and created intense excitement. The moment the premiere ended, the clamour to book the film erupted. The *Daily Film Renter's* correspondent was amazed by the scenes at BIF's distributors, as exhibitors appeared in person to make arrangements for the delivery of the film. In a shrewd comment on the film's power, he noted that what found favour with film critics was often very different from the tastes of the wider public, but this was an instance where the two coincided fully.[32] The enthusiasm for the film from hard-nosed businessmen driven by box-office potential reveals powerfully that British people were intensely interested in celluloid interpretations of the war and would patronize them. In producing its series of documentaries, BIF had also played a role in broadening the demographic of cinema attendance in Britain. By concentrating on respectful reconstructions of wartime events, BIF was part of a wider mid-twenties shift in which cinema wooed a middle-class audience to a form of entertainment once felt to be the preserve of the working class.[33] Given the dominance of the middle class as a proportion of the British wartime armed forces, the war film was the ideal medium for assisting in this transformation.

Of great importance to the professional film critics were the technical and aesthetic qualities of the production. C.A. Lejeune, on her way to becoming one of Britain's most influential film commentators, lavished praise stating, "in theme, acting, technical efficiency and high spirit, 'The Battles of the Coronel and Falkland Islands' is without question the best motion picture that a British director has ever made."[34] It was a judgment echoed in the *Westminster Gazette*, which declared it "excellent from the technical point of view."[35] German newspapers were equally enthusiastic about its quality. Leo Hirsch, writing in the *Berliner Tagesblatt*, called it "a fine film, with images that are fantastically effective," while the *Deutsche Allgemeine Zeitung* commented on its "powerful delivery."[36] Even Hans Rompel, an Afrikaans nationalist, filmmaker, and critic for *Die Burger*, the Cape Province's leading Afrikaans newspaper, agreed, judging "the filming outstanding."[37] Many critics stated that the technical and aesthetic highlight of the film was the dockyard scene in which the *Inflexible* and *Invincible* were made ready for war. Summers's direction of the sequence remains impressive to this day, for, like Eisenstein, he used rapid editing and montage to create a sensation of dynamism and industry in which red-hot rivets are driven, welders' torches spark, and hammers beat rhythmically. Some critics were clearly aware of the similarity with Eisenstein. Mordaunt Hall, reviewer for the *New York Times*, stated: "These episodes are among the best that have ever been filmed, equal to the trenchant glimpses in the Soviet picture 'Potemkin.'"[38] (However, to state that Summers had learnt the technique from Eisenstein would be wrong, for there is no evidence that he had seen the film, which had yet to be screened in the UK.)

Perhaps of more direct appeal to wider audiences were the film's other obvious qualities. Although the film is by no means a totally detached and unbiased interpretation, as will be discussed below, looking across the range of newspaper and journal reactions, it is clear that BIF's claim to impartiality was taken seriously. The fan magazine *Cinema World Illustrated* told its readers that, "full justice is done to the gallantry of our foes"; the *Daily Chronicle* believed the film showed "that the men of the German and British fleets were brothers in that both respected a fine fight," and a similar sentiment was expressed by the Adelaide *Register*, which admired the depiction of the "splendid qualities of both British and German men."[39] German commentators were equally impressed by this element. The *Deutsche Allgemeine Zeitung* noted, "The film is unbiased. This is perhaps the highest praise," while the *Berliner Illustrirte Zeitung* judged it "a scientific study.... Both [sides] are shown with strict impartial symmetry."[40] Indeed, so strong was this emphasis that both the *Daily Mirror* and the *Evening News* worried that the film might be "too modest in depicting the triumph of our naval victory."[41] The perception of impartiality was often linked to the concept of chivalry. According to the writer and critic T.P. O'Connor, the film was a "picture of war showing chivalry on both sides."[42] The *Deutsche Allgemeine Zeitung* came to the same conclusion, lauding the "chivalrous fighting from both sides, with duty carried out to the death for the victors and for the Fatherland."[43] Chivalry is, of course, widely regarded as an immensely positive attribute in those who show it. *The Battles of Coronel and Falkland Islands* shows both sides as chivalrous, but it is the British who tip the balance both in terms of the film's narrative, by being the ultimate victors, and subsequently by making the film. It can be argued that on both levels chivalry could be exercised only by having been victorious, and its cinematic expression was in itself a reminder of Britain's victory.

The most complicated references to the depictions of chivalry and nobility came from the populist film magazine *Picturegoer*, which referred to the production as a record of a 1914 battle "before the dark days of black manufactured 'hate.'"[44] Such a comment provides a fascinating insight into multiple, and occasionally contradictory, states of consciousness. At one and the same time, it tells its readers that the film is about a noble incident, but noble in more ways than one—first, due to the genuine and verifiable actions of those who were present, and second, because the people who were informed of it on the home front were purer, having not yet been corrupted by propaganda machines working at full power. The film therefore depicted an all-around "better" moment in the war. But did such an admission then imply that war under such conditions was acceptable? Those watching the on-screen reconstruction of the battle and old enough to remember the war were empowered by experience, and could judge just how far they had, subsequently, been polluted by the darker side of the war in the form of material disseminated by the mass media. This entailed a further irony, for it was a piece of cinematic artifice specifically produced by and for a mass communication medium that was thought to be the restorer of lost truth. The acceptance of *The Battles of Coronel and Falkland Islands* as a corrective to hateful and hate-filled propaganda was due to its "purity" of cinematic form and the acceptance of the claims made about it by its producers. By continuing to apply only partially the key techniques of mainstream cinema—melodrama, actor-led plot, and narrative devices—in favour of "documentary realism" in the form of maps, independently verifiable data in the intertitles and scenes, and deliberate eschewal of the attributes usually associated with high-profile actors, the shaping of audience preconceptions began even before the film started to roll. This fetishizing of the historical incident imposed a double-consciousness over the production process: the film was lionized for being painstaking in its reconstruction, but it was so good that it was not consciously considered as an act of artifice in its own right, with possible concomitant implications for its alleged aloofness and impartiality. BIF's commitment to the creation of a history-book page in cinematic form can be seen in its deliberate decision to issue no cast list to journalists nor as part of the film's titles. Aside from the production crew, the only other items listed in the credits are the ships themselves: real Royal Navy ships comprise the cast and heroes (or, probably more correctly, heroines); they are real, the actors are shadows—ghosts in the naval machines. The insistence on this degree of detachment had important implications for how the film was viewed against Hollywood products, as will be discussed below.

Detachment, impartiality, and the even-handed depiction of gallantry on both sides were therefore taken as guarantees of realism and authenticity. "The merit of this remarkable film consists in the producer having spent his energy on the essential and realistic points of the battles themselves," stated the New Zealand *Evening Post*.[45] According to the *Glasgow Herald*, it was "a film of grim realism," and the *Westminster Gazette* judged it a "marvellous piece of kinema realism."[46] Much of the explanation for the realism and authenticity was thought to lie in the collaboration extended by the Admiralty. The insistence that Admiralty assistance was a crucial component of the film's quality reveals the degree of trust invested in British state institutions and the belief that their involvement raised the production about cheap partisan sentiment. However, not all were prepared to subscribe to this view. Unsurprisingly, *Die Burger* felt that despite the tribute to the Germans the film contained a "glorification of British militarism."[47] Mordaunt Hall, writing in the *New York Times*, was also less than impressed by what he called "a tendency toward patting the British a little too much on the back."[48] But few others within the Anglophone world felt such qualms, and certainly saw nothing to shake their faith in its overall authenticity. But this realism did not deny the thrilling spectacle of warfare, and naval warfare in particular. The *Liverpool Echo* called it an "exciting and exhilarating" film, and an "epic episode," and Caroline Lejeune pronounced it "an epic of the sea."[49] For the London *Evening News*, it represented "a glorious hour and a half of thrills and enthusiasm," which was a sentiment echoed in the *Portsmouth Evening News*'s belief that it was "one of the most thrilling spectacles that anyone could wish to see."[50]

It was the element of excitement that provoked the ire of the film's few ardent negative critics. Leading the onslaught was Bryher, pseudonym of Winifred Ellerman, who had immigrated to Switzerland soon after the end of the war in disgust at the atmosphere of revenge and retribution. A regular contributor to the left-leaning and self-consciously intellectual-aesthetic film magazine *Close Up*, she took the film to task for celebrating a redundant and pernicious vision:

> war is presented *entirely* from a romantic boy-adventure book angle, divorced from everyday emotions and that thereby the thousands who desire unreality are forced further and further away from the actual meaning of battle.... We want a race that understands what acceptance of warfare means. By all means let us have war films. Only let us have war straight and as it is; mainly disease and discomfort, almost always destructive (even in after [sic] civil life) in its effects. Let us get away from this nursery formula that to be in uniform is to be a hero; that brutality and waste are not to be condemned provided they are disguised in flags, medals and cheering.[51]

The Battles of Coronel and Falkland Islands can be said to fall short of Bryher's definition of realism, for although it shows death, and on a large scale, and destruction it certainly does not show scenes of mutilation, dismemberment, or drowning, and death is invested with nobility even though the moment of passing may not be particularly dignified.

The *Daily Herald*, the mouthpiece of British organized labour and the Labour Party, took a similar line. After initial praise of the film, it concluded on a questioning note:

> Yet when all has been said there is yet something more serious to consider. Those who launch such a film as this have a responsibility to those who see it. Passions are so easily inflamed, and this persistent war romanticism is the most subtle form of propaganda. Here is everything calculated to create an atmosphere of mild hysteria. You can feel it in the house. The music; the guns; the pulsing rhythm of men working in frantic co-operation; the gallantry of all concerned; the beauty of the scene's setting; all invest the struggle with poetry and beauty. But romanticism can be bought too dear.[52]

Critics of the BIF approach, especially Bryher, therefore implied that realism about war could mean one thing only—its horrors and miseries. This ideological position then categorically denied that chivalry, honour, or bravery were part of the reality of war. Alternatively, if they were accepted, they were either wasted in such an ignoble pursuit and/or such a tiny component of war as to be irrelevant. In turn, this meant that any depiction that foregrounded these qualities was inherently flawed, and, worse still, fundamentally immoral.

Others took a diametrically opposite point of view. The Adelaide *Advertiser* believed the film was, in fact, effective peace propaganda: "a war picture that should help end war."[53] For the *Berliner Tagesblatt*, the film made it clear "how foolish the war was," and even *Die Burger* admitted that in its realistic depiction of naval battles it revealed "the dreadful conditions of war."[54] However, such interpretations can be read as attempts to launder sensations some were uncomfortable admitting openly. While "realistically" visualizing combat, *The Battles of Coronel and Falkland Islands* woos the audience into experiencing certain aspects of naval warfare vicariously, which is precisely what the audience expected and wanted. The *Observer*, a highbrow British Sunday paper, which in the mid-twenties began to take film seriously, produced a subtle and highly insightful review that included an analysis of audience motivations: "For the love of truth, do not close your ears to the plain fact that spectators at the New Gallery are exhilarated. Perhaps you yourself can look at no picture of war without a shudder. If so, you are in a very small minority. For hearts to glow at the spectacle of naval or military adventure is natural. To pretend that this glow arises from righteous horror is a falsehood more dangerous than disagreements at disarmament conferences."[55] Few, however, seem to have taken this call for close self-analysis to heart.

What, perhaps, audiences were also reacting to was another irony in the film, for although it self-consciously foregrounds the ships through the device of listing them as the cast, it is also an attempt to reinforce human agency in the outcome of modern battles. The mechanized slaughter of the Great War challenged pre-existing ideas about combat as the ultimate expression of human wit, bravery, skill, and dexterity. During the war, propagandists countered this by either "organicizing" the machines—for example, visualizing tanks as dragons, dinosaurs, or other great beasts, or turning the new weapon into a platform for long-lauded martial skills, as in the case of fighter pilots.[56] In *The Battles of Coronel and Falkland Islands*, the key narrative moments of explanation and decision occur as a direct result of human action and resolution: the determination of Cradock and von Spee to fight to the end regardless of the logic of technological advantage; the insight and drive of Fisher and Churchill in London; the dedication to duty and sharp wits of the lookouts in the ships and on the Falkland Islands; the humanity of Sturdee, as he most reluctantly closes in for the final kill; the skill with which all the crews perform their tasks; and, importantly, the flashes of humour that consciously stop it being an experiment in scientific detachment, regardless of the comments by critics. Not all read the film in these terms, however. Leo Hirsh, a German journalist reviewing the film for the defeated people, questioned the essential moral: "Is it a heroic tale? At Coronel Spee had more guns, more ship-power; he won. In the Falklands Sturdee was the stronger and he won. A heroic tale? ... we know ... that the outcome of the battles was decided in advance by each side's relative strength in terms of machinery, tonnage and firing power."[57]

The film therefore fulfilled different functions and had different meanings for different audiences. At the level of the British state, *The Battles of Coronel and Falkland Islands* proved the viability of British cinema as a competitor on the international stage, vindicated the Cinematograph Act, and protected the role of Britain in the Great War and the moral status of the nation in the conflict—it fought a just war honourably. Much the same can be applied to the bulk of British film critics and their employers in the popular publishing industry. For those who regarded themselves as of the avant-garde or higher-brow end of film criticism, the film's technical excellence, adherence to a documentary structure, and promise of an emerging, distinctively British cinematic form of expression, allowed it to overcome any taint of cheap jingoism. Only very few, left-of-centre critics failed to find it entirely laudable.

For the general public across the British Empire, particularly the Anglophone world of the dominions (including the Irish Free State), the film's popularity reveals a number of trends. Veterans of the battles, and of the war in general, were given the opportunity to relive, and contextualize, their part in the conflict.[58] History with a capital "H" met personal memory and provided an over-arching, explicable story. Veterans were also given the chance to share aspects of their experience with family and friends without having to talk about it directly. With many veterans unable to express themselves about their war experiences, society required an alternative mode of bridging the gap between those who had fought and those left behind. Historians of literature and high culture have identified the dual bind in terms of communications that the war appeared to create for many: the experience was so emotionally and intellectually overwhelming that it sparked a crisis of communication in that the English language did not contain enough words adequately to describe it—and even if there had been enough words and existing literary devices, would they ever be able to shape them into a response even remotely proximal to the experience?[59] According to Paul Fussell and Samuel Hynes, the path lay in new forms of literary expression and the intentional inversion of older ones. Although this may explain the nature and form of high-cultural interpretations of the war, it does not provide an overview of British and dominion society. The seeming lack of high-profile testimony from the "ordinary" masses of the British and imperial armies has led some to the conclusion that most veterans simply retreated into silence. Such a judgment appears solid when backed up by the ample testimony from the families of veterans stating the much-repeated mantra, "Dad never spoke much about the war." But concluding that veterans never spoke about the war from this evidence base is problematic. Rather, as anyone who has ever studied regimental associations, or other ex-service organizations, the literature can testify that veterans never stopped talking (and very often singing) about the war. There was a communication problem, but it did not mean total silence. When among their own, veterans found that blanks in communication were automatically compensated for by dint of shared experience. For veterans, the genius of BIF lay in its ability to externalize aspects of their war experiences for both themselves and their families. The films became a proxy for personal interaction with their families. Walter Summers's own wartime experiences doubtless helped him achieve this substitute language. His genius, and that of his production crew, was about creating enough of an insight to impress veterans with BIF's output. The new language of cinema found a way of expressing and interpreting the war acceptable to the veteran. Veterans spoke about the war through the act of going to the cinema with their families.

Thus, for women and children, and especially for war widows, a cinema visit to see a BIF film was to understand what daddy had done in the war. Witnessing a film like *The Battles of Coronel and Falkland Islands* paid homage to him in much the same way as contributing to a local war memorial scheme or attendance at an Armistice Day ceremony. This transformed a trip to the cinema into something beyond entertainment and into an act of remembrance—just as a visitor to the battlefields was not a tourist, but a "pilgrim." The films also gave women an insight into the most enclosed and exclusive of male realms—serving in the very front line of war and the act of fighting and killing in battle. Children were certainly identified as a discrete audience for the film. Special showings for children were organized in cities across the empire, including Canberra, Liverpool, and Toronto, as well as Stanley, capital of the Falkland Islands (where it was a special Empire Day treat). In Canberra and Stanley, the importance of the film to children was reinforced by essay-writing competitions.[60] The didactic value of the film was fully appreciated by the *Tamworth Herald*, which told its readers that, "it is a picture that will teach boys and girls something of the might of Britain, something of the spirit that has gone into the making of the great Empire."[61]

For the former enemy, interpretations of the film depended on precise political standpoint. For the conservative *Deutsche Allgemeine Zeitung*, it provided solace by stressing the loyalty, bravery, dedication, and honour of the Imperial German armed forces. In fact, the review became a platform for a wider onslaught on those Germans who sought to denigrate the reputation of the services:

> One ought to watch this film. It will shock many. It will give new courage to some already aware of this heroism; it will be a lesson to others. Namely those who—in surprising conformity with the postwar period—are dishonourable enough to have forgotten the war and its achievements and who continue lying. In particular, there is a man,

whose name shall not be mentioned, who has issued speeches which he recommends as models for celebrations of the constitution in schools. This German now brazenly claims that there was no opportunity for chivalrous battle in the past world war. One should permit the pupils who had to listen to his babble to see the film about the German–English sea battles—so that the children will know what chivalrous battle means [...][62]

Far from being a paean to peace and the pointlessness of war, this review appears to support Bryher's interpretation, for it was clearly read as a glorification of the armed forces and implied that war could be honourable. By stressing the importance of the Imperial German Navy's ensign, *The Battles of Coronel and Falkland Islands* also crept unwittingly into a fierce debate about symbolism in Weimar Germany, for in 1926 President Hindenburg had forced through a regulation requiring German government agencies abroad to fly the old imperial colours alongside those of the new state. This move caused consternation among social democrats and led to great sensitivity on all issues of iconography in the new Germany.[63] This controversy perhaps coloured the views of those approaching the film from a centre-left perspective, for Leo Hirsch of the *Berliner Tagesblatt* drew an entirely different conclusion, seeing it as a warning against the futility of war.[64] On the whole, the film was very well received in Germany and added to a spate of popular German-made naval films.[65] Having agreed to take up distribution and exhibition rights, Ufa's determination to promote the film probably influenced the decision of the lavishly illustrated film magazine, *Film Kurier*, to devote a special edition to its release complete with dramatic descriptions of the battles.[66] In this way the production also served to further the idea of Anglo-German collaboration in the cinema industry, especially as it was premiered in Berlin during the first conference of European cinema exhibitors.

Somewhat ironically, the film caused the most controversy in the tiny part of the empire it did so much to celebrate. Sir Leo Amery, secretary of state for the colonies, was made aware of the fact that Falkland Islanders who had seen the film while in the UK felt insulted by their depiction. The scenes they found objectionable were those involving the Falkland Islands Defence Force, which was portrayed as a dedicated, loveable, but slightly comic bunch, who, although enthusiastic, might not be capable of making a skilful stand against a German onslaught. The governor of the Falkland Islands, Arnold Hodson, was extremely angry and took up the case, and was even more piqued by the fact that no filming was carried out on the actual islands! (The Scilly Isles were used, and its local militia portrayed their South Atlantic counterparts.) Hodson's passionate communications to the Colonial Office give away something of the power commonly attached to film and its ability to influence the image and prestige of the British Empire. He was particularly concerned by the idea of ridiculing white men, and sent an extract from an islander's letter: "Good, healthy, honest laughter can be obtained in any film without going to the trouble of ridiculing the Only White Colony under the British Crown, a Colony which is so little known, and which has been rather neglected, but where, nevertheless, white men of British stock earn their livelihood and maintain the traditions of the Old Country."[67] The islander queried whether anyone would allow Australians to be depicted in this manner and added that the local volunteers should be portrayed in "their true colours, as stalwart Britishers of the Caucasian race, rough riders, good shots, good oarsmen, hard-toiling peat-cutters and daring seamen." The emphasis on rural virility, here, is very similar to that used in popular representations of Anzacs and Canadians, and probably also reflects the Falkland Islanders' determination to distance themselves from the Latin "other" of the South American mainland. Amery took the case seriously and interviewed representatives of BIF, who proclaimed their utter remorse at causing offence and agreed to produce a specially edited version for exhibition in Stanley.[68] This was duly carried out, ensuring that the film was warmly received in the islands and given an equally enthusiastic reception in the whaling station at South Georgia.[69]

Box-office figures confirmed the appeal of the film, broadened as it was by its British credentials in the cultural war against Hollywood.[70] These wider patriotic impulses helped it fulfill its apt billing as flagship for British film. According to many critics, *The Battles of Coronel and Falkland Islands* allowed British cinema to reveal inherent advantages over Hollywood, particularly when it came to interpretations of the Great War. The skill lay in the ability to avoid cheap melodrama and mawkish sentimentalism. Michael Orme, one of a gaggle of emerging British film critics, took the opportunity pointedly to delineate between the two cinema cultures and celebrate the flowering of more discerning cinema audiences:

> I have been struck of late with the slow but steady defeat of sentimentality on the screen. Public taste is gradually finding its feet. I can only put it that way, for if ever any form of entertainment pandered to the

least desirable demands of the public, it has been, alas! that of the kinema. When, in the first fine frenzy of discovering that real tears could run down real faces at a moment's notice, the public wallowed in emotionalism. Hollywood gave it glycerine tears *ad lib* and is still inclined to do so. Now, it seems to me, the moment has come to realise that familiarity with all that claptrap and false sentiment, all the "bathos" and sob-stuff, of bad pictures has eventually bred, if not contempt, then at least a better appreciation of better films.[71]

What Orme is actually conveying is the fear of the British middle and ruling classes over the struggle for the soul of the nation, and nothing was more important in this regard than the depiction of its war effort and war dead. Taking cinematic possession of the meaning of the war was regarded as a national crusade, and *The Battles of Coronel and Falkland Islands* was a reason to cheer. However, as *Cinema World Illustrated* revealed, vigilance had to be maintained:

These two War pictures [the other new British release, *The Somme*] demonstrate at least one thing, and that is the absolute superiority of this country in this branch of film production. One has only to compare either with the classical farce, "The Big Parade," to realise how far behind the Americans are in this respect. And now, to crown all, an American company has arrogated to itself the right to present the epic of the Royal Air Force. "War Hawks" will, unfortunately, be seen by thousands in this country, attracted to the picture house by the false description, but, after seeing it, the picturegoer will wonder why Buster Keaton or Harold Lloyd was not included on the cast, and on realisation that the film is not *meant* to be funny, will register a vow not to look to American pictures if he or she really wish to learn something about the War in Europe, as distinct from that in Hollywood.[72]

It is ironic to note that Bryher considered *The Big Parade* far superior to BIF's output and far more sincere in its anti-war message.[73]

Despite some variants in interpretation, the remarkable thing about the public discourse on BIF's output is the degree of consensus over its meaning and qualities. This agreement resulted in the creation of a common vocabulary of terms to describe, interpret, and analyze the films. Certain words came to be privileged by reviewers and commentators: realism, authenticity, humour, epic, glorious. Such words combined two narrative devices for dealing with the war in the 1920s. Realism and authenticity were thought to be the cornerstones of the written histories, particularly the official histories project, with their sense of cool detachment and over-arching analysis. Glorious was the adjective to describe the fallen as deeply inscribed on the Cenotaph in Whitehall, "The Glorious Dead," who had made the ultimate sacrifice in the most noble of causes. Epic and humour were part of the "lower"/popular language of war, as used in boys' comics and the pulp literature on the conflict aimed at the lower middle class, with their hints at what Mike Paris has called "the pleasure culture of war."[74] Their combined use in rhetoric about BIF films shows that instead of a new diction of modernist discordance forged in the cataclysm of the Great War, a hybrid language merging older, popular images of war with the sober dissection of the historian attempting to make sense of the experience came into being. Thus, BIF's films successfully balanced three seemingly incongruous concepts: historical detachment, respectful remembrance, and thrilling excitement.

BIF and *The Battles of Coronel and Falkland Islands* served to remind the world that the British Empire had fought honourably, gallantly, and successfully against a powerful and worthy foe. Through strong narrative lines consciously designed to appear realistic, and given weight by the lavish assistance of the armed forces, the films put a containing frame on the past and invested it with positive meaning. For a society wracked by the trauma of loss, disfigurement and disability, BIF's films were a palliative imparting the war with structure and value: they were cinematic war memorials. In addition to this, they told the world that the British Empire was not prepared to let Hollywood dictate the popular history of the Great War, and that the USA was not going to monopolize the economic and cultural laurels of victory. So intense was the feeling that BIF was prepared to depict the former enemy positively, creating a link between Britain, its empire, and Germany that excluded the US as a peripheral interloper. The ships portrayed in *The Battles of Coronel and Falkland Islands* hoisted battle ensigns in more ways than one.[75]

NOTES

1. See Charles Barr, "Before *Blackmail*: British Silent Cinema," in *The British Cinema Book*, ed. Robert Murphy (London: BFI, 1997), 5–16.
2. *Times*, 25 February 1926, quoted in Sarah Street, "British Film and the National Interest, 1927–1939," in *British Cinema Book*, 17–26.

3. For a full discussion of this issue, see Mark Glancy, *Hollywood and the Americanization of Britain: From the 1920s to the Present* (London: I.B. Tauris, 2014), 14–75. See also D.L. LeMahieu, *A Culture for Democracy: Mass Communication and the Cultural Mind in Britain Between the Wars* (Oxford: Clarendon, 1988).

4. See Richard Maltby and Ruth Vasey, "'Temporary American Citizens': Cultural Anxieties and Industrial Strategies in the Americanisation of European Cinema," in *"Film Europe" and "Film America": Cinema, Commerce and Cultural Exchange, 1920-1939*, ed. Andrew Higson and Richard Maltby (Exeter: University of Exeter Press, 1999), 32–55.

5. See *Film Renter* (Manchester), 30 October 1926.

6. For a full discussion of the Act, see Margaret Dickinson and Sarah Street, *Cinema and State: The Film Industry and the British Government 1927-84* (London: BFI, 1985), 5–75.

7. *Times*, 5 September 1921.

8. See review in *Variety*, 25 November 1921.

9. *Times*, 19 November 1923.

10. *Register* (Adelaide), 2 February 1925.

11. *Advertiser* (Adelaide), 5 February 1925.

12. *Times*, 17 October 1924.

13. *Daily Express*, 30 August 1924.

14. *Film Renter* (Manchester), 15 November 1924.

15. *Toronto Daily Star*, 21 March 1925; *Mercury* (Hobart), 1 March 1926; *Evening Post* (New Zealand), 28 March 1927.

16. *Irish Times*, 11 February 1926. See also Kevin Rockett, *Irish Film Censorship: A Cultural Journey from Silent Cinema to Internet Pornography* (Dublin: Four Courts Press, 2004), 319–20.

17. *Film Renter* (Manchester), 21 and 28 November, and 5 and 12 December 1925; *Auckland Star*, 5 June 1926; *Toronto Daily Star*, 2 February 1926; *Register* (Adelaide), 8 July 1927.

18. *Daily Express*, 17 September 1926.

19. *Irish Times*, 31 May 1927.

20. *Kinematograph Weekly*, 11 November 1926.

21. *Daily Express*, 5 November 1926.

22. *New York Times*, 23 October 1927.

23. See Christine Gledhill, "Remembering the War in 1920s British Cinema," *British Silent Cinema and the Great War*, ed. Michael Hammond and Michael Williams (Basingstoke: Palgrave, 2011), 94–108.

24. *Kinematograph Weekly*, 11 November 1926; for further material on BIF's relationship with the Admiralty, see National Archives of the United Kingdom (hereafter TNA UK), ADM 116/2490 "Flag Lieutenant—Naval Assitstance," File Minute 18 November 1925.

25. *Daily Express*, 5 November 1926; *Times*, 7 September 1927.

26. See Kristin Thompson, "The Rise and Fall of Film Europe," and Thomas J. Saunders, "Germany and Film Europe," *"Film Europe" and "Film America,"* 56–81, 157–80.

27. For mid-twenties international relations and the "Locarno honeymoon," see Anthony D'Agostino, *The Rise of Global Powers: International Politics in the Era of the World Wars* (Cambridge: Cambridge University Press, 2011), 192–93.

28. For good examples of press updates on the production, see *Daily Mirror*, 17 and 23 April, and 7 May 1927; *Daily Express*, 10 May 1927; *Illustrated London News*, 10 September and 1 October 1927; and the *Times*, 11 May 1927.

29. For examples of the press coverage of the royal viewing, see *Daily Express*, 12 September 1927; *Times*, 16 September 1927; and *Kinematograph Weekly*, 22 September 1927. For an example of how it was recounted in dominion press, see *Toronto Daily Star*, 1 March 1928.

30. *Kinematograph Weekly*, 8 September 1927.

31. See *Daily Chronicle*, 16 September 1927.

32. *Daily Film Renter*, 17 September 1927.

33. See Haidee Wasson, "Writing the cinema into daily life: Iris Barry and the emergence of British film criticism in the 1920s," in *Young and Innocent: The Cinema in Britain, 1896–1930*, ed. Andrew Higson (Exeter: University of Exeter Press, 2002), 321–37.

34. *Manchester Guardian*, 16 September 1927.

35. *Westminster Gazette*, 16 September 1927.

36. *Berliner Tagesblatt*, 5 August 1928; *Deutsche Allgemeine Zeitung*, 3 August 1928.

37. *Die Burger*, 17 April 1928. For further details on Rompel's work as a film critic, see Michael Eckhardt, *Film Criticism in Cape Town, 1928–1930* (Stellenbosch: Sun Press, 2005).

38. *New York Times*, 19 February 1928.

39. *Cinema World Illustrated*, October 1927; *Daily Chronicle*, 16 September 1927; *Register* (Adelaide), 8 October 1928.

40. *Deutsche Allgemeine Zeitung*, 3 August 1928; *Berliner Illustrirte Zeitung*, 7 October 1927.

41. *Daily Mirror*, 6 November 1926; *Evening Standard*, 16 September 1927.

42. *Manchester Guardian*, 27 January 1928.

43. *Deutsche Allgemeine Zeitung*, 3 August 1928.

44. *Picturegoer*, November 1927.

45. *Evening Post* (New Zealand), 11 December 1928

46. *Glasgow Herald*, 16 September 1927; *Westminster Gazette*, 16 September 1927.

47. *Die Burger*, 17 April 1928.

48. *New York Times*, 9 February 1928. The US version also appears to have had a scene of the Niagara Falls added at the end, which was, according to Hall,

"unneccesary footage … to symbolize the lasting amity between the United States and Great Britain."

49. *Liverpool Echo*, 8 November 1927; *Manchester Guardian*, 18 February 1928.

50. *Evening News*, 16 September 1927; *Portsmouth Evening News*, 1 October 1927.

51. *Close Up*, 4 (October 1927).

52. *Daily Herald*, 16 September 1927.

53. *Advertiser* (Adelaide), 8 October 1928.

54. *Berliner Tagesblatt*, 5 August 1928; *Die Burger*, 17 April 1928.

55. *Observer*, 18 September 1927.

56. For discussions of these weapons as propaganda symbols, see Patrick Wright, *Tank. The Progress of a Monstrous War Machine* (London: Faber and Faber, 2000); Michael Paris, *From the Wright Brothers to Top Gun: Aviation, Nationalism and Popular Cinema* (Manchester: Manchester University Press, 1995).

57. *Berliner Tagesblatt*, 5 August 1928.

58. See Laurence Napper, "Remembrance, Re-membering and Recollection: Walter Summers and the British War Film of the 1920s," in *British Silent Cinema*, ed. Hammond and Williams, 109–17.

59. See Paul Fussell, *The Great War and Modern Memory* (Oxford: Oxford University Press, 1975); Samuel Hynes, *A War Imagined: The First World War and English Culture* (London: Bodley Head, 1991).

60. *Liverpool Echo*, 7 November 1927; *Toronto Star*, 3 March 1980; *Canberra Times*, 27 September 1928; *Falkland Islands Magazine and Church Paper*, July 1928; TNA CO 78/178/1, Letter from Governor A. Hodson, 3 May 1928.

61. *Tamworth Herald*, 21 January 1928.

62. *Deutsche Allgemeine Zeitung*, 3 August 1928.

63. For details, see Franklin C. West, *A Crisis of the Weimar Republic: A Study of the German Referendum of 20 June 1926* (Philadelphia: American Philosophical Society, 1985), 227–32; see also Benjamin Ziemann, *Contested Commemorations: Republican War Veterans and Weimar Political Culture* (Cambridge: Cambridge University Press, 2013), 125–26.

64. *Berliner Tagesblatt*, 5 August 1928.

65. See Bernadette Kester, *Film Front Weimar: Representations of the First World War in German Films of the Weimar Period (1919-1933)*, trans. Hans Veenkamp (Amsterdam: Amsterdam University Press, 2003), 160–92.

66. *Film Kurier*, 3 August 1928.

67. TNA CO 78/178/1, letter from Hodson, 15 December 1927.

68. TNA CO 78/177/5. See correspondence and memoranda, 27 and 30 September, 6, 10, and 15 October, and 9 November 1927.

69. TNA CO 78/178/1, letter from Hodson, 3 May 1928.

70. The producer H.B. Woolfe later claimed it grossed £70,000 in the UK alone, having cost £18,000 to make. Rachael Low, *The History of the British Film, 1918-1929* (London: George Allen and Unwin, 1971), 181.

71. *Illustrated London News*, 1 October 1927.

72. *Cinema World Illustrated*, October 1927. See also *Irish Times*, 24 May 1927 for an onslaught on *The Big Parade* when compared with BIF products.

73. *Close Up*, 4 (October 1927).

74. Michael Paris, *Warrior Nation. Images of War in British Popular Culture, 1850–2000* (London: Reaktion, 2000), 223.

75. A final, and somewhat amazing, irony should be noted. In December 1939, the German pocket battleship *Admiral Graf Spee* scuttled itself in the estuary of the River Plate, northwest of the Falkland Islands. HMS *Exeter* retired to Stanley harbour to repair its damage before returning home. In 1956 the British film-making duo, Michael Powell and Emeric Pressburger, made a large-scale semi-documentary account, *The Battle of the River Plate*, utilizing the services of the Mediterranean Fleet and depicting Captain Karl Langsdorff, commander of the *Graf Spee*, as a gallant and honourable foe. The only Americans included were a journalist in Montevideo and the USS *Salem* impersonating the *Graf Spee*!

"CAN ONE GROW USED TO DEATH?"

Deathbed Scenes in Great War Nurses' Narratives

ALICE KELLY

"We will send you the dying, the desperate, the moribund," the Inspector General had said. "You must expect a thirty per cent mortality." —Mary Borden, *The Forbidden Zone: A Nurse's Impressions of the First World War* (1929)[1]

A common truism of the Great War is that it turned men into numbers. In her 1920 memoir *A Scottish Nurse at Work*, the Voluntary Aid Detachment (VAD) nurse Henrietta Tayler explains that in the military hospital in which she worked in La Panne, Belgium, they received "ten or twenty patients every night, an hour or so after they had been wounded, and [during] any local attack *many* more ... we had many, many deaths."[2] The numbers of dead are only described indirectly, with the emphasis on mass death compounded by the lack of specific numbers. The confrontation with death that nurses, doctors, and medical orderlies encountered in casualty clearing stations and military hospitals in the First World War was unprecedented. Much has been written on the culture shock of "these gently nurtured girls who walked straight out of Edwardian drawing rooms into the manifest horrors of the First World War," but relatively little on how the nurses encountered and coped with such large numbers of dying men.[3] This chapter explores how women serving in hospitals in the war zones and on the home front witnessed and wrote about military death in contemporary and retrospective diaries, memoirs, and eyewitness accounts.

The First World War prompted a crisis in attitudes towards death. In 1915, Freud presciently noted that, "we cannot maintain our former attitude towards death, and have not yet discovered a new one."[4] Jay Winter has suggested that the ten million deaths of the Great War represented a "puzzling, unprecedented catastrophe" for contemporaries.[5] David Cannadine argues that, "the impact of the First World War on attitudes to death has been underrated by sociologists and historians, that its significance was profound for at least a generation; and that interwar Britain was probably more obsessed with death than any other period in modern history."[6] Adrian Gregory refers to the war and postwar period as "a transitional moment in the history of attitudes towards death."[7] Pat Jalland argues that the First World War was "a major turning-point in the history of death in its own right, since it shattered what remained of the Victorian way of death for many bereaved families."[8] Here I consider how this crisis in attitudes was represented and played out in wartime writing.

This chapter focuses on deathbed scenes, which are ubiquitous in the nurse narratives and the primary narrative trope for expressing anxiety over the changed modes of dying caused by the war. I argue that the majority of nurse narratives turned back to conservative literary tropes, such as the deathbed scene, in an effort to impose meaning and dignity on the mass deaths that were occurring. Although this trope was frequently inadequate for the immensity of the loss of life the nurse was trying to represent, the choice of a conservative aesthetic mode is revealing. Focusing on the sites of intensely proximate encounters between nurses and the dying mostly written while the war was still ongoing, this chapter argues for the importance of these accounts as a type of immediate proto-memorialization, before more official modes of commemoration were established.[9] I hope to demonstrate that nurses were implicitly positioned at the forefront of the contemporary debate about death, burial, and adequate memorialization, and their viewpoint was unique and warrants further critical attention. I examine a selection of texts that present themselves as "authentic" accounts—by Olive Dent, Enid Bagnold, Henrietta Tayler, Lesley Smith, and Pat Beauchamp—and read them as representative of the larger body of nurses' writings.[10] These texts were all written as firsthand accounts by women who served as voluntary nurses, although in separate branches. My use of the term "nurses" therefore applies to volunteer rather than professional nurses.[11]

In recent years there has been a re-evaluation of what Margaret Higonnet has termed "an alternate history of World War I traumas," through a critical appreciation of nurse narratives in First World War literature.[12] Angela K. Smith has similarly argued for the nurses' "establishment and recognition as active and important contributors to the dialogue of war."[13] Social and cultural histories of nursing have increased our understanding of the organization and work of nursing groups, including the Voluntary Aid Detachment (VAD) nurses, Queen Alexandra's Imperial Military Nursing Service (QAIMNS), and the First Aid Nursing Yeomanry (FANY), as have more general studies of the medical profession during the war.[14] These studies have focused on the emancipatory potential of women's war work and the ideologies inherent in the interpellation of women as military nurses. More recent work has examined the connections between modernist and First World War writing.[15] The republication of some nurses' accounts has prompted further interest, and the prefaces and afterwords to these new editions have provided excellent critical commentary on the genre as a whole.[16] However, despite the acknowledgement in every commentary of the sheer number of dead in the First World War, of whom a high proportion died in field hospitals and convalescent units, there remains little critical discussion of the nurses' depictions of death.[17]

The nurses' eyewitness accounts provide a record of what it was like to be present at the site of death: the lived experience of those who witnessed the unrelenting numbers of deaths firsthand. This bestowed on nurses what Margaret Higonnet terms "the first kind of knowledge about war trauma," which is "often symbolized by a confrontation with death that civilians can never understand," as well as responsibility for comforting grieving relatives in person or by letter. Higonnet is therefore right to suggest that the texts of the nurses, like the nurses themselves, "both observe and participate in the experiences of trauma."[18] The peculiarly liminal status of the nurses, with their "marginalised identity—one in, but not of, the war," as Sharon Ouditt suggests, makes their accounts particularly valuable.

The nurse's heavily gendered role and ambiguous military positioning was compounded by her contradictory roles of healer and griever, as well as participant and witness. Quoting from Mary Borden's satirical 1929 text *The Forbidden Zone*, Higonnet argues that it was the "nurse's business ... to create 'a counter-wave of life.'"[19] The image of women as life-givers was utilized in recruiting efforts for war work, particularly nursing. This sentiment was made explicit on a particularly graphic American Red Cross poster, depicting a nurse supporting a wounded soldier and summoning another seated at a desk with the words "If I Fail He Dies" in capital letters at the top.[20] Nurses were simultaneously asked to fulfill the culturally constructed role of primary mourner usually attributed to women.[21] This had immediate historical precedent: women were, as Jalland notes, the primary carers around the nineteenth-century deathbed.[22] Nurses appropriated the specifically determined narrative trope of the deathbed scene for representing the dead, partly because it reflected the reality of what they were experiencing, but more importantly because it imposed a meaningful and immediately recognizable structure on the deaths they were attempting to represent, dignify, and begin to memorialize.

John Morley, Michael Wheeler, and Pat Jalland have written extensively on changing death practices and customs from the Victorian period to the twentieth century.[23] During the nineteenth century, the deathbed scene was recognized as a trope for representing the dying and the dead, and was consciously constructed and heavily determined. It was predominant in religious ideology and further consolidated by its reproduction in painting, literature, and other cultural forms. Jalland outlines the conventions of the mid-Victorian "Evangelical version of the good death":

> Death ideally should take place at home, with the dying person making explicit farewells to each family member. There should be time, and physical and mental capacity, for the completion of temporal and spiritual business, whether the latter signified final Communion or informal family devotions. The dying person should be conscious and lucid until the end, resigned to God's will, able to beg forgiveness for past sins and to prove his or her worthiness for salvation. Pain and suffering should be borne with fortitude, and even welcomed as a final test of fitness for heaven and willingness to pay for past sins.

These conventions demonstrate an idealized and communal experience of a death: death has been accepted by the dying person, who has sought spiritual atonement in preparation for the afterlife. The moment of death was significant in religious terms because of the "immediate divine judgement on each individual at death, making constant preparation essential." Conversion could happen on the deathbed, and instruction for "dying well" was therefore greatly important. From late medieval England onwards, "a vast body of devotional literature known as the *ars moriendi*, the art of dying, taught people how to die well," and during the Evangelical revival, "thousands of didactic deathbed scenes in nineteenth-century Evangelical tracts and journals attested to the zeal to save souls by showing people how to die."[24]

The personal significance of the deathbed for those caring for the dying person is demonstrated in the Victorian tradition of deathbed memorials. Kept in diary form, these attest to the significance of the last days and hours of the dying person:

While these memorials were chiefly intended as spiritual accounting to God, they also served as personal therapy for the writer and as a written record to preserve the memory of the loved one for the immediate family. They usually recorded daily, even hourly, events in the sickroom, including the symptoms, medical treatment, visitors, and conversations.... The medical and spiritual accounts were often uneasily juxtaposed, even within the same paragraph, as the diarist moved between a prosaic clinical narrative and a symbolic spiritual discourse.[25]

These memorials complemented the *ars moriendi* as literature that sanctified and privileged the final expressions and emotions of the dying. Few of these memorials survive, but their influence on later nurses' narratives is evident, as demonstrated by the nurses' recording of daily and hourly changes in their patients.

The deathbed as narrative convention was further reproduced and thereby reinforced in the Victorian period through well-known literary deathbed scenes, which were usually lengthy, memorable descriptions, highly sentimentalized and laden with pathos.[26] Jalland observes:

Deathbed scenes in novels were usually melodramatic occasions of moral judgement and emotional farewell.... These stereotypical scenes often included proof of spiritual salvation, with minor miracles, haloes of light, and edifying last words. Death scenes in Victorian fiction tended to be more melodramatic and sentimental than those in Evangelical tracts, but it was often a matter of degree. However, the fictional scenes made no claims to historical accuracy; they were deliberate devices for emotionally engaging the reader in an age when sentimental stories were very popular.[27]

Literature became a means of consolidating the myth of the good death and its conventions, alongside *ars moriendi* literature, Evangelical tracts and journals, deathbed memorials, and paintings. In depicting the deaths of their patients through deathbed scenes, nurses were invoking a longstanding, recognizable, and consolatory narrative trope for representing death.

Among her other responsibilities, the nurse's role involved keeping vigil by the deathbed. Christine Hallett has written of this practice of "specialing":

Caring for the dying was one of the most important elements of the nurse's work. In the urgently busy scenario of a casualty clearing station or field hospital, where the emphasis was on containing the lives of those with a chance of survival, nurses struggled to be present with their dying patients. In the more controlled environment of a base hospital, it was often the most highly trained nurses who stayed with patients who were dying; the practice was known as "specialing." The nurse worked to ensure that everything possible was done to provided [*sic*] the patient relief from pain and trauma at the time of his death. Nursing the dying was as much a process of containment as nursing the living; the nurse protected both the dying patient and those around him.[28]

The convention that it was the trained nurses who stayed with the dying does not seem to have been absolute. Numerous volunteer nurses recorded their experiences of attending deathbeds, and the shock of the frequently distressing death scenes and the altered nature of the corpse, as well as the emotional burden of comforting the dying, meant that this could be particularly disturbing.

A brief survey of the contemporary nursing handbooks and manuals demonstrates that volunteer nurses were not formally prepared for this aspect of their role. The handbooks collectively attest to the detailed care and attention nurses were encouraged to give to their patients, and stress their increased responsibility in wartime. However, the difficult situations that nurses would face were only implicitly discussed, with nurses at most knowing the physical and the legal procedures for dealing with a dead body. The 1912 *British Red Cross Society Nursing Manual, No. 2* was aimed at VADs whose nursing was largely limited to "the temporary care of patients until they can be transferred to the general hospitals" and "duty in ambulance trains." The last page, unusually, provides information on "Laying Out the Dead":

When a person dies, remove the blankets and throw the sheet over the corpse, covering the face as well as the body. After an interval pass a bandage or handkerchief beneath the lower jaw and tie off on the top of the head, so that the mouth is closed. Spread a mackintosh beneath the corpse to protect the bed, and proceed to wash the whole body with soap and water; dry thoroughly; shut the eyelids and place a pad of cotton-wool on either eye to ensure the lids being kept closed. Push a piece of cotton-wool up the bowel for a short distance. Put on stockings or socks, and pyjamas or nightdress; tie the feet together.

A clean sheet is spread beneath the body, which is then completely covered by another clean sheet.[29]

The information is solely concerned with the physiological practice of dealing with a corpse and provides no indication of what the nurse may be required to do to console or comfort the patient before death, or the emotional aspect of this experience. Although aimed at "nurses, orderlies, and Red Cross workers," Duncan C.L. Fitzwilliams's 1914 *Nursing Manual for Nurses and Nursing Orderlies* does not deal with the question of dying at all.[30] Under the index entry for "Breathing," we find "Cheyne-Stokes, nature of" and "stertorous, cause and nature of," although there is no reference to this in relation to dying (known colloquially as the "death rattle"). Violet Young's *Outlines of Nursing* similarly does not discuss dying patients.[31] M.N. Oxford's *Nursing in War Time: Lessons for the Inexperienced*, explicitly aimed at volunteer nurses, does, by contrast, include a short section on "The Last Duties to a Patient." Oxford outlines a physiological methodology similar to that of Cantlie's 1912 handbook, and the manual ends with a paragraph on the necessity for respect for the dead: "It is unnecessary to say that we do these last offices for our patients with the same reverent care that we should like used for our own relations, and for ourselves when our turn comes; without unnecessary talking, and with exactly the same decency that we observe in washing a living person."[32] Although this does not concern the emotional impact of the death itself, this manual is unusual in going beyond physical details to discuss the significance of death. A.S. Woodwark's *Medical Nursing* (1914) includes a chapter on "The Care of the Dead: Dying Declarations and Will Making," although this was not intended for wartime nursing.[33] The French physiologist Charles Richet's translated Red Cross lectures, *War Nursing: What Every Woman Should Know* (1918), which asserts on its cover that it "will be found particularly useful for members of the V.A.D.," does not include any reference to death, presumably assuming that women should already know this from their assistance at peacetime deathbeds.[34]

Although these handbooks did not formally or explicitly prepare the nurses for the mass death they encountered, it is possible that some passages refer implicitly to the care of the dying. This is most evident in Fitzwilliams's 1914 nursing handbook, which notes that a nurse's training "now ranges over anatomy, physiology, pathology or the knowledge of disease ... and also all that is meant by the word nursing as applied to the comfort and care of the sick," which presumably refers to the care of the dying. Fitzwilliams stresses the difficulty of nursing, noting the "health, strength and endurance" needed by the nurse, and that training is "a great tax upon her," where "many nurses break down under the strain."[35] Such passages perhaps indicate both the physical and emotional difficulties of nursing, without explicitly naming them. Oxford discusses the problems of war nursing in her "Introductory," which is more explicit in its acknowledgment of the frequently gory situations that nurses would encounter: "A woman who means to nurse, especially in war time, must possess courage. The sight of blood need not alarm you; a very little blood makes a very great mess, and if you will set yourself to *help*, instead of gazing helplessly at the mess, you will not be troubled by faintness nor sickness. There is a great deal too in determining not to be frightened."[36]

Many of the handbooks include in their introductions or preliminaries the qualities of a good nurse. Fitzwilliams cites "[g]entleness and refinement, sympathy and tact, patience and perseverance" as "all qualities to be cultivated."[37] Under the virtue "gaiety," Richet comes closest to discussing the role of the nurse as comforter: "The patients, heroic men who have just escaped death, require cheering or consoling by some comforting word," but he warns that "such expressions of friendship and sympathy should not overstep certain limits."[38] These qualities of bravery, sympathy, tact, kindness, and the ability to comfort and console were the characteristics that nurses would most need to cultivate in caring for the dying during the First World War.

The failure of the nursing handbooks and manuals to mention death made the mass numbers of dying men all the more shocking for the nurses. Even if they implicitly discussed the types of scenes a nurse might encounter in wartime, these examples were woefully inadequate. The nurse narratives show again and again that "specialing" was virtually impossible in the wartime hospital. Writing and recording the deaths of the men became the best tribute that nurses were able to provide.

Each nurse narrative I examine includes a number of individually described deaths among the depersonalized passages of the numbers dying. Re-invoking Victorian pieties, these individual deaths act as a type of memorialization, and may be written as a single, lengthy, descriptive passage, or as a repeated return to one individual patient in the narrative, mimetically described as the nurse would have experienced the death on her routine and schedule of duty. Each deathbed scene is usually remembered by the nurse for something in particular: the nurse's regret that she could have done more for this patient, the patient's seemingly superlative vulnerability, or that their injuries and death were especially painful. These individual deaths are an important means of personalizing the multiple anonymous deaths that the nurse wished to portray, despite the fact that the patient concerned is not always named, but instead known by his injury or bed number. The particularizing of a scene, whether or not the patient is named, insists that *all* deaths are *individual* deaths. However, these narratives signal a stylistic break with many lengthy, highly sentimentalized nineteenth-century literary deathbed sequences. Instead, the nurses' narratives are frequently notable for the brevity of their description and the distanced mode of narration, and we see the tension between an engaging individualization and sympathy and a disengaging generality. Although nurses frequently employed the narrative model of the deathbed scene, their writings repeatedly demonstrate that these models were no longer adequate.

The nurses' narratives demonstrate the changed nature of dying that arose as a direct result of the war. Many of the soldiers died in pain far from home and apart from loved ones, and many of the anonymous dead depicted by nurses left corpses broken or incomplete and therefore difficult to accommodate to Victorian convention.[39] In *Four Years Out of Life* (1931), Lesley Smith, a VAD in France, records the break with traditional modes of dying, which prompted women at home to take the war and their new VAD roles seriously:

> I looked hastily at the list and found, not only Douglas's name but the names of five other boys who had been friends of his and ours; sons of people we knew—our friends! It was a queer crashing start to one's own personal war. Before that it had been the government's affair, and now we were all in it just because some boys we knew had been killed outright instead of dying with the usual paraphernalia of doctor and nurses and wreaths. It suddenly seemed to be necessary after that to try to stop muddling, and do some one thing tidily and properly.

The nurses were clearly disturbed by the broken, deformed and frequently incomplete male bodies resulting from warfare. Comparing these descriptions with the Victorian urge toward realism—the desire that the corpse should look the same in death as it had in life, aptly documented in the popularity of Victorian memorial photography—we see how the war was an unexpected assault on traditional aesthetics of death. Smith records that there was no longer the conclusiveness of death permitted by an entire corpse: "Death has its own clean finality; but these men, whose admirable bodies lay inert and helpless at the mercy of a grotesque, obscenely rolling head, seemed a denial of everything beautiful and fair." The approach to death similarly lost its sanctity and pathos. Smith describes the death of a patient known as "Ninety-nine" because of his tendency to count continually:

> I ran back to look at him, there had been nothing to be seen through the mass of bandages but two eyeholes and a gash for the mouth, but at last there was a change, a trickle of blood was dribbling slowly out of the gash and soaking the white bandage. Old Ninety-nine would not count much further. The new rhythm was strangely disturbing:
>
> "Ninety ninety ninety—hic—seven, ninety ninety-nine, hic, ninety hic, ninety hic." He was obviously just going. Well, there wasn't anything to be done and it was no use disturbing Sister, she was having a heavy night in "Chests" … old "Ninety-nine" gave a last triumphant shout of "Ninety ninety hic nine" and was silent for the first time since he had come in three days ago. A breathless pause held us stationary for a moment, then Matron tramped out saying, "I'll send Sister."[40]

The man is dehumanized and almost corpse-like, and his impending death is only apparent because of blood trickling through his bandages. Although Smith demonstrates her urgent engagement with the scene ("I ran back"), the deflationary death sequence is notable for its deliberate ordinariness and lack of ceremony. Smith's resignation to, and disengagement from, Ninety-nine's death is stated before it even occurs, and the bathos of his last moments is seen in his "triumphant" hiccupping, rather than dying a dignified death. Smith and her Matron are "held … stationary" only to validate that the man has actually died; it is not any type of reverential or ritual pause. The moment of death has moved from being the sacred movement into another realm, which the nineteenth century narrative depicted in extended, sentimentalized sequences, to being one so commonplace that it does not even qualify interrupting others from their work.

The nurses' writing reveals the multiple roles they were expected to play at the deathbed: the final sitter present at the men's deaths, sometimes a surrogate priest and final confessor, and primary mourner. A large part of the nurse's role was comforter, and all of the nurses' accounts record the men seeking comfort from the author, physically and mentally. An extended passage in Smith's narrative concerns the death of Railton, a young corporal who has lost one leg and severely injured the other. This particular death is given considerable narrative space, most likely because of the pathos and personal element of his story—that he "came in determined to live," that he "had a girl to go back to," and because his mother is allowed to visit the hospital when his condition worsens. Smith prefaces this account by recounting that in this period they "had one case after another who *might* have recovered, whose lives we fought for, and who died in spite of us after days of agony," which adds further pathos. The detail in the long description of Railton's death suggests the multiple, conflicting pressures on the nurse: both to attend to all of her patients, and to give reassurance and comfort to individual patients—the tension between general duties and the traditionally personalized attention at a deathbed:

> I waited while the champagne revived him and then laid him back on the pillow. He still held my hand and I couldn't leave him, but a chest wound had slipped off his air pillow and was in a bad position, and an amputation back from the theatre that afternoon was being very sick. There were two fomentations due and Sister had run over to the mess for a cup of tea. I still waited, but I couldn't help being conscious of all these clamorous duties.
>
> Railton could hardly move his head, but he lifted his eyes to my face and panted:
>
> "Sorry to keep you, Nurse—I won't be long now—Am going fast, ain't I?"
>
> I choked and fumbled stupidly for a word, and finally managed to tell him to hold on, there might be a change at any moment. He just brushed that aside and still holding me with his eyes said:
>
> "I'm frightened, Sister. Is it all true what they say in church?" His voice had dropped to an agonised whisper and I had to bend down to catch what he said. "Will I be forgiven?"
>
> I tried to say what he wanted to hear and he slowly lifted his hand off mine and said "Thank you."
>
> I fled down the ward to roll over the amputation's head and prevent him choking himself.

The individualization of Railton in this scene of an intensely intimate encounter between a nurse and her patient initially seems to return the reader to the world of the Victorian deathbed. However, this passage highlights the tension between engaging individualization and a disengaging generality, where the other patients are represented by distancing epithets—"a chest wound" and "an amputation"—a necessary troping of people as wounds that was both horrific and anonymous. Smith's comment,

"I couldn't help being conscious of all these clamorous duties," works as an admission that this individualized deathbed scene is impossible to maintain in the wartime hospital, and that a focus on one patient—even at the moment of his death—is impossible due to multiple other demands on her attention. Her uncomfortable description of her reaction to his anxious questions demonstrates her lingering feelings of helplessness and impotence. Once Railton has died, the narrative moves on quickly: Smith writes that, "in the morning there was another man in Railton's bed."[41] As Carol Acton has noted, "[t]here is literally no further space for Railton and no time for Smith to grieve."[42]

Pat Beauchamp's patriotic 1919 memoir *Fanny Goes to War* provides a recording of an individualized death, but one that is elided in the narrative. Beauchamp records watching a man slowly dying from a distance and tells us that this deathbed image—another curious mixture of distance and intimacy—has remained with her:

> I shall always see the man in bed sixteen to this day. He was extremely fair, with blue eyes and a light beard. I started when I first saw him, he looked so like some of the pictures of Christ one sees; and there was an unearthly light in his eyes. He was delirious and seemed very ill. The sister told me he had come down with a splendid fighting record, and was one of the worst cases of pneumonic typhoid in the ward. My heart ached for him, and instinctively I shivered, for somehow he did not seem to belong to this world any longer.... Each time I passed No. 16 I tried not to look at him, but I always ended in doing so, and each time he seemed to be thinner and more ethereal looking. He literally went to skin and bone. He must have been such a splendid man, I longed for him to get better, but one morning when I passed, the bed was empty and a nurse was disinfecting the iron bedstead. For one moment I thought he had been moved. "Where—What?" I asked, disjointedly of the nurse. "Died in the night," she said briefly. "Don't look like that," and she went on with her work. No. 16 had somehow got on my mind, I suppose because it was the first bad typhoid case I had seen, and from the first I had taken such an interest in him. One gets accustomed to these things in time, but I never forgot that first shock.[43]

The characterization of the man through superlatives, as "extremely fair ... with a splendid fighting record ... one of the worst cases' and her likening him to Christ makes literal the motif of sacrifice and adds pathos to his inevitable fate. However, the patient remains nameless, identified only by his bed number. Beauchamp records her distance, even repulsion, from the man, noting the "unearthly light in his eyes." He is already distanced through his delirium, seemingly already a corpse: "instinctively I shivered, for somehow he did not seem to belong to this world any longer." However, Beauchamp is simultaneously attracted to him, writing in the language of popular romance that that, "[m]y heart ached for him," that "I longed for him to get better." However, she is prevented from any actual engagement or sympathy with the man. Caught between an intense desire for him to recover and the knowledge that his death is inevitable, Beauchamp's feelings toward the man are manifested in a compulsion to look; a looking that is eventually frustrated. His death is elided in the narrative, but symbolized, as in many other nurse narratives, by the empty bed. Beauchamp records her initial denial of the death, where her own reaction is elided but made clear by the recorded reaction of her fellow nurse. This death is the first of a series of similar deaths: "One gets accustomed to these things in time." The absent nurse and the distant reader are not sure what to conclude from his death.

The fear that the nurse "gets accustomed to these things in time" is analogous to the sentiment expressed with some concern by Enid Bagnold in *A Diary Without Dates*, her popular 1918 memoir of her nursing experiences at the Royal Herbert Hospital in London.[44] One of the most poignant deathbed scenes concerns "a boy of seventeen" brought in with pneumonia.[45] The description of the infantilized boy serves purposefully to heighten the pathos and emotive effect of the scene. Bagnold emphasizes both his physical pain, "so ill that he couldn't speak," and his youth, stating, "it gave me a shock to see how young his feet were," and highlights his child-like vulnerability when he asks her to brush his hair. The Sister speaks in a soothing, maternal tone to the boy: "There you are, Sonnie, it's almost finished…." The boy is clearly in grave danger after a rapid decline, referred to in euphemistic diction as being "on the edge of the world—to-night looking over the edge." The boy "submits with a terrible docility" to whatever medical procedure the nurses and doctors attempt, but Bagnold acknowledges that his illness exceeds their expertise. She is "preoccupied with the mystery that is his lungs' and documents her helplessness at the lack of a physical wound to treat, that '[t]here is no shell, no mark, no tear…. The attack comes from within.'"

Although it seems there is nothing she can do medically to ease the boy's suffering, Bagnold wishes to demonstrate her emotional and mental engagement with him, stressing that "he is all the centre of my thoughts."

She nervously anticipates his death, and her lack of control over his fate reveals her feelings of inadequacy as a nurse. The desperate actions of the boy's mother (who has been summoned to his bedside), seeking some alleviation of her son's suffering by bringing each day a cake as "a bribe, dumbly offered" to the Sisters, is a ritual that Bagnold states "hurts me," further compounding her sense of impotence and guilt. She withholds from the reader whether the boy survives his illness. The description of the sky "like a pale egg-shell" hints at the fragility of his situation, as does the inconclusiveness of Bagnold's unanswered question: "I think from time to time, 'Is he alive?'" When the boy comments that the ward is pretty, Bagnold takes comfort in this small gesture: "It isn't, but I am glad it seems so to him." The key element of the scene is the truism that results, suggesting the traumatic impact on the nurses of keeping vigil over so many deathbeds: "Can one grow used to death? It is unsafe to think of this.... For if death becomes cheap it is the watcher, not the dying, who is poisoned."[46] This fear of normalizing death, of becoming "used" to death because of its frequency, was of serious concern to the nurses. Even heavily propagandistic narratives, such as Olive Dent's 1917 text *A V.A.D. in France*, do not conceal the enormous emotional burden of deathbed scenes or the universal concern at this prolonged exposure to death.

The nurse's role was a mode of keeping vigil, where she might simultaneously deny the possibility of death to the patient and provide comfort to him, but privately acknowledge her anticipation of death, where it was inevitable and would actually be a relief. Beauchamp writes, "When I became more experienced I could tell if patients were going to recover or not; and how often in the latter case I prayed that it might be over quickly."[47] Recounting the extended but inevitable death of a French soldier who has left a wife and five children at home, Beauchamp notes, "'Why must they go through so much suffering?' I wondered miserably. If they *are* to die, why can't it happen at once?'"[48] Smith, having done some work in the head injuries ward, writes, "I stayed in 'heads' for eight weeks, and at the end my only happiness was in remembering how few during that time had recovered enough to go home." She writes later: "We 'took in' three times in that one month, and each time there were half a dozen cases who swung between life and death for days and whose lives seemed, to our exaggerated conscientiousness, to be bound up with our own. Again and again we gave in to death, angry, dogged by a sense of our failure, resenting our powerlessness, and then began the struggle all over again as another convoy replaced the last." The mention of "our exaggerated conscientiousness" demonstrates that nurses were highly aware of the disproportionate burden of responsibility concerning death that was conferred on them. Sometimes the nurse recorded her personal discomfort in acquiescing to the men's need for comfort by telling them something they do not actually believe. As Smith notes, "I tried to whisper that it would probably be better to-morrow, but the lie stuck in my throat."[49]

The nurses' narratives contain frequent expressions of their feelings of inadequacy, a sense of an inability to console or to relieve the suffering of the men. Bagnold writes: "We sit on the floor of the bell tent and gaze out into the night, a night when the sound of the guns is insistent … we suddenly feel a helpless band of futile women, agonisingly impotent."[50] They attempted to make the best of situations, such as the withholding of bad news from home from very ill patients, but frequently the conclusive feeling was the inability of the nurses to change the situation in which they find themselves or to alter the fates of those they nursed, fighting against the "insistent" relentlessness of the guns. In *A Scottish Nurse at Work*, Tayler similarly notes the relentlessness of incoming patients: "though many died, being only sent to us at the last gasp, there always seemed to be others to take their places…. Poor miserable objects, dying like flies, because only arriving when at the point of death; though, of course, the French doctors were goodness itself, and we had the necessary tinned milk and drugs for the patients, only so many were too far gone to profit by these things." Tayler praises the medical service and the provisions available, but emphasizes that little can be done for many of the patients. The sense of helplessness, seen in the depersonalizing reference to the men as "Poor miserable objects, dying like flies," is frequently tempered elsewhere by a justification that "nothing at all could be done" for the patient, that there was sufficient medication and that "we were able to soothe the last days and hours." Tayler discusses the deaths of many of her patients in an increasingly depersonalized, passive voice, suggesting that the deaths were entirely out of the nurses' control: "a sad number of deaths occurred of hopeless heart disease, cancer, dropsy, nephritis, lupus, tuberculosis and other cruel illnesses."[51]

The dominant impression of the deathbed scenes, then, is the sheer numbers of deaths and the emotional burden this put on nurses to play multiple, often contradictory roles. At times, even Dent's usually propagandistic narrative becomes intensely graphic:

So the day wore on and night came. Without—a night of glorious July summer, with palest saffron, flamingo and purple lights, and one gem-like star, a night of ineffable beauty and peace, and within—a vision of Hell, cruel flesh-agony, hideous writhings, broken moanings, a boy-child sitting up in bed gibbering and pulling off his head bandages, a young Colonial coughing up his last life-blood, a big, so lately strong man with ashen face and blue lips, lying quite still but for a little fluttering breathing.

This positive account full of patriotic rhetoric does not conceal the enormous emotional burden of deathbed scenes. She writes, "'I am too tired to sleep … too tired to do anything but think, think, think, too tired to shut out of sight and mind the passionate appeal of two dying eyes, and a low faint whisper of "Sister, am I going to die?"'"[52]

There has been a critical lack of attention paid to First World War nurses' representations of death. As the field of First World War studies diversifies, we can read these texts, written by women in the war zones but marginalized from the front, with a greater awareness of their importance in demonstrating the effect of the war on perceptions of and attitudes toward death. The nurses' narratives show the wartime renegotiation of death, and a very early version of what governments and individuals would be involved in for many years in the postwar period: the drive to commemorate and memorialize, what Samuel Hynes has called "monument-making."[53] Consciously or unconsciously, nurses used the trope of the deathbed scene to give meaning to otherwise meaningless deaths, and thereby constitute a type of proto-commemoration of the men who died. Giving the men—only a few of very many men—a deathbed scene meant that they were not forgotten. Turning to a traditional structure—one that had been consolidated through the *ars moriendi* literature, Evangelical tracts, deathbed memorials, and Victorian paintings and literature— demonstrates some attempt to find comfort in the salvaging of traditional death rituals and to derive meaning from these deaths. However, the narratives repeatedly demonstrate that these deathbed scenes were no longer adequate to the mass death the nurses attempted to represent, that war death could not be contained by its conventions. Earlier modes of writing death and commemoration had outgrown their usefulness, but there were not yet new ones to take their place.

Looking back to the first responses to mass mortality in the mechanized warfare of the First World War, the nurses' narratives present us with the war's ideological assault on traditional modes of dying and the efforts of ordinary people to ensure dignity at the moment of death, rather than the posthumous nationalistic attempts to apply dignity retrospectively. As the Great War moves from memory to history, our work as scholars is to make public memoirs by nurses and others, to remind us of the terrible death in warfare experienced by so many, and the traumatic effects on those who witnessed it.

NOTES

1. Mary Borden, *The Forbidden Zone: A Nurse's Impressions of the First World War*, ed. Hazel Hutchison (New York: Doubleday, 1930 [1929]).
2. Henrietta Tayler, *A Scottish Nurse at Work: Being a Record of What One Semi-Trained Nurse Has Been Privileged to See and Do during Four and a Half Years of War* (London: John Lane, 1920), 38.
3. Lyn Macdonald, *The Roses of No Man's Land* (London: Papermac, 1990 [1980]), 3.
4. Freud, "Thoughts for the Times on War and Death [1915]," in *Sigmund Freud: Collected Papers*, vol. 4, trans. Joan Riviere (New York: Basic Books, 1959), 307–8.
5. Winter, "Representations of War on the Western Front, 1914–18: Some Reflections on Cultural Ambivalence," in *Power, Violence and Mass Death in Pre-Modern and Modern Times*, ed. Joseph Canning, Harmut Lehmann, and J.M. Winter (Aldershot: Ashgate, 2004), 205.
6. Cannadine, "War and Death, Grief and Mourning in Modern Britain," in *Mirrors of Mortality: Studies in the Social History of Death*, ed. Joachim Whaley (London: Europa, 1981), 188–89.
7. Gregory, *The Silence of Memory: Armistice Day, 1919–1946* (Oxford: Berg, 1994), 22.
8. Jalland, "Victorian Death and its Decline: 1850–1918," in *Death in England: An Illustrated History*, ed. Peter C. Jupp and Clare Gittings (Manchester: Manchester University Press, 1999), 251.
9. Here I appropriate Jay Winter's term "site"—both a literal and narrative site— to refer to the deathbed as a conservative site of grief and mourning. Winter's very influential argument that the social response to the enormous death toll of the First World War was a reversion to traditional modes of mourning provokes the question of whether or not we can trace this conservative turn in writing. Winter, *Sites of Memory, Sites of Mourning: The Great War in European Cultural History* (Cambridge: Cambridge University Press, 1998).
10. Dent, *A V.A.D. in France* (London: Grant Richards, 1917); Bagnold, *A Diary Without Dates* (London: Virago, 1978 [1918]); Tayler, *A Scottish Nurse at Work* (1920); Smith, *Four Years Out of Life* (London: Philip Allan, 1931); and Beauchamp, *Fanny Goes to War* (London: John Murray, 1919).

11. Hallett is right to point out that previous critics tend to "conflate the two [voluntary and trained nurses] as if they formed a homogenous group." Christine E. Hallett, *Containing Trauma: Nursing Work in the First World War* (Manchester: Manchester University Press, 2009), 10.

12. Higonnet, "Authenticity and Art in Trauma Narratives of The First World War," *Modernism/Modernity* 9, no. 1 (2002): 92. See Nicola Beauman, *A Very Great Profession: The Woman's Novel, 1914–39* (London: Virago, 1983); Sandra M. Gilbert and Susan Gubar, *No Man's Land: The Place of the Woman Writer in the Twentieth Century. Volume Two: Sexchanges* (New Haven: Yale University Press, 1989); Claire Tylee, *The Great War and Women's Consciousness: Images of Militarism and Womanhood in Women's Writing, 1914–64* (Iowa City: University of Iowa Press, 1990); Sharon Ouditt, *Fighting Forces, Writing Women: Identity and Ideology in the First World War* (London: Routledge, 1994); Jane Potter, *Boys in Khaki, Girls in Print: Women's Literary Responses to the Great War, 1914–1918* (Oxford: Oxford University Press, 2008); Santanu Das, *Touch and Intimacy in First World War Literature* (Cambridge: Cambridge University Press, 2005).

13. Angela K. Smith, *The Second Battlefield: Women, Modernism and the First World War* (Manchester: Manchester University Press, 2000), 71.

14. Anne Summers, *Angels and Citizens: British Women as Military Nurses, 1854–1914* (London: Routledge and Kegan Paul, 1988); Janet Lee, *War Girls: The First Aid Nursing Yeomanry in the Great War* (Manchester: Manchester University Press, 2005); Yvonne McEwen, *It's a Long Way to Tipperary: British and Irish Nurses in the Great War* (Dunfermline: Cualann Press, 2006). More general studies are Jeffrey S. Reznick, *Healing the Nation: Soldiers and the Culture of Caregiving in Britain during the Great War* (Manchester: Manchester University Press, 2004), and Mark Harrison, *The Medical War: British Military Medicine in the First World War* (Oxford: Oxford University Press, 2010). See also Joanna Bourke, *Dismembering the Male: Men's Bodies, Britain and the Great War* (London: Reaktion, 1996), and Anna Carden-Coyne, *Reconstructing the Body: Classicism, Modernism, and the First World War* (Oxford: Oxford University Press, 2009).

15. See Allyson Booth, *Postcards from the Trenches: Negotiating the Space between Modernism and the First World War* (Oxford: Oxford University Press, 1996), and Ariela Freedman, "Mary Borden's *Forbidden Zone*: Women's Writing from No-Man's-Land," *Modernism/Modernity* 9, no. 1 (2002). Jane Marcus observes that "the fragmentation described as typical of modernist texts has an origin in the writing practice of women nurses and ambulance drivers," in "Corpus/Corps/Corpse: Writing the Body in/at War," in *Arms and the Woman: War, Gender, and Literary Representation*, ed. Helen M. Cooper, Adrienne Auslander Munich, and Susan Merrill Squier (Chapel Hill: University of North Carolina Press, 1989), 129.

16. For example, Borden's *The Forbidden Zone*. This had previously only been partially reprinted, with extracts from Ellen N. La Motte's *The Backwash of War: The Human Wreckage of the Battlefield as Witnessed by an American Hospital Nurse* (New York: G.P. Putnam's Sons, 1934 [1916]), in *Nurses at the Front: Writing the Wounds of the Great War*, ed. Margaret Higonnet (Boston: Northeastern University Press, 2001). For useful prefaces and afterwords, see Jane Marcus, "Corpus/Corps/Corpse: Writing the Body In/At War," afterword to Helen Zenna Smith, *Not So Quiet: Stepdaughters of War* (New York: Feminist Press, 1989); Jane Marcus, "Afterword: The Nurse's Text: Acting Out an Anaesthetic Aesthetic," in Irene Rathbone, *We That Were Young* (New York: Feminist Press, 1989).

17. Only two critics explicitly address this, both of which are very valuable: Margaret Higonnet, "Women in the Forbidden Zone: War, Women, and Death," in *Death and Representation*, ed. Elisabeth Bronfen and Sarah Webster Goodwin (Baltimore: Johns Hopkins University Press, 1993), and Carol Acton, "'Can't Face the Graves Today': Nurses Mourn on the Western Front," in *Grief in Wartime: Private Pain, Public Discourse* (Basingstoke: Palgrave Macmillan, 2007).

18. Higonnet, "Authenticity and Art in Trauma Narratives of The First World War," 101.

19. Higonnet, quoting from Borden, *The Forbidden Zone* (New York: Doubleday, 1930 [1929]), in "Women in the Forbidden Zone: War, Women, and Death," 204.

20. Arthur G. McCoy, *If I Fail He Dies, Work for the Red Cross* (Duluth: J.J. LeTourneau, 1918 [copyright Rev. S.A. Iciek, 1918]).

21. Ouditt, 9. The culturally constructed position of the mourning woman, already a recognized type during the Victorian period, was consolidated during the Great War, and a number of postwar official commemoration efforts were specifically aligned with female mourners. See Gregory, *The Silence of Memory*, 34, 39–41. As Carol Acton argues in her examination of wartime grief, "we cannot examine the individual experience of loss and grief without considering that experience as gendered, both in terms of the particular wartime environment and the more general way cultures prescribe different grief responses and mourning behaviour for men and women," in *Grief in Wartime*, 6, 7. Her study of multiple wars suggests that "in the public discourse such 'gendering' privileges women, particularly mothers, as mourners," 7.

22. Jalland, *Death in the Victorian Family* (Oxford: Oxford University Press, 1996), 12.

23. John Morley, *Death, Heaven and the Victorians* (London: Studio Vista, 1971); Michael Wheeler, *Heaven, Hell and the Victorians* (Cambridge: Cambridge University Press, 1994), abridged edition of *Death and the Future Life in Victorian Literature and Theology* (Cambridge: Cambridge University Press, 1990); Jalland, "Victorian Death and its Decline: 1850–1918" (1999); *Death*

in War and Peace: Loss and Grief in England, 1914–1970 (Oxford: Oxford University Press, 2010).

24. Jalland, *Death in the Victorian Family*, 17, 21, 26.

25. Jalland, *Death in the Victorian Family*, 10.

26. For example, Little Nell's death in Charles Dickens's *The Old Curiosity Shop* (serialized 1840–41).

27. Jalland, *Death in the Victorian Family*, 24.

28. Hallett, *Containing Trauma*, 65.

29. James Cantlie, *British Red Cross Society Nursing Manual, No. 2* (London: Cassell, 1912), v–vii, 185.

30. Duncan C.L. Fitzwilliams, *A Nursing Manual for Nurses and Nursing Orderlies* (London: Henry Frowde, 1914), v.

31. Young, *Outlines of Nursing* (London: Scientific Press, 1914).

32. Oxford, *Nursing in War Time: Lessons for the Inexperienced* (London: Methuen, 1914), 52–53. This text is "intended for the use of those women who by the fortune of war may find themselves obliged to undertake the care of the sick or wounded, without any previous knowledge of the art of nursing" (Preface).

33. Woodwark, *Medical Nursing* (London: Edward Arnold, 1914), 280–84.

34. Richet, *War Nursing: What Every Woman Should Know, Red Cross Lectures*, trans. Helen De Vere Beauclerk (London: Heinemann, 1918).

35. Fitzwilliams, *A Nursing Manual*, v, 9–10.

36. Oxford, *Nursing in War Time*, 1–2.

37. Fitzwilliams, 10.

38. Richet, *War Nursing*, x. Richet discusses the problem of romantic or sexual relationships between nurses and patients, which was wholly forbidden and would result in disciplinary action. Although fascinating, this topic is beyond the scope of this chapter.

39. Patients were often identified by their injury, such as Dora M. Walker's discussion of "The Spine Case," in *With the Lost Generation, 1915–1919: From a V.A.D.'s Diary* (Hull: A. Brown and Sons, 1970), 3.

40. Smith, *Four Years Out of Life*, 3, 93, 85–86, 90.

41. Smith, *Four Years Out of Life*, 125–27.

42. Acton, 149.

43. Beauchamp, *Fanny Goes to War*, 42–44.

44. Beauchamp, *Fanny Goes to War*, 44.

45. Bagnold's book led to her dismissal from her nursing position within thirty minutes of its publication of fifteen thousand copies. By April 1918, the book was already in its third impression. "Advertisement: Mr. Heinemann's List," *The Bookman*, April 1918, 29. Contemporary reviews did not consider the book to be unpatriotic or offensive: "Miss Bagnold has served as a V.A.D. nurse in a military hospital and has pictured her day by day experiences there with stark and simple truthfulness. She recreates the whole thing, gives it its

native hue and atmosphere, and touches in portraits of sisters, nurses, patients and visitors with that imaginative sympathy which always goes with a sense of humour." Unsigned review, "A Diary Without Dates," "News Notes," *The Bookman*, March 1918, 174. The text was even initially patriotically billed as "An intimate account of the life of a V.A.D. in one of our great military hospitals." "Advertisement: 'Mr. Heinemann's Autumn List,'" *The Bookman*, December 1917, 39.

46. Bagnold, *A Diary Without Dates*, 77–79.
47. Beauchamp, *Fanny Goes to War*, 48.
48. Beauchamp, 48.
49. Smith, *Four Years Out of Life*, 93, 254, 123.
50. Bagnold, *A Diary Without Dates*, 267.
51. Tayler, *A Scottish Nurse at Work*, 94–95, 42, 62.
52. Dent, *A V.A.D. in France*, 335, 338.
53. Hynes, *A War Imagined: The First World War and English Culture* (London: Pimlico, 1992 [1990]), 270.

KITSCH, COMMEMORATION, AND MOURNING IN THE AFTERMATH OF THE GREAT WAR

MARK A.R. FACKNITZ

[Kitsch] is a vivid reminder that the human spirit cannot be taken for granted, that it does not exist in all social conditions, but is an achievement that must be constantly renewed through the demands that we make on others and on ourselves.[1] —Roger Scruton

Kitsch is false beauty. Kitsch is junk, and junk of two kinds. The first and commonplace type of kitsch is pleasant, sometimes bathetic, always guileless, and never more offensive than a random belch in an elevator. The second kind of kitsch, with which I concern myself here, is an entirely different matter.

As the antithesis of beauty, kitsch is an important aesthetic concept for which there is remarkably little published comment, though the term can be useful in cultural studies and historicist discussions. Indeed, kitsch is a complicated idea, which most people use without critical forethought, assuming it to be unproblematic. And kitsch, as a concept, is of recent emergence. In German it began to mean what we take it to mean in the late nineteenth century, and we can presume that it was fully consolidated in that language by the time Walter Benjamin used it in the 1920s, or about the time the first English dictionary included it. It entered colloquial French in the decade after the Great War, though it continued to be excluded from Larousse and Robert through the 1960s and '70s. Kitsch, it would appear, is a category that Western Europe did not much need before the war and the efflorescence of modernism. The obvious question, then, is why do we need it after?

More particularly, how do the paralyzing and commodifying tendencies of kitsch characterize the commemorative monuments of the Great War? As Saul Friedlander wrote, "as an aesthetically inadequate mode of expression, an imitation of art, [kitsch] aims at getting an unreflective, immediate, emotional response; its function will *either* be to promote something—mainly in commercial terms—without contextual restrictions, or ... to reinforce identification within a specific ... context, mainly in ideological terms."[2]

In this sense "kitsch" does *not* mean what most people think of first— the frou-frou clutter of ceramic kittens with eyes that light up, or big-eyed stuffed animals from county fairs, mementoes of evenings that may have ended in seduction but never in aesthetic transcendence of ordinary circumstance. Hummels and bric-a-brac are merely material objects, sometimes fetishized, often ugly and a bit pathetic, but in themselves harmless. To a large extent, we often, as Robert Solomon contends, respond with "a deep but undeserved suspicion of emotions, especially those tender emotions that would seem the most humane." Solomon ends with the comment that "incidents" of bad art can make us smarmy, but that does not condemn our taste or reveal our emotional juvenility; rather, they reveal a "virtually universal concern" that is innocuous to the idea of art, but fundamental to our constant need to refresh our humanity as creatures who feel and whose feelings of tenderness, empathy, and vulnerability are as legitimate as any other emotions.[3] In other words, kitsch can provoke the always salutary reminder that we are not dead inside.

It would be feckless to argue against a person's right to feel what they feel. However, the notion of kitsch that I intend implies an arrest of aesthetic process and a substitution of static object for dynamic subject, and, in the instances that I treat, the inchoate and almost entirely irrational responses of mourners are preserved in the presence of a kitsch monumentalism, which proposes order and beauty to perceivers whose compelled response is morbidly to repress the disorder and horror of their emotions. In this, kitsch is fundamentally damaging to psychic and cultural integrity, for it demands the individual's complicity in an agreement to prefer fictitious value to real value, or shared postures of public grief to private processes of healing. Indeed, participation in kitsch-culture is symptomatic of an acceptance of a world without the possibility of full interiority.

The modern subject might also complain that one is crippled by a nostalgia for such experience as debilitating as its actual loss. Hence, the modern genealogy of kitsch returns through Pater's aestheticism to Baudelaire's preference for cosmetics and *paradis artificiels*, though in its popular forms—for example, the cheap ceramics in the booths of "Araby" in Joyce's *Dubliners* or the vapidly pious bric-a-brac in any narthex gift shop of a cathedral—kitsch is not cosmetic, rather it is evidence of a widespread coarsening of human experience and vitiation of symbolic culture. Ultimately, it derives from a Romantic elevation of the intensity of experience and boisterous sincerity of expression over decorum and idealism: indeed, it may be Kant's notion of beauty as disinterested interest, which, in needing an antithesis, provides the germ from which the concept of kitsch develops. In Kantian terms, if beauty is disinterested, kitsch would codify *interested disinterest*, or the deceitful posture of a borrowed enthusiasm. Kitsch is "always already" acknowledged to be impermanent, its value only negotiable or contractual, never intrinsic or durable.

In this essay, I intend something close to what Matei Călinescu means when he writes, "kitsch represents the triumph of immediacy—immediacy of access, immediacy of effect, instant beauty." Kitsch, he recognizes, "appears as designed to both 'save' and to 'kill' time ... in the sense that its enjoyment is effortless and instantaneous," and also because "like a drug it frees [us] temporarily from [our] disturbed time consciousness, justifying 'aesthetically' and making bearable an otherwise empty, meaningless present." Călinescu's *Five Faces of Modernity* included the first extended effort to deal with kitsch historically, specifically as an ideological characteristic of modernity. For Călinescu, the premise is simple: "Kitsch is one of the most typical products of modernity." Moreover, rather than a consequence of "aesthetic modernity," he writes, "the appearance and growth of kitsch are the results of the intrusion of the other modernity—capitalist technology and business interest—in the domain of the arts."[4]

By all appearances, kitsch has had an unswerving evolution, creating remarkable patterns of desires and melancholies, reflections of frustrated longings for liberal values and a functional free will. Such desire for freedom bespeaks a futile nostalgia for a long-discredited myth of free agency, which Marx classed as a fetish of bourgeois humanism, one belonging to that optimistic set of delusional confidences that built industry, empire, and modern nations, and none of which made it safely through the Somme in 1916, or at the very latest across No Man's Land at Passchendaele in 1917. Kitsch becomes characteristic of western culture in the "age of extremity," Eric Hobsbawm's description of the period 1914 to 1989. As also the age of kitsch, the period marks the low point of western confidence in categories of value such as idealism, transcendence, and beauty. Kitsch much more efficiently describes the ironic and desultory compensations of materialism and hedonism, for the central challenge to art was to persist in a time when its "kitschification" was made inevitable by the press of history—post-Great War, and soon enough post-Auschwitz, post-Hiroshima. Kitsch became the primary value, beauty its shadow.

In reflecting on the consequences of this inversion of value, Giorgio Agamben commented that we confront in kitsch, at its extreme, the commodification of human experience, a presupposition that our value as persons is relative to our accumulating weight of being as we conceive of ourselves not as subjects but as objects. Self-possession, once a question of liberty and consciousness, becomes self-ownership, being that we earn and bank, so to speak. As once at Verdun and Passchendaele, in this manufacture of temporary selfhood: "[At] Auschwitz, people did not die; rather, corpses were produced. Corpses without death, non-humans whose decease is debased into a matter of serial production. And, according to a possible and widespread interpretation, precisely this degradation of death constitutes the specific offence of Auschwitz, the proper name of its horror."[5] At this most abject limit of its devolution, kitsch prefers the cadaver to the vital body, a disabling irony strikingly familiar to visitors to the ossuary at Douaumont where around the back one can peer into the deep bins of collected bones. Or it characterizes the monument at the Mort-Homme, near Cumières-Chattancourt, an early memorial addition to the blighted landscape of the Verdun sector, erected in 1922 by the sculptor Froment-Meurice.[6] Among the more striking of commemorations, insisting on the one hand that this was a place of death, the soldier who cradles the flag of France and hoists a broken sword (or is it a torch?) toward heaven is well decayed before he stands, but also he reminds the world that the promise that the Boche would not pass was one the French soldiers kept. Dead, he is of more value to the *patrie* than were he alive. The memorial is triumphalist, to be sure, yet cadaverous; in fact "cadaverous triumphalism" is an oxymoron that makes sense within the inverted logic of kitsch, the conundrum of interested disinterest. Austrian novelist Hermann Broch expressed the idea in "Evil in the Value-System of Art" (1933): "every era of disintegration of values was also an era of kitsch" in which evil is accepted, even congratulated for preventing art from entering with its corrective revelations and healing force, "for times of final loss of values are grounded on evil and the fear of evil, and the art that is to be their most obvious expression must also be an expression of the evil at work within them."[7]

Where that evil is disclosed, or when the pseudo-art of kitsch is recognized as manipulative, we confront "deathworks," the coinage of Philip

Rieff. Kitsch dismantles the authority of truth by suggesting that the "commanding truths are grandiose," when in fact, Rieff continues, "the lies are grandiose, for they can never be lived modestly, as the truths can be lived."[8] It is as if beauty must be quiet in a din—or small, fragrant, and ephemeral in a vast ocean of shit for which the Western Front provided a material metaphor. Edmund Blunden caught the irony of minor beauty in "Vlamertinghe: Passing the Chateau (July 1917)":

> Bold great daises, golden lights,
> Bubbling roses' pinks and whites—
> Such a gay carpet! poppies by the million:
> Such damask! such vermillion!
> But if you ask me, mate, the choice of colour
> Is scarcely right; this red should have been much duller.[9]

In this new environment, inhospitable to beauty, the soldier's loss, fragility and ephemerality make hurtful effects of nature that once sustained and delighted. This effect is clear and iconic in the final moments of Lewis Milestone's 1930 film version of *All Quiet on the Western Front*; as Paul Baumer reaches out into the detritus of No Man's Land to lift a butterfly into his hand, a French sniper sights and kills him. Beauty has become random and brief; our attraction to it is now lethal. The moment is brusquely unambiguous.

However, kitsch is not always without guile, so to speak. In matters of official remembrance—by which I mean monuments, cemeteries, and commemorative texts, paintings and statuary—the line tends to be anything but stark. Sargent's painting *Gassed*, John McCrae's poem "In Flanders Fields," and Lutyens's Thiepval Memorial to the Missing of the Somme are treated as kitsch by some, as art by others. About such works it is possible to have differences of opinion, to wonder if the work is truth or tripe. I would like to articulate this paradox, this positing of an impossible place where the antitheses disappear—or are shed—by looking at two monuments, one of which is disingenuous, and the other of which seems to embody its designer's awareness of a rhetorical instance that called for consolidation and arrest even while the ethical instance demanded emotional access to grief, intellectual access to idealism, and spiritual access to transcendence.

The first, kitsch *par excellence,* is the *Tranchée des baionettes*, or Bayonet Trench, at Verdun, a French monument funded by the American millionaire George Rand (d. 1919), and the second, chosen among several, is the Canadian Memorial at Vimy, the work of Walter Allward (1875–1955). Each of these monuments has a transparency, a rhetorical extensity, and a reliance on a populist vernacular characteristic of kitsch, not art. And so they should have, for in the first instance—the moment of inauguration, most notably—they must be sufficiently intelligible to victims/survivors/mourners who assemble for the unveiling. Ceremonially, and narratively, they must make an immediate sense sufficient to needs of the moment—creating a space in which participants are awestruck by the experience of the dead and the afflicted can grasp that their private grief has public extensity. All monuments have incontrovertible lowbrow functions. Some have only that.

Interestingly, some monuments seem quickly to take on a pathetic fixity, as if the unintended consequence of commemoration were to demonstrate the futility of acts of commemoration. Others remain more nearly open, more possibly transparent and evocative. How can this be? Where the Bayonet Trench veers into deceit and didacticism, the Vimy Ridge monument foreshadows Maya Lin's Vietnam Veterans Memorial in its capacity to surprise and move its viewers, to inform the heart well beyond the limits the mind might predict. By comparison, Bayonet Trench more nearly resembles Frederick Hart's grouping of three Vietnam soldiers adjacent Lin's memorial; had it been placed any closer it would have travestied her work.[10] I propose that we can begin to understand how completely we have misunderstood what we thought we were saying when we talked so glibly about kitsch. Indeed, in its relationship to the Great War, I think we can discern why this empty idea has appeared to bear a great weight, and perhaps why, at last, it is time to take it seriously.

Antoine Prost understands that the duplicity of memorials is at once necessary and corrupt. Something must mark the unintelligible boundaries of human experience, and it would be rather feckless of us to expect those markers to be perpetually sincere. At Verdun, a place of limits, no place is as extreme as Bayonet Trench. "Like Auschwitz," Prost concludes, "Verdun came to symbolize the limits of the human condition," and even today it "marks the boundary between two worlds":

> The old world in which men were capable of enduring conditions that have become unimaginable and of sacrificing their lives for the sake of duty ended at Verdun in a blaze of glory.… The specter of war remains, and slaughter on a vast scale is still possible, but, now it is mankind as a whole that is threatened and not France as such. With today's tanks, missiles, and nuclear weapons, war no longer means a slow accumulation of individual deaths through a lengthy ordeal of suffering. The

world may again experience horror, but in new, more brutal, more rapid and massive forms that do not require the inward consent of their victims.[11]

That "inward consent" of the victims is the key. As secondary witnesses at the site, we know we don't share it, and are the lesser for desultory participation; moreover, we are grateful and guilty that we don't share it, for it was precisely the profitless sacrifices of the Great War that taught us not to trust large motives, towering myths. Prost understands that the spot commemorated at Verdun, once known as Rifle Trench for the dead men's rifles that marked where the bodies were buried, was forcefully renamed Bayonet Trench because "the bayonet conjured up a comic-book ideal of heroism, a false idea of courage and sublimity according to which soldiers quivering with patriotic emotion and joy yearned for nothing better than to attack the enemy." In fact, the legend of the trench was a "pious fraud." That preposterous legend advanced the notion that about a hundred soldiers, bayonets fixed and at attention, were buried alive by shell bursts. On this messiest of battlefields, strewn with rotted body parts, where terror and abjection reigned, an impossible lie stands for the type. Writes Prost, "the commemoration of a myth like this one meant that the memory of the rear echelon was silencing that of the combatants."[12]

Entrance to Bayonet Trench. *Photograph by author.*

One enters the memorial site through a low and narrow passage, one that could be closed at any moment by a heavy gate, itself an iron fraud painted to resemble patinaed bronze.

Over the supposed trench of the standing dead rests an enormous slab of *béton armé*; the gate is ornamented with a cruciform sword, and the trench shelter has two enormous crosses in relief on the lower end that look less like swords or crosses than great testaments to the longevity of poured concrete. Perhaps it takes such mass to hold down a lie.

Ian Ousby, in the epilogue to *The Road to Verdun*, recalls the origin of the myth of Bayonet Trench, mentioning how tidily it dovetails with the myth of the fighting dead, or *les morts debout*, commonplace as early as 1915, the year before the Verdun cataclysm. Certainly the macabre and aggressively enforced mythos of Bayonet Trench is consistent with the monument of the Mort-Homme, a few kilometres north-northwest. Indeed, unlike mortuary architecture, which must make literal reference to the presence of the

Gate to Bayonet Trench.
Photograph by author.

remains of the dead, battlefield markers like Bayonet Trench and the Mort-Homme don't suffer the same requirement for decorum and sincerity—real or sham—to which makers of cemeteries and ossuaries must attend. Instead, here cadaverous triumphalism is a kitsch intention that heroic myths can sometimes sustain for several generations. In an obscene inversion, the dead become the ultimate warriors, for virility derives from their annihilation. Their claim to our attention, as Abel Gance shows us at the end of his film *J'Accuse* (1919, 1938), depends primarily on their capacity to frighten us, because, as maimed and stinking as their bodies are, they are not truly dead. (Zombies are the kitsch dead.) Our panic in their presence quite abolishes our ability to respond intelligently and freely. The heroics of *les morts debout* conflate valour and triumph with cinematic fantasies and pop-horror.

Yet, obviously the men at Bayonet Trench died with the same measures of cowardice or heroism as elsewhere. Consequently, we can discern in the Bayonet Trench memorial a desire to quell the excesses of superstition, sentimentality, and the contentious iconography of the Catholic Church against the phallic impertinence of Masonic symbols (such as the tower at the Ossuary at Douaumont), or indeed any compensatory totems that crowd other areas of the Verdun *lieu sacré* and other major *lieux de mémoire* elsewhere in France, such as Notre Dame de Lorette, the Chemin des Dames, Les Éparges, and Hartmannswillerkopf or Vieil Armand. Noncombatants may have wanted conventional—and convenient—master narratives to negate the relentlessly modern and crushing allegories that the battlefields suggested, but in the immediate postwar years, as Ousby decides, "Verdun still appeared unfinished in the imagination of the veterans. It still beckoned for them to return; it demanded more if it was to be brought to anything like closure."[13]

In such a circumstance, imposing "kitsch closures" resolves nothing, but does more or less vulgarly suggest that a premature adoption of a decisive finality would be the decent and patriotic thing to do. "Stop sniffling and salute the flag," would be the cruel and simple way to make the point. How and when one should feel a satisfactorily tragic emotion the kitsch-object proposes without hesitation or ambiguity. "Right now and right here feel X, Y, and Z" are its uncompromising demands. And once you have felt those emotions, shelve them with the other detritus and memorabilia of a life lived in half-contact with reality. In this respect, as Adorno soon comes to understand the process, "kitsch is a parody of catharsis," for its "one enduring characteristic ... is that it preys on fictitious feelings, thereby neutralizing real ones."[14] Kitsch mourning, then, is a peremptory and repressive emotional gesture, guaranteeing the residual debilitation of the sufferer, not quite the same as but certainly adjacent in its working to postcards of piles of bones and snow-globes of killing fields. Preposterous myths of good death, or the fighting dead, prevent the mourner from fully confronting what Vera Brittain called "the final and acute question of loyalty to the dead," or of adequately gauging "the grief for … unfulfilled lives that no time could diminish." Such tendentious constructions impeded "halting endeavours to control … political and social passions," substituting "destructive impulses" where there ought to be "the vitalizing authority of constructive thought."[15]

André Ventre, official departmental architect for the Marne, designed Bayonet Trench with the idea that, in his words, "nothing could typify the tragedy and heroism of the trench better than the trench itself," and so declared his intention to do "everything possible to ensure durability." The giant block of concrete enforces that guarantee, though it squats over a spot that is not the trench itself, but one dug some thirty metres distant at a spot where the terrain was more suitable for construction. It would, Ventre promised, last for five hundred years, and so it shall, though already its surface is roughening and beginning to crumble. Whatever its native deceits, it resists at least symbolic erosion. Winter writes, "the preference for the traditional is explicit," citing the block's resemblance to prehistoric Breton structure, and though I see nothing even vaguely druidical about mammoth blocks of reinforced concrete, Winter's key point is correct: "The Trench of the Bayonets is a war memorial of a special kind: a tomb frozen in time and preserved not *by*, but *from* art."[16]

If kitsch is failed art, then Winter's judgment of Bayonet Trench amounts to saying that the memorial can never be vulgar because it was never intended to exalt or in any way to confound ethical and aesthetic experiences. On the other hand, if kitsch is anti-art, deliberate travesty and deconstruction of art's capacity dynamically to negotiate the space between cultural conventions and the interior life of the individual, then Bayonet Trench accepted the condition of kitsch and asserted the superiority of kitsch-experience to aesthetic (or spiritual, or lyrical) experience from the very first moment. However, one consequence of the Great War may well be the modernist contempt for transcendentalist notions of art, reduced so often to mawkish and appallingly insincere sacramentalism, like the bland *Pietà* that the village of Beaumont-Hamel in the Somme erected for its dead.

At a historical intersection of aesthetics and ethics, can we say that the problem of Bayonet Trench is its failure to create a work that dignifies and perpetuates the love we feel for the dead, our gratitude, and to do so in a form that will never make itself available to cheapening or parody? Or is the success of Bayonet Trench its staunch and simple ideology? Does it intend such a thoroughly persuasive piece of kitsch that no one witnessing it will ever feel other than a static and entirely unproductive grief, a bored recognition of suffering, perhaps, but never any lifting of the repressive weight, the sheer monumentality of horror contained? Here, no one will ever question if what happened here was not local heroics; rather, this is merely another spot where many died for no good reason. So, for visitors to the places that Siegfried Sassoon called the world's worst wound, where the shibboleth that Christ died at Passchendaele was invented, and where banal nationalism won out over all other human concerns, we have at the French symbolic anchor point the *concrete* and tyrannizing lie of Bayonet Trench.

Memorial of the village of Beaumont-Hamel to its dead. *Photograph by author.*

Such massive and ideologically ponderous commemorations should not be confused with the elegant trifles one might find among a dead soldier's kit. Annette Becker, in her study of the bric-a-brac that fills the collection of the *Historial de la grande guerre* in Péronne, rightly points out that kitsch is one of those words (like totem, fetish, or talisman) that arrests meaning, blocking in effect any process of examining the imagination that a less strident term might have in opening to us the human imagination, or that seductive and spurious thing we all wish we could know, the mind of the past. Becker understands that the eclectic stuff she handles in her work, her "insolent" articles, are more than quaint and pathetic collectibles, astutely understanding that "these ex-votos say that even the most industrial of wars leaves a place for miracle." Ultimately, the wonder is that the individual who made or cherished these talismans ever existed at all, and that they were individuals, at least right up to the point of annihilation and the pulverization of the body. In this context, the peculiarly German habit of painting scenes and writing names on the scapulae of horses killed in combat reveals "an obsession with naming, with saying that one still exists, still loves one's own people, that one has not abandoned them."[17] To subvert the lie of kitsch, Becker is suggesting, we must look at the attention paid to the dead who were once free, once quick, as Wilfred Owen wrote, and still missed as individuals who made and owned things unique to them, as ephemeral as they. The humble and unique debris left behind by the dead, personal relics, often inscrutably encrypted with carved marks or enigmatic words and numbers, in their potency and privacy sharply contrast with the anesthetizing and constricting message of a site like Bayonet Trench.

If there is a monument that can do both—consolidate and express the national trauma at the same time that it permits and provides for private contemplation and grief—it is the Canadian Memorial at Vimy. Walter Allward embraced kitsch motives sufficiently to get the Vimy monument built in the first place. He also injected enough insolence—swerved sufficiently from the ordinary discourse of nationalism—to allow it to develop ambivalences and resonances in the moment and beyond. Vimy sits on ground every bit as sanctified and spoiled as the ground at Bayonet Trench. Yet Allward's Vimy rises to the condition of art, for it articulates the condition of the possibility of a transcendent truth, an escape from cultural and historic gravity, in the widening V of the monument as the regard moves upward. Allward, it seems, at once discovered an idiom that makes adequate and compassionate reference to the survivors' real need to mourn and yet does not settle into a repression, rather opening more vantages on suffering and doubt the longer we linger. Unified and symmetrical from a distance, on closer approach one sees that each individual figure and grouping has an asymmetrical relationship to the unifying horizontal and vertical centre lines of the whole, as well as to the centre line of his or her own body or the bodies nearest at hand. Some grieve, some express anger at others or at God, some cling to aspiration, some seem sunken into contemplation of the dead. One, at the top of the northern pillar, suggests a precarious grasp on hope. The longer one spends with the monument at Vimy, the more complex and personal it becomes, and the less it appears to articulate a simplistic and nationalist sentiment of heroic sacrifice.

Or, unlike Bayonet Trench, the more one's experience is private, personal, and transformative, the more the "reading" of Vimy reveals not the totalitarian claptrap of kitsch but rather a premise more adequately expressed by Herbert Read in "The Problem of Pornography." For ex-soldier Read, art implies that "memory cannot be entirely extinguished"; instead, aesthetic encounters entail "experiences which transcend the cultural *schemata* ... which transcend the conventional memory *schemata*," and in which "every new insight and every true work of art have their origin."[18]

Canadian Memorial at Vimy. *Photograph courtesy of Bart Keeton.*

In his 1939 essay "Avant-Garde and Kitsch" (in *Art and Culture*), Clement Greenberg opened the postmodern phase of the debate on kitsch, and later, in "Intuition and Esthetic Experience" (in *Homemade Esthetics*), tried to convince an increasingly reluctant (post–Jasper Johns, post–Jackson Pollock, nearly post–Andy Warhol) world that, "moral value, insofar as it is final and intrinsic, is … accessible only to intuition." The premise is a hard sell given that fewer and fewer people can be convinced that anything we experience can be final or intrinsic, so deeply invested are we in ephemerality and alterity. Indeed, Greenberg acknowledged that many were apt to be howling with irritation (or laughter) by the time he asks them to accept that, "the affect or pleasure of art … consists in a 'sensation' of exalted cognitiveness—exalted because it transcends cognition as such." If we strip away all extrinsics—all contaminations and ideology—would there really be anything left, any *thing* to experience at all, much less as purity, beauty, or truth? This longstanding aesthetic conundrum Greenberg sets aside with the contention that, "the pleasure of esthetic experience is the pleasure of consciousness: the pleasure that it takes in itself."[19] There is no consciousness of some thing, however. So it would seem that the aesthetic experience is not at all dependent on exposure to certain objects, but simply on the reaction we have to them? If this is so, then there may not be any hierarchies; "to each his own" would become a rule we would be obliged to enforce rigorously. Thus the whole point of the kitsch/art distinction disappears.

The crucial point about kitsch is not its relation to the consumer, or in the manner of consumption, but in the way we misunderstand the commerce between objects and memory, and how infrequently we see this commerce as consequent to the impossibility of aestheticizing first the Great War, later the Shoah and Hiroshima. Celeste Olalquiaga calls kitsch "the attempt to repossess the experience of intensity and immediacy through an object," and "since this recovery can only be partial and transitory, as the fleetingness of memories well testifies, kitsch objects may be considered failed commodities."[20] Art, by contrast, is what we experience in those instances in which we converse with a virtual entity that arises in some mysterious alternation of our being and the object of our attention. Art leaves us persuaded that whatever has changed within us has reduced the burden of repression upon us and does not leave us longing to possess the lost experience but rather makes us more open to other, new experiences. In this equation, art is to healing and mourning as kitsch is to repetition and arrest.

Finally, in the case of commemorative architecture, artfulness would reside in the capacity of a work to replace desperate stoicism with a painful but nevertheless dynamic mourning, that sort of generative granting of dignity and awareness of loss that Allward extended toward Canadian widows, parents, and siblings, and that W.G. Sebald—however melancholically, however tentatively—was beginning at the time of his death to explore in the context of contemporary Germany's memory of Holocaust and Reich.[21] As a growing literature about the Shoah and other world paroxysms more recent than the Great War can teach us, the supposed inauthenticity of art remains a central concern of the modern or postmodern moment, one that manifests itself whenever the cusp between ethics and aesthetics is at issue. My contention is that this is merely a trick of the historical moment, not an essential failing. If it is self-evident that the twentieth century ended with some ugly wounds still open, my final point is that we need to seek out those instances of successful and failed efforts to figure commemoration as a form of healing, as opposed to continuing to visit and venerate instances of repression or institutionalized deceit. In this, of course, we find a workable distinction between art and kitsch, and understand what Hermann Broch meant by "kitsch is the element of evil in the value system of art."[22] Art thrives. Kitsch kills. Seeking to evade that simple equation takes us back at least to 1914, when kitsch was still a concept without menace or complexity.

NOTES

1. Roger Scruton, "Kitsch and the Modern Predicament," *City Journal* (winter 1999), http://www.city-journal.org/html/9_1_urbanities_kitsch_and_the.html.
2. Saul Friedlander, "Preface to a Symposium: Kitsch and the Apocalyptic Imagination," *Salmagundi* 85/86 (winter/spring 1990), 203.
3. Robert Solomon, "On Kitsch and Sentimentality," *Journal of Aesthetics and Art Criticism* 49/1 (winter 1991), 2, 13.
4. Matei Călinescu, *Five Faces of Modernity: Modernism, Avant-Garde, Decadence, Kitsch, Postmodernism* (Durham: Duke University Press, 1987), 7–9.
5. Giorgio Agamben, *Remnants of Auschwitz: The Witness and the Archive*, trans. Daniel Heller Roazen (New York: Zone, 2002), 72
6. Philippe Rive et al., *Monuments de mémoire: les monuments aux morts de la premiere guerre mondiale* (Paris: MPCIH, 1991), 120.
7. Reprinted in Hermann Broch, *Geist and Zeitgeist: The Spirit in an Unspiritual Age* (London: Counterpoint, 2003), 37.

8. Philip Rieff, *My Life among the Deathworks: Illustrations of the Aesthetics of Authority* (Charlottesville: University of Virginia Press, 2006), 141–42.

9. Edmund Blunden, "Vlamertinghe: Passing the Chateau, July, 1917," in *The Penguin Book of First World War Poetry*, ed. Jon Silkin (Harmondsworth: Penguin, 1981), 106.

10. See Mark Facknitz, "Getting It Right by Getting It Wrong: Maya Lin's Misreading of Edwin Luytens' Thiepval Memorial to the Missing," *Crossings: A Counter-Disciplinary Journal* 7 (2004–05): 47–69.

11. Antoine Prost, "Verdun," in *Realms of Memory: The Construction of the French Past*, ed. Pierre Nora (New York: Columbia University Press, 1998), 397, 401.

12. Ibid., 385, 401, 386.

13. Ian Ousby, *The Road to Verdun* (London: Pimlico, 2003), 266.

14. Theodor Adorno, *Aesthetic Theory*, trans. C. Lenhardt (London: Routledge and Kegan Paul, 1984), 340.

15. Vera Brittain, *Testament of Youth* (New York: Penguin, 1989), 655–56.

16. Jay Winter, *Sites of Memory, Sites of Mourning: The Great War in European Cultural History* (Cambridge: Cambridge University Press, 1995), 101–2.

17. Annette Becker, "Kitsch, désordre esthéthique, ferveurs et superstitions," in *Petites histoires de la grande guerre: les objets insolites de l'Historial* (Péronne: Historial, 2001), 69, 73.

18. Herbert Read, *To Hell with Culture and Other Essays on Art and Society* (London: Routledge, 1963), 158.

19. Clement Greenberg, *Art and Culture* (Boston: Beacon, 1965); *Homemade Aesthetics: Observations on Art and Taste* (Oxford: Oxford University Press, 1999), 6, 9.

20. Celeste Olalquiaga, *The Artificial Kingdom: On the Kitsch Experience* (Minneapolis: University of Minnesota Press, 2002), 291.

21. W.G. Sebald, *On the Natural History of Destruction*, trans. Anthea Bell (New York: Modern Library, 2004).

22. Broch, op. cit., 63.

"ASK HIM IF HE'LL DRINK A TOAST TO THE DEAD"

The Cinematic Flyer-Hero and
British Memories of the Great War
in the Air, 1927–1939

ROBERT MORLEY

Royal Flying Corps (RFC) pilots have a lasting persona in British popular culture: they are drunken and jovial, but also stoic and lethal. After 1927, Hollywood films energized and disseminated this image of the aviator to the point where, by the outbreak of the Second World War, it was accepted as the realistic portrayal of British Great War flyers. Indeed, interwar film played a central role in establishing this enduring memory of First World War aviators. However, interwar cinema did not simply reproduce British and American propaganda distributed during the Great War, nor did it faithfully convey the realities of the air war. Instead, the aviator's screen image fit certain wartime propaganda images, while also infusing it with pacifism, a common interwar motif. Also, drinking as an aviator's pastime was firmly established by the cinema during the interwar period, despite being absent from wartime imaginings of the pilot.

This chapter will first briefly consider the foundational role of the interwar years in the construction of British popular memories about the Great War. It will then shift to discussing two films, Howard Hughes's *Hell's Angels* (1930) and Edmund Goulding's *The Dawn Patrol* (1938), both considered to be at the pinnacle of the First World War aviation film genre.[1] Specifically, it will examine the depiction of aviators, including their characterization, camaraderie, and war-weariness. Third, it will look at how the image of the flyer-hero was used to market the films to the British public.

Finally, a sampling of British newspaper and trade reviews of the films will demonstrate how this image of the aviator was agreed upon as realistic and accurate. Through Hollywood films, the First World War aviator was established as a powerful warrior who coped with the strain of combat through overt pacifism and bouts of heavy drinking.

Though aviators were getting considerable public attention before the war, the stereotypical image of the First World War flyer-hero did not emerge in the British public sphere until mid-1916. Britain, unlike Germany and France, had been reluctant to make heroes out of its aviators.[2] It was not until the disaster on the Somme and increasing image concerns (RFC difficulties in defending against Zeppelin raids, and shockingly high RFC casualty rates) that the RFC decided to make heroes out of their individual aviators.[3] The RFC seemed to be a natural place to look for heroes, despite having a higher casualty rate than the infantry. Flying still allowed individual agency, or at least the semblance of it, something that by the Battle of the Somme the infantryman had been stripped of.[4] Simultaneously, the decidedly unheroic poems of servicemen like Siegfried Sassoon appeared in British print, along with more realistic and graphic portrayals of British soldiers and life in the trenches started to dominate British culture.[5]

Britain's first celebrity flyers began to receive public attention in the summer and fall of 1916; initially their successes were mentioned in the House of Commons or their feats leaked to the press.[6] Flyers such as Albert Ball, James McCudden, and Mick Mannock soon became darlings of the British press and developed "cult-like" followings.[7] They also appeared more heroic in British literature from the works of aviatrix Hilda Beatrice Hewlett (*Our Flying Men*), or of Henry Newbolt, who called them the "knights of the air" in his *Tales of the Great War*.[8] Boys' papers like *Chums* published recruitment material for the RFC and willingly ignored the dangerous realities of the air war. Some RFC aces such as McCudden also contributed to this by publishing memoirs that glorified the service.[9] The British movie industry also aided in the heroic presentation of the flyer by releasing films like *The Eyes of the Army* in early 1916. In the end, the flyer proved to be the hero the British press was looking for; they gave the war a positive spin while conveniently avoiding the realities of the trenches.[10]

As Linda Robertson argues, the public image of the stoic, patriotic, dutiful, and skilled flyer-hero became the RFC's greatest contribution to the war effort.[11] Conveniently, however, British propaganda imagery glossed over or ignored the rowdier elements of RFC pilots—the customary tomfoolery and drinking, sometimes even before missions. Also, these

propaganda images were becoming dominant right when the nature of the air war was changing; aerial combat had ceased to be a duel between individuals and was becoming a rigid, choreographed engagement between formations. It was in the British propagandizing of pilots—modeled on the French, German, and American methods—that the stoicism and strength of the flyer-hero was entrenched in British popular culture.

The interwar years were uniquely important for British constructions of national and personal First World War memories, as Mark Connelly's chapter in this volume has argued. The dominant narrative, exemplified by the work of Paul Fussell and Samuel Hynes, argues that the trauma of the Great War created a lack of a demand for war stories for most of the 1920s, but also a literary and cultural schism between the prewar and interwar periods.[12] This changed in 1928, when, according to Fussell and Hynes, literary interest in the war rose dramatically. It was during this period that some of the now-canonical accounts of the war were published: Robert Graves's *Goodbye to All That*, Siegfried Sassoon's *Memoirs of an Infantry Officer*, Vera Brittain's *Testament of Youth*, and, of course, Erich Maria Remarque's *All Quiet on the Western Front*.[13]

More recently, historians such as Michael Paris, Jay Winter, and Jonathan Vance have contested the arguments put forward by Fussell and Hynes.[14] Paris argues that Hynes's and Fussell's focus on the poetry and novels of Britain's elite has distorted the memory of the war in contemporary accounts, making it appear more disillusioned than the actual popular feelings of the 1920s and the 1930s. He contends that interest in the war can be traced to well before the 1928–30 literary boom. This can be corroborated by the surge of traditional commemoration immediately after the war chronicled by Jay Winter. Also important, Jonathan Vance has emphasized that all cultural artifacts, like the cinema, must be considered of value when evaluating the memories of the Great War.[15] Similarly, other historians, such as Karel Dibbets, Modris Eksteins, Bert Hogenkamp, Pierre Sorlin, David Williams, and Winter, have argued for cinema's fundamental importance in the shaping of opinions, the construction of myths, and the forging of memories about the Great War.[16] Echoing these points, Paris argues that the unrivalled popularity of the cinema makes it "a valuable reflection of popular opinion"—or, for our purposes, popular memory.[17] Directly related to this chapter, Dominick Pisano has argued that cinematic stereotypes are what "persist in the popular memory" regarding the Great War in the air.[18]

Paris convincingly argues that British interwar popular culture—specifically youth culture—was inundated with images of the Great War that presented the conflict as horrible and violent, but also glorious, romantic, and worthwhile.[19] As early as 1918, boys' periodicals like *Chums* and *Boys Own Paper* published articles written by ex-servicemen that made the war appear to be an adventure.[20] Here, Paris asserts, is a continuation of the warrior culture forged during the nineteenth century by the likes of H. Rider Haggard, Rudyard Kipling, and Edgar Wallace; there was no schism between British culture before and after the war, nor does it imply a previous lack of interest in the war before 1928. To Paris, this also represents a deliberate effort by the writers and editors of these collections to gloss over the grim realities of the Great War (including the air war) and focus on the heroism and justification.[21] The new, interwar flyer-hero simply supplemented these Victorian and Edwardian imperial adventurers and the newly added Great War soldier.[22] Boys' papers like *Chums* were particularly interested in the adventures of RFC pilots.[23] No other aviator personified this new flyer-hero better than Captain W.E. Johns's adventuring character Biggles, whose stories were immensely popular among British youth during the 1930s. The heroic yet tragic flyer-hero was exactly the type of Great War aviator that could be found on screen between 1927 and 1939.

Much of Britain's heroic understanding of warfare during the interwar years was imported from Hollywood.[24] From the outbreak of hostilities, film was an important medium in the construction of myths and memories about the Great War. It became the most popular leisure activity of children in Great Britain during the 1930s—the very same children who read periodicals like *Boys Own Papers* or *Chums*. In Britain and the United States, fifty films about the war were made between 1914 and 1918. Immediately after the armistice, the first film of the Great War in the air was made: *A Romance of the Air*.[25] However, it was not until the mid-1920s that films about the Great War were produced in large numbers. Despite societal pressure to know what the war had been like, filmmakers felt it was too soon to make films about the war, and few appeared until *The Big Parade* (1925) and *What Price Glory* (1926).[26] Both of these were well received, demonstrating to Hollywood executives that films depicting the First World War could be commercially successful.[27]

It is not surprising that at least twenty-six films about the First World War in the air were produced between *Wings* in 1927 and the release of the second version of *The Dawn Patrol* in the United Kingdom in early 1939.[28] The action, tempo, and romance could appeal to the working classes, while the historical content and social commentary attracted the middle classes.[29] Coupled with star power and marketed with a highly sophisticated publicity campaign, they had the potential to appeal across class, age, and gender lines. Despite the large number of First World War aviation films, this chapter will focus on *Hell's Angels* and *The Dawn Patrol* (1938 version), with briefer references to other pictures. *Hell's Angels* and *The Dawn Patrol* are two parts of the trilogy of Great War flying films (*Wings* being the first) that Michael Paris sees as the most expensive, best made, most well-received, most popular, and most culturally significant; all others were mere "imitations."[30] These qualities make them ideal case studies. Also important, both films were American-made, but depict British aviators, something that was, considering Hollywood's love for British characters and stories, surprisingly rare during the period.[31]

Hell's Angels and *The Dawn Patrol* both present stereotypical, albeit complicated, flyer-heroes. In doing so, they attempt to rehabilitate the warrior's masculinity that had been fractured by the war. *Hell's Angels* provides a mixed depiction of the stereotypical flyer through two brothers, Roy (James Hall) and Monte (Ben Lyon), as neither fully embodies the pilot persona.[32] Monte, the more carefree and personable of the two brothers, embodies many of the flyer attributes: he is fun-loving, drinks heavily, and is a womanizer. Yet, he is a coward. Roy, on the contrary, is dutiful, nationalistic, violent, and a skilled aviator. In contrast, the aviators portrayed in *The Dawn Patrol* perfectly represent the pilot stereotype during the interwar period; they are portrayed as an amalgam of drinking playboys and stoic warriors. Most of the film's notions of the pilot are conveyed through its four major characters: squadron commander Brand (Basil Rathbone), his adjutant Phipps (Donald Crisp), and pilots Scott (David Niven) and Captain Courtney (Errol Flynn). Their hairstyles and posh accents convey a sense of elitism. Each possesses unique characteristics that contribute either to the flyer persona during the 1930s or to the views of war presented in the film. Brand and Phipps have been hardened by the war and stoically carry out their duties, despite clear signs that Brand's strength is being sapped by the stress of ordering other flyers to their deaths.

David Niven's character in the film, Scott, while less complex than Courtney, embodies particular elements of the flyer-hero archetype. His excessive drinking, sometimes while sporting polka-dot pyjamas over his uniform, is one of his defining traits. However, Scott remains serious about his work as a flyer and is quite good at it. His skill, fatalism, and understanding of the brutalities of the war are most clearly demonstrated in his reaction to the arrival of his younger brother Donny at the squadron. Donny is quickly killed, expelling the flyboy element of Scott's personality.

Captain Courtney is the film's most important character. Flynn was Warner Bros.'s biggest star during the late 1930s, thanks to swashbuckling and manly performances in hits like *Captain Blood* (1935), *Charge of the Light Brigade* (1936), and *The Adventures of Robin Hood* (1938).[33] He portrays Courtney as the quintessential interwar flyer-hero, beginning with the first shot of him at the controls of his Sopwith Camel, wearing a helmet and goggles, his face dirtied by the oil of his engine.[34] Over the course of the film, he downs numerous German planes and conducts bombing raids with precision. He proves to be an equally effective partier as he is a flyer; he drinks heavily, is often intoxicated, gets into mischief, plays tricks, and enjoys singing.

Like many films of the period, including *The Eagle and the Hawk* (1933) and *Ace of Aces* (1933), much of the flyer-hero persona is established in the boisterous mess halls, where the pilots escaped the horrors of war by sharing anecdotes, reading newspapers, or drinking. The mess in *Hell's Angels* fits this image perfectly; the pilots sing, drink, and trade insults and stories as they eat, while music plays in the background. Still, it is in *The Dawn Patrol* that the mess is used to greatest effect. Like in *Ace of Aces*, their mess is decorated with wreckage of German airplanes and a sign on the wall that reads "The Binge Patrol."[35] The atmosphere is even more boisterous than in *Hell's Angels*, and drink is immediately established as the preferred recreational activity; almost all of the pilots are singing "hurrah for the next man that dies!" as they drink.[36] *The Dawn Patrol* only reinforces the cinematic precedent of flyers enjoying drink to avoid addressing their fears and emotions.

One of the most important themes conveyed through the mess halls in both films is the pilots' camaraderie. Not only does it create an image of brotherhood on the screen, it serves to reinforce interwar notions of the flyer-hero. Camaraderie is less overt in *Hell's Angels* than in *The Dawn Patrol*, largely due to the story's emphasis on the relationship between the two brothers and their love interest. Yet there is a strong bond between soldiers and airmen in scenes in the French canteen and in the officers' mess, where pilots can be seen drinking and joking together.

Camaraderie is the dominant theme of *The Dawn Patrol*. It is evident in how the RFC pilots interact both with each other and with their German adversaries. There is a paternalistic relationship between aviators that can be seen in how the veteran pilots treat the often very young replacement pilots. Courtney makes an effort to greet the enthusiastic replacement pilots with respect, asking them how many hours solo they have had before telling them to get ready to go up. Further, as the replacements stand at attention or try to salute, Courtney tells them, "stand at ease, we don't have any formality here," immediately signalling their place in the squadron.[37] However, at no point in the film do the replacement pilots drink with the senior flyers.[38]

Perhaps the most important scene in the establishment of the flyer-hero ethos and their camaraderie is the arrival of a captured German pilot—Hauptmann Müller—the man thought to have shot down and killed Scott. The thought of the meeting thrills Müller and the RFC pilots; Courtney asks if he would "drink a toast to the dead" and "to the day they'll blow us out of the skies." The men continue to drink and sing together, only interrupted by Hollister, who had recently lost a friend on a mission. When a British pilot collapses sobbing, Müller asks Courtney if he is a flyer. The question implies that such behaviour is unusual, even inappropriate for a pilot.[39] This fraternity is also apparent in the film's climax, when Courtney is shot down after his solo attack against the German munitions depot; as Courtney dies he exchanges salutes with the German pilot who shot him down.[40]

As Graham Dawson notes, the war-weariness of the 1920s and 1930s presented serious challenges to the warrior-hero narrative that had dominated British culture since the Napoleonic Wars.[41] Great War aviation films in the 1930s handled the issue of pacifism to varying degrees of effectiveness. Nearly every picture depicting the First World War in the air, including *Hell's Angels* and *The Dawn Patrol*, addresses the issue that Michael Paris has labelled the "prevailing mood" of the period.[42] Typically, filmmakers advanced their anti-war arguments by emphasizing the psychological trauma of the war or killing the protagonist. The 1933 film *Ace of Aces* is a prime example of Hollywood trying clumsily to send a pacifist message. Another work by screenwriter John Monk Saunders tells the story of a pacifist sculptor who becomes a cold-blooded killer after enlisting in the American aviation section. This is taken even further in *The Eagle and the Hawk*, when the film's protagonist gives an impassioned speech decrying war before committing suicide.[43] However, his comrades cover up the suicide to preserve his honour. In *Hell's Angels*, Roy and Monte die helping an Allied offensive, while in *The Dawn Patrol* Courtney dies destroying a German munitions depot.

In *Hell's Angels*, the pacifist message is clear, if clumsy. Roy, of course, is proud of his military service and his abilities as a pilot: he glows when Helen (Jean Harlow) compliments his uniform, and answers back quickly and with pride to correct a woman who mistakes him for an infantry officer. When he returns from his first solo flight (the first time the viewer sees him in his flight gear), he greets his comrades with enthusiasm. Clearly, he embodies the warrior elements of the flyer persona: he has a firm sense of duty and responsibility, and is an accomplished combat pilot.[44] Yet, Roy is portrayed in contrast to his brother—he reacts to military service less enthusiastically, but more vocally. When one of the brothers' fellow pilots returns from a mission with graphic details about the death of another aviator, Monte finds it intolerable: "Stop! I can't stand it!" After he is accused of cowardice, Monte yells out: "I'll get it sooner or later, we'll all get it! Isn't there any end?" Monte continues his awkward pacifist rhetoric after their commanding officer issues orders for that evening. He proclaims: "What are you fighting for—patriotism, duty? Are you mad? They are just words that politicians and profiteers use to get you to fight for them!"

The Dawn Patrol has a considerably more anti-war tone than *Hell's Angels*. The social and political contexts had changed significantly since 1930. By the release of *The Dawn Patrol* in Britain in early 1939, a malaise had settled in the liberal democracies of the West as the Great Depression continued to grip the United States, and Great Britain was only modestly recovering. Worse still, totalitarianism had spread across much of Europe and the continent seemed to be moving toward war. Also, ample evidence of the airplane's destructive potential had collected since 1930: the Italians had used it to drop mustard gas during the Ethiopian war; Japan had launched extensive bombing raids in China; and, most infamously, the German Condor Legion had razed Guernica in April 1937.

The nervous, fidgety, tattered Major Brand clearly advances the anti-war message of the film. First, Brand acts as a source for much of the anti-war tone of the film; at numerous points he laments what the war has done to the young men of Britain, and the country itself. He is often shown on the telephone defending his undertrained and poorly equipped pilots from the dangerous orders of his superiors. He also acts as a champion for the British flyer, saying on more than one occasion that they do their best and never complain about their missions. Still, his sense of duty outweighs his feelings for the flyers under his command: "you know what this place is? A slaughterhouse and I'm the butcher!" Courtney, despite his clear disdain for Brand, seems to understand his commanding officer's position, stating "I'm not blaming anyone" when they argue over inexperienced pilots. The statement implies that he blames the war and those who got Britain involved; he will reiterate this point later. This contrast is also seen in his relationship with drink. Unlike the other flyers, who enjoy alcohol and the company that comes with it, Brand sips sherry alone while sitting in front of a fire.

Brand's stress comes to a head when he receives word that he will be promoted, and chooses Courtney to replace him as squadron leader. He declares that Courtney will now have to endure the stress and pain that comes from the responsibility of command. Once promoted, Courtney is transformed from a flyer-hero to a tortured commander. The change is captured by Major Brand's parting words:

> So far the war has been a personal adventure for you, full of boom and glory. As an individual flyer you have been admirable and you have evaded responsibility with equally supreme skill, disobeyed orders, blamed me, accused me of putting kids into canvas coffins. Well listen to this, HQ loved your raid this morning so much that they've appointed me up to wing. And before I go, I am ordered to appoint someone in my place, here at my place at this little desk. That somebody is going to be you. See you how you like it, Mr. Squadron Commander Courtney![45]

Courtney is quickly and harshly introduced to the other side of the air war with the arrival of a new group of replacements to send into combat, including Scott's younger brother, whom he ultimately sends to his death.

The filmmakers also used the Courtney character to advance an anti-war agenda. A conversation between Courtney and Donny is especially interesting and clearly reflects the pacifism of the time. In the conversation, Courtney takes a very different position than in the 1930 version of the film, when he instructs Donny to "take it like a man."[46] Instead, he delivers a pacifist monologue on the ills of war and those who cause it:

> [War is a] great big noisy rather stupid game that doesn't make sense at all. No one knows what it's all about or why. Here we are going at it hammer and tongs. I betcha those fellows over there feel the same way, the enemy. Then one day I suppose it'll all end as suddenly as it begun and we'll go home. 'Til some other bunch of criminal idiots sitting around a large table shoves us into another war and we'll go at it again.[47]

Courtney goes on to mention his father, a biology professor at Queen's (presumably Queen's University Belfast, where Flynn's actual father was a biology professor), who once told him "man is a savage animal who periodically, to relieve his nervous tension, tries to destroy himself." After Donny's death, the relationship between Courtney and Scott fractures, as do Courtney's nerves; he starts to resemble Brand. In the end, Courtney atones for Donny's death by flying a dangerous mission in Scott's place. Even before his death, the horrors of the Great War in the air had victimized Courtney. Indeed, Courtney, Scott, and Brand in *The Dawn Patrol* and Roy and Monte in *Hell's Angels* were and remain the classic image of First World War flyer-heroes: men who dutifully, swiftly, and with profound individuality inflicted death and destruction on their enemies, while escaping the guilt and realities of their deeds by drinking, singing, and carousing.

In addition to exploiting the star power, the studios deliberately evoked the memory of the war to promote the films. The First World War in the air featured prominently in the promotion of both pictures. In the case of *Hell's Angels*, images of the stars always included the men in RFC uniform, often gazing upward toward the sky, with looks of wonder on their faces. In an attempt to exploit the film's most famous scene—a Zeppelin attack on London—and ongoing British fears of aerial bombardment, numerous promotional posters featured a Zeppelin hovering above London or being attacked by RFC airplanes (in British promotional materials, the RFC roundel was conspicuous on the wings).[48]

More telling are the posters' taglines: "Aces Fight Terrific Air Battle for Film," "The Only Authentic Picture of Air Warfare Ever Produced," and "An Experience Brimming with the Essence of Life." These taglines were a clear attempt by United Artists to appeal to the popularity and commonly held views that First World War aviators duelled in a thrilling, exciting, and dangerous environment. Despite numerous other films made on the very same subject, the taglines sought to portray *Hell's Angels* as the first authentic depiction of the First World War in the air, implying there was a popular interest in how aviators fought.[49] There are a number of attempts in the promotional materials for *Hell's Angels* to emphasize the realism of the film. This realism was intended not only to provide a true depiction of the war in the air, but also to shock viewers and create interest in the film. To support their claims about the realistic depiction of aerial warfare, the promoters stated that members of the Overseas Aviators Club viewed the film and were impressed by how effectively it depicted the air war.[50] Indeed, studio attempts to promote the film actually went beyond the cinema and high street. They suggested collaborating with local RAF bases to promote the film, and recruited RAF officers to appear at premieres and speak to the accuracy of the aviation sequences. What can be said with certainty is that the stars and the characters they played (with the exception of Jean Harlow's sex appeal) were unimportant in the promotion of *Hell's Angels* in

Britain, especially when compared to how the memory of the Great War was evoked.

Shifting to *The Dawn Patrol*, without romantic subplots, Warner Bros. had little choice but to focus on Errol Flynn's star power and the air war. The use of Flynn as the primary marketing angle was not unusual in an era when cinemagoers often chose films based on the star.[51] However, *The Dawn Patrol's* marketing campaign used not only Flynn's star power, but also his aviation hobby. He, like many other celebrities of the period, was a licensed pilot. The campaign tried to connect the adventurous actor to the character he played in the film, claiming that Errol Flynn "could be the real-life version of the character he plays in *The Dawn Patrol*."[52]

In the promotional material, Flynn was depicted as the squadron's ace. An image of him standing in his flight gear holding a pistol, or in a flight helmet wearing goggles, occurs in almost all the marketing materials; nearly every poster, cutout, and newspaper advertisement featured Flynn as an aviator. In most photos he appears to be war-weary and tired (certainly representative of the popular perceptions of warfare at the time). In the photo of Flynn in flight gear, his character is obviously meant to be distressed; his face is dirty and carries an expression of fatigue and disillusionment. This image becomes even stronger when contrasted with how Flynn is depicted in the film before he is promoted—a rebellious, fun-loving, drinking, lethal ace flyer. In the only promotional material in which Flynn's character—and the other squadron members, for that matter—appear to be smiling and enjoying themselves, they are drinking alcohol either from sherry glasses or straight from bottles.

Along with Flynn, Warner Bros. also emphasized the masculinity and acting talents of each of the leads: Niven, Rathbone, and Flynn were all praised in the promotional materials for their ability to project "strong, virile honest masculine emotion." Cinemagoers would have been used to seeing Niven, Rathbone, and Flynn sharing the screen in swashbuckling roles. Warner Bros. claimed that the men in *The Dawn Patrol* were the greatest collection of male actors ever to share the screen.[53] What is especially interesting about this is Warner Bros.'s focus on the actors' presentation of masculinity, both on screen and in the promotional materials. Their weathered uniforms, grooming, behaviour, and postures all convey notions of strength, virility, and toughness.[54]

The flyers presented in the marketing materials for *The Dawn Patrol* were personifications of the film's pacifist tone, appearing more war-weary and restless than the strictly heroic depictions in promotional materials for films like *The Eagle and the Hawk*. For example, promotional material for the original *The Dawn Patrol* (1930) and *The Eagle and the Hawk* emphasized the star-power of the two leads (Richard Barthelmess and Cary Grant) rather than making them seem tortured or weathered. Conversely, in the promotional material for *The Dawn Patrol*, Flynn and his comrades were presented as tragic heroes: "untrained, unknowing and unafraid, they roared into each blood red dawn on fighting wings of glory! Gay reckless gallant, boys all … they battled for women they'd never seen, for love they might never know!" At the same time, there was an effort to connect this fatalism to other popular perceptions of the pilot as reckless and rebellious: "their laughter is louder, their love gayer, their courage more reckless, for every dawn may be their last."[55] Still, the fact that these warriors were pilots—and in the public's eye a unique form of warrior—was not lost on the film's promoters, who were always sure to connect them to their reckless and hedonistic personas: "the frolicking flyers who night after night before they take off on their death-dealing dawn patrols join in mad fun are real men whose spirit it is easy to understand."[56] This theme is echoed in numerous newspaper articles supplied by Warner Bros., all of which emphasized the dangers of flying during the First World War and the gallantry of British aviators. Another such article declared the film to be "a story of British wartime aviation, a moving and exciting compound of the pitiful, needless, gallantry of youth and the calmer courage of maturity."[57]

Warner Bros. also tried to emphasize the dangers of aerial warfare. They claimed that most Great War aviators did not survive more than 4.5 hours in the air and that pilots were "sent to certain death" when they enlisted in the RFC.[58] While this was true of British aviators during the air war's worst period (spring 1915), it certainly does not speak for the whole conflict. It seems that Warner Bros. tried to create a sense that these were typical British aviators during the First World War, and the film was merely capturing an ordinary time in the service of RFC pilots. The characters' effort to cope with the dangers of flying, and, more sensationally, "certain death," was an important selling point for Warner Bros.[59] Additionally, the studio suggested that it was "timely" to use the newspaper as a forum for discussion of the warlike nature of human beings, the prospect of future war, and the role that bombers would play.[60] Indeed, film promotional angles are closely related to popular sentiments of the time, including those regarding war and flying.

Presumably taking a cue from the promoters of *Hell's Angels*, Warner Bros. suggested that local cinema owners encourage the RAF to help promote the film and enhance its authenticity by having airmen share their war stories at screenings. It was also thought the RAF might help by donating surplus uniforms, propellers, airplane parts, and literature for cinemas to display in lobbies.[61] An especially interesting anecdote that highlights not only how the film was marketed to the British public, but also reveals the level of interest in the Great War, involves the premiere of *The Dawn Patrol* in the town of Keighley, West Yorkshire. For the premiere, the Ritz Keighley was turned into a miniature aerodrome: windsocks were placed on the theatre's flagpoles; planes were brought in from the local flying club and placed on the street adjacent to the theatre; local RFC veterans attended the showing in uniform; Marks and Spencer donated toy airplanes to decorate the lobby of the cinema; and the local air cadets held a parade in front of the cinema. The locals used the premiere of the film as a way to remember the Great War, not unlike the Cenotaph, cemeteries, or other cultural forms. This was not just a film distribution company pushing thrills and ideas on a population, but people acting out of their own interest in the film's subject matter.[62]

Assessing public responses to film during the interwar years is exceptionally difficult, but as Janet S.K. Watson has established it is possible to get a general sense of public reception using newspapers and trade reviews.[63] Reviews, while praising the aerial sequences and adventure in each film, also praised the films as realistic portrayals of the Great War in the air. *Hell's Angels* was generally well received by British film critics.[64] The *Bioscope* judged it an "amazing picture of aerial warfare [that has] wonderful artistic value"; these qualities, said both the *Bioscope* and *Picturegoer Weekly*, would have "impressed any audience."[65] All told, the *Bioscope* stated that the "amazing picture of aerial warfare" with "wonderful artistic value … will be acclaimed by the British public."[66] *Picturegoer* stated that the film was a comprehensive and realistic look at aviation during the First World War. In some cases, the realism of the film went too far—pilots being shot and coughing up blood was seen as unnecessary and overly intense.[67] This, as in Connelly's findings regarding the Royal Navy, suggests a pacified and glorified interest in realistic cinematic depictions of war during the interwar years.

The presence of government officials and members of the British aviation community at the premiere lent credibility to reviewers' claims about the film's realism. Some of the notable attendees were Thomas Shaw, secretary of state for war, James Henry Thomas, secretary of state for dominion affairs, the ambassadors from Belgium, Hungary, China, and Argentina, and celebrity flyer Sir Alan Cobham. Undoubtedly, Cobham's star-power was meant to do more than simply confirm the film's historical accuracy.

He was arguably the most famous aviator in Great Britain at the time, and his appearance at the premiere would have drawn the attention of the British public. Along with cabinet ministers and dignitaries, a large number of current and former RAF pilots attended, including Lieutenant-Colonel J.T.C. Brazon, assessor of the R101 disaster, Lieutenant P. Connor, a transatlantic aviator, and Canadian pilot Captain J.L. Boyd.

The Dawn Patrol was also well received by British film critics, especially for its realistic depiction of aerial warfare. *Picturegoer Weekly*'s review emphasized the character development in the film, particularly its depiction of the men as tortured yet rebellious, citing their heavy drinking and theft of a motorcycle as examples. The review also explores the darker elements of being an RFC pilot during the First World War, and how they were "dealing death" as they flew through the sky. The fatalism of the squadron's pilots is also a focus of the *Picturegoer Weekly* review. It claims that the film tried to create a story in which the viewer could understand the daily mental anguish of aviators. To corroborate the film's realism, it also mentions that most pilots were pushed through flying courses in England, leaving them woefully unprepared for combat. To this end, the review specifically mentioned Brand's comments about the squadron being a "slaughterhouse," and he (later Courtney) the butcher.[68]

The review of *The Dawn Patrol* in the *Monthly Film Bulletin* also explored the film's depiction of the air war's darker elements. It discussed at length the importance of Courtney's transformation from a reckless aviator to a tortured and serious commander, and emphasized the sacrifice that Courtney ultimately makes to atone for sending Scott's brother to his death.[69] Indeed, *Monthly Film Bulletin* signalled "the strain and tension on those who have to command in war" as the main theme of *The Dawn Patrol*. The *Cinema* also emphasized the realistic depiction of the struggles of aviators during the First World War, praising the film for its exploration of the tortured characters of the squadron without "recourse to sentimentality or theatrical effect."[70] British newspaper reviews also emphasized the realistic treatment of the pilots' struggles with the reality of war. The *Times* praised *The Dawn Patrol* while critiquing previous, more sanitized depictions of the air war: "The sphere of modern war, which appears to be still made for individual heroism, has often been used as a pretext for the heroics of popular fiction, but here it is treated with consistent, implacable, and extremely impressive realism."[71] According to reviewers, the film's sombre tone was only enhanced by the strong performance of the leads. Flynn, Rathbone, and Niven were lauded for their ability to portray First World War aviators.

The *Times* also praised the performances, especially Niven's, who was "brilliant" in his portrayal of the descent of Scott from a reckless and friendly flyboy to a disillusioned pilot. The reviewers of *The Dawn Patrol* clearly saw the film for what it is: a sombre and cynical depiction of life in an RFC squadron during the First World War, which, despite *Hell's Angels*'s claims of realism, actually hit closer to the mark.

NOTES

1. *Hell's Angels*, directed by Howard Hughes, Caddo Company, 1930, and *The Dawn Patrol*, directed by Edmund Goulding, Warner Bros., 1938.

2. Germany was the first country to make celebrities of its flyers, and France was the first to adopt the ace system. Germany's exploitation of them is well documented. See Peter Fritzsche, *A Nation of Fliers: German Aviation and the Popular Imagination* (Cambridge, M.A. thesis: Harvard University Press, 1992), and Robert Wohl, *A Passion for Wings: Aviation and the Western Imagination, 1908-1918* (New Haven: Yale University Press, 1994). Michael Paris, "Boys Books and the Great War," *History Today* 50, no. 11 (2000): 49.

3. Michael Paris, *Over the Top: The Great War and Juvenile Literature in Britain* (London: Praeger, 2004), 61.

4. Linda Robertson, *The Dream of Civilized Warfare: The First World War Flying Aces and the American Imagination* (Minneapolis: University of Minnesota Press, 2003), 209–13.

5. Susan Kent, *Making Peace: The Reconstruction of Gender in Interwar Britain* (Princeton: Princeton University Press, 1993), 49.

6. Robertson, *The Dream of Civilized Warfare*, 95, 161.

7. A. Bowdoin Van Riper, *Imaging Flight: Aviation and Popular Culture* (College Station: Texas A&M Press, 2004), 36.

8. Goldstein, *The Flying Machine and Modern Literature* (Bloomington: Indiana University Press, 1986), 91; Henry Newbolt, *Tales of the Great War* (London: Longman's Green, 1916), 248–49; Michael Paris, "The Rise of the Airman: The Origins of Air Force Elitism, 1908-1918," *Journal of Contemporary History* 28, no. 1 (1993): 123–41. Newbolt is often cited as the instigator of this idea of the "knights of the air." Robertson, *The Dream of Civilized Warfare*, 157–63. The British Government used not just the ideals of the medieval knight—honour, duty, chivalry, courage—but also their participation in crusades to try to encourage conscription. Goldstein, *The Flying Machine and Modern Literature*, 87. The idea of a crusade fit well with the broader British propaganda effort during the Great War. It focused on depicting the German "Hun" as a barbaric, savage, and ruthless murderer.

9. Paris, *Over the Top*, 68

10. Ibid., 56. Goldstein, *The Flying Machine and Modern Literature*, 88; Van Riper, *Imagining Flight*, 41; and Robertson, *The Dream of Civilized Warfare*, 97–104.

11. Ibid., 87, 98.

12. Samuel Hynes, *A War Imagined: The First World War and English Culture* (London: Bodley Head, 1990); Paul Fussell, *The Great War and Modern Memory* (Oxford: Oxford University Press, 1975).

13. Janet S.K. Watson, *Fighting Different Wars: Experience, Memory, and the First World War in Britain* (Cambridge: Cambridge University Press, 2004), 188–95. Vera Brittain, *Testament of Youth: An Autobiographical Study of the Years 1900–1925* (London: Virago Press, 1933), Robert Graves, *Goodbye to All That* (London: Cassell, 1957), Erich Maria Remarque, *All Quiet on the Western Front* (London: Little, Brown, 1929), Siegfried Sassoon, *Memoirs of an Infantry Officer* (London: Faber and Faber, 1931). For more, see Modris Eksteins, *Rites of Spring: The Great War and the Birth of the Modern Age* (Toronto: Lester, Orpen and Dennys, 1989), and Fussell, *The Great War and Modern Memory*.

14. Michael Paris, "Boys Books and the Great War"; Michael Paris, *Warrior Nation: Images of War in British Popular Culture 1850–2000* (London: Reaktion Books, 2000); Jay Winter, *Sites of Memory, Sites of Mourning* (Cambridge: Cambridge University Press, 1995). Watson also argues that because pacifist works became so popular with the British public during the 1930s, they also became extremely popular with scholars (Fussell and Eksteins are examples), homogenizing the public discourse around anti-war commemoration and ignoring other reactions.

15. Jonathan Vance, *Death So Noble: Memory, Meaning and the First World War* (Vancouver: UBC Press, 1997), 3–11.

16. Winter, *Sites of Memory, Sites of Mourning*; Karel Dibbets and Bert Hogenkamp, eds., *Film and the First World War* (Amsterdam: Amsterdam University Press, 1995); Pierre Sorlin, "Cinema and the Memory of the Great War," in *The First World War and Popular Cinema*, ed. Michael Paris (New Brunswick, NJ: Rutgers University Press, 2000); Modris Eksteins, "The Cultural Impact of the Great War," in *The First World War and Popular Cinema* (New Brunswick, NJ: Rutgers University Press, 2000).

17. Michael Paris, "Enduring Heroes: British Feature Films and the First World War, 1919–1997," in *The First World War and Popular Cinema*, 53. For example, Fussell does not consider the film version of *All Quiet on the Western Front* (directed by Lewis Milestone, Universal, 1930), despite its importance to the construction of interwar (and beyond) notions of the Great War. Williams, *Media, Memory and the First World War*, 31. Sorlin also points to the importance of *All Quiet* in shaping both the memory of the Great War and the history of the cinema. Sorlin, "Cinema and the Memory of the Great War," 13–22.

18. Dominick A. Pisano, "Constructing the Memory of Aerial Combat in the First

World War," in *Legend, Memory, and the Great War in the Air*, ed. Dominick A. Pisano, Thomas J. Dietz, Joanne M. Greenstein, and Karl S. Schneide (Washington: Smithsonian, 1992), 13.

19. Paris, *Warrior Nation*, 154; and "Boys Books and the Great War," 49.

20. Paris, *Warrior Nation*, 147, 156.

21. Paris, "Boys Books and the Great War," 49.

22. Francis, *The Flyer*, 14.

23. Paris, "Boys Books and the Great War," 49. Other flying stories often included spy adventures.

24. Ibid., 160–63. Paris more specifically notes the adventurous aviation film.

25. Michael Paris, *From the Wright Brothers to* Top Gun (Manchester: Manchester University Press, 1995), 33–34.

26. John Whiteclay Chambers, "The Movies and the Anti-war Debate in America, 1930–1941," *Film and History* 36, no. 1 (Fall 2006): 413, and Paris, "Wings," 11.

27. Rudy Behlmer, "World War I Aviation Films," *Films in Review* (August–September 1967): 414.

28. *The Kinematograph Year Book: 1940* (London: Kinematograph Weekly), 1940.

29. Richards, *Age of the Dream Palace*, 12–24.

30. Michael Paris, "Wings," in *The Movies as History: Visions of the Twentieth Century*, ed. David Ellwood (Gloucestershire: Sutton Publishing, 2000), 11–15.

31. Mark H. Glancy, *When Hollywood Loved Britain* (Manchester: Manchester University Press, 1999). The other films were *Body and Soul*, *The Eagle and the Hawk*, and *Lilac Time*.

32. James Farmer, *Celluloid Wings* (New York: McGraw-Hill 1984), 49; Beril Skogsberg, *Wings on the Screen* (New York: A.S. Barnes, 1981), 8.

33. Skogsberg, *Wings on the Screen*, 23.

34. This image of the aviator was taken with the camera mounted directly behind the propeller, facing backwards—the legacy of cinematographer Harry Perry, who had also done camerawork for *Wings*, *Hell's Angels*, and the original *The Dawn Patrol*. Behlmer, "The First World War Aviation Films," 415.

35. *The Dawn Patrol*, 12 min.; *Ace of Aces*, 12 min. The mess in *Ace of Aces* is adorned with cartoons, airplane wreckage, and empty liquor bottles.

36. *The Dawn Patrol*, 12 min. It should be noted that Major Brand, the men's squadron leader, is also drinking. However, he is sipping sherry in his office while writing a letter to the recently killed pilot's widow.

37. *The Dawn Patrol*, 23 min. Youthful replacements feature in a number of aviation films.

38. Separation in mess halls was common practice in the RFC during the First World War. The National Archives, London, Air 1/2391/228/11/145, The Service Experiences of Flt. Lt. G. Martyn, L.N. Hollingsworth, T.H.G. Downing, C.J. MacKay, N.M. Bottomley, R.M. Hill, N. Leslie, and E.M. Pollard.

39. Hawks deliberately inserted this scene to show audiences how important chivalry was to aviators during the war. Farmer, *Celluloid Wings*, 62.

40. *The Dawn Patrol*, 52 min.

41. Dawson, *Soldier Heroes*, 236.

42. Paris, "Wings," 9.

43. *Picturegoer Weekly*, 11 May 1935. This story can also be found in films like *Hell in the Heavens* (1934), in which the lead (played by Werner Baxter) is a tattered and nervous aviator, as well as in *Legion of the Condemned* (1928) and *Young Eagles* (1930).

44. *Hell's Angels*, 69 min.

45. *The Dawn Patrol*, 58 min.

46. Farmer, *Celluloid Wings*, 125.

47. *The Dawn Patrol*, 70 min.

48. *Special Souvenir Number, Gaumont-British Pictorial: Hell's Angels*, British Film Institute (BFI) Library.

49. *Exhibitors' Campaign Book: Hell's Angels*, BFI Library.

50. *Special Souvenir Number, Gaumont-British Pictorial: Hell's Angels*.

51. Richards, *Age of the Dream Palace*, 24.

52. *Warner Bros. Campaign Plan: The Dawn Patrol* (London: Warner House, Wardour Street), BFI Library. Ironically, Flynn was rejected for military service because of numerous, and sometimes embarrassing, health concerns.

53. *Warner Bros. Campaign Plan: The Dawn Patrol*.

54. One publicity photo shows Flynn, Rathbone, and Niven gazing skyward with obviously distressed looks on their faces; despite the concern, there is still an air of confidence and strength. This image is contrasted by a photo on the same page of the lead characters toasting while smiling. *Warner Bros. Campaign Plan: The Dawn Patrol*.

55. *Warner Bros. Campaign Plan: The Dawn Patrol*. There were many references to love and romance in the marketing materials for *The Dawn Patrol*, even though there are no love interests in the film and (unlike most aviation films in the period) no woman even appears on screen.

56. "The Dawn Patrol Is a Thrilling and Inspiring Film," *Warner Bros. Campaign Plan: The Dawn Patrol*.

57. "The Dawn Patrol Arrives," *Warner Bros. Campaign Plan: The Dawn Patrol*.

58. *Warner Brothers Campaign Plan: The Dawn Patrol*.

59. The National Archives, London, Air 1/39/15/7, "Casualties RFC/RAF for Entire War."

60. "Timely Topic for Debate," *Warner Bros. Campaign Plan: The Dawn Patrol*.

61. "Other Exploitation," *Warner Bros. Campaign Plan: The Dawn Patrol*.

62. "Air Cadets Parade for Dawn Patrol," *Kinematograph Weekly*, 27 July 1939.

63. Watson, *Fighting Different Wars*, 187. Trade reviews such as *Kinematograph Weekly*, *Bioscope*, *Monthly Film Bulletin* (published by the British Film Institute itself), and the *Cinema* were published to help British cinema proprietors choose what film reels to rent. They provided comprehensive reviews that discussed plot, production value, actors, and critical points of appeal. Their assessments of films were almost entirely focused on gauging public attitudes and tastes. As a result, their opinions of films can be considered important in determining what appealed to the British public at a given time.

64. This is the consensus view of the picture, and is echoed in Wohl, Paris, and Skogsberg. Skogsberg contends that the film was better received by the public than by critics, but offers no evidence of this.

65. "Box-Office Film Reviews: Hell's Angels," *Bioscope*, 29 October 1930; Lionel Collier, "Realism Costs £800,000," *Picturegoer Weekly*, December 1930.

66. "Box-Office Film Reviews: Hell's Angels."

67. Collier, "Realism Costs £800,000."

68. *Picturegoer Weekly*, 2 April 1939.

69. "Dawn Patrol," *Monthly Film Bulletin*, 1 December 1938, 278.

70. "The Dawn Patrol," *Cinema: News and Property Gazette*, 1 December 1938, 37.

71. "New Films in London," *The Times*, 20 February 1939, 10.

OTTO DIX AND THE GREAT WAR

Reality, Memory, and the Construction of Identity in *The Trench* (1923) and the Portfolio *The War* (1924)

MICHÈLE WIJEGOONARATNA

Otto Dix was one of the few German artists who served on the Western Front for the duration of the Great War and who survived the horrors of trench warfare. His direct combat experience yielded a deeply subjective visual chronicle of his days as a soldier, and, in a series of self-portraits and hundreds of drawings done from 1914 to 1918, Dix both imagined and experienced the war.[1] Before he had even completed military training, Dix anticipated battle. He aligned his own identity as a soldier with existing cultural precepts of German wartime identity that combined enthusiasm for battle with national loyalty and a perceived heroic masculinity.[2] Once he was released from active service, he initially internalized his war encounters only to resurrect them from memory in his 1923 painting *The Trench* (now lost), and in a 1924 print cycle of fifty etchings simply titled *The War* that had been commissioned by his dealer, Karl Nierendorf, who exhibited them in his Berlin Gallery in August 1924.[3] In the introduction to the print portfolio, the poet and writer Max Hermann Neisse wrote that Dix's *The War* should be distributed as a "document of truth" to counter bloodthirsty, military propaganda that was being publicly disseminated in the Weimar Republic by 1924.[4] Though *The War* and *The Trench* depicted Dix's wartime experience with verisimilitude, their credibility as "document[s] of truth" about the war is problematic and raises questions. Do these images represent an accurate testimony of Dix's experience, or an untrustworthy reconstruction of it based on postwar political influences? Furthermore, is the intention of Dix's painting *The Trench* and his subsequent *The War* portfolio to privilege reminiscence or remembrance? Are the depictions of death, sex, and violence that are hallmarks of *The War* portfolio a reification of Dix's war experience that he simply could not commit to paper between 1914 and 1918, or do they express a conflation of Dix's war and postwar experiences and reflect a particular narrative agenda designed to solidify his reputation as an artist? Two self-portraits, one made after the war and the other during the hostilities, emphasize these issues.

In the second set of artist proofs of *The War* portfolio that was dedicated to Nierendorf, Dix included a self-portrait.[5] The pen drawing *How I*

Otto Dix, *How I Looked as a Soldier* (*So sah Ich als Soldat aus*), 1924. Watercolour, pen, and wash on paper · 16 15/16 x 13 3/8 in. (43 x 34 cm). Berlinische Galerie, Landesmuseum für Moderne Kunst, Fotografie und Architektur. © 2014 Artists Rights Society (ARS), New York/VG Bild-Kunst, Bonn.

Looked as a Soldier depicts an inexorable Dix, stern-faced in his worn field artillery uniform cradling the threatening shaft of a machine gun.

His grim countenance roughened by an unshaven jaw and his belligerently alert eyes glaring from under his cold, steel helmet portray Dix as a pugnacious fighter and war hero. The callousness of the image is reinforced by the medium. The thin, sparse pen strokes have been rendered with a swift but precise linearity that stresses the cold brutality of warfare. The tears on the uniform sleeves and the (presumed) bullet hole in the helmet authenticate the image.[6]

However, the visible trace of warfare and its impact on Dix's uniform both support and moderate his heroic self-portrayal. On one hand, he is a soldier who has championed the war; on the other, he is just a man who has survived where others have fallen. Dix's self-possessed stance and authoritative manner endow the image with a performative quality that adds to its ambiguity.[7] By attaching this image to his 1924 *The War* portfolio, Dix identifies himself as a witness to and participant in the war, and projects himself as both survivor and hero. The implication is that the self-portrait is a rendering of a personal *Kriegserlebnis*, which stood in stark opposition to official remembrance of the soldier's experience. Dix portrayed himself from memory, but with an alleged realism that should leave the viewer with no doubt about his unflinching vigour during the war. His relentlessly penetrating gaze conveys the impression that he has seen and experienced the atrocities of war and, thus, his image stands in stark contrast to his 1916 *Self-Portrait with Cap* that was painted while he was active in the trenches.

Here, Dix is recognizable from his angular face, Greek nose, and high cheekbones that he emphasized by careful shading in soft charcoal. Instead of a steel helmet, a soft uniform cap identifies him as a soldier, but the eyes are shut and replaced by heavily shaded quadrilateral patches—a shadow caused by the brim of his hat. Dix's face shuts out the viewer, but also prevents him from seeing out. Though the face exudes strength and resolve, the closed eyes indicate that Dix could not, or would not, bear witness to the events surrounding him while he was in the trenches in 1916. If knowledge is acquired through the visual apprehension of the surrounding world, then seeing is the origin of knowing. By shielding his own vision and blocking our ability to see his eyes, Dix invites a reading of his wartime work in which his knowledge about war is based on a purely subjective construction of his own experience. In contrast, *How I Looked as a Soldier* declares an objective, external experience that corresponds to, but also challenges, the way war was collectively visualized in 1924. Memory is the mediating factor that bridges the temporal distance and perceptual span between these two works. In the ironic disparity between his two self-portraits, one drawn during the height of hostilities yet failing to reflect their impact, and the other contrived as a memory of them ten years later, we realize that Dix's war-related works are part of a complex creative process. In particular, when contrasted with the drawings done while in the trenches, it becomes apparent that Dix's *The War* portfolio and *The Trench* are the results of the unconscious absorption of experience and a conscious manipulation of memory. They function as rhetorical devices that deliberately fuse memory and reality to establish Dix's postwar identity as an arbiter and interpreter of the First World War.

The Trench and *The War* helped establish Dix as the social and political critic of his time, a reputation that endures to this day. With their focus on death and destruction, they are assumed to portray realistically the atrocities of war, and their veracity as a historical record of Dix's wartime experience has rarely been questioned. Some scholars view these works as an indictment of the horrors of the First World War and Dix as an artist who mercilessly unmasked these events. In this scenario Dix, the critical realist and political radical, becomes the purveyor of a pacifist credo, a righteous harbinger of the terrible course of events to which Germany would succumb by 1939.[8] The other, more frequently expressed construct emphasizes the psychological impact of the war on the artist. Here, an apolitical Dix devotes himself to depictions of the war as a way to purge himself of his own traumatic experience.[9] Both of these analyses are problematic, and though Dix was generally laconic when discussing his war works, he emphatically maintained that, "I just needed to experience everything exactly. That's what I wanted. So, therefore I am not a pacifist at all."[10] In the same context, when asked about the compulsion to paint particular images, Dix dismissed the idea that he made these works as a form of self-therapy. "It is not as if one does something to make peace with one's soul. In my opinion one does not think of that at all," he stated in an interview a few years before he died. *The Trench* and the *The War* portfolio thus question whether Dix returned to the subject of war in the 1920s to confront the "rubble that was constantly in my dreams," or as a strategic maneuver to enhance his reputation and confirm his artistic identity.[11]

Even the most superficial research into *The Trench* and *The War* portfolio reveals that there is a difference between a realistic portrayal of events and the interpretation of personal experience. In order to create his *The War* portfolio, Dix plumbed a variety of external sources, including documentary photography, to create brilliantly detailed etchings. These works are rendered with a dramatic realism that gives the illusion of the precise reproduction of memory. However, memory is often elusive. As the instrument of thought and feeling, it does not always correspond to the truth. Memory is socially and culturally constructed. It is a private mental contemplation that traverses the public sphere to function as a source for recognition of a shared experience. The analysis that follows seeks to address how *The Trench* and *The War* portfolio emerged from Dix's desire to become "famous an⌐   ⌐se works were not necessarily created as a therapeu   ⌐f the war or as a pacifist credo, but as a conscious   ⌐e on a scandalous reputation, and to be taken seriously a⌐   ⌐caustic postwar social conditions Dix encountered in Dres⌐   ⌐o 1922 ignited and fueled this ambition and provided visual fc⌐   ⌐s oeuvre of prostitutes and war cripples. The Dresden to which⌐   ⌐ed after the war was fraught with political tensions and socia⌐   ⌐. The failed 1918 November Revolution in Berlin spread to Dres⌐   ⌐inging clashes between workers' and soldiers' councils, and between the Social Democratic Party (SPD) and its rival Independent Social Democratic Party (USPD).[13] The city was also ravaged by the same social problems that beset Berlin after the war. Public health initiatives and resources were severely stretched by the need to treat wounded and mutilated war veterans, as well as contain contagious and sexually transmitted diseases. Economic deprivation forced women, especially war widows, into prostitution, and infant mortality rose. The artist Hans Grundig, whose studio was next to Dix's, reported: "The sexual question encroached everywhere in the lives of people. It was ... not only discussed as a problem of class warfare and the battle for a new morality, but also thrust itself upon the question of general destitution that had above all forced women and girls into prostitution."[14] The social problems resulting from Germany's defeat in the war and not the war itself were the ones that captivated Dix upon his return to Dresden; as Willi Wolfradt would note, "Dix, with a whore in one arm and a war cripple in another, calls out their century before the court of an annihilating judgment."[15]

Dix began work on *The Trench* in 1921, and, soon after it was finished in 1923, embarked on *The War* portfolio. Both works were created at a moment when Dix needed to develop his critical reputation while retaining his position as an avant-garde artist. In a photograph taken at the inauguration party of the Dresden Secession Group 1919, Dix sits among the most important founding members: the publisher Hugo Zehder and the artists Lasar Segall and Conrad Felixmüller. He is distinguishable by his detachment from the others and strikes a pose for posterity. Dix's ambition to be noticed, apparent in the photograph, translated into an unfailing ambition for professional and commercial success. This desire was captured in a 1919 letter in which Dix berates Felixmüller for publicly disparaging his work—"you seem to have put my light under a bushel so that yours could shine more brightly"—while acknowledging that he needed money as well as recognition.[16]

In terms of his immediate postwar reputation, Dix struggled to be taken seriously at first. Even the galleries most open to exhibiting the latest contemporary trends balked at some of Dix's work. In a letter to Kurt Günther, he wrote: "Richter is shitting his pants and doesn't want to exhibit me … absolutely no art dealer has the guts to exhibit me."[17]

In fact, Dix needed to counter a great deal of unenthusiastic criticism. The established critics not only failed to recognize Dix's talents, but his raw energy, anger, and effusive desire to be noticed unleashed a barrage of negative publicity. The Dresden publisher and art critic Rudolf Kaemmerer referred to Dix as a "wild, completely untamed temperament [for whom] a clear development is not yet recognizable."[18] In a review that criticized Dix's *Self Portrait as Mars* (1914–15) for being a "futurist salad, just not a painting," Carl Puetzfeld, critic for the *Dresdner Neueste Nachrichten*, referred to his nature as "wild and unruly."[19] As Dix began to adopt the meticulous realism that would result in his *The War* portfolio, critics still reacted with derision. Paul Fechter, the highly esteemed critic for the *Dresdner Neueste Nachrichten* who had supported the Expressionists before the war, pejoratively declared: "Dix is also represented once again with his monstrosities, proving himself to be the Richard Müller of the younger generation."[20] As did Max Osborn, cultural editor of the *Vossische Zeitung* in Berlin, who wrote that Dix's work was a "combination of fierce humor and dogged, Richard-Müller-esque accuracy."[21] Perhaps the most damning complaint about Dix came from the esteemed modern poet Theodor Däubler, who claimed that Dix was a "surprise," but someone who failed to dazzle: "Almost everyone passes over his paintings, mostly without even shrugging their shoulders," he judged dismissively.[22] Even Dix's colleague Conrad Felixmüller, who in 1921 had published a monograph on the author, wrote: "Dix is lonely, desperate and totally impoverished. He knows that no one will buy these pictures from him; he knows that he is not happy."[23]

While most of this criticism can be categorized as a reactionary or premature judgment on Dix's work (Däubler, after all, commissioned a portrait from Dix in 1927), Dix's intentions to help found the Dresden

Secession Group 1919 were probably motivated as much by a desire to gain critical recognition and an opportunity to exhibit as they were to develop post-expressionist art in Dresden.

Dix enjoyed good exposure in Dresden with the Secession Group, if not critical or commercial success, and his brief participation in the Berlin Dada movement in 1919–20 provided sufficient distinction that Lovis Corinth invited him to participate in the 1921 summer exhibition of the Berlin Secession. This external recognition culminated in 1923 when Max Liebermann, president of the Berlin Academy, invited Dix to exhibit at the Prussian Academy of Art.[24] The interest in Dix taken by the Berlin Dada artists, his participation in the 1920 International Dada Exhibition in Berlin, and his inclusion in the Berlin-based November Group all conferred notoriety on Dix. It was the scandalous confiscation of the painting *Girl in Front of a Mirror* (1921) and the resulting trial for indecency, however, that turned his critical fortunes. In a letter to Dix, the editor and publisher of the communist paper *Die Freiheit*, Felix Stössinger, congratulated Dix on his troubles: "The confiscation of your paintings pleased me greatly. Talent becomes most effective with the indignation of bourgeois society."[25] The publicity created by Dix's trial provided the opportunity for his work to gain recognition in Berlin and the rest of Germany.[26]

Instrumental to Dix's success was the sudden interest in the artist taken by Paul Ferdinand Schmidt, the director of the Städtisches Museum in Dresden. Schmidt lent his support to several contemporary artists, including Kandinsky, Nolde, Rousseau, and Grosz, and built up a considerable collection of their works for the museum. Other museum directors soon emulated Schmidt's commitment to Dix's work by purchasing it for their collections, the most controversial being the Wallraf-Richartz Museum's purchase of *The Trench* in 1923.[27]

The support of German museums for Dix's art coincided with the most important professional contact Dix was to make: his dealer Karl Nierendorf, who quickly became Dix's most avid supporter, and, in 1920 and 1921, purchased several works from him. It is probable that Nierendorf suggested to Dix in 1923 that he should bring out a war portfolio to coincide with the ten-year anniversary of the First World War, though there is no hard evidence to substantiate this claim. Nevertheless, it must also have been Dix's painting *The Trench*, and the controversy that surrounded it, that occasioned the series of etchings for *The War* in 1924. *The Trench* and the scandal it unleashed have been extensively analyzed elsewhere, though little attention has focused on the effect it had on Dix's reputation.[28] The cultural capital earned from the public storm surrounding *The Trench* provided Dix with the opportunity to create *The War* portfolio. The two works also share similar characteristics: a heightened sense of realism and a similar means of reproducing memory through a combination of actual experience and accumulated knowledge.

The Trench depicts an exposed trench in the grey light of day following a brutal shelling whose savage explosions have torn apart landscape and human flesh. It is filled with dismembered bodies and bodily fragments. Brains and entrails spill from exploded bodies, with faces partially blown away. Life has been brutally extinguished and there is no dignity in death. One soldier has been hurled out of the trench only to lie impaled on stakes driven into the slithering mud. His place of eternal rest functions as a banner to mark the carnage below. In place of sympathy or outrage, however, Dix elicits revulsion from the viewer while retaining a sardonic wit. The dead soldier lies rigidly impaled on the stakes of the trench, but a sharp stake or sword rises up between his legs like an erect penis. The hand of the soldier's outstretched arm, clenched and stiff with rigor mortis, cannot quite grasp this perpetual priapism. Through this indication of sexualized vigour in the face of death, Dix recognized the visual equivalency between the life and death instincts. He understood that the same psychical energy fuelled sex and violence. Even in his 1916 war notebook he had cryptically observed, "Actually, in the end all wars are fought for, and on account of, the vulva."[29]

Dix began the painting while he was still in Dresden in 1921 and completed it following his move to Düsseldorf. Initially, Dix and Nierendorf planned to exhibit the work in Berlin, but because the French occupied the Rhineland/Ruhr where Dix was keeping the painting, it was impossible to transport it to Prussia. Hans Friedrich Secker, the director of the Wallraf-Richartz Museum in Cologne, entered into an agreement with Nierendorf to purchase the painting, but the cultural storm that attended its exhibition forced Secker to refuse the painting and Nierendorf was compelled to take it back.[30] Dix must have thought that the painting would cause a tremendous critical stir, and certainly Secker recognized that it would be the biggest sensation on opening night. It was displayed by the Wallraf-Richartz Museum on 12 January 1923 behind a curtain so that visitors to the museum would not feel obliged to see such provocative material.[31]

Critics recognized that concealing the painting was physically and metaphorically controversial, and Dix was both accused and applauded for unveiling the truth about the war. The critical reception of the work was divided along political lines, with writers on the left reveling in its documentary, accusative realism and conservative critics such as Julius Meier-Graefe castigating it as an insult to the heroic, palliative battle scenes rendered by Anton von Werner and Ludwig Dettmann. *The Trench* not only polarized the art world and offended bourgeois propriety, but was also a political affront on the German nation.[32] As Dora Apel points out, *The Trench* became the most explosive intervention in the Weimar debate between anti-war and patriotic forces.[33] By 1924, the year he published his *The War* portfolio, Dix's reputation was reaching a crescendo. On 24 August 1924, Nierendorf wrote enthusiastically to Dix, "you are now a famous man and known all over Germany."[34] Even the dealer Alfred Flechtheim, who had allegedly referred to Dix's work as "dirt" and the artist as a "painter of farts," had to concede: "with the exception of Dix nothing is of interest anymore, Dix is the big man ... today's Stuck."[35]

Dix cannot have known that *The Trench* would solidify his reputation when he conceived of and executed the painting between 1921 and 1923, so what was his purpose in painting it and following it up with *The War* portfolio some six years after the end of the war? The contemporary critic Curt Glaser seems to have identified Dix's intention when he called *The Trench* a "massive still life of horror.... The painting is a talent test, but it is also an act of violence, it is a hermaphrodite that neither works to ravish the viewer, nor give him pleasure."[36] The idea that Dix might have embarked on *The Trench* as a reception piece to display his painting ability gains credence from its unusually large size and the fact that Dix began the painting in Dresden and completed it in Düsseldorf, where he became the master student of Heinrich Nauen at the Düsseldorf Academy.[37] It seems just as likely, however, that Dix wanted to vilify the academic tradition of history painting. In the size of the painting and in the nature of the depiction, Dix followed established tenets of history painting as set out by Gottfried Ephraim Lessing in his *Laocöon: An Essay on the Limits of Poetry and Painting*: "Painting in its coexistent compositions, can employ only a single moment of the action, and must therefore choose the instant that is most laden with significance: that which makes most clear all that has preceded and is to follow."[38] *The Trench*, however, generates the opposite response from a conventional academic history painting. Instead of the grandeur of warfare, Dix exposed the underbelly of war in order to be seen as the "anti-Anton von Werner."[39] While his supporters applauded the "realism" of the picture, many critics decried it precisely for its lack of realism or *ésprit*. The work was not painted with the fine brushstroke that Dix had mastered in his prewar self-portraits, but with a materiality that led Meier-Graefe to complain that Dix had not *painted* brains, blood, and entrails, but that they physically garnished the canvas so that all that was missing was "to stick prepared clumps of blood [onto the work] like the cubists with their bits of newspaper and cigar lids."[40] Glaser picked up on the dissonance of the painting that extrinsically purported to be a history painting, but actually railed against the genre, by describing the painting as a "hermaphrodite." He detected that the painting combined contradictory elements, but did not further elucidate his comments except to say that it failed to satisfy.

In *The Trench*, Dix rendered the carnage of war with precision, but in spite of the meticulous attention to detail and emphasis on the gruesome human cost of battle, the painting represents a visual implausibility. The apparent eidetic nature of the image is demolished by its sophisticated theatricality. The corpse flung out of the trench and impaled in a state of eternal rigor mortis on the left, and the gas-mask glasses that dangle precariously on the right, form a rudimentary proscenium arch under which the scene is carefully staged. On this *theatrum mundi*, contorted bodies and burnt out vegetation are artfully constructed on the picture plane. Following a trip to the local hospital and morgue, where he made watercolours of brains and entrails and observed two female corpses that had been crudely gutted and sewn together, Dix rendered the various phases of human death and decay, which were then transferred onto the canvas.[41] The sketches he made in the morgue were also used as preparation for *The War* portfolio. In many other instances, Dix did not operate from memory but made generous use of the mangled faces of war cripples who populated the German streets. Glaser perceptively stated that the painting was both a still life and an act of violence. It is this element of contradiction combined into one image that jars the viewer. These two opposing forces, the stillness of death in the present and the petrified energy of the massacre from the immediate past, come together in an extreme close-up that evokes a distillation of memory that is at once reminiscence and remembrance.

The indication is that Dix came upon such a trench scene while he was serving at the front. Since he allegedly based his painting on his own experience, his vision of the trench became his indisputable bedrock of evidence about conditions during the war. Alfred Salmony empathized with Dix's depiction of war in *The Trench*, writing: "This is a healthy reaction to ... Salon peinture. Dix paints as he must with uninhibited creative power from the abundance of *seen* experiences."[42] Salmony regarded Dix as an authority on war because the artist had experienced it and his representation of the trench was therefore based on observed knowledge. However, this assessment fails to take into account how Dix might have conflated conscious observation with subsequent reflection and external stimuli. Other critics seemed to intuit this problem and exposed it in their reviews of the work. On the conservative side, Karl Scheffler dismissed Dix's realism: "He does not depict a trench with dismembered, decaying human cadavers clearly and objectively, but [paints] rather like Strathmann: preciously ornamental. His painting has the effect of a deep ocean, like an aquarium. This crass, unsparing art is perfumed, the inhumanity sentimental."[43] Even Glaser, who responded neutrally to *The Trench*, saw Dix's style as one in which the horrors of the dismembered corpses "do not stink of rot, but of perfume."[44]

These nuanced critiques that were at once repulsed by the painting, but could not accept it as visual evidence of a lived experience, point to the problems inherent in depicting war from memory. As historian Joan Wallach Scott has pointed out, experience and authenticity do not necessarily equate: "Experience is at once already an interpretation *and* something that needs to be interpreted. What counts as experience is neither self-evident nor straightforward, it is always contested and therefore always political."[45] This politicization is especially noticeable when an experience, such as war, is shared collectively, but expressed individually. The visceral and horrified reactions that critics such as Julius Meier-Graefe had to *The Trench* illustrate this point. While Meier-Graefe railed against the content and form of the painting (which made him want to "puke"), it was not as significant as his principal worry, that Dix had created a "German cultural document" that would damage the country's reputation. In his review of the painting, he wrote despairingly: "In Cologne I saw a few officers from over there standing in front of the document and made myself scarce so that I would not take in their objectively justified criticism."[46]

In 1923, British and French troops occupied Cologne and the German Ruhr was reeling from Franco-Belgian occupation. Paul Fechter echoed Meier-Graefe in his concerns that the Allies would view the painting as an official document of German attitudes that would lead to new disrespect of the Germans. There is no concrete evidence to suggest that Dix was being deliberately political *or* pacifist when he painted *The Trench*, but in comparison to his other war works, which until then were dominated by an affiliation with Berlin-Dada and therefore outside of the purview of conservative critics such as Meier-Graefe and Fechter, Dix had launched a determined salvo against academic art and officially sanctioned war paintings.

The effect of *The Trench* on the viewer thus throws up a critical conundrum; it is unclear whether Dix reconstructed his own experience, or used his experience to construct his artistic self. *The Trench* may have been a visual depiction of actual experience, but it was a subjective one devised specifically to represent who Dix was as an artist in 1923. Dix interpreted the war hermeneutically in *The Trench*, but he also engaged in an epistemological sleight-of-hand. Dix's war experience was not just an immutable transmission of an external event, but one calculated to illustrate his sense of self.

The experience conveyed in both *The Trench* and *The War* portfolio is expressed on two levels, according to the subtle distinction in the German language between "Erlebnis" and "Erfahrung"; the former is a direct occurrence and the latter is based on accumulated knowledge. There is a temporal difference between the two. An *Erlebnis* is an event that occurs to you; it has a defined beginning and an identifiable end. *Erfahrung* is something that you undergo; it draws you into an event and allows you to acquire a deeper knowledge about its effects. *Erlebnis* happens once, but *Erfahrung* is based on a set of cumulative experiences. Where the former can be immediately assigned to memory as a discrete unit, the latter will be processed with other occurrences of a similar nature in order to build a reservoir of understanding. *The Trench* and *The War* portfolio are therefore works of *Erfahrung*, but not necessarily of *Erlebnis*. In *The Trench*, Dix has compounded several recollections of bloodshed into one scene, presumably based on experience but also through information acquired about the war in its aftermath. Paul Ferdinand Schmidt perceived this layering of memory, knowledge, and narrative, and understood Dix's modus operandi: "With iron nerves, Dix has documented this bath of steel for all posterity; every square centimeter of this huge canvas ... is filled with horror, fetid stench and a feast of teeming maggots. In this painting nothing is exaggerated—it is only compressed. What remained of the non-living at ten [separate] places in a bombed out trench, Dix lumped together in a single spot."[47] Schmidt recognized that Dix overlapped several war experiences to produce the most dramatic image possible. It is this conflation of several remembered events and images onto one scene for dramatic effect that also informs the cumulative effect of the etchings from *The War* portfolio. In the portfolio, this premise works in reverse. Instead of layering several memories into one scene, Dix separated several, related actions into single, static events.

Schmidt's contention, that Dix had compressed his experience of war in *The Trench* to heighten its impact, contradicts the artist's later recollection of his war work in which he stated his commitment to a realistic depiction of events: "I was striving to paint the war objectively without wanting to arouse pity, without propaganda. I avoided depictions of battles. I didn't want any ecstatic exaggerations."[48] While Dix later chose to remember that his war work was not intended as a form of propaganda, in 1924 Nierendorf treated *The War* portfolio precisely in that vein with Dix's full support.[49] Nierendorf did not hesitate to take advantage of the publicity surrounding *The Trench*, and launched an aggressive marketing ploy for the portfolio as part of the anti-war movement. Having sent *The Trench* to accompany Ernst Friedrich's pacifist travelling exhibition Nie Wieder Krieg, Nierendorf deliberately published *The War* portfolio in early 1924 to coincide with the ten-year anniversary of the outbreak of the Great War. He brought out five separate portfolios of ten leaves of aquatints and etchings totaling fifty different images. Nierendorf also arranged for twenty-four images to be published as a book for which Henri Barbusse wrote a foreword. In a letter to Dix, Nierendorf confirmed that, "A bigger propaganda effort for a portfolio has never been made."[50]

In spite of Nierendorf's efforts, the portfolio was commercially unsuccessful. However, it aroused enough critical attention to promote it as an accurate, visual anti-war message. The renowned *Vossische Zeitung* claimed that the portfolio was a "first rate document of our time," whereas the *Berliner Zeitung am Mittag* suggested that, "whoever is not an avowed opponent of the war … can hardly be called a human being anymore," and the *Neues Tageblatt* in Stuttgart claimed the portfolio was "on par with Goya's *Disasters of War*."[51] Conservative critics accused Dix's work of harbouring a latent "romanticism of decay," and that, in spite of its manifesto quality, *The War* portfolio failed as a comprehensive assessment of war just as much as the "bright and beautiful" academic depictions of battles could not do justice to the enormity of the Great War.[52] Dix later said about his war work: "Well, I paint still-life. One has to render things as they are. One cannot paint indignation."[53] Dix's desire in choosing his subject matter was not an attempt at personal recollection, but aimed to shock his viewers and remind them of the human cost and suffering of war.

Dix was certainly not the first artist to indict the human outcome of war in this way. In 1916 Willibald Krain, a pacifist student from the Munich Academy of Art who counted Käthe Kollwitz as his mentor, brought out a series of seven lithographs in a portfolio simply called *War*. They were some of the earliest images that contradicted the prevailing notion that Germany was going to win the war. In the same year, Willy Jaeckel, who had served for a few months as a cartographer on the Russian Front, brought out a portfolio of lithographs titled *Memento 1914/15*, which evoked the carnage in a dramatic way. In spite of the overt expressionist style, the content of works such as *Direct Hit*, *Shelling*, and *Rape* were a frank portrayal of the human horrors that the war was unleashing. Dix's etching *House Destroyed by Aerial Bombs (Tournai)*, from *The* War portfolio, depicts a bombed-out house with bodies flung outward by the explosion. The alleged realism of the image has its art-historical referents in Goya's plate *Ravages* from the 1810 portfolio *Disasters of War*, but also bears a striking resemblance to Willy Jaeckel's *Dead Mother and Small Child* lithograph from *Memento 1914/15*. Dix, who only turned to the horrors of war years after it was over, used a similar close-range technique to that of Jaeckel in his war portfolio. It is likely that Dix was familiar with Jaeckel's portfolio, since *Memento* was published and distributed by the Graphisches Kabinett J.B. Neumann, a gallery that Nierendorf had taken over by 1923.[54] Though possibly stimulated by *Memento*, Dix also used other art-historical and contemporary sources for *The War* portfolio that throw the notion of a personal memory into stark relief.

Horse Cadaver and *Skin Graft* are based on photographs from Ernst Friedrich's book *Nie Wieder Krieg*, and the Dresden photographer Hugo Erfurth supplied other photographs that Dix used as source material.[55] Other etchings in the portfolio reference prints from the sixteenth and nineteenth centuries. "Goya, Callot and, even earlier, Urs Graf, I looked at prints by those artists in Basel," Dix remembered in the 1960s.[56] Certainly, *Visit to Madame Germaine at Méricourt* bears an affinity with Urs Graf's *Prostitute* (1521), and the devastated landscape of *Near Langemarck (February, 1918)* shares the fine detail of Graf's *Horrors of War* from 1521. The same Graf image informs the burnt-out trees, crumbling earth, shreds of barbed wire, and skeletal remains in Dix's *Disintegrating Trench*, and reflects Dix's desire to emulate the linear delicacy of sixteenth-century drawing and print-making techniques. Dix deliberately chose the medium of etching for *The War* portfolio, claiming that, "with this simple medium one can say everything more penetratingly and vividly."[57] This is not only true for visually disturbing images such as *Shot to Pieces* or the viscerally repugnant image of *Mealtime in the Trench (Loretto Heights)*, where Dix has effectively used various graphic techniques to emphasize festering wounds and contrasted living flesh with the opacity of skeletal remains. It is also evident in images such as *Crater Field near Dontrien Lit by Flares*, where the tonal gradations of the ink yield an eerie desolation, or *Machine-Gun Squad Advances (Somme November, 1916)*, in which Dix has differentiated the energy of the active soldiers from the pale morass of the dead.

The War portfolio is considered to be an accurate memory of war on account of the realism of the subject matter that matched the painstaking, detailed technique. The images were visually shocking; as the poet and writer Max Hermann-Neisse would write, "[they] faithfully depict what the war really looked like ... what the steel bath period truly means and what a return to the years of slaughter would bring us anew."[58] This is only partially true. In a conversation specifically about *The War* portfolio with Hans Kinkel in the late sixties, Dix admitted that it had not been necessary for him to witness the events depicted. "Once you have been out there, you know what it is like—one does not need to have seen anything," he said. The medium also provided him with the ability to transmute reality: "when one etches, one becomes a pure alchemist."[59] Thus, Dix transformed documentary photography and fused art-historical references in his detailed etchings

Otto Dix, *Dead Men before the Position near Tahure* (*Tote vor der Stellung bei Tahure*), from *The War* (*Der Krieg*), 1924. Etching, aquatint, and drypoint from a portfolio of fifty etchings, aquatints, and drypoints. Plate: $7^{11}/_{16}$ x $10^{3}/_{16}$ in. (19.6 x 25.8 cm); sheet: $13^{7}/_{8}$ x $18^{7}/_{16}$ in. (35.3 x 46.8 cm). *Publisher:* Karl Nierendorf, Berlin. Printer: Otto Felsing, Berlin *Edition:* 70. Gift of Abby Aldrich Rockefeller. © 2014 Artists Rights Society (ARS), New York/ VG Bild-Kunst, Bonn. Digital Image © The Museum of Modern Art. Licensed by SCALA/Art Resource, NY.

that are rendered with dramatic realism. However, if a picture's realism is measured by the extent to which it is a successful illusion, then the test of fidelity becomes deception. Some of the etchings in *The War* portfolio are rendered with a fastidiousness that seems to undermine them as reliable testimonies of witnessed events. The vanitas image *Skull* is an obvious example, but in *Dead Men before the Position near Tahure* Dix takes this artifice to the extreme.

He has etched two apparently bodiless skulls in close-up. They have one disintegrating eyeball between them, the black sockets and burnt-off noses and hair perhaps a testimony to death by mustard gas, which the Germans had introduced at Ypres in 1915. With macabre wit, the skulls appear to be in conversation, with the one on the left almost laughing and the other curling its lip in horror. The skulls were not based on actual observation, but resulted from trips to the morgue in Dresden, where Dix made watercolour studies of skulls, and one to Italy in 1923, when he interrupted work on the etchings and visited the catacombs in Palermo. Dix transformed these skulls from studio objects or documentary photographs by personalizing them and assigning an identity to them, thus constructing a false memory of the war. The art-historical and contemporary references that Dix appropriated for artistic purposes further confuse the extent to which Dix's *The War* portfolio can be viewed as personal memory of war. After the war, Dix said, "I don't think anyone else saw the reality of this war in the way that I did, the deprivation, the wounds, the suffering. I chose the truthful coverage of the war. I wanted to show the disturbance of the earth, the corpses, the wounds."[60] While this is evident in his choice of subject matter for the etchings, Dix's *The War* portfolio as a memory of the war is still complex. He did not attempt to make an emotional appeal on behalf of the millions of individual tragedies resulting from the war like Käthe Kollwitz's war imagery, nor did he participate in the type of official memorial that sought to promote the heroic necessity of war and justify its human sacrifice. As a set of independent moments of wartime experience, Dix's portfolio thus functions more as an *ars memoria*, where separate mental images have been deliberately construed to evoke a shared, mnemonic response from the viewer and to offer a didactic reminder about war's violence. The result is an epic cycle of images that artfully combines reminiscence and remembrance, and crosses the line between personal and universal memory.

Taken in its entirety, the portfolio is not a sequential narrative, nor can Dix be reliably identified as a participant in the action. Instead, each image is a separate occurrence, a story thematically linked to the other images.

As vignettes, the etchings provide insight into the war experience, but offer no conclusion or closure. In *The War* portfolio, Dix is a "storyteller" in the sense that Walter Benjamin referred to in his essay on the works of Nikolai Leskov: "The storyteller takes what he tells from experience—his own or that reported by others. And he, in turn, makes it the experience of those who are listening to his tale."[61] In *At Langemarck (February 1918)*, Dix shows the abandoned and devastated battlefield. Skeletons litter the front of the image and the earth bulges from exploded shells. Burnt-out trees haunt the background. Dix fought several times in Ypres, only four miles away from Langemarck.[62] The specific locale and date are significant, turning the reminiscence into a politicized remembrance. The image probably refers to the aftermath of the Third Battle of Ypres, a British offensive that began in July 1917. The battles in Flanders that raged throughout 1917 resulted in some of the heaviest Allied and German casualties of the war, and the terrible conditions of battle were worsened by rain and glutinous mud. "The whole of West Flanders is one large, steaming pot, in which death and destruction are brewing ... it is like the bowels of the earth exploding," wrote an anonymous German soldier on 31 July 1917.[63] Between 16 and 18 August 1917, German and British armies fought each other at Langemarck, causing enormous casualties on both sides. By early 1918, Langemarck was already devastated and deserted. Though Dix participated periodically in the summer battles in Flanders from 22 July until 4 October 1917, by 1 August he was actually on leave in Bruges with his sisters. A card to his friend Helene Jacob postmarked 14 August and signed "Dix on holiday!" shows him standing in uniform with his sisters: "Hopefully you are still well. For the past 14 days we have been in the vicinity of Bruges after having endured terrible battles in Y[pres]."[64]

The choice of February 1918 as the remembered date for the Langemarck etching is puzzling. In January 1918, Dix was on the Belgian coast, probably in Knokke, from where two undated postcards were sent to Jacob; by February 1918, Dix was not even at the front, but on leave in Gera following an illness. He only returned to combat to participate in Germany's last large-scale offensive on the Western Front, Operation Michael in March 1918.

So why did Dix specify that this etching depicted Langemarck in February 1918? In terms of war strategy, by February 1918, under the leadership of General Erich Ludendorff, Germany was regrouping to prepare for its last major assault on the British. It would prove to be a devastating failure and result in ultimate triumph for the Allies. In his memoirs, Ludendorff glossed over Germany's collapse. Even when he acknowledged Germany's severe losses, he depersonalized the human dimension of violence and death at Ypres and turned human suffering into heroic sacrifice: "What the German soldier experienced, achieved and suffered in the Flanders' battles will be his everlasting monument of bronze erected by himself in the enemy's land." [65] In reality, the German military leadership had submitted soldiers to a quagmire of mud and blood in Ypres, and particularly at Langemarck. However, by 1919 and certainly by 1924, public memory was being manipulated to celebrate German soldiers' heroism in the face of adversity. Dix's invocation of Langemarck, which had attained a cult status by 1924, was a deliberate choice to debunk the heroic myth associated with it. Langemarck, the site of the 1914 "Massacre of the Innocents," held a particular resonance with the German populace. "The Day of Langemarck will forever remain a day of honor for the German youth," the papers wrote in 1914; after the war, the anniversary of the battle became a National Day of Remembrance as well as a propaganda tool for the National Socialists. It was celebrated on many occasions, including 1919 and in 1924, when a memorial was dedicated to the site of the first Battle of Langemarck. [66] Dix's memory in *Langemarck (February 1918)* is therefore both personal and socially constructed, encompassing reminiscence and remembrance. In another etching devoted to the site, *The Ruins of Langemarck*, Dix depicts rubble that is based on one of his many drawings of the same subject from the front. During the war, he rarely specified a location in his drawings, particularly those almost abstracted views of ruins and rubble. In doing so in the etching cycle, Dix forces the viewer to make specific associations about the historical import of war. Dix thus becomes a storyteller, a man who, in Benjamin's words, "has counsel for his readers." [67]

Written in 1936, Benjamin's essay on the storyteller focuses on the transition from oral to written narrative, the dependence of the former on memory, and modern society's preference for information, which threatens to extinguish the story. The demise of communicable human experience after the Great War that Benjamin refers to, and its effect on the construction of memory, is particularly applicable to Dix's *The War* portfolio. Benjamin blames the inability of people to communicate personal experience that is of universal value on the social and economic caesura created by the destruction of Great War: "Was it not noticeable at the end of the war that men returned from the battlefield grown silent—not richer, but poorer in communicable experience? ... For never has experience been contradicted more thoroughly than economic experience by inflation, bodily experience by mechanical warfare, moral experience by those in power." The narrative of the storyteller was valuable, Benjamin wrote, because it imparted a useful message (usually moral), a maxim, or some practical advice, but did not attempt to explain anything or offer psychological insight: "The most extraordinary things ... are related with the greatest accuracy, but the psychological connection of the events is not forced on the reader. It is left up to him to interpret things the way he understands them, and thus the narrative achieves an amplitude that information lacks."[68]

Dix echoed this about his own work in general: "artists must not try to improve or convert. They are far too meager for that [role]. They must only bear witness."[69] This type of "storytelling," in which the narrator presents memories or experiences as facts but spurs other associations in the viewer, is evident in several of Dix's etchings. In *Dead Man in the Mud*, Dix shows a corpse lying on his back submerged in mud, his clenched fist raised skyward. The image resembles the manner in which soldiers were laid to rest on the battlefield, as shown in the photograph of a dead Russian soldier in a ditch from 1915. These were the palatable types of photographs published during the war, images that remembered and honoured death. In Dix's image he adopts a similar pose, but the acid from the etching plate has eaten into the flesh of the soldier's face and arm to emphasize his deadly wounds. The overall effect of Dix's image is very different from his other depictions of the dead and wounded in *The War* portfolio. Where the twisted bodies in *Corpse in Barbed Wire (Flanders)* or *Dead Man (Saint-Clément)* show the gruesome and random nature of death in battle, *Dead Man in the Mud* gives the impression of a man who, in spite of his suffering, has been carefully laid out in eternal rest. After 1918 there was a vogue for representing a soldier's death as a deep sleep, and statues of the recumbent soldier were built as memorials to fallen soldiers. In 1924, several of these memorials were unveiled in Germany as public sites of mourning.[70] In *Dead Man in the Mud*, Dix skilfully manipulates memory to describe the reality of a soldier's death, but also invokes an association with this most public of commemorations. Dix not only exposed the hypocrisy of the heroic death, but also used memory in his etchings to confront social taboos about sex and violence.

In the fourth series of plates for *The War* portfolio, Dix alternates between sexualized, earthly pleasures and meaningless, violent deaths.[71] Sexual pleasure is always centred on men in works such as *Sailors in Antwerp*, but it is women who possess sexual power, as in *Frontline Soldier in Brussels* or *Visit at Mme Germaine's in Méricourt*, where the size and voluptuousness of the prostitutes dwarf the soldiers relying on their services. These images seem to be based on Dix's personal experiences or witnessed events. Sexualized violence is highlighted in *House Destroyed by Aerial Bombs (Tournai)*, and women and children flee an aircraft attack in *Lens Being Bombed*. Violence was also perpetrated without any physical sign of combat. In *Sleeping Soldiers in Fort Vaux (Gassed)*, Dix shows countless soldiers who have succumbed to gas poisoning, and, in *Gas Victims*, two soldiers stand outside the infirmary where the swollen, blackened bodies of gassed infantrymen have been lined up for burial.

Although the war was generally regarded as the site of anonymous and mass death, hand-to-hand combat was not completely unknown. In *Surprise Attack on a Trench Position*, Dix depicts the brutal slaughter of a soldier stabbed in the chest. Stéphane Audoin-Rouzeau has pointed out that combatants chose to remain silent about these types of individual attacks after the war. Presenting the war as mass slaughter exercised through industrial warfare, rather than by an individual, rendered the violence anonymous and exonerated soldiers from responsibility for it.[72] The general message about war was that men die, but they do not kill. Dix did not shy away from challenging this taboo; he even emphasized the energetic intoxication associated with killing at close quarters. The soldier lunges forward on his belly out of the dark trench and gleefully stabs the enemy whose hand is raised in futile self-defence.

In her analysis of the act of killing in warfare, Joanna Bourke notes that "the act of killing another person may invoke a wave of nervous distress, it may also incite feelings of pleasure."[73] Conrad Felixmüller contended that one of the reasons his relationship with Dix deteriorated after 1919 was because Dix admitted to feeling pleasure when he bayonetted someone in battle.[74] In her book, Bourke describes the close relationship between the pleasure of killing and the carnivalesque. She recites stories of soldiers who, with black humour, manipulated corpses into sitting positions with adornments on their heads, and positioned their hands and feet as a form of comic relief to heighten their own sense of being alive in the face of death. In *Seen on the Escarpment at Cléry sur Somme*, Dix comically presents two ossified soldiers with their exploded bodies propped up as if in animated conversation.

This image that appears so artificial and constructed may well have been based on an actual wartime memory. Dix's most accusatory etching is *Dead Sentry in Trench*, which exposes a suicide, the most fundamental of all taboos.

The decomposing skeleton of a German soldier, identifiable by his steel helmet, is shown leaning against the trench. His gun is pointed in his face, the butt of the gun against the ground. The soldier has removed his boot, his bare foot positioned to pull the trigger while his hand steadies the gun. Dix lifted the veil of silence about these wartime realities. In so doing, he reconstructed memories to rework their impact on the viewer as self-contained stories complete with residual associations.

Otto Dix, *Seen on the Escarpment at Cléry-sur-Somme* (*Gesehen am Steilhang von Cléry-sur-Somme*) from *The War* (*Der Krieg*), 1924. Etching, aquatint, and drypoint from a portfolio of fifty etchings, aquatints, and drypoints. *Plate:* 10 1/8 x 7 11/16 in. (25.7 x 19.5 cm); sheet: 18 1/2 x 13 11/16 in. (47 x 34.7 cm). *Publisher:* Karl Nierendorf, Berlin. Printer: Otto Felsing, Berlin. *Edition:* 70. Gift of Abby Aldrich Rockefeller. © 2014 Artists Rights Society (ARS), New York/VG Bild-Kunst, Bonn. Digital Image © The Museum of Modern Art. Licensed by SCALA/Art Resource, NY.

As Benjamin explains, for a story to be effective, it must be remembered so that it can be repeated. It resonates most fully with the listener if it can be integrated into his own experience. If we regard each etching in the portfolio as an episode of the war and the portfolio as a whole as an epic cycle of

Otto Dix, *Dead Sentry in the Trench* (*Toter Sappenposten*) from *The War* (*Der Krieg*), 1924. Etching, aquatint, and drypoint from a portfolio of fifty etchings, aquatints and drypoints. *Plate:* 7 11/16 x 10 3/16 in. (19.6 x 25.8 cm); sheet: 13 7/8 x 18 7/16 in. (35.3 x 46.8 cm). *Publisher:* Karl Nierendorf, Berlin. Printer: Otto Felsing, Berlin. Edition: 70. Gift of Abby Aldrich Rockefeller. © 2014 Artists Rights Society (ARS), New York/VG Bild-Kunst, Bonn. Digital Image © The Museum of Modern Art/Licensed by SCALA/Art Resource, NY.

several stories, an analogy can be made between Dix's approach to memory and Benjamin's explanation of it. For Benjamin, memory is "the epic faculty *par excellence*"; it "creates the chain of tradition which passes on from generation to generation." Epics, according to Benjamin, combine the "perpetuating remembrance of the novelist with the short-lived reminiscences of the storyteller. The first is dedicated to *one* hero, *one* odyssey, *one* battle; the second to many diffuse experiences."[75] For Dix, the memory of war was at once personal and collective. Many of the etchings comment on the war's impact on human destiny; as Dix put it, "I showed conditions, conditions that the war caused and the consequences of the war as conditions."[76]

This declaration in itself confirms that Dix regarded his etchings as witnessed events and therefore as memories of his own experience. However, only a few of the images can be traced back to drawings made while Dix was in combat. *Shell-Crater with Flowers (Spring 1916, near Reims)* and *Crater Field near Dontrien Lit by Flares* emerged from several wartime drawings derived from Dix's fascination with the effect of the war on nature. His enthrallment with the picturesque effects of destruction caused by rhythmic explosions and blasts of colour while in combat are remembered in these delicately detailed etchings. The images are probably the most authentic memories in the portfolio, since they are closely aligned with actual war drawings and convey, pictorially, the second part of Dix's entry on experience in his 1916 War Notebook:

> Experience only consists of a main tone or thought around which countless side tones or thoughts orbit, they overlap, flood, transcribe it—Following the main line [of thought] one encounters the many mutations, variations and byways; Intellect makes experience more labyrinthine and complicated until one finally reaches the point of departure once more. This process is repeated in the execution of the work. A system of circles at the end of which one no longer remembers anything about the beginning.[77]

During the war, Dix recognized that he was translating a diffuse range of raw, sensory experiences into concrete, visual form. His analysis of experience accounts for the near abstraction and lack of realism in many of his wartime drawings. By the time he made *The War* portfolio, the nebulous nature of experience Dix described was impossible to recapture even had he wanted to. Instead, he recalled those experiences, and with the aid of artistic referents transformed his memory of war into a hardened message about war that corresponded to his self-image in *How I Looked as a Soldier*. This is not to suggest that the images in *The War* portfolio do not represent the reality of war, or, as Dix would have it, the conditions and the consequences of war. Rather, the bitingly realistic etchings are a distillation of personal *Erlebnis* combined with postwar *Erfahrung*: a sequence of images that was deliberately forged as part of a self-constructed identity.

NOTES

1. The exact number of drawings and works on paper that Dix made during the war is not verifiable. In her *catalogue raisonné* of Dix's drawings and pastels, Ulrike Lorenz has catalogued more than 470 works. Ulrike Lorenz, *Das Werkverzeichnis der Zeichnungen und Pastelle* (Weimar: VDF Verlag, 2003). Also, Susan Pfäffle, *Otto Dix: Werkverzeichnis der Aquarelle und Gouachen* (Stuttgart: Verlag Gerd Hatje, 1991).
2. Dix painted four self-portraits as a soldier before he had seen active service.
3. Anja Walter-Ris, *Kunstleidenschaft im Dienst der Moderne: Die Geschichte der Galerie Nierendorf Berlin/New York 1920–1995* (Zurich: Zurich Inter-Publishers, 2003), 93.
4. Max Hermann-Neisse, "Otto Dix. Der Krieg," *Die Aktion* 15 (1924), reprinted in Heinz Lüdecke, *Der Krieg* (Berlin: Deutsche Akademie der Künste, 1963), 5.
5. The dedication on the self-portrait reads, "I dedicate this second artist proof of the war portfolio to Karl Nierendorf in June 1924." Sabine Rewald, *Glitter and Doom: German Portraits from the 1920s* (New York: Yale University Press, 2006), 205.
6. Stefan Goebel has shown that in visual war propaganda the steel helmet was an emblem of German endurance amid industrialized warfare. Stefan Goebel, "Chivalrous Knights versus Iron Warriors: Representations of the Battle of Materiel and Slaughter in Britain and Germany, 1914–1940," in *Picture This: The First World War Posters and Visual Culture*, ed. Pearl James (Lincoln: University of Nebraska Press, 2009), 93.
7. Paul Fox has perceptively analyzed this image and Dix's *The War* portfolio in relation to the status of war veterans in German society and the politics of postwar shame and trauma through a comparison to the narrative structure of Ernst Jünger's *Storm of Steel*. See Paul Fox, "Confronting Postwar Shame in Weimar Germany: Trauma, Heroism and the War Art of Otto Dix," *Oxford Art Journal* 29, no. 2 (2006): 249–67.
8. See Löffler, *Otto Dix* (1981); Conzelmann, *Der andere Dix* (1983); Cork, *A Bitter Truth: Avantgarde Art and the Great War* (1994); Dietrich Schubert, *Kunsthistorische Arbeitsblätter*, Heft 9 (2002).

9. Most recently, Olaf Peters has articulated this interpretation in *Otto Dix*, exhibition catalogue (New York: Neue Galerie/Prestel Verlag, 2010).

10. Otto Dix, "Über Kunst, Religion, Krieg: Gespräch mit Freunden am Bodensee," recording (St. Gallen: Erker Verlag, December 1963), transcript in Dieter Schmidt, *Otto Dix im Selbstbildnis* (Berlin: Henschelverlag und Kunst, 1981), 255–60.

11. Quoted in Maria Wetzel, "Ein harter Mann, dieser Maler," in *Diplomatischer Kurier* [Cologne] 14 (1965): 731–45. The entire interview is reprinted in Schmidt, *Otto Dix im Selbstbildnis*, 269–70.

12. Schmidt, 270.

13. Joan Weinstein, *End of Expressionism: Art and the November Revolution in Germany, 1918–1919* (Chicago: University of Chicago Press, 1990), 107–61.

14. Hans Grundig, *Zwischen Karneval und Aschermittwoch. Erinnerungen eines Malers* (Berlin, DDR, 1958), 141.

15. Willi Wolfradt, *Otto Dix*, originally published in 1924 as a monograph in the series Junge Kunst, translated and quoted in Peters, ed., *Otto Dix*, 117.

16. Letter from Otto Dix to Conrad Felixmüller, 1919, reprinted in ABK, Germanisches National Museum, *Conrad Felixmüller Werke und Dokumente* (Klagenfurt: Ritter Verlag, 1982), 76.

17. Letter to Kurt Günther, in *Kunst im Aufbruch Dresden 1918–1933* (Dresden: Staatliche Kunstsammlungen Dresden, Gemäldegalerie Neue Meister/ Albertinum, 1980), 41.

18. Rudolf Kämmerer, "Die erste Austellung der Dresdner Sezession Gruppe 1919," *Cicerone* 11, no. 2 (5 June 1919): 340.

19. Carl Puetzfeld, "Dresdner Secession," *Dresdner Neuesten Nachrichten*, 18 April 1919, quoted in Rainer Beck, *Otto Dix: Die kosmischen Bilder: Zwischen Sehnscht und Schwangerem Weib* (Dresden: Verlag der Kunst, 2003), 141.

20. Paul Fechter, "Juryfreie Kunstschau," *Deutsche Allgemeine Zeitung*, 15 October 1922, quoted in Andreas Strobl, *Otto Dix: Eine Malerkarrier der zwanziger Jahre* (Berlin: Reimer Verlag, 1996), 64.

21. Max Osborn, "Die Juryfreien" in *Vossische Zeitung* [Berlin], 14 October 1922, quoted in Strobl, 66.

22. Theodor Däubler, "Otto Dix," *Das Kunstblatt* 4, no. 4 (April 1920): 118–20.

23. *Conrad Felixmüller: Werke und Dokumente*, ed. Archiv für Bildende Kunst am Germanischen Nationalmuseum, Nürnberg (Klagenfurt: Ritter Verlag, 1982), 78.

24. Strobl, 84.

25. Letter from Felix Stössinger, Verlag der Neuen Gesellschaft Berlin to Otto Dix in Düsseldorf, 12 December 1922. Germanischen Nationalmuseum, Nürnberg (hereafter GNM): I,C. 752.

26. Although Dix had exhibited at the *International Dada Messe* in Berlin in 1920, this had barely been reviewed or attended by the general public. He had

greater success with his paintings in the Berlin Secession of 1921 (*Barricade, Skat Players*, and *Prague Street*) and his participation at the Große Berliner Kunstaustellung in the section devoted to the Novembergruppe, where he exhibited *Suleika the Tatooed Wonder*. For more information on the trial and related publicity, see Strobl, 72–79.

27. Denis Crockett, "The Most Famous Painting of the 'Golden Twenties'? Otto Dix and The Trench Affair," *Art Journal* 51, no. 1 (1992): 72–80.

28. Andreas Strobl has provided evidence that the scandal caused by *The Trench* and the attending press coverage gave Dix the opportunity to exhibit in renowned institutions and cemented his reputation; Strobl, 88–108. Cf. Wolfgang Schrock-Schmidt, "Der Schicksalsweg des Schützengraben," in *Dix* (Stuttgart: Verlag Gerd Hatje, 1991), 161–65. See also Brigid Barton, "Die Enstehung eines Kunstlerrufs: Otto Dix und der Schützengraben," in *Otto Dix zum 100. Geburtstag, Symposium* (Albstadt: Städtische Galerie, 1991).

29. Conzelmann (1983), 133.

30. Wulf Herzogenrath, ed., *Dix* (Stuttgart: Verlag Gerd Hatje, 1991).

31. Press release from the Wallraf-Richartz Museum for the reopening of the museum in 1923, quoted in Schrock-Schmidt, 161n8.

32. Kira van Lil, "Ein perfekter Skandal: der Schützengraben von Otto Dix zwischen Kritik und Verfemung," in *Das verfemte Meisterwerk: Schicksalswege moderner Kunst im Dritten Reich* (Berlin: Akademie Verlag, 2009), 49–74.

33. Dora Apel, "'Heroes' and 'Whores': The Politics of Gender in Weimar Antiwar Imagery," *Art Bulletin* 79, no. 3 (1997): 366–84.

34. Postcard from Karl Nierendorf to Dix, 18 August 1924, quoted in Jorg Martin Merz, "Otto Dix' Kriegsbilder. Motivationen—Intentionen—Rezeption," *Marburger Jahrbuch* 26 (1999): 196.

35. Alfred Flechtheim to J.B. Neumann, 23 May 1924, in Hans Albert Peters and Stephan von Wiese, eds., *Alfred Flechtheim—Sammler—Kunsthändler—Verleger* (Düsseldorf, 1987), 175.

36. "Die Fruhjahrsaustellung in der Akademie," *Berliner Börsen Courier*, 12 April 1924, quoted in Strobl, 91.

37. Lothar Fischer, *Otto Dix: Ein Malerleben in Deutschland* (Berlin: Nicolaische Verlagsbuchhandlung, 1981), 47.

38. Gotthold Ephraim Lessing, *Laocoon: An Essay on the Limits of Painting and Poetry*, trans. Edward Allen McCormick (Baltimore: Johns Hopkins University Press, 1962), 19.

39. Hans Kinkel, *Die Toten und die Nackten: Beiträge zu Dix* (Berlin: Galerie Remmert und Barth, 1991), 14.

40. Julius Meier-Graefe, *Deutsche Allgemeine Zeitung*, 2 July 1924, reprinted in Merz, 225–26.

41. Conzelmann, 136.

42. Alfred Salmony, "Die neue Galerie des 17. bis 20. Jahrhunderts im Wallraf-Richartz Museum in Köln," *Cicerone* 16, no. 1 (10 January 1924): 8.

43. Karl Scheffler, "Frühjahrsaustellung der Akademie," *Kunst und Künstler*, 10 July 1924, quoted in Strobl, 92.

44. *Berlin Börsen Courier*, 11 May 1924, quoted in Strobl, 91.

45. Joan Scott, "The Evidence of Experience," *Critical Inquiry* 16 (1991): 780.

46. Julius Meier-Graefe, "Die Austellung in der Akademie," *Deutsche Allgemeine Zeitung*, 2 July 1924, quoted in Strobl, 94.

47. Strobl, 95.

48. Birgitte Reinhardt, "Dix a Painter of Facts?" in *Otto Dix: Inventory Catalogue of the Galerie der Stadt Stuttgart* (Stuttgart: Edition Cantz, 1989), 33.

49. Anja Walter-Ris, *Kunstleidenschaft im Dienst der Moderne: Die Geschichte der Galerie Nierendorf Berlin/New York, 1920–1995* (Zurich: Zurich Interpublishers, 2003).

50. Heinz Lüdecke, *Der Krieg* (Berlin: Deutsche Akademie der Künste, 1963), 5.

51. Kinkel, 51.

52. Strobl, 88–90.

53. Schmidt, 280.

54. J.B. Neumann exhibited Willi Jaeckel's *Memento* portfolio in the autumn of 1916. See H.S., *Cicerone* 4 (October 1916): 412.

55. See letter from Erfurth confirming the supply of war photographs to Dix in exchange for graphic work, GNM I,C 205.

56. Quoted in Schmidt, 279.

57. Quoted in ibid., 280.

58. Max Hermann-Neisse, *Die Aktion* 15 (1924), reprinted in Heinz Lüdecke, *Otto Dix: Der Krieg* (Berlin: Deutsche Akademie der Künste, 1963), 22.

59. Otto Dix in conversation with Hans Kinkel, reprinted in Kinkel, 42.

60. Schmidt, *Otto Dix im Selbstbildnis*, 273.

61. Walter Benjamin, "The Storyteller: Reflections on the Works of Nikolai Leskov," in *Illuminations* (New York: Schocken Books, 1985), 83–109.

62. See the chronological reconstruction of Dix's active war service in Ulrike Rüdiger, *Grüsse aus dem Krieg, Die Feldpostkarten der Otto Dix—Sammlung in der Kunstgalerie Gera* (Verlag Kunstgalerie Gera, 1991), 22–23.

63. *Source Records of the Great War*, vol. 5, ed. Charles F. Horne (National Alumni, 1923), 272–73.

64. From the postcard "Dix on Holiday!", in Rüdiger, 34.

65. Erich von Ludendorff, *Ludendorff's Own Story August 1914–November 1918: The Great War from the Siege of Liège to the Signing of the Armistice as Viewed from the Headquarters of the German Army*, vol. 2 (New York: Harper, 1919), 105.

66. Goebel, 102.

67. Benjamin, 86.

68. Ibid., 84, 89.

69. Otto Dix, *Gespräch im Wartezimmer*, 1958, reprinted in Schmidt, 228.

70. Goebel, 9.

71. Conzelmann, 113.

72. Stéphane Audoin-Rouzeau and Annette Becker, *14–18 Understanding the Great War* (New York: Hill & Wang, 2000), 39.

73. Joanna Bourke, *An Intimate History of Killing: Face-to-Face in Twentieth-Century Warfare* (London: Granta Books, 1999), 6.

74. Lothar Fischer, *Otto Dix: Ein Malerleben in Deutschland* (Berlin: Nicolaische Verlagsbuchhandlung, Berlin, 1981), 30.

75. Benjamin, 94.

76. Schmidt, 273.

77. Conzelmann, 131.

CONTRIBUTORS' BIOGRAPHIES

Zachary Abram (University of Ottawa) is a doctoral candidate working on a dissertation about the representation of the soldier in Canadian war fiction. His written work has appeared in the *Dalhousie Review, Studies in Canadian Literature,* and *Papers of the Bibliographical Society of Canada.*

Carol Acton (St. Jerome's University, University of Waterloo) is associate professor of English at St. Jerome's University at the University of Waterloo, Ontario. She has recently completed a study of medical personnel in war from the First World War to the current wars in Iraq and Afghanistan (with Jane Potter) entitled *Working in a World of Hurt: Trauma and Resilience in Narratives by Medical Personnel in Warzones* (Manchester University Press).

Dan Bullard (York University) completed his doctoral dissertation in European and colonial history at York University in 2012. Grounded in extensive research in Africa and Europe, his dissertation explores the remembrance of German colonial rule in the former metropole and colonies in Africa, Asia, and Oceania between 1919 and 1943.

Mary G. Chaktsiris (Queen's University) is a doctoral candidate in the Department of History. She specializes in gender history and the First World War in Canada, and her research explores connections between masculinity and war in Toronto between 1914 and 1918.

Mark Connelly (University of Kent) is professor of modern British history at the University of Kent. His main research interests are in the fields of commemoration and military history. Among his publications are *The Great War: Memory and Ritual* (2002), *We Can Take It! Britain and the Memory of the Second World War* (2003), and *Steady the Buffs! A Regiment, a Region and the Great War* (2006).

Mark A.R. Facknitz (James Madison University) is Roop Distinguished Professor of English at James Madison University, in Virginia, where he has taught since 1983. His academic interest in the Great War depends largely on a family history that included a grandfather in the German army, a grandfather in the America Expeditionary Force, and a great-uncle who died for Canada.

Thomas Hodd (Université de Moncton) is assistant professor in Canadian literature at Université de Moncton. His work on Atlantic-Canadian writers has appeared in *Canadian Literature*, *Canadian Poetry*, and *Studies in Canadian Literature*. He is currently preparing an anthology of selected war stories by Nova Scotia writer Will R. Bird.

Geoff Keelan (Western University) is a SSHRC postdoctoral fellow at Western University. He completed his doctorate at the University of Waterloo working with Dr. Whitney Lackenbauer. His dissertation examines Henri Bourassa's perspective of the First World War, though his research reflects upon many aspects of the French-Canadian war experience.

Alice Kelly (Yale University) completed her Ph.D. in English at the University of Cambridge in 2014. Her dissertation examines the impact of the vast mortality of the Great War on literary representations of death and memorialization in British and American women's writing. She is currently a visiting scholar at Yale University.

Kimberly J. Lamay Licursi (Siena College) is a visiting assistant professor of history at Siena College in Loudonville, New York. Her dissertation explores American collective memory of the First Word War, specifically focusing on the ways in which war stories might have been shared with the next generations during the interwar period.

Bette London (University of Rochester) is a professor of English at the University of Rochester. She is the author of *The Appropriated Voice: Narrative Authority in Conrad, Forster, and Woolf* and *Writing Double: Women's Literary Partnerships*. She is currently completing a book entitled *Posthumous Lives: World War I and the Culture of Memory*.

Brian MacDowall (York University) is a doctoral candidate in the Department of History at York University.

Jane G.V. McGaughey (Concordia University) is assistant professor of Irish Diaspora Studies at Concordia's School of Canadian Irish Studies. She is the author of *Ulster's Men: Protestant Unionist Masculinities and Militarization in the North of Ireland, 1912–1923*. Her current research explores violence, gender, and notions of identity and loyalty in Ireland's 1798 Rebellion and the Canadian Rebellions of 1837.

Robert Morley (University of Saskatchewan) recently completed his Ph.D. in history at the University of Saskatchewan, where he wrote a dissertation exploring the depiction of aerial warfare on the screen in Great Britain between 1927 and 1939.

Veysel Şimşek (McMaster University) is a doctoral candidate interested in the political, social, and military history of the later Ottoman Empire. His dissertation examines the "Grand Strategy" of the Ottoman leadership between the 1820s and the 1840s, and the broader impact of their decisions on the Ottoman state and society.

Marzena Sokolowska-Paryz (University of Warsaw) is an associate professor at the Institute of English Studies, University of Warsaw, Poland. She is the author of *Reimagining the War Memorial, Reinterpreting the Great War: The Formats of British Commemorative Fiction*, and *The Myth of War in British and Polish Poetry, 1939–1945*. Her collection *The Great War in Post-Memory Literature and Film*, co-edited with Martin Löschnigg, was published in 2014.

William F. Stewart (independent scholar), after a brief, thirty-year hiatus in management, graduated from the University of Birmingham, UK, with a Ph.D. in 2012. He examines the tactical, operational, and administrative aspects of the Canadian Corps in the First World War. His book, *The Embattled General: Sir Richard Turner and the First World War*, is forthcoming.

Michèle Wijegoonaratna (Metropolitan Muscum of Art) received her Ph.D. in art history from the Institute of Fine Arts, New York University. She is a research associate at the Metropolitan Museum of Art in New York. This paper was distilled from her dissertation, titled "Tradition, Innovation and the Construction of Identity in Otto Dix's Portraits and Self-Portraits 1912–1927."

INDEX